Jonathan Arnold is Chaplain and Senior Research Fellow at Worcester College, Oxford. He is a Fellow of the Royal Historical Society, holds a Ph.D. from King's College, London and is the author of *Dean John Colet of St Paul's: Humanism and Reform in Early Tudor England* (I.B.Tauris, 2007).

For Mum and Dad

THE GREAT HUMANISTS

AN INTRODUCTION

JONATHAN ARNOLD

I.B. TAURIS

LONDON · NEW YORK

Published in 2011 by I.B.Tauris & Co Ltd
6 Salem Road, London W2 4BU
175 Fifth Avenue, New York NY 10010
www.ibtauris.com

Distributed in the United States and Canada
Exclusively by Palgrave Macmillan
175 Fifth Avenue, New York NY 10010

ISBN: 978 1 84885 081 1 (HB)
      978 1 84885 082 8 (PB)

A full CIP record for this book is available from the British Library
A full CIP record is available from the Library of Congress

Library of Congress Catalog Card Number: available

Typeset by Newgen Publishers, Chennai
Printed and bound by TJ International Ltd, Padstow, Cornwall

MIX
Paper from
responsible sources
FSC   FSC® C013056
www.fsc.org

CONTENTS

ACKNOWLEDGEMENTS

I would like to thank all those who have helped and encouraged the completion of this book. My appreciation goes to those who have helped me to develop my ideas by offering feedback on papers given in seminars: to Dr. Sarah Apetrei and members of the Oxford University Ecclesiastical History Seminar; Dr. Susan Gillingham and members of the Worcester College Theology Seminar; as well as Gresham College in London. My sincere appreciation is offered to those who have assisted my research by reading extracts from the thesis and offering helpful criticism and advice. In particular, I thank the meticulous work of historian Tim Stuart-Buttle of Worcester College for his painstaking proof-reading, editing and sound advice; to Prof. Caroline Barron for all her support over the years; to David Kennerley for taking the time to read some of the work and for his comments; and to Joanna Godfrey and Victoria McHugh at I.B.Tauris, for all their help. Their work has assisted me immeasurably and any mistakes that remain our entirely my own.

I have not the words to express my gratitude for the love, support and faith of Emma, my wife, and the indefatigable *joie de vivre* of our wonderful children, Katie and Thomas, without whom no book would be worth writing. I am also in debt to Amy our cat for her mystical and profound wisdom of silence, for being a good listener and for her company as I wrote much of this book.

Finally, I wish to thank my parents, Brenda and Christopher, for all their unfailing love and kindness over the years. I dedicate this work to them with gratitude.

INTRODUCTION

Renaissance humanism has shaped the way we think and what we do: our education, the cultural world we inhabit, the literature we read, the plays we watch, the music we listen to, our religion, politics and philosophy; the very language we speak. To hear the poetry of Milton, Spenser or Shakespeare, or to read the prose of Erasmus, More or the words of a Tyndale Bible, for instance, is to encounter language that has been shaped by the humanist ideas and assumptions that have permeated the Western world. Thus, humanism is a phenomenon that transformed the study of literature in Renaissance Europe and has left its imprint on society today. The *studia humanitatis*, a discipline embracing grammar, rhetoric, poetry, moral philosophy and history, involved the study of classical literature and languages, philology and the art of debate. It gave birth to a new age of eloquence, in which education and literature, as well as the way in which philosophy and theology were expressed, changed forever. Humanism revolutionized European culture by means of relating to its classical literary past. The term *humanitas* is still employed in almost every university in the world in the form of the word 'humanities'.

This book is not about the secular humanism of the twenty-first century, it is about Renaissance humanism in a broad sense, Christian and civic. This work, for the general reader and student alike, offers an introduction to humanism, from its birth to the Reformation, by means of examining some of its key figures as well as those closely related to humanism through their work as philosophers. It attempts to create a picture of the movement and its influence in pre-Reformation and Reformation Europe by juxtaposing a series of inter-related sketches of scholars, priests, theologians and philosophers, now known as humanists, active in the Renaissance and early modern periods. The aim is not only to provide an overview of intellectual thought in Europe at the time, but also to offer the reader individual portraits of the key humanists involved which can be read as free-standing chapters, or used for reference. After a definition of humanism, this introduction will give a brief summary of the rise of humanism in Europe and survey some of the important scholarship written about it, before providing a brief justification of those humanists included, and those omitted, and an outline of the book.

What is Humanism?

Any attempt to give a working definition of humanism is always a precarious venture, but it must be done. In fact, the term 'humanism' is not a term from the Renaissance at all, but was developed in the nineteenth century from the Latin *humanitas*, as used by Cicero (106–43 B.C.) in classical times and those *humanista*, of the fifteenth century, who studied and taught the *humanae litterae* (liberal arts) in universities. As James Hankins has observed, it was Georg Voigt who first used the word 'humanism' to refer to the Renaissance study of classical texts and languages. In the same century, a philosophical sense of humanism was developed in the work of Ludwig Fauerbach (1804–1872), leading eventually to the common understanding of the term 'humanism' in modern society as a secular philosophy of humankind. However, any notion of Renaissance humanism as a 'philosophy of man' was largely discredited by Paul Kristeller (1905–99), who cogently argued that Renaissance humanism is best seen as a 'movement, rooted in the medieval rhetorical tradition, to revive the language and literature of classical antiquity. Humanists were not philosophers, but men and women of letters'.[1]

As for the origins of humanism, we have to look to the *Trecento* and *Quattrocento* in Italy, as it was here that humanism emerged through the thirteenth and fourteenth centuries in the works of Italian scholars such as the Paduan Lovato dei Lovati (*c.* 1240–1309), Geremia da Montagnone (1255–1321), Rolando da Piazzola (d. 1325) and Albertino Mussato (1261–1329).[2] Most of the early humanists were lawyers and, of the Paduans, Mussato became the most widely renowned. The humanist Paduans were basically secular and civic in their outlook, not least Mussato, whose writings demonstrated no special religious interest until he converted to Christianity late in life (1328–9).[3]

The term 'humanist' (in the Latin *humanista* or Italian *umanista*) was used in the fifteenth century. However, as Lewis Spitz points out, the term did not travel outside of Italy until the early sixteenth century, appearing in Germany (in the Latin text of the *Epistolae Obscurorum Virorum*) in 1515.[4] The term made its way also to France by the mid-sixteenth century, to England by the late-sixteenth century, and the German word *humanismus* was in use at the end the eighteenth century, so that, by 1809, humanism stood for 'devotion to the literature of ancient Greece and Rome, and the humane values that may be derived from them'.[5] These *literati, poetae* or *oratores* were often prominent figures in Italian society, such as university teachers, political secretaries, or other officials and poets – they all specialized in language.[6] This new Graeco-Roman inspired culture placed great emphasis on the *studia humanitatis*, which tended to involve the study of classical literature and languages along with the rhetorical arts, such as debating skills, philology and the eloquent use of language. Other terms used to describe their pursuits were '*studia humaniora* (more humane studies), *studia honestarum artium* (the study of honourable arts), *bonae litterae* (good letters), *bonae artes* (the good arts), *eruditio legitima et ingenua* (noble and legitimate learning)'.[7] The aim of these humanist pursuits, occupying a central space between the practical studies of law, medicine, or the mechanical arts and more theoretical occupations such as natural philosophy, metaphysics and theology, was therefore to improve individual and corporate wisdom, piety and eloquence:

> The scope of the humane studies was to improve the quality of human beings *qua* human. The humanists claimed that study of good letters made people better, more virtuous, wiser, and more eloquent. It made them worthy to exercise power and made them better citizens and subjects when not exercising power. Humane studies embellished life, brought pleasure, and nourished piety. The humanities did not save souls, but living a good life would bring men favour in the eyes of God and strengthen piety, or at least not damage it. The fundamental assumption of all humanists, as of the Renaissance movement in general, was that the remains of classical antiquity constituted a great reservoir of excellence – literary, intellectual, artistic, and moral – to which debased and decadent modern times could turn in order to repair the damage wrought by the barbaric and corrupt *medium aevum* [Middle Ages] that had followed the fall of the Roman Empire.[8]

One thing humanism was not was 'New Learning': a term that has been incorrectly used in connection with Renaissance humanism. The phrase 'New Learning' was employed in the sixteenth century but only in a pejorative sense, as 'an abusive Catholic term for Protestant or evangelical theology, and that is by no means the same as humanism'.[9] Nor can we simply equate humanism with philosophy and theology.

Humanists tended to extol moral philosophy at the expense of meta-physics, psychology and natural philosophy, which they largely ignored. Of the seven parts of the medieval arts curriculum (*septennium*), con-sisting of the *trivium* (grammar, rhetoric and dialectics) and the *quad-rivium* (arithmetic, geometry, music and astronomy), the *trivium* was more attractive to the humanists. Rhetoric was preferred to logic, dia-logue to analysis, philology to philosophical substance; eloquence was more important than powerful thought.[10] Nevertheless, humanism, in its insistence upon eloquent expression and civilized self-improvement, served philosophy and theology well. Although the *studia humanitatis* had developed from the so-called *ars dictaminis*, the medieval rhetorical tradition, and those who taught the subject (the *dictatores*) were largely interested in secular issues and rarely addressed Christian themes, the Christian branch of humanism which developed north of the Alps nev-ertheless encouraged the appreciation and study of languages such as Hebrew, Greek and Latin. These languages were considered to be of importance in allowing for a proper understanding of Christian texts (scripture and patristic writings), which were consequently subjected to scholarly and philological treatment by humanists. Christian human-ists were particularly concerned with Church reform, the provision of an incorrupt, educated clergy and a preaching ministry:

> Christian humanists are often defined by their wish to reach the bedrock of Christian belief without some of the accretions of subsequent tradition. They apply humanist philological technique to the scriptures, seeking to achieve a more reliable text and to make from it a more accurate Latin translation than that provided in the Vulgate. Typically, they wish to base their religion, as far as possible, on the gospels and to inves-tigate the practices of the primitive church where this can be deduced from the Acts of the Apostles and the writings of the early Church fathers.[11]

In fifteenth-century Italy there was a belief that Francesco Petrarca (or Petrarch) (1304–74) had been the 'father of Italian humanism' and made a break with the medieval past in terms of the study and use of language, grammar, and eloquence,[12] but as scholars have shown Petrarch was the most significant member of a third generation of Italian humanists, whose real importance was an establishment of new literary studies that survived and flourished beyond his own lifetime.[13] Petrarch and his disciples, Giovanni Boccaccio (1313–1375) and Coluccio Salutati (1331–1406), were thus indebted to earlier scholars.[14] Nevertheless, early humanism 'culminated in Petrarch and Boccaccio, who in turn considerably accelerated its development ... Petrarch and Boccaccio were the forerunners of the Renaissance of the fifteenth century'.[15]

Thus, this work begins with the life of Petrarch, whose father was exiled from Florence in 1302 and who grew up in Provence, where he learned and translated the works of Cicero (106–43 B.C.), Virgil (70–19 B.C.) and Horace (65 B.C.–8 A.D.). Following a spiritual crisis, perhaps precipitated by his brother's decision to become a Carthusian monk, the Christian element in his writings became considerably more pronounced. One of his great works, his *Secretum*, is an exercise in self-analysis, examining his inner conflicts, and is dedicated to his chief Christian authority, St. Augustine (354–430). The *Secretum* is a drama set between the personas of Franciscus and Augustinus, with the latter presented as the embodiment of wisdom and truth.[16] However, Petrarch also continued to admire the pagan works of classical antiquity. The combination of classical and Christian ideas in Petrarch's mature thought mirrored that of medieval writers such as Dante Alighieri (*c.* 1265–1321), for whom the pagan Virgil was a primary guide, whilst his beloved Beatrice (embodying Christian wisdom) became increasingly important for Dante later on. Indeed, Dante would have concurred with Petrarch's statement that:

> If to admire Cicero means to be a Ciceronian, I am a Ciceronian ... However, when we come to think or speak of religion, that is, of supreme truth and true happiness, and of eternal salvation, then I am certainly not a Ciceronian, or a Platonist, but a Christian. I even feel sure that Cicero himself would have been a Christian if he had been able to see Christ and to comprehend His doctrine.[17]

As we shall see, building upon the earlier humanists, Petrarch became the key figure of Renaissance humanism of the fourteenth and fifteenth centuries. Its influence was greatly felt in society as it became embedded in education curricula, elevating grammar and rhetoric as beautiful forms of expression but also emphasizing the value of truth in the content of language. A popular quotation for humanist educators was taken from Cicero: 'Eloquence is nothing else than wisdom speaking copiously'.[18]

In attempting to achieve this eloquent expression of wisdom, humanism developed in several ways, encouraging the study of grammar, the huge growth in epistolary literature (letters), the use of dialogue as a literary technique, translations from Greek to Latin, an emphasis on moral philosophy and theology and an interest in historical interpretation. For instance, letter writing, as an art, originated in antiquity and grew through the Middle Ages: 'Humanists wrote letters with the public in mind', and 'with Petrarch there begins the long line of humanists who collected their own letters and at the same time carefully polished and revised them.'[19] Translations also assisted those, in schools, universities or society more generally, who had good Latin but little Greek. Humanist literature avoided the pedantic methods of proof demanded by the scholastic learning of the late-Middle Ages. Moreover, humanism's emphasis was on moral problems and practical wisdom rather than logic or metaphysics.[20]

As for historical interpretation, Lorenzo Valla (1407–57) employed historical criticism to great effect, especially in his influential *Elegantiae Linguae Latinae* (1444). Valla's work pioneered techniques that would become essential to the Reformation: he corrected errors in the vulgate, criticized exegesis, even that of Augustine, and he declared that the religious life was not a higher spiritual calling than the civic life of a lay person.[21]

However, it was in the latter part of the fifteenth century that humanist techniques were used in a more philosophical realm, with the rise of Neoplatonism in the works of Marsilio Ficino (1433–99) and Pico della Mirandola (1463–1494).[22] Thus, the 'humanistic' subjects among the medieval arts (grammar and rhetoric) provided the tools for the Florentine thinkers. Although considered by some more as philosophers than primarily humanists, the Platonic ideals that these scholars assimilated into their work emphasized ethics, the cultivation of the mind and will and the goodness of the soul.[23] For Plato (429–347 B.C.), the Demiurge (or, for Christian humanists, God), who brought the world into being, enabled it to share in His perfection by putting the image of the eternal into the human mind.[24] The body of thought generated by Plato's Athenian Academy, and by the middle Platonic schools that followed, was expanded into a philosophical movement by Plotinus (205–70 A.D.), who stressed the transcendence of 'the one', who was the highest principle and above human understanding: in Christian terms, a transcendent God. However the human soul, according to Plotinus, was by its nature divine, even though it had fallen into a human body, and longed to return to 'the one'.[25] Platonism was revitalized in the late Renaissance, partly by Ficino in Florence, and for many philosophers, including Pico, following Plato, Plotinus and Ficino, every Christian's destiny was to be reunited with divine perfection.

Ficino edited Plotinus' *Enneads*, as well as works by Proclus (410–485), Porphyry (232/4–c.305) and Pseudo-Dionysius (sixth century). His great works *De Religione Christiana* and *Theologia Platonica* sought to reconcile Renaissance classical thought with Christian theology. Many wealthy theologians, philosophers and writers, from all over Europe, travelled to Italy in the late-fifteenth century in order to learn at the cultural and intellectual centre of this new thinking. Although Italian universities were primarily law or medical schools, which offered some lectures on liberal arts subjects in the medical faculty, many students were also attracted to the humanistic teaching fashionable in most university towns. Likewise, most foreign students travelled to them in order to gain professionally desirable doctorates in law or medicine, but also to benefit from the humanistic teaching emanating from university and pre-university towns. John Colet (1467–1519), for instance, visited Italy between 1492 and 1496, corresponding with Ficino admiring and praising his transformative works.

Ficino and Pico had been trained, as had all scholars of their age, in scholastic philosophy, which provided the basis for their study of ancient philosophy.[26] Whereas humanists held the art of rhetoric in high regard, Pico and Ficino 'placed rather strict limits on the value of the rhetorical humanism of the earlier *Quattrocento*'. In fact Ficino 'regarded a rhetorical approach as a possible, but not a properly philosophical attitude toward philosophy'. Pico likewise regarded eloquence and wisdom as separate.[27]

Nevertheless, the Greek and Latin revival of rhetorical eloquence in Italy soon spread throughout Europe and this work seeks to explore some of the main humanists who helped disseminate its principles. If Petrarch was a key figure in the acceleration of this process in the fourteenth century, then Desiderius Erasmus of Rotterdam (1467–1536) was responsible for expanding and broadening humanism's influence in fifteenth-century Northern Europe, through his travels, letters, translations, colloquies and numerous other works. Many clerics and scholars visited Italy in the late-fifteenth and early-sixteenth centuries, and subsequently put the humanist principles they encountered there into practise upon their return home. Thus, men such as Thomas More (1478–1535), William Grocyn (1463–1519) and Thomas Linacre (c. 1460–1524) in England, Lefèvre d'Étaples (c. 1460–1536) in France and Johannes Reuchlin (1455–1522) in Germany helped to establish the *studia humanitatis* as the key method of intellectual pursuit, paving the way for the religious and political reforms of the sixteenth century even as they remained to some degree independent of those reforms with a legacy that went far beyond the Reformation. Even if we examined only one aspect of humanism, for instance its use of the Ciceronian model of oratory, we could nonetheless observe its significant impact:[28]

> Their identification with the Ciceronian orator made the humanists blind to some important features of classical thought, but at the same time it allowed them to see much that no one had glimpsed for centuries. By identifying themselves

with the idealized figure of the classical orator and refashioning existing rhetorical culture in the Ciceronian image, the humanists radically changed – even revolutionized – the relationship of European culture to the classical past.[29]

The great humanists provided a methodology and ethos for the study of the scriptures, literature, theology and philosophy, which were used as the basis of the criticism that led to subsequent changes to civil and religious institutions and ideas in the Reformation. They were more than an overture to a greater drama. Their achievements stand alone, and their works have been, and continue to be, drawn upon for inspiration and wisdom by generations of poets, politicians and priests through the centuries.

Humanism and Theology

All humanists were, of course, at least nominally Christian, but many wore their religious allegiance very lightly. Indeed, it has been argued, perhaps excessively, that humanism's connection with Christianity had to be invented by Erasmus and Lefèvre d'Étaples in the early-sixteenth century.[30] Certainly Petrarch made a close connection between humanism and Christianity. However, humanism was neither 'a high road to Reformation', as Rex has convincingly shown,[31] nor was the revival of classical learning a *praeparatio evangelica*.[32] Humanism was 'civic' in certain decades and in certain places, most notably in Florence in the age of Salutati and Leonardo Bruni (*c.* 1370–1444). In general terms, a republican polity was more likely than a despotic regime to produce humanists who linked their studies to active participation in public service. Although there were some humanists who were hired to discharge certain functions within some despotic cities, they tended to be less drawn to Roman republicanism. For some, the primary purpose of the humanist was that of gaining virtue (*pietas* in the Christian context) and learning, and this did not necessarily require the active participation in public service espoused by Roman republicanism.[33]

In more recent scholarship it has been argued that 'most humanists aspired to serve the State, and ... most servants of the State had been formed in the curriculum of Renaissance humanism'.[34] Indeed, most Italian civic officers (and especially secretaries and other officials at the Curia) had been exposed to humanistic education, at least from the mid-fifteenth century and many humanists aspired to public service.

Humanism's influence was, nonetheless, felt deeply in the religious and political upheavals of the European Reformation, although its contribution might be better seen as complementing rather than directly causing reform, by advocating and practicing the skilled use of languages, sources, rhetoric, eloquence, philology, and all the techniques of the *studia humanitatis*.

Born out of a love of language, text, books, classical learning, philosophy, and philology, humanism did not thereby necessarily entail or lead to the rejection of the Roman Catholic Church. Rather the Protestant reformers saw in humanist techniques a means by which they could profitably be put to that (preconceived) end, taking the humanist technique of '*ad fontes*' (a return to the original sources) and using it for a reformation far beyond the rebirth, or Renaissance, desired by the humanists. Both Luther and Calvin fully embraced humanist education and culture.[35] Indeed, in Germany and the Netherlands, a high proportion of young humanists followed Luther, but by the 1520s the older humanists, such as Erasmus, Reuchlin, Wimpheling (1450–1528) and Pirckheimer (1470–1530), had rejected Luther: theological convictions and humanist affiliation were not coextensive.

The humanists' criticism of both traditional Roman Catholic Church authority and practice, as well as new evangelical thought, led to battles: Valla against Pope Eugenius IV, Pico della Mirandola against Pope Innocent VIII, Erasmus against Luther, More against Henry VIII, Lefèvre d'Étaples against the Paris Faculty of Theology, Colet against the London clergy, Reuchlin against Pfefferkorn, and so on. Each battle demonstrated the power of humanist techniques and thought to challenge all areas of Church and society and, although humanism was used as a tool for the Protestant Reformation, the humanist project continued beyond the turmoil of sixteenth-century Europe to survive in a new form in post-Reformation thought. From a humanist perspective, humanity's capacity for reason had not been defeated by the Fall, as some Augustinians had claimed, and belief in it withstood the Reformation. Humanism's quest for reasoned and eloquent reform is as relevant today as it was in the late Middle Ages; its concern for truth in expression, language, eloquence and for humanity's need to improve itself in understanding and wisdom through the study of essential ancient texts and scripture is essential for a new Renaissance in religion today. Only in the light of a programme of rational reform through a love of text and language can sensible and wise leadership of change occur.

Humanism and Philosophy

In a famous exchange of letters, in 1485, between Pico della Mirandola and the Italian humanist Ermolao Barbaro (1454–93), Barbaro had sharply criticized scholastic philosophers as 'rude, dull, uncultured barbarians'. Immortality, the goal of any great writer, could only be conferred, Barbaro argued, on an author of 'shining eloquence'.[36] Pico disagreed vehemently with this thesis, but his reply in defence of the substance of philosophy is so eloquent that he was surely seeking to prove that he, as a philosopher, could 'equal, if not surpass, the best of his contemporaries' in the art of humanist persuasion.[37] Pico's argument was that philosophy and rhetoric address different subjects; that philosophy uses its own particular method; that Latin is a useful language for scholastic and philosophical purposes; and that humanist pursuits are fine, but limited. Being a full human being involves engagement with content as well as form.[38]

Thus, Pico rigorously but eloquently defended his opinion that the scholastics, whom Barbaro called 'barbarians', did not need humanist eloquence for their philosophical task. Wisdom need not be joined to eloquence, Pico argued. Indeed, it might even be wicked to do so:

> The barbarians have had the god of eloquence not on the tongue, but in the heart... if eloquence they lacked, they did not lack wisdom... eloquence should not have been joined to wisdom; only their not being joined perhaps is free from fault, so that it were wicked to join them...[39]

Pico's aversion to the advancement of rhetoric in the realm of philosophy was stark: 'So great is the conflict between the office of the orator and the philosopher that there can be no conflicting greater that theirs'.[40] The correspondence, which of course became public, aroused great interest amongst philosophers and humanists, so that even as late as 1558, Philip Melanchthon (1497–1560) in Germany wrote a response to Pico's argument, defending the place of rhetoric in the expression of philosophical ideas.[41]

Nevertheless, Pico cannot be depicted as anti-humanist. The elegant style of his letter to Barbaro is enough to indicate his strong affinity with, and mastery of, humanist technique. Moreover Pico and Ficino spent much of their time engrossed in the eloquent texts of what they considered to be theosophical wisdom from ancient Egypt, Persia, Greece and Israel.[42] Without the spur of humanism, and the philological tools it provided for both discovery and expression, the study of philosophy and theology would have been impoverished:

> Prodded by humanists, university philosophers tried to enhance the quality of their teaching by learning Greek, by improving the quality of translations and by acquiring a much more thorough knowledge of the ancient Muslim, Jewish and medieval Christian commentary tradition... Outside the universities, humanists were busily engaged in recovering the

heritage of ancient pagan philosophy and theology, reconstructing and promoting as philosophical alternatives ancient Platonism, Skepticism, Epicureanism, and Stoicism.[43]

However, as we shall now see, the extent to which humanism was linked to philosophy and theology is, historically, a matter of some division amongst scholars.

Scholarship

In order to distinguish more precisely between what humanism is and what it is not, it is necessary to conduct a brief survey of some of the scholarship on the subject.

By the seventeenth century, the term 'Renaissance', first used by Giorgio Vasari (1511–1574) in his *Lives of the Artists* (1550), had been accepted to mean the European blossoming of literature and culture that signified a break with the Middle Ages. This idea was further developed in the Enlightenment, reaching its height in the nineteenth century with scholars such as Jules Michelet, Georg Voigt, and Jacob Burckhardt.[44] For Michelet, the Renaissance in France was less to do with literary, philological and artistic renewal, and more to do with the birth of the modern age through the discovery of the world and man.[45] Voigt took up this adulation of the human spirit in his work *The Revival of Classical Antiquity* (1859), in which humanism was defined by its capacity to release humanity from the darkness of the medieval and transform civilization.[46] Building on these works, but going beyond them in scope and ideas, was Burckhardt's *The Civilization of the Renaissance in Italy* (1860). Burckhardt extended the argument that the Renaissance marked humanity's break from the past, but distinguished between political and social change in Italy and the rise of humanism. Humanism, he argued, was a separate phenomenon to the Renaissance, which was specifically related to the development of the individual. The Renaissance would have occurred without humanism, he argued, because the rise of 'individualism' was the chief cause of change.[47] Thus, as Zachary Schiffman has observed, 'nineteenth century views of the Renaissance as "the discovery of the world and the discovery of man" tend to bathe humanism (a literary movement) in the diffuse light of *humanitas* (a reawakening of the human spirit)'.[48]

Scholars since Burckhardt have attempted to reclaim the importance of the ancient revival as the basis for the Renaissance. Burckhardt's theory was challenged by Johan Huizinga in *The Waning of the Middle Ages* (1919) and by Charles Homer Haskins in *The Renaissance of the Twelfth Century* (1927), who both located the origins of the Renaissance in the Middle Ages themselves. Erwin Panofsky questioned this shift back to medieval roots in *Renaissance and Renascenes in Western Art* (1969) and emphasized, once again, the unique nature of the Renaissance.[49]

Hans Baron emphasized the civic nature of humanism in fourteenth- and early fifteenth-century Italy, and especially in Florence from 1402 until Leonardo Bruni (1369–1444).[50] Baron's argument was that humanism arose, in this specific context, in response to the crisis precipitated by the military threat presented by the Visconti rulers of Milan. Jerrold E. Seigel, who saw rhetoric as the fundamental theme in humanism of which civic humanism was merely an adaptation, has criticized this idea. Quentin Skinner and Anthony Grafton, who both asserted the rhetorical nature of humanist writings, expanded Seigel's revisionism, whilst questioning Cassirer's attempt to demonstrate a 'mystical' element in the works of writers such as Ficino and Pico.[51] However, the foremost scholar on humanism was undoubtedly Paul Oskar Kristeller, who reclaimed the idea of humanism as a literary curriculum but provoked the question of whether Renaissance humanism was merely a natural development in the history of culture, or whether it was a new start for humanity and civilization.[52]

One of the fundamental questions raised within the context of this debate was the degree to which humanism ought to be considered a philosophy, and whether humanism was indebted to, or broke away from, scholastic philosophy. At a conference held in Mirandola (the family home of Giovanni Pico della Mirandola) in 1963, there was a famous and revealing debate between two great scholars of late-Renaissance humanism: Eugenio Garin and Kristeller. Garin argued that:

> The difference between humanist-philosophers and scholastic-philosophers is not – as assumed by Kristeller – a fundamental distinction between scholastic metaphysicians, representing philosophy, on the one hand, and humanist *grammatici* or *oratores*, often ignorant of philosophy or opposed to it, on the other hand. Both scholastic philosophers and humanist philosophers, as Garin maintained, should be equally regarded as philosophers – of two different types.[53]

Thus, Garin argued, there were humanist philosophers and theologians who were wholly in a different category to scholastic theologians and philosophers, or, for instance, Dominican preachers, such as Girolamo Savonarola. This slightly anachronistic argument imposes an artificially rigid divide between humanism and theology, as to be a theologian in early-modern Europe one had to gain a degree from a university, and thus pass through its faculty of theology. For this reason, Erasmus was keen to claim his Turin doctorate, as it gave him the legal right to speak in public on theology. In this respect he was a humanist and a theologian. However, with regard to philosophy, Kristeller's argument, dating back to the 1930s, stressed that humanism and philosophy were only linked in the respect that humanist philological techniques were useful in approaching ancient texts, such as Plato, afresh:[54]

> The *studia humanitatis* includes one philosophical discipline, that is, morals, but it excludes by definition such fields as logic, natural philosophy, and metaphysics, as well as mathematics, and astronomy, medicine, law and theology.[55]

Yet, as recently as 1994, Garin questioned what skills we need when approaching a humanist work, for instance, Pico's *Commentary on a Canzone of Benivieni*:

> In this case, do we find ourselves on the terrain of poetry, mythology, the figurative arts, religion or philosophy? Are we dealing here with Girolamo Benivieni or Marsilio Ficino, Plato or Jewish mysticism? In order to annotate the text properly, is our knowledge of Greek and Latin – in addition to the Florentine vernacular – sufficient, or do we need ancient Hebrew as well? It seems reasonable to claim that it is the entire field of the so-called *Quattrocento* humanism that is being transformed. Poetry and philosophy, but likewise literature and the sciences, converge in new formations as techniques and arts experience shifts in methods, boundaries, and relationships.[56]

Garin's argument, however anachronistic, has had several followers including Charles Trinkaus and, most recently, Amos Edelheit.[57]

Trinkaus was one of the first to devote his entire career to the study of humanism. In his work *In our Image and Likeness* (1970), he attempted to demonstrate how humanists, through the pursuit of eloquence, exhibited a Christian philosophy in their work, seeking to learn about philosophical and theological matters and the human condition. Moreover, William Bouwsma sought to describe how humanists managed to reconcile both the Stoic and Augustinian elements of their thought into a coherent approach. He concluded that, far from being a movement solely concerned with rhetoric and form, humanism explored the deepest philosophical and theological questions.[58]

Building upon Garin's work, Edelheit further suggests that, in order to understand late-Renaissance and early-modern humanists, we cannot 'study intellectual, religious, and political history separately from each other, since many of these figures were deeply involved in

all these areas of activity or, at least, in more than one of them'.[59] This
attempt at an integrated approach to history and the study of humanism, philosophy and theology, seeks to form a balanced and rounded
portrait of these fifteenth- and sixteenth-century thinkers, who would
not have considered themselves 'humanist' as such, given that the term
was only coined long after their deaths. Thus, Edelheit, in a minority amongst modern scholars, argues that 'a sharp distinction between
theology and humanism, professional theologians and humanists, has
no historical validity'.[60] Edelheit's use of the term 'humanist theology'
is provocative, given that Kristeller, and his followers today, would see
it as a contradiction in terms. Edelheit's argument is that:

> the same figure can be a humanist in terms of his education
> and with regard to the main part of his activity, but can also
> be a philosopher, whose philosophical thinking is influenced
> by his humanist background; moreover, he can be a theolo-
> gian as well, one who creates a new kind of theology, influ-
> enced by his humanist and philosophical perspectives.[61]

According to Edelheit, this 'humanist theology', at least in Florence
between 1460 and 1490, was a product of rediscovering Plato and
the Neoplatonic philosophers.[62] He also considers that the 'secular'
scholars of the past few decades have chosen to ignore both the religious works of Renaissance writers, such as Pico's *Apologia* (*Defence*,
1487) or Ficino's *De Christiana Religione* (*On the Christian Religion*,
1484), and the fact that 'almost all humanists were observant Catholic
Christians, and that some of them held high offices in the Church
hierarchy'.[63] This is perhaps, he suggests, the legacy of Burckhardt's
distinction between culture and religion.

On balance the weight of scholarship sides with Kristeller on the
issue of separating humanism from philosophy and theology. Given
that most humanists were indeed Christian, and many ordained, it is
also true that, in order properly to define humanism, one must make
a clear distinction between the literary, rhetorical and philological
aims and preoccupations of most humanists, and the metaphysical,
logical and analytical focus of most philosophers. Moreover, being
a Christian, then as now, did not make one a theologian – that title
was given only to those who had gained, like Erasmus, a doctorate in
the subject. Therefore some humanists were theologians, that is, they
were educated as both and used humanist techniques in their theology
(indeed all the major reformers adhered to humanist literary methods,
especially with regard to scripture and patristics), but that fact does not
mean that there existed a 'humanist theology' as such.

It is clearly not possible to review all the scholarship relating to humanism in this work and many recently published volumes have been essential for researching this book.[64] However, it is worth mentioning that *The Cambridge Companion to Renaissance Humanism* (1997) is a masterly thematic survey covering humanism from its origins to the seventeenth century. Likewise, the three volumes of *Renaissance Humanism* (1988), edited by Albert Rabil Jr., give a near comprehensive overview. Alister McGrath's *The Intellectual Origins of the European Reformation* (1987) traces the development of thought from patristic and medieval times to humanism's engagement with biblical scholarship and translation. *The Renaissance in Europe: The Impact of Humanism* (2000), edited by Lucille Kekewich, begins with an assessment of Burckhardt as historian and proceeds to examine humanism's origins in culture and philosophy. Charles Nauert's *Humanism and the Culture of Renaissance Europe* (1995) gives an excellent survey of humanism from its origins to the mid-sixteenth century, with a reverence to Burckhardt and a thesis emphasizing the discontinuity between the medieval world and the Renaissance from Petrarch onwards. *The Impact of Humanism on Western Europe*, (1990) edited by Anthony Goodman and Angus Mackay, attempts a more geographical approach, taking the reader from Italy, to the Low Countries, France, Germany, England and the Iberian Peninsula. Zachary Schiffman's *Humanism and the Renaissance* (2002) usefully presents extracts from the most important works of humanist scholars, from Burckhardt and Huizinga to the late-twentieth century. A more complete collection of scholarship is *Renaissance Thought: A Reader* (2001), edited by Robert Black, which eschews the nineteenth century writers in favour of later ones from Kristeller to Nauert. Jerry Brotton's *The Renaissance Bazaar* (2002) contains a neat survey of humanism's impact. Anthony Levi's magisterial work *Renaissance and Reformation* (2002) represents the culmination of a whole career working on the subject. From Plato to the Swiss Confederation of the sixteenth century, Levi interweaves characters and historical events throughout Europe with great skill. One other work, from the most recent literature, *Christian Humanism: Essays in Honour of Arjo Vanderjagt* (2009) is a wonderful resource, covering humanism's association with Christianity, Stoicism, philosophy, arts and sciences as well as writing and education.[65] This work demonstrates the enduring appeal of Christian humanism as an academic discipline as well as an intriguing subject for anyone interested in the history of ideas.

Of course, each of the humanists explored in this current work has been scrutinized by scholarly experts. Some have been researched more than others: much scholarly attention has naturally been paid to the writings of Erasmus, but the important work of Rudolph Agricola (1442/3–1485), for instance, has been relatively neglected. The lesser known humanists are no less important for that and it is to be hoped that, as humanism continues to be scrutinized, the importance, influence and continued historical interest of even those less well known humanist figures of Renaissance and pre-Reformation Europe will be recognized.

Omissions: Women and Humanism[66]

This work is necessarily selective and subjective, given the constraints of space imposed by a book of this length. Some justification is necessary to explain why certain humanists of the pre-Reformation period have been included and others not.

Women humanists have largely been omitted from this work, not because they did not exist but because those humanists who made the greatest impact were those who had access to the education that was deemed necessary for professional life, and they were almost exclusively men.[67] Although there were many women who possessed the resources to pursue a humanist education and implement the techniques of the *studia humanitatis*, their involvement in professional life was heavily circumscribed and recent scholarship has demonstrated how most of them did not leave records.[68]

However, there were many women of considerable ability in the field of humanism in the pre-Reformation period. In Italy, the first generation of women humanists included Maddalena Scrovegni (1356–1429), from a noble Paduan family,[69] and Battista da Montefeltro Malatesta (1383–1450), the youngest daughter of the Count of Urbino.[70] The first generation also included Isotta Nogarola (1418–66), author of *Of the Equal or Unequal Sin of Adam and Eve*, a dialogue in which she defended Eve's ignorance as natural compared to Adam's deliberate and greater sin; Isotta's sister Genevra Nogarola (1417–1461/8); Costanza Barbaro (born after 1419); Cecilia Gonzaga (1425–51); Costanza Varano (1428–47), and Caterina Caldiera (d. 1463).[71] The next generation of Italian women humanists were led by Ippolita Sforza (1445–88), and the third generation, active between 1480 and 1500, included Cassandra Fedele (1465–1558), Laura Cereta (1469–99) and Alessandra Scala (1475–1506).[72] Of course, there were also prominent women humanists in other parts of Europe, such as Christine de Pisan (1365–1434) in France and, in England, Lady Margaret Beaufort (1443–1509), whose patronage was responsible for establishing great centres of humanist learning. Also in England, Margaret Roper (1505–1544) was one of the most highly praised intellects of her generation and the product of Thomas More's educational project within his own home.

Margaret King has suggested that Giovanni Boccaccio (1313–75) was a good example of a man who praised learned women, yet in doing so robbed them of their sexuality:

> The ambiguous sexual identity of learned women was assumed from the early age of humanism. In dedicating his book *De Claris Mulieribus* (*Concerning Famous Women*) to Andrea Accaiuoli, Boccaccio declared learned women to have so far exceeded the rest of womankind that her sexual being had in fact been transformed by a miraculous divine act…Her very greatness, Boccaccio reasons, in which she equals male greatness, suggests that Andrea was not so much a talented female as a woman transformed by the Creator himself and made – not a man – but a being of compound and indefinite sexuality.[73]

The attitude of learned men to learned women, as Boccaccio's dedication might suggest, was often one of fear. Intellectual women were perceived as being fierce and powerful, and therefore must also be chaste. This notion is demonstrated in a poem and expository letter from Antonio Loschi to Maddalena Scrovegni, written in 1389. The poem is revealingly entitled 'the Temple of Chastity'.[74] In it, the role of learned women is confined: '[Loschi] erects for Scrovegni a temple in her honour and binds her captive within it'.[75]

Likewise, Leonardo Bruni, writing to Battista da Montefeltro Malatesta in 1405, outlined how learned women should study.[76] Unsurprisingly, Bruni extolled the virtues of classical Latin, the Latin theologians (Augustine, Jerome, Ambrose, Cyprian and Lactantius), the Greek theologians (Gregory of Nazianzen, Chrysostom, Basil) and the classical Latin authors, such as Cicero, Virgil, Livy and Sallust. However, he advised that there are some studies that women should not undertake, namely arithmetic, geometry, astrology, and above all rhetoric, which has no practical value, he wrote, as women never enter public debate.[77] The only reason for a woman studying the great orators, Bruni argued, would be to improve their writing. Bruni further suggested that a woman's scholarly priorities should be to learn religion and morals (and not just from Christian writers), history and poetry, 'for we cannot point to any great mind of the past for whom the poets had not a powerful attraction'.[78]

Bruni's prohibition of rhetoric and his emphasis upon the greater importance of religious instruction for women became a feature of the work of women humanists, who rarely spoke in public (although it did happen on occasion) and tended to focus upon religious studies, but also wrote poetry, letters, orations, moral philosophy, biography and autobiography.[79]

Whilst humanist men, fearful lest educated women should forget their domestic place, tended to put women on the metaphorical pedestal, in order to keep them from intruding into their masculine world, women could be equally vicious in their condemnation of the pursuits of female humanists. Both Laura Cereta and Isotta Nogarola were victims of aggressive criticism from other women. Cereta defended herself vehemently, attacking those 'who strive for no good but exist to adorn themselves and do not understand that their condition is one of servitude', whereas Nogarola preferred to defend her interest in humanism on the grounds of its inherent benefits: 'For knowledge is not given as a gift, but through study ... The free mind, not afraid of labour, presses on to attain the good'.[80] Thus, the lot of the Renaissance humanist woman has immense relevance for today:

> The achievement of the learned women of the Renaissance ... was enormous, and has not wholly been surpassed ... What learned women of the Italian Renaissance attained, we have attained, in greater quantity; but what they suffered we have not escaped. We have confined their demons in a pandoran box, from which they erupt to haunt us: book-lined cells; armed maidens; the thwarting of ambitions.[81]

Many women humanists came from a similar socio-economic background: most were from very wealthy families and from great cities. In these rich, urban dynasties, education had often been available to women for many generations. Virtually all learned humanist women received encouragement and support from their fathers, and were recognized by their families to be talented. However, once they came of age, there was no place for them in public life. Of the alternatives available (marriage or religious vows), of those who chose marriage very few continued their humanistic studies afterwards. The convent perhaps offered an opportunity to study in peace, but was also a restricted environment and there is no evidence of any works written by those who entered the religious life.[82]

Selectivity

So what were the criteria in selecting humanists to be included in this work? It would have been easy enough to fill several volumes with just Italians, or Englishmen for that matter, so many claims are there for the title 'great humanist'. However, I have based my choices on three criteria. First, those selected represent a diverse variety of figures across time, geography and intellectual background in order to convey some idea of the sheer breadth of pre-Reformation and Reformation humanism. Second, the chosen figures were also diverse in their achievements: some are known only for their humanism; some used humanism in order to promote philosophy; some travelled widely, others hardly at all; some helped the spread of humanist ideas, others fought important battles. Third, those whom scholars have considered to be 'great' and to leave a lasting mark upon Europe have invariably been included. Thus, Francesco Petrarca was an inevitable choice, as his life and work symbolize a period of accelerated growth for the movement, building upon the works of late-thirteenth and early-fourteenth-century Italian humanists. Likewise, Erasmus, the 'prince' of humanists, and arguably the greatest of them all, was a certain choice.

Beyond these, the key humanist figures from various nations have been selected, in order to offer an overview of Europe on the eve of the Reformation. Thus, in England, John Colet, Thomas More, and Thomas Linacre, along with William Grocyn and Thomas Lupset, represent a close circle of friends who all made a significant contribution to learning and society. It is, however, inevitable that some may argue that Richard Fox (Bishop of Winchester and founder of Corpus Christi College, Oxford), William Lily (Grammarian and Headmaster of Colet's St. Paul's School), and several others could all fall into the same category. For Italy, the pre-Petrarchan humanists have been omitted due to lack of space, but of the fifteenth-century, Lorenzo Valla, perhaps the greatest of all Italian humanists, must be included. Alas, Ambrogio Traversari (1386–1439), Ermolao Barbaro (1454–1493), Pietro Pomponazzi (1462–1525), Pietro Bembo (1470–1547) and Angelo Poliziano (1454–1494) are some of the great Italians omitted.

As for Marsilio Ficino and Pico della Mirandola, we have seen above how divided the scholarship is concerning these figures. Were they humanists or philosophers? My belief is that they were primarily philosophers, but of such importance and widespread popularity that their influence was felt well beyond the Italian border. They were both humanists in that they knew the Greek language and ancient texts, made translations, used dialectic techniques and, even when arguing against the role of rhetoric, wrote eloquently and used all the armoury of humanist philology. Therefore for this reason, and for their influence upon northern European humanism, they are included.

Johannes Reuchlin, that fascinating German Hebraist and humanist who fought the 'battle of the books' with Pffefforkorn, was an irresistible choice, albeit one made at Sebastian Brant's (1458–1521) expense. Likewise closer scrutiny of Phillip Melanchthon's humanism and relationship with Luther, and of the work of Rudolph Agricola, who brought humanism from Italy to Northern Europe, was considered too valuable to be excluded. Lefèvre d'Étaples, the greatest of all French humanists, and Juan Luis Vives in Spain complete the selection. Each of the great thinkers and writers briefly surveyed in this work became humanists, or were closely associated with humanism, because they took the techniques and language of the *studia humanitatis*, learning from ancient culture, philosophy and theology, and combined it with their own individual passion for text, reasoning and debate. The differences between them not only create a fascinating patchwork of thought, but also highlight the manner in which humanism was used in a variety of ways to attempt to bring about moral and intellectual improvement in religion and society.

Structure

The book will follow a geographical trajectory and, to some extent, a chronological one. Each biography will not only include the main facts of each humanist's life – their education, career and works, with examples, as well as brief references to other relevant humanists with whom they dealt – but also offer an assessment of their influence amongst their contemporary colleagues and society, as well as their lasting legacy. Each chapter will also include a timeline of significant dates and events, as well as a digest of key works summarized for each humanist. For ease of reference, the two appendices contain brief sketches of other notable humanists and a glossary of terms.

ITALY

1

FRANCESCO PETRARCH (1304–1374)
and the Growth of the Renaissance

Francesco Petrarca (Petrarch in the anglicized version) was a huge influence in the growth of Italian and, by extension, Northern European humanism.[1] Although he never mastered Greek, his own words aptly summarize his intellectual work and thought: 'Platonic wisdom ... Christian dogma ... Ciceronian eloquence'.[2] Building on the work of the Italian humanists before him, Petrarch's passion for classical learning, philosophy and eloquence provided the basis for his life's work. Primarily a poet, he believed in a 'Rinascita' ('Renaissance'), a concept that brought about the transformation of literary culture in Europe. Petrarch, like Lovato dei Lovati before him, emphasized both a discontinuity with the more recent past, or the 'dark ages' of medievalism, in terms of the use of literature, language, eloquence and philology, and the need to return to ancient (classical) standards. Although in many areas of society there was continuity with the cultural past, such as in economics and politics, Petrarch believed in the transformative powers of the revival of ancient culture.

Introduction

Petrarch may not have been the first to express humanist ideas, or indeed the first writer to turn his whole life over to the discipline of humanist thought, but he was perhaps the greatest humanist influence in the Italian *Trecento*.[3] He not only loved the Latin works of Cicero and Virgil, but was captivated by the idea, if not the reality, of the Greek literature of Homer and philosophy of Plato, even though he could not speak or read Greek and there existed only a handful of Latin translations. Petrarch's Platonic interest, for instance, was derived from translations by Cicero and Augustine, and he probably only knew Plato's *Timaeus* and *Phaedo*, from which he nevertheless developed a dislike of scholastic Aristotelianism. He Christianized this Platonic thought in the light of Augustine, for him the greatest spiritual authority, as demonstrated in the fictitious dialogue with Augustine presented in his *Secretum*.[4]

Scholars have hailed Petrarch as the first humanist on the basis of his emphasis upon the centrality of Christian spirituality to the humanist approach:

> Francesco Petrarch deserves the title 'Father of Italian Humanism' in that, first, his compelling writings, dramatized by a life self-consciously lived and publicly reported, served to win support for humanism among the rich and powerful; and, second, in these writings he clearly formulated humanism's spiritual goal as a moralising force within contemporary Christian society.[5]

The origin of the term 'father of humanism' may perhaps be found in Petrarch's own comment, made late in his life, when he declared himself to be *'omnium senior qui nunc apud nos his in studiis elaborant'* ('the first of all who now in our time labour in these studies').[6] As we have seen in the introduction, there were several Italian humanists before Petrarch.[7] Petrarch's disciple, Salutati, in a letter of 1395 to the Paduan Bartolomeo Oliari, recognized that:

> The study of letters emerged to a degree in our century: the first cultivator of eloquence was Mussato of Padua, your fellow countryman, and there was Geri d'Arezzo, the greatest imitator of the orator Pliny the Second.[8]

Nevertheless, from its northern Italian base, Petrarchan humanism spread throughout Italy in the fourteenth and fifteenth centuries. Its influence was greatly felt in civic society as an ideology for the common good. It became embedded in education curricula, elevating grammar and rhetoric as beautiful forms of expression, but also emphasizing the value of truth in the content of language. He has been acknowledged as 'among the outstanding humanist philosophers',[9] notwithstanding the difficulties we have encountered with ideas of 'humanist philosophy' and 'humanist theology'.[10] Petrarch was at the forefront of humanist advances, 'since his authority and influence gave the whole movement a strong impulse'.[11] Petrarch enabled a transition in Europe from the medieval world to the Renaissance. He was, in a sense, a kind of prophet:

> Petrarch did not merely anticipate later Renaissance developments because he was unusually talented or perceptive. He also had an active share in bringing them about, because of the enormous prestige he enjoyed among his contemporaries and immediate successors. Like most philosophical (and political) prophets, he was one of those who foresaw the future because they helped to make it.[12]

Petrarch is best known for his Italian poems, particularly the *Canzionere*, a love poem written to his lifelong and unrequited love, Laure de Noves (Laura). But his Latin writings (poems, orations, invectives, history and letters) were also influential upon later humanism, particularly in his emphasis upon moral philosophy, in his love of Cicero, Virgil and Latin classical authors, in his preference for Plato over Aristotle, and in his reverence for other Greek works of literature, even though his knowledge of the latter was based entirely on secondary sources, mainly Cicero and Augustine. One of the characteristics of his humanism was his insistence upon the primacy of the Christian life, whilst at the same time rejecting scholasticism and reconciling classical learning with religious faith.

Life

'I was born in Arezzo. In a back street, Garden Lane, was the seed cast, and there sprang that arid flower, that insipid fruit that was I'.[13] Petrarch's colourful life began as part of an exiled family, as his father had been expelled from Florence for supporting the cause of the conservative White Guelphs (a political party in opposition to the radical Black Guelphs).[14] Petrarch was born on 20 July 1304 just south of Florence to Pietro di Parenzo di Garzo (Ser Petracco dell' Incisa) and Eletta Canigiani. Soon after, the family moved to Ancisa (Incisa), not far away and Gherardo, Petrarch's brother, was born two years later. Thereafter, Ser Petracco was offered employment in the Papal curia in Avignon and so the family moved to the nearby small town of Carpentras. Petrarch's first formal education was given by his school master at Carpentras, Convenevole da Prato. He learned elements of grammar and rhetoric and, even at this age, was attracted to the works of Cicero.[15] As Levi notes, Petrarch was captivated by Virgil and Horace, but it was 'his concern with the moral potential of human nature which he found in Cicero rather than the stylistic polish which marks in literature the inauguration of the Renaissance'.[16]

At the age of twelve, Petrarch was sent to the University of Montpellier with his brother Gherardo in order to study Law, which was his father's wish. Here Francesco required a surname and so he chose Petrarca, a name by which his father had once been known (Petracco/Petraccolo). Francesco's named appeared as 'Franciscus Petracchi' in the university's register.

Following the death of his mother in 1319, Petrarch travelled to Bologna to continue his legal studies with Gherardo, along with a friend, Guido Sette, where they stayed for six years. Nearly all Italian universities were primarily law or medical schools, but the study of law proved unfruitful for Petrarch. Instead, he turned his attention to philosophy and theology, purchasing a copy of Augustine's *City of God*. After his father's death Francesco returned to Avignon, abandoning the study of law. He wrote the comic *Philologia* (no longer extant) and embarked upon a literary career, supported by ecclesiastical benefices and patrons. Thus, like most literary figures of the time, he became an itinerant intellectual who was reliant upon patronage for his living.

In Avignon Petrarch had led a promiscuous life without commitment to any single woman. However, according to Francesco himself, in Holy Week, 1327, on seeing Laure de Noves (Laura) for the first time in the church of Sainte-Claire d'Avignon, he fell in love. Thus the legend of Petrarch's lifelong love affair began, which, even though Laura was already married, inspired the 366 poems of his *Canzoniere*, on which he worked for the rest of his life. The work is an 'autobiographical novel in verse, telling the story of a man's love-life' and is divided into two parts, roughly corresponding to Laura's life and death.[17] The passionate desire depicted in the poems is exemplified in Canzone LXXVI:

> Love with his promises cajoling me,
> to his old prison led me; clapped the door
> upon me; and the keys he handed o'er
> to my relentless foe, his votary.

Alas, bemused and blind, I could not see
until too late their guileful secret war.
And it is only now I come once more,
struggling and halting, to my liberty.
And though there be an end of durance now,
under familiar chains I still must bend.
I've writ my heart upon my eyes and brow,
and you will read it, you will comprehend.
And seeing my prison pallor, you will vow:
'You've but a little walk to death, my friend.'[18]

The passionate *Canzionere* became tremendously influential in later humanist and poetic writings, especially in the English Renaissance.[19]

In 1330, Petrarch took minor orders in the Church and entered the service of Cardinal Colonna, travelling to Lobez and Toulouse. The next few years proved significant for Petrarch: he became a devoted admirer of Augustine's *Confessiones* and made the remarkable discovery of Cicero's *Pro Archia*, adding it to his collection. By the beginning of his thirties, he had collected a significant library of philosophy, poetry, and history. Indeed, he made many significant discoveries of manuscripts from the ancient Latin world and acquired (but could not read) a Greek copy of Homer. His library became 'the largest private collection of classical literature in existence in his day'.[20]

By 1336 Petrarch had completed the first eighty or so poems of his *Canzionere*, completing an account of the first stage of his love for Laura. By now he seemed tormented by Laura's memory and sought many distractions, including mountain climbing. When he penned a description of climbing a certain Mount Ventoux, he described his love for Laura as evil and a calamity.

Meanwhile Petrarch's private life was made more complicated by the birth of an illegitimate son (whose mother is now not known), born in Francesco's newly purchased country house at Vaucluse. In this house Petrarch wrote *De Viris Illustribus*, a series of short biographies on the lives of illustrious men, and his Latin epic about the Roman general Scipio and the Punic Wars, entitled *Africa*. For his work he was offered a poetic crowning both from the University of Paris and the Senate in Rome. Petrarch's 'coronation' as poet laureate took place in Rome, on Easter Sunday (8 April) 1341, conducted by Orso dell' Anguillara, a Roman noble. In his acceptance speech Petrarch called for a rebirth of classical wisdom and poetry. Indeed, he was so enamoured with the honour that he developed the notion of the laurel as the symbol for poetic and literary immortality. Even five years earlier, one of his closest friends, Giacomo di Colonna, accused Petrarch of inventing the character of Laura and of really being in love with the 'Laurel', to which Petrarch had replied:

> You say that I have invented the beautiful name of Laura to have something to talk about and to get everyone talking about me, and that there's no Laura in my life except the poetic Laurel, to which obviously I aspire through long and persistent toil…I am afraid you are making fun of my disease, with the Socratic humour that is called irony.[21]

Probably around 1342/3 Petrarch underwent a profound spiritual crisis (although he later dated it to around 1350), which may have been connected to his brother's decision to become a Carthusian monk.[22] Whatever the cause of the crisis, Francesco seems to have responded by examining his own faith, thus developing ideas for his *Secretum*, begun in 1342 and completed between 1347 and 1353; it was also known as *Liber de Contemptu Mundi*.[23] The *Secretum* is composed of three imaginary dialogues between Petrarch and St. Augustine, who speak in the presence of 'Lady Truth'. It is a 'secret' book, intended for private meditation, and reflects his sense of inner crisis and depression, resolved only by Augustine's wise counsel and the recollection of his readings, particularly Virgil, Ovid (43 B.C.–17 A.D.), and Augustine's own *Confessions*.

This period also saw the birth of Petrarch's daughter, Francesca, the mother of whom is (once again) unknown. In the following two years Petrarch resided in Parma and Verona, before returning to reside in the solitude of Vaucluse, where his spiritual journey continued to be expressed in two works on the solitary and religious life: *De Vita Solitaria* and *De Otio Religioso*.

According to Petrarch, on 6 April 1348, Good Friday, Laura died:

> Laura, illustrious for her own virtues and long celebrated in my poems, first appeared to my eyes in my early manhood, in the Church of St. Clare in Avignon, in the 1327th year of our Lord, on the sixth of April, at the early morning service. And in the same city, in the same month of April, on the same sixth day, at the same first hour in the year 1348, her light was subtracted from that of the world, when I, by chance, was in Verona, ignorant, alas, of my fate.[24]

The cause of death may have been either the Plague or consumption: that same year Avignon suffered its worst epidemic of the former disease. Laura's death is reported by Petrarch to have occurred exactly twenty-one years since he first saw her, although some scholars have doubted that she existed at all.[25] Whatever the case, the 1350s saw

Petrarch briefly in Florence, a city he never knew well (where he met Giovanni Boccaccio, author of *The Decameron*, for the first time), Rome, Milan, Padua and Venice. By the end of the decade, Francesco had sent his son to live in Avignon, and his daughter had married. Francesca gave birth to her first daughter, Eletta, in 1361, and, in order to avoid the plague, moved to Venice in order to join her father. A second child, Francesco, was soon born and Petrarch adored him, but he only survived two years. Perhaps conscious of his own mortality, Petrarch wrote his last will and testament in Padua on 4 August 1370. On 19 July 1374 Francesca found her father dead, slumped over his desk as he worked on yet another opus. He was buried in the parish church and, six years later, his remains were transferred to a sarcophagus built in Arquà (south of Padua) by his son-in-law.

The Humanist

Petrarch's reputation as a pioneer of humanism has arisen because of his insistence on the contrast between 'his' new ideas – the revival of ancient language and culture, a 'Renascita' (Renaissance) – and medieval literature. The introduction to this book briefly outlined how scholarship, from the nineteenth-century Burckhardtian view onwards, debated the question of whether Renaissance humanism actually brought about a massive change that occurred between the 'middle' millennium of history, or medieval times, and the new flourishing of ideas and a renewal of humanity's outlook in the Renaissance. Charles Nauert, writing in the 1990s aptly summarized the enormity of Petrarch's influence on this issue:

> The distinctive Renaissance way of reading classical literature was a direct outgrowth of a new way of thinking about history, a way that is embedded in the term *Renaissance* itself. Petrarch invented this new way, and his invention explains why, even in his own lifetime, he was regarded as the crucial innovator, responsible for the emergence of a new era in civilization.[26]

This view credits Petrarch with the highest of accolades: not just of being the foremost in his field, but as wholly responsible for the change of a civilization. If we take civilization to mean everything in our entire culture then this is a claim too far. Nevertheless, the 'concept of historical discontinuity'[27] that had begun with Lovato dei Lovati in early thirteenth-century Padua was developed by Petrarch into the notion of the 'dark ages' an era wrongly maligned by later European historians – it was in fact far from bleak, either intellectually, religiously or culturally. Indeed, in the Middle Ages, there was a sharply developed sense of historical discontinuity, defined by the primitive Church, which was seen as spiritual and pure, in contrast to the corrupt later Church, which had become secularized, an idea subscribed to by Dante amongst others.[28] Moreover, European Renaissance culture shared the same social, economic and political characteristics as late-medieval Europe.

Nevertheless, following Petrarch, the division of history into the three periods of antiquity, medieval and Renaissance (a rebirth of antiquity) brought about a new emphasis on the importance of historical context when approaching literature of the past. The obsession, therefore, with text and its original context and meaning led to a new interpretation of the past through its literature. As Nauert has noted, 'humanism was not a comprehensive system of philosophy as scholastic Aristotelianism had been and continued to be, but it was a distinct method of intellectual procedure'.[29]

The debate surrounding this matter, therefore, is whether this new historical perspective alone constituted the fundamental element of Renaissance humanism and was sufficiently important and powerful definitively to alter the character of European literary culture, or whether there was another crucial ingredient, namely the humanists' desire for fame and glory that led to the spread of their ideas and to an increased 'individualism' which, for Burckhardt and others, was the defining characteristic of the Renaissance.[30] However, just as Nauert has shown that humanism can neither be defined purely in terms of a new philosophy, nor as the glorification of human nature, nor as a new spirit of individualism, so Petrarch's new sense of 'historical consciousness' cannot alone be considered as wholly responsible for such a seismic shift in European intellectual thought.

Petrarch was a Christian humanist, and any balanced assessment of Petrarch's historical outlook must emphasize his combination of 'pagan' classical culture with Christian faith, which prepared the way for the *Philosophia Christi* (philosophy of Christ) of later humanists, such as Erasmus. Like famous humanists throughout Europe yet to come, such as John Colet, Thomas More, and Juan Luis Vives, Petrarch considered Christianity, not philosophy, as primary. Indeed, he wrote, one cannot be a true philosopher without Christianity: 'In order to philosophize truly, we must above all love and worship Christ' as 'to be a true philosopher is nothing but to be a true Christian'.[31]

Petrarch gives us a clear example that it was possible for the humanists to reject scholasticism while remaining convinced Christians, and to reconcile their classical learning with their religious faith. He is thus an early Italian forerunner of that 'Christian Humanism', which recent historians have emphasized in the work of other north European Renaissance scholars.[32]

However, it was Petrarch's revival of classical scholarship itself that would drive a wedge between the past and Petrarch's adherence to the religious, political and cultural norms of his own age. His rediscovery of Cicero's *Pro Archia* at Liège in 1333 (a work which stresses the power of poetry) and of Cicero's personal letters at Verona, in 1345, were crucial in this development. The Cicero that Petrarch encountered in these texts was not only a great orator and politician but also a moral philosopher. For Petrarch, Cicero was admirable because of his works on moral questions, but his political career was, according to Francesco, a sad departure from the conduct expected of a wise man. In fact, Petrarch had no understanding of the values of the Roman ruling class, for whom office-holding and political power were both a right and a duty. The classical emphasis upon the virtue of giving one's life to public service clashed with Petrarch's desire to be a faithful Christian; the medieval emphasis upon monasticism and the contemplative life was a great influence upon Petrarch, particularly following his brother's decision to enter the religious life in 1343. The conflict between Christian and classical republican conceptions of virtue, with the latter emphasizing the active life of public service, the former the contemplative life of ascetic withdrawal from the corrupting influences of political society. Petrarch's inner battle between the active and contemplative life became a characteristic concern of humanists to come, as did his attempts to reconcile his Christian faith, as demonstrated in his *Secretum*, with his reverence for the eloquence and moral insights of classical authors, such as Cicero.[33]

Thus, Petrarch, wittingly or otherwise, established the twin pillars of Renaissance humanism: virtue (or *pietas* within the Christian tradition) and learning (or wisdom and eloquence). Petrarch's Christian faith was the basis for his philosophy of life, but his passion for Roman literature and the eloquence of expression through learning that could stir the emotions and lead humanity to greater heights was the means by which Christian humanism became established. For Petrarch, the truth of scripture combined with the beauty of classicism was a powerful combination that could persuade people to devote themselves to 'public service and...[to] put the welfare of society before personal advantage'.[34] The educational goals of moral improvement and social reform were therefore to be achieved through the wise application and expression of Christian tradition and classical idealism, rather than the intellectualism and cool logic of scholasticism.

Thus in Petrarch, the contemplative, reflective Christian of his *Secretum* resided alongside the active reviver of Roman culture – a combination resulting in a new and vibrant period in the history of ideas.

The Author and Scholar

Apart from his great Italian love poems, Petrarch's Latin works fall into several categories, all of which made a significant impact upon later humanist thought. These include moral philosophy, work on Greek and Roman literature, Plato, Aristotle and Christianity.

His works on moral philosophy comprise *De Remediis Utriusque Fortunae*, 1366 (On the Remedies of Good and Bad Fortune); *De Secreto Conflictu Curarum Mearum*, or *Secretum*, completed before 1358 (On the Secret Conflict of my Worries); *De Vita Solitaria*, 1356 (On the Solitary Life) and *De Sui Ipsius et Multorum Ignorantia*, 1367–1370 (On his Own and Many other People's Ignorance).[35] One of the common characteristics of these works is Petrarch's hostility to scholasticism, astrology, logic, jurisprudence, physicians and Aristotle, including the Arabic commentator on Aristotle, Averroës (1126–1198).[36] Petrarch's orthodoxy is revealed in his account of a heated exchange that resulted when he was visited by an Averroist cleric:

> 'I [Petrarch] quoted scripture'; he said, in a rage: 'Keep your little Doctors, yours and the Church's! I know whom to follow, whom to believe!' Said I: 'You have just used the words of the Apostle [Paul]; would you had also his faith!' 'That Apostle was a mere wordmonger, and mad into the bargain!...Paul and Augustine and all the rest were a lot of gabblers! Read Averroës!' 'Go to the devil with your heresies, and never come back!' Petrarch seized his interlocutor's clerical gown and pushed him out the door.[37]

Petrarch's attacks on scholasticism and Aristotelianism were personal and subjective and were not made in a systematic fashion. What we piece together from Petrarch's writings on moral philosophy is a reaction against theories such as the eternity of the world, or the attainment of happiness in this world, or 'double truth', meaning adherence to both Aristotelian philosophy and Christian theology. Petrarch objected to these three ideas on the grounds that they were against the Christian religion. But, as Kristeller points out, Petrarch's suspicion of scholasticism and Aristotelian logic was not based upon a new science, or religious grounds, but upon the basis of a conflict with knowledge from classical antiquity.[38] It was his passion for classical Latin (and to some extent Greek) culture and their texts that would provide the foundations not only for his own humanism, but for that of all the great humanists of Europe to come:

> The reading of the ancient Latin writers, and the sight of Rome's ancient monuments, evoked in Petrarch as in many other Italian humanists a strong nostalgia for the political greatness of the Roman republic and Empire.[39]

Indeed, for Petrarch, the purpose of studying ancient Roman authors was to gain, through the elegance of the writing, a love of virtue and aversion to vice:

> Thus the true moral philosophers and valuable teachers of virtues are those whose first and last purpose is to make their students and readers good. They not only teach the definitions of virtue and vice, haranguing us about virtue's splendour and vice's drabness. They also instil in our breasts both love and zeal for what is good, and hatred and abhorrence of evil.[40]

Likewise, Petrarch argued, had the scholastics taken due notice of the greatest of ancient philosophers, Plato, they would have had a better concept of God and immortality, instead of worshipping Aristotle, 'whom they don't understand; and they accuse me for not bending my knee before him, ascribing to ignorance what stems from my faith'.[41]

One of Petrarch's manuscript discoveries was that of Cicero's *Letter to Atticus*, made whilst he was in Verona, but it was one of many such works in his collection. He also deeply admired the works of Virgil and imitated him in his poem *Africa* as well as giving the *Aeneid* an allegorical interpretation in Book II of his *Secretum*. Petrarch also adopted ideas from Seneca's *Moral Epistles*, such as his dislike of dialectic forms of thought and emphasis on moral problems, and the Stoic ideas of Virtue and Fortune, which are apparent in Francesco's *De Remediis* and *Secretum*.[42] In *De Remediis* (Remedies for Good and Bad Fortune, 1366), Petrarch harmonized Stoic and Christian ideas, so that '...Job, and above all Christ himself' were seen as 'heroic figures who had endured tribulation and excruciating pain more stoically than the Stoics themselves'.[43]

In terms of Greek scholarship, Petrarch had less success, although he may have been something of a herald. He never learned ancient Greek, but his copy of a Greek manuscript of Homer (which he could not read) became the basis of the earliest Latin translation. He also owned a Greek manuscript of Plato's *Dialogues*.[44] Thus, one could argue that he opened up, albeit indirectly, a new interest in Greek poetry and literature beyond philosophy and theology. He knew Plato's *Timaeus* and *Phaedo*, and made a claim for Plato's prominence over Aristotle, arguing that Aristotle may be praised by a greater number of men but Plato is praised by greater men.[45] However, Plato never achieved equality with Aristotle even in the sixteenth century let alone in the fourteenth. The argument that, 'when Raphael painted his School of Athens in the early sixteenth century, Plato had achieved equal stature with Aristotle, and had become as widely known', is outweighed by the fact that there remained many more sixteenth-century editions of Aristotle than of Plato.[46]

With the combination of religious faith and classical learning, the classic Christian texts of the Patristic period became of vital importance for Petrarch, and none more so than those of Augustine. In his *Secretum* Petrarch examined his own life by inventing a dialogue between himself and Augustine, and Petrarch kept a copy of Augustine's *Confessions* with him wherever he went.

Petrarch was not without his critics, and his four invectives demonstrate his responses to attack from four important sources: the medical profession, the Church, scholasticism and French culture.[47] For instance, his *Invective Against a man of High Rank with No Knowledge or Virtue* was directed against the prominent churchman Cardinal Jean de Caraman (d. 1361), and attacked the cleric's pious arrogance, accusing him of being a slave to his position.[48] Written in the style of a classical satire, Petrarch's words are strong:

> You seemed so dignified, I confess, that a sane person might easily have overlooked your insanity. Yet it is not your virtue, but your dignity that makes you deserve to be stung by words rather than silence, although I pity your dignity – if dignity it is, rather than an illusion and a sham...By now, the populace is fed up with you.[49]

Apart from the major influence of the revival of classical learning, the rejection of scholasticism and the combination of philosophy with faith, there were other, minor elements in Petrarch's work that were, nevertheless, new. The personal, subjective and individualistic character of his writings, such as a pronounced self-consciousness, would become a feature of future humanist writers; his love of fame (although he condemns it) and travel can also be recognized in later humanists. His devotion to solitude, as expressed in his *De Vita Solitaria*, and the exquisite pleasure of melancholy ('acidia' of mood) that he enjoys in his *Secretum* are also features that were later adopted.[50] Marsilio Ficino and Pico della Mirandola would subsequently develop Petrarch's notion that the object of all thought and philosophy for humanity is its moral progress and happiness, as well as the idea that knowledge of humanity requires a knowledge of God: 'To know God, not the gods, this is the true and highest philosophy'.[51] Likewise, Petrarch's emphasis, following Augustine, on the primacy of the will over the intellect would also take hold:

> It is safer to cultivate a good and pious will than a capable and clear intellect. The object of the will is goodness, the object of the intellect, truth. It is better to will the good than to know the true … Hence those are in error who spend their time in knowing rather than in loving God. For God can in no way be fully known in this life, but He can be loved piously and ardently … It is true that nothing can be loved that is completely unknown. Yet it is enough to know God and virtue up to a certain point (since we cannot know them beyond that point), so long as we know that he is the source of all goodness by whom we are good (insofar as we are good), and that virtue is the best thing after God.[52]

Petrarch's moral philosophy and Christian reasoning have to be extracted in fragments from his works. They are not presented to us as fully developed ideas but are more akin to 'aspirations',[53] encapsulated in his mantra: 'Platonic Wisdom … Christian dogma … Ciceronian eloquence'.[54] Thus, his life's work formed the basis of the lives and careers of all other authors examined in this current work.

Petrarch's Influence and the Growth of Renaissance Humanism

As we have seen in the brief outline of the events of his life above, Petrarch was an itinerant man who never settled for long in any one place. Nevertheless the establishment of his ideas in the Italian consciousness was assured by their adoption in Italian cities, particularly by wealthy intellectuals and especially in Florence.[55] Florence became the centre of Italian humanism, ironically perhaps because of its lack of a university (until 1349); this however meant that it was relatively unencumbered by traditionalist ideas, whilst its republican status (until 1532) might have made the revival of ancient Roman republican values attractive.[56] More specifically, however, the establishment of Petrarch's ideas in Florence can be attributed to one man: Giovanni Boccaccio. Until 1350, Boccaccio's life and work had been dedicated to 'vernacular prose tales in the medieval tradition', including his greatest and most famous work, the *Decameron*.[57] However, in 1350, Petrarch passed through Florence as part of a pilgrimage to Rome and spent some time with Boccaccio, whose acquaintance he had not previously made. The meeting was to have such a profound effect on Boccaccio, then thirty-seven years old and well established in his career, that it changed his intellectual and moral outlook as well as his literary output for the rest of his life.

Rejecting the 'dark age' of the medieval past, not only did Boccaccio devote himself to classical studies from then on, but he also spent much time promoting the cause of Petrarch's Christian Renaissance humanism in Florence, engaging with the learned of the city and amassing a group of followers. Thus, the key city of Florence was captured by humanism's ideology, even though Petrarch spent very little time there himself.

With Petrarch's death in 1374 and that of Boccaccio soon after, in 1375, it was again Christian teachers who continued to promote humanism in Florence, through the fellowship of Christian humanists led by the theologian and Augustinian friar Luigi Marsili (1342–94). However, it was the work of the chancellor of the Florentine republic from 1375–1406, Coluccio Salutati (1331–1406) that was most influential in propagating humanist ideals.

Salutati was born in 'the small rural commune in the village of Stignano in the Valdinierole', on the border between Florence and Lucca. After the Ghibelline victory, his family fled to Bologna until 1350/1, where Salutati was educated by the skilled rhetorician Pietro da Moglio (d. 1384) before, on the death of his father, he returned to Buggiano.[58] Although Salutati never knew Petrarch personally,[59] he helped cement humanist methodology among the intellectual and political elites by making frequent use of the works of Cicero and by collecting and making available to the learned an enormous library of classical manuscripts. Moreover, his personal contacts throughout the area ensured the dissemination of humanist ideas into fifteenth-century Italy. Thus, as reflected in both official documents and letters, humanism was able to grow from the shared interest of a few individuals to 'the cultural norm of the educated classes'.[60]

Salutati was a humanist before he encountered Petrarch's ideas. It was the 'pre-Petrarchan, the secular, civic variety espoused by those earlier scholars that Petrarch endeavoured to transform into a Christian humanism by reconciling what he considered the best elements of pagan culture with Christianity'.[61] Nevertheless, Salutati developed Petrarch's humanist agenda by improving the standards of humanist textual and linguistic scholarship, undertaking the work of textual emendation, whilst being aware that Latin style had changed since classical times. He also espoused the study of Greek texts, a task only begun by Petrarch, realizing that Latin culture had been profoundly influenced by its Greek heritage. Salutati persuaded the government to employ

Manuel Chrysoloras, a leading Byzantine scholar, to teach in Florence from 1396–1400, resulting in the further establishment of humanist disciples.[62]

Salutati eventually followed Petrarch's Christian slant on humanism, but he 'only succumbed to the attractions' of it 'at Rome in his late thirties after protracted contact with the latter's writings'.[63] Nevertheless, Salutati's 'conversion' in 1369 was 'permanent and justifies considering his humanism as Petrarchan'.[64] In a letter written to Ugolino Orsini, consoling him on the death of his father, Salutati describes heaven for those who have Christian faith:

> We live with the indulgence of nature and this is common to us and other animals; to live well, however, is peculiar to a human being and is the mark of a good and virtuous man. This capacity is not within our power but we acquire this by ourselves, through the cooperating grace of God, by means of virtues and a good disposition of mind.[65]

This idea of living well and improving oneself and society through the correct disposition of mind was a key idea that permeated humanism for the next two centuries. Salutati's Christianity was also reflected in his reverence for the contemplative life and the reward of a peaceful afterlife, but he also passionately believed in the good to be achieved through a life of action and public service. Thus, the twin pillars of Christian humanism lay at the heart of his diplomatic and political work: the art of eloquent rhetoric in work of persuasive diplomacy and the search for moral virtue in political decisions. Salutati was a devout, publicly minded man. Thus, 'Burckhardt's impression that the typical humanist was an impoverished intellectual without much stake in society' can hardly be sustained in Salutati's case.[66]

Baron's theory of 'civic humanism' begins with this period in Florentine history, arguing that, following the advances of the Duke of Milan, Giangaleazzo Visconti, between 1385 and 1402, Florence's resistance led its humanists to emphasize a political ideal based upon Roman republicanism, which held public service as the highest of goals. Salutati's life and works only partly reflect this view of society, as it omits the Christian aspect of his humanist ideal. Although Salutati can be seen to have assisted in the rediscovery of ancient Roman republicanism, at times he also upheld monarchy as a form of governance, which reflected the hierarchy of God's kingdom.[67]

One of Salutati's most famous pupils and one of those most responsible for the furtherance of the humanist programme in Italy was Leonardo Bruni of Arezzo (1369/70–1444), who began as a scholar, translator and historian, rose to public life (Secretary to the Papal Curia, 1405–15, Chancellor of the Florentine Signoria, 1427–42), and became one of the main defenders of Roman republican values. Bruni translated many Greek works into Latin, including those by Aristotle, Plato, Plutarch, Xenophon and Polybius. He translated Aristotle's *Nichomachean Ethics* and *Oeconomics*, which were widely published in the fifteenth and sixteenth centuries.[68] Bruni wrote a life of Aristotle (1430) and a biography of Dante. But his most famous work, and his masterpiece, was the *Historiarum Florentini Populi Libri XII* (*History of the Florentine People*) (c. 1416–42), in which he extolled ancient Roman governance as the best model for Florentine society. Bruni denied that the Holy Roman Empire of Augustus was the pinnacle of achievement, arguing instead that, in the Athens and Rome of ancient times, the free expression of dialogue and discourse was the basis for the societal model. This republican ideal, he argued, was swept away by tyrannical imperial rule, but was to be realized anew in fourteenth-century Florence.[69] This rebirth, he suggested, first became evident in twelfth-century Tuscany with the rise of republican, self-governing cities, thus marking a distinctive break with the past, a Petrarchan notion. As Nauert observes, for Bruni the image of the ideal man was Dante: 'father, active citizen, poet, and philosopher'.[70]

Bruni's republicanism is also evident in his 1403/4 composition *Laudatio Florentinae Urbis* (*Panegyric of the City of Florence*). Based upon the ancient Latin author Sullust's notion that 'harmony makes small states great while discord undermines the mightiest empires', Bruni's work vindicated 'Florence's republican form of government' and refuted 'the princely humanist orthodoxies which organized the self-presentation of the Visconti Dukes', from whom Florence was under threat.[71] In the work, Bruni praised the city in true republican humanist style by imitating the rhetoric of the Athenian orator Aelius Aristides:

> [Florence's] founder is the Roman people – the Lord and conqueror of the entire world ... What nation in the entire world was ever more distinguished, more powerful, more outstanding in every sort of excellence than the Roman people? Their deeds are so illustrious ...[72]

Bruni's argument concerning the illustrious heritage of Florence emphasized that it was a city founded at exactly the same time as Rome's great flourishing, when the likes of Caesar, Tiberius and Nero had 'not yet deprived the people of their liberty'.[73] For Bruni the most shining quality of this great republic in action is the rule of law: 'There is no place on earth where there is greater justice open equally to everyone'. For Bruni,

Florence is self-evidently at liberty, because justice is evident, and justice is impossible without liberty.[74] Humanism consisted of two strands by the end of Bruni's life. On the one hand it was a practical preparation of young men for their work in civic life, exemplified in the life and work of Niccolò Machiavelli (1469–1527), author of *The Prince*. On the other hand, humanism was the means of improving a contemplative life of philosophical investigation and textual scholarship. This kind of Christian philosophy would reach its height in Italy with the philosopher Marsilio Ficino. However, before the Neoplatonism of Ficino and Pico, there was the important development of the critical humanistic method as practised by and lived out in the person of Lorenzo Valla.

Petrarch: Dates and Events

October 1302:	Pietro (Francesco Petrarch's father) is exiled from Florence.
20 July 1304:	Petrarch is born in Arezzo to Pietro di Parenzo di Garzo (Ser Petracco dell' Incisa) and Eletta Canigiani.
1305:	the family move to Ancisa (Incisa).
1307:	Gherardo, Petrarch's brother is born.
1310:	Laura de Noves, daughter of the Knight Audibert de Noves is born in Avignon.
1311:	family goes to Pisa to meet the new Emperor Henry VII.
1312:	family moves to Carpentras near Avignon.
1316:	Petrarch goes to school in Montpellier with Gherardo. Acquires the name Petrarca, based on one of the names his father was known as (Petrarcco/Petrarccolo). His named appeared as Franciscus Petrarcchi in the school's register.
1319:	Petrarch's mother dies.
1320:	Petrarch goes to Bologna to study law with Gherardo. Petrarch despises the law.
16 January 1325:	Laura de Noves marries Hugues II de Sade. Petrarch buys his first book: Augustine's *De Civitate Dei*.
1326:	Petrarch's father dies. Petrarch abandons law and returns to Avignon. He writes *Philologia*, a comedy.
6 April 1327: (**Good Friday**)	sees Laura de Noves (Laura) for the first time.

1330: Petrarch enters the service of Cardinal Colonna. Travels to Lobez and Toulouse.

1333: Boccaccio reads Petrarch's work. Petrarch travels to various European cities and discovers Cicero's *Pro Archia* at Liège.

1336: Petrarch climbs Mount Ventoux. and begins to write *Rerum Vulgarium Fragmenta* (*Il Canzionere*) between 1336 and 1338.

1337: travels to Flanders and the Brabant and to Rome. Petrarch's first child, Giovanni, is born.

1338: Petrarch begins to write *Africa* and *De Viris Illustribus*.

1340: Petrarch offered a poetic crowning from the University of Paris and the senate in Rome at the same time; he accepts Rome's offer.

1341: crowned poet laureate in Rome on Easter Sunday (8 April).

1342: reorganizes his *Il Canzionere* between 1342 and 1347. Writes *Rerum Memorandarum Libri*, on the cardinal virtues.

1343: writes *Psalmi Poenitentiales*: seven prayers and confessions. Gherardo becomes a Carthusian monk. Petrarch writes *Secretum*. Francesca is born.

1344: writes *Italia Mia* in Parma.

1345: discovers Cicero's letters in Verona and makes a collection of his own letters, *Familiares*.

1346: writes *De Vita Solitaria* and *Bucolicum Carmen*.

1347: writes *De Otio Religioso*. 6 April 1348, Good Friday: Laura dies.

1350: Petrarch and Boccaccio meet for the first time. Travels to Rome for the Jubilee Year.

1352: begins to write *I Trionfi*.

1353: moves back to Italy for the rest of his life.

1353–61: lives in Milan under Visconti patronage.

1354: writes *De Remediis Utriusque Fortunae*.

1356: travels to Basle and Prague.

1357: sends his son Giovanni to live in Avignon.

1359: begins compiling *Epistolae Familiares*.

1360: travels to Paris. In October writes *To Homer*.

1361: Giovanni, Petrarch's son, dies of the plague. Francesca marries. Petrarch moves to Padua. Begins *Seniles*.

Moves to Venice. Francesca gives birth to Eletta.
Francesca and family move to Venice to avoid the
plague.

1361–8: Venice.

1365: writes to Boccaccio.

1366: Francesca gives birth to a second child, Francesco.

1367: Petrarch moves to Arquà. Writes *De Sui Ipsius et
Multorum Ignorantia.*

1368: Francesco, Petrarch's grandson dies. Petrarch moves to
Padua.

1370: writes *Testamentum.*

1372: writes *The Trials of a Man of Letters* to the Abbot of
St. Benigno.

1373: finishes *Il Canzionere.*

19 July 1374: Petrarch dies.

Petrarch's Key Works

1336–1373: *Il Canzioere*: also known as *Rime sparse* or *Rerum
Vulgarium Fragmenta* (Fragments of Vernacular
Matters). 366 'Canzons', or poems on his love for
Laura. Over two hundred poems are from Laura's
lifetime and over one hundred written after her
death.

1337: *De Viris Illustribus*: short biographies on the lives of
illustrious men (from classical times).

1337: Petrarch begins his work *Africa*: a Latin epic in the
mould of Virgil's *Aeneid* about the Roman general
Scipio and the Punic Wars.

1342: *Rerum Memorandum Libri IV sive Memorabilia*: an
incomplete treatise on the cardinal virtues.

1342–1353: *Secretum*: also known as *Liber de Contemptu Mundi*,
it contains three imaginary dialogues between
Petrarch and St. Augustine in the presence of 'Lady
Truth'. A book for meditation, which expresses
Petrarch's inner religious crisis and depression, eased
by Augustine's counsel.

1343: *Psalmi Poenitentiales*: seven prayers and confessions.

1345: *De Vita Solitaria*: a treatise of two books on the
virtues of the religious, solitary and contemplative
life, dedicated to Philippe de Cabassoles, Bishop of
Cavaillon, and inspired, perhaps, by Petrarch's brother
becoming a monk.

1345: *De Otio Religioso*: another work extolling the religious life and dedicated to the Cartreux monks of Montrieux, of whom Gherardo, his brother, was a member.

1345–1366: *Bucolicum Carmen*: a poem in twelve eclogues. Each poem deals with a different subject, such as an allegory on Petrarch's crowning, the plague of 1348 and the death of Laura.

1351: *I Trionfi*: a series of Italian poems inspired by his love for Laura.

1354–66: *De Remediis Utriusque Fortunae*: his most famous Latin work. A moral treatise on good and bad fortune. Two books of 122 and 131 dialogues between 'Joy' and 'Reason' (concerning good fortune) and 'Sorrow', 'Fear' and 'Reason' (regarding ill fortune).

1359–66: *Epistolae Familiares*: a collection of letters written between 1325 and 1366, compiled in twenty-four books and dedicated to Ludwig van Kempen.

1361–73: *Seniles*: Petrarch's second collection of letters. Begun in 1361, it contains one hundred and twenty-eight letters written between 1361 and 1373 and sorted into seventeen books. The final letter, the first and only of the eighteenth book, is his incomplete letter to Posterity, an autobiographical letter, written in 1351.

2

LORENZO VALLA (*c.* 1406/7–57)
The Confrontational Philologist

Many, many books have issued from my pen in almost every area of learning, and in these I have disagreed with some great authors of long established reputation ... I am one who writes not only against the dead, but against the living as well – not one or two of them, but many – and not merely against private persons but even against those who hold high office![1]

Thus begins Lorenzo Valla's 1440 treatise on the '*Forged and Mendacious Donation of Constantine*' (*De Falso Credita et Ementita Constantini Donatione Declamatio*). The quotation reflects not only Valla's audacity as a writer, but also his vanity and combative nature, which gained him many enemies during his short, itinerant lifetime. Lorenzo Valla lived at a time when humanism was developing into a grand educational and philosophical movement that would permeate civic, religious and intellectual life. Valla's works are mainly adversarial and polemical in style, reflecting the growth of humanistic ideas that would, after Valla's death and by the end of the fifteenth century, become mainstream in Italian universities: the *studia humanitatis*.[2] In the first half of the fifteenth century, Valla was the epitome of the humanist scholar and critical thinker. He was a great humanist, so much so that his critical works were too sophisticated for even the most learned men of his generation. Although many other humanists were learning Greek and teaching at Italian universities, it was not until Erasmus championed Valla in the sixteenth century, realizing his importance and publishing his most challenging works, that Valla's worth was justly recognized. Today, he is acclaimed as one of the greatest humanists:

> Lorenzo Valla's contributions to humanism can hardly be overestimated. He gave the humanist program some of its most trenchant and combative formulations, but also put it into practice by studying the Latin language as no one had done before, discussing a host of morphological, syntactical, and semantical features in his widely influential *Elegance in Latin* (*Elegantiae Linguae Latinae*, 1441). But he went even further than this. His aim was to show the linguistic basis of law, theology, philosophy, and in fact all intellectual activities, thus turning the study of language into a sharp-edged tool for exposing all kinds of errors and misunderstandings.[3]

Life[4]

Valla was born in Rome, probably in 1406/7, and educated there and in Florence where he learned Greek from Giovanni Aurispa (1376–1459). Valla lived through the time of the schism when claims to the papacy became divided with one contender for the papacy residing in Avignon and the Italian claimant in Italy, but itinerant. Sometimes the papal court resided in Florence, and here Valla probably nurtured his ambition to become a papal secretary. The schism ended in 1417, when Valla was only around ten years old, but it was not until 1443 that Pope Eugenius IV returned the papal court to Rome.[5] His ambition to become a papal secretary there was possibly fuelled by admiration for his uncle, Melchior Scrivani, who held that position. However, Valla, even at the age of twenty-four, was considered too young for the post. Thus, after the death of his father, he moved to Pavia in 1429–31, in order to take up the post of Professor of Eloquence at Pavia University.

In Pavia, Valla taught rhetoric, and wrote his treatise *De Voluptate* (*On Pleasure*) in his first year there. The treatise was an eloquent examination of Stoic, Epicurean and hedonistic ethics. Valla argued for the right of humans to indulge in natural pleasures, as Epicurus had done in the fourth century B.C. In the work Leonardo Bruni (called Aretino) argued that life should conform to nature; Antonio Beccadelli (Panormita), argued in favour of Epicureanism (the gratification of sensual desires); and Niccolò Niccoli argued for Christian hedonism, where virtue is practiced in order to achieve pleasure, but that virtue is not an end in itself. Valla later emended the work and re-titled it *De Vero Bono* (*On True Good*). In the book, Valla considers the fable of Gyges, 'in which Gyges' ring enabled him to become invisible and to do wicked things', a fable Valla rejected on account of its internal inconsistency: 'the fable does not square with itself and lacks coherence'.[6] The work begins thus:

> When I undertook the discussion of the cause of the true and the false good, which is dealt with in the three following books, it seemed best to follow a most compelling division of the subject according to which we are to believe that only two goods exist, one in this life, one in the next. I have to deal with both of them, but in such a way that I shall seem to have gradually moved from the first to the second. All of my treatise is directed to the matter of this second good, which, as tradition holds, we reach through two means: religion and virtue. However, it is not my purpose to speak of religion, since others, especially Lactantius and Augustine, have dealt with it sufficiently and fully: one of them, as the earlier, appears to have confuted the false religions; and the other to have confirmed the true one with greater distinction. I have been seized instead with the desire of dealing as far as is humanly possible with those true virtues through which we reach the true good.[7]

Thus, Valla did not ignore the role of religion in the matter, but simply deferred to Lactantius and Augustine as greater authorities on the subject.

Valla was forced to leave Pavia in 1433 following a dispute with the jurists, in which he attacked the language of one of their main authorities, Bartolus of Sassoferrato (1313–1357). Lorenzo journeyed to Milan and then to Genoa, returning to Rome, but eventually settling in Naples, where he was employed, by 1437, as secretary to Alfonso of Aragon (1396–1458), who was making military advances on Naples. Alfonso's court had a reputation for riotous and debauched living, temptations to which Lorenzo was not immune. However, during this period Valla was prolific in his output: in 1439 he finished the first version of his critique of scholastic philosophy; in 1440 he wrote *De Libero Arbitrio*, which discussed the concept of free will. In the work Valla conceded that God's foreknowledge of events (given His omniscience), is not incompatible with free will, for our minds are unable to comprehend the mystery of God's power. At this time he also composed *Dialecticae Disputationes*, a work that strongly opposed Aristotle and the scholastics, more on the grounds of their use (or misuse) of language than of their philosophical tenets. Although the work made little contribution to philosophy, it did help discredit scholasticism. Lodi Nauta has noted that Valla, along with Rudolph Agricola, was influential in the development and promotion of humanist dialectic:

> [Valla and Agricola] are generally responsible, each in his own way, for having inaugurated the transformation of Aristotelian-Scholastic logic into a humanist dialectic. Humanist dialectic is marked by a study of argumentation and forms of reasoning that were tailored to the practical goal of analyzing the argumentative structures of classical texts, then using this knowledge in composing one's own persuasive discourse of whatever kind.[8]

Another work from this period is his great *De Falso Credita et Ementita Constantini Donatione Declamatio*, which argued that the document purporting to transfer much of Europe into the jurisdiction of the papacy, entitled the 'Donation of Constantine', was a fake. Thus, Valla argued, the temporal authority of the papacy was invalid. Valla cited four main objections to the legitimacy of the Donation document:

> First, I shall show that Constantine and Sylvester were not such men that the former would choose to give, would have the legal right to give, or would have it in his power to give those lands to another, or that the latter would be willing to accept them or could legally have done so.
>
> In the second place, if this were not so, though it is absolutely true and obvious, [I shall show that in fact] the latter did not receive nor the former give possession of what is said to have been granted, but that it always remained under the sway and empire of the Caesars.
>
> In the third place, [I shall show that] nothing was given to Sylvester by Constantine, but to an earlier Pope (and Constantine had received baptism even before that pontificate), and that the grants were inconsiderable, for the mere subsistence of the Pope.

Fourth, that it is not true either that a copy of the Donation is found in the Decretum [of Gratian], or that it was taken from the History of Sylvester; for it is not found in it or in any history, and it is comprised of contradictions, impossibilities, stupidities, barbarisms and absurdities.[9]

In the *Donatione* Valla further considered whether this was a direct attack upon the Pope or upon the legitimacy of the Emperor at Constantinople:

'But what shall I do?' you will say. Shall I try to recover by force what the Pope has in his possession? But he, alas, has now become more powerful than I. Shall I seek to regain it by law? But my right is only such as he is willing for it to be. For I came to the throne, not through an inherited title, but by a compact that if I wish to be Emperor I should promise the Pope in turn such and such considerations. Shall I say that Constantine did not give away any of the Empire? But that way I should be arguing the cause of the Greek Emperor, and I should rob myself of all imperial dignity. For the Pope says he makes me Emperor with this very thing in view, as a kind of vicar of his; and unless I bind myself, he will not make me Emperor; and unless I obey I shall have to abdicate. If only he gives me the throne I will acknowledge everything, I will agree to everything. Only, take my word for it, if I had Rome and Tuscany in my possession, I would act quite differently and Paschal would sing me that old song of the Donation, spurious in my opinion, in vain. As things are, I yield what I neither have nor hope to have. To question the right of the Pope is not my concern but that of the Emperor yonder at Constantinople.[10]

Valla's treatise on the Donation of Constantine was a devastating attack upon the papacy, partly motivated by his belief in the truth of his discovery, and partly in order to serve his employer, Alfonso, who was in a battle with the papacy over land.

Two years later he finished his *Elegantiae Linguae Latinae*, a manual for the correct use of Latin syntax and vocabulary. In its six books, comprising 235 chapters, 'Valla criticizes, corrects, and expands on explanations of words, grammar, syntax, and morphology offered by late classical grammarians such as Priscian, Donatus, Servius, and Nonus'. His aim was to correct others in their use of language: 'by "right usage" he means grammatically correct and rhetorically effective'.[11] In the same years, he composed a dialogue on free will and began working on his annotations to the standard Latin translation of the Bible, comparing it with the Greek text of the New Testament. He also wrote a dialogue *De Professione Religiosorum (On the Profession of the Religious)*, in which he attacked the vow of obedience and asceticism taken by members of religious orders.[12]

Alfonso had made peace with the Pope in 1443, and Valla's denial of the apostolic origin of the *Symbolum Apostolicum (Apostle's Creed)* resulted in a row with Fra Antonio da Bitonto and Valla's eventual trial for heresy by the Curia at Naples, for which Valla wrote a self-defence (and later an 'Apology'), and had to be rescued by the king. Even his manual of Latin, the *Elegantiae*, caused controversy when certain literary figures considered themselves to be criticized in the work, although they had not been explicitly named. One such writer was Poggio Bracciolini (1380–1459), who not only pointed out stylistic weaknesses in Valla's work, but also accused him, in a much more personal way, of degrading moral behaviour. Valla answered these accusations in his equally aggressive *Invectivarum Libri Sex*. However, as Valla was still keen for a position as papal secretary, he wrote his *Apologia ad Eugenium IV*, which promised repentance of his ways and a defence of his own character. The *Apologia* was an attempt to pacify the Vatican by tempering some of his previous statements, especially in his *Invectarium Libri Sex*.

Having 'repented', he travelled to Rome to become, in 1448, an apostolic *scriptor* (scribe). By 1455, he was a papal secretary and a canon at St. John Lateran. Valla thrived in the post: under Pope Nicholas V, his work included translating many works from Greek into Latin. During this time, he also revised his anti-scholastic *Repastinatio Dialectice et Philosophie (Re-ploughing of Dialectic and Philosophy*, also known as his *Dialectic*) and his notes on the New Testament, and translated Thucydides and Herodotus into Latin. His work on Thucydides, in particular, was to have an important impact on the study of this difficult Greek author. He continued to quarrel with men such as Poggio, until, on 1 August 1457, Lorenzo died in Rome, and was buried in the Lateran.

The Humanist

In his *Repastinatio Dialectice et Philosophie*, Valla attacked scholastic and Aristotelian philosophy. *Repastinatio,* for Valla, meant not only 're-ploughing', but 'weeding out' the Aristotelian and scholastic ground and a re-planting of rhetoric and grammar. The work is divided into three books, the first dealing with Aristotelian-scholastic metaphysics, ethics and natural philosophy, and books two and three dealing with dialectic. As Nauta has rightly noted, in book I of *Repastinatio*, Valla 'attacked Aristotelian-scholastic metaphysicians' by criticizing their complicated and confusing terminology: the ten categories ('ten supreme and irreducibly different genera of being – substance, quality, quantity, and so forth'), six transcendental terms, such as 'being', 'good' and 'one', and concepts such as 'genus', 'species', 'form and matter', and 'act and potency'. These terms, Valla argued, should be replaced by a simplified, common sense approach:

> The principal task he has therefore imposed on himself is to cut back this useless superstructure of technical jargon and empty concepts by reducing them to what he considers the basic elements of a common-sense world view.[13]

One of his objections to Aristotle's philosophy was that rationalistic determinism and materialism detracted from the notion of God's power. Valla emphasized God as the creator of heaven and earth, rather than seeing the cosmos in terms of a living animal or the heavens in terms of celestial orbs moved by intelligences. Valla's Christianity also led him to reject Aristotle's ideas concerning the soul and to adhere to Augustine's picture of the soul as a wholly spiritual and immaterial substance made in the image of God, and consisting of memory, intellect, and will. For Valla, the soul is dignified in nature, immortal, autonomous, and superior to the body. It is like the sun at the centre of the cosmos.[14]

During the early fifteenth century, humanist ideas were forged by use of the 'Dialogue'.[15] The Dialogue was a literary form in which fictitious characters, usually based upon real-life ones, would argue over a philosophical point, using all the rhetorical, literary and philological skill they could muster. Celenza rightly points out that the value of such a technique was that it took into account many voices and opinions before coming to a conclusion about a subject, even if all the voices and characters were the work of just one man. Thus the discussion was broader, more ambiguous and less dogmatic than merely one person's proclamation from a single point of view. Conversation was important for the early humanists, whether it was 'external or internal'.[16]

For Valla, however, the strength of any argument was best assessed by whether it worked or not. What mattered was not how well formulated it was, but how persuasive it was when given in public oration:

> For him [Valla], language is primarily a vehicle for communication, debate, and persuasion, and consequently arguments are to be evaluated in terms of their validity ... Dialectic, Valla argues, is merely a species of confirmation or refutation, and as such merely a part of one of the five parts of rhetoric, invention.[17]

Thus, for Valla, rhetoric was superior to logic. Rhetoric, argued Valla, comprised of five parts: the easiest part was dialectic, or dialogue, the aim of which was to teach.[18] The other parts of rhetoric, following the Aristotelian model, were syllogism (a conclusion drawn from two independent statements using logic), enthymeme (incomplete syllogism), epicheireme (a kind of extended reasoning) and example. Thus the task of the orator was to teach, but also to entertain, move and persuade. But Valla preferred assessing arguments in terms of persuasion and usefulness rather than syllogism. Valla's approach was partly based on Quintilian's idea that 'the whole point of argumentation is to prove what is not certain by means of what is certain'.[19]

Perhaps the best example of Valla's writing on morality is to be found in his dialogue, *De Voluptate*, of 1431, in which an Epicurean (follower of Epicurus (341–270 B.C.) and advocate of sensual pleasure), a Stoic, and a Christian discuss what ought to be considered as the highest ethical good. The result is a mixture of Pauline theology and Epicurean hedonism, in which the Christian concepts of charity and beatitude are identified with hedonistic pleasure, and the Stoic concept of virtue is rejected. Valla thus treats Epicureanism as a stepping-stone to the development of a Christian morality based on the concept of pleasure, and repudiates the traditional synthesis of Stoicism and Christianity, popular among scholastics and humanists alike.

Valla wanted to reduce the four theological virtues – prudence, justice, fortitude, and temperance – into one, fortitude, and then to equate fortitude with charity and love. For Valla, fortitude is the essential virtue, since it shows that we do not allow ourselves to be conquered by the wrong emotions, but instead act for the good. Fortitude is the only true virtue, because our actions, to which we assign moral qualifications, proceed from the will. Thus Valla equated strength of action with love, because we are tested, according to St. Paul (II Cor. 12:10[20]): virtuous behaviour (love) requires fortitude (strength) because it is hard to achieve.

Because Valla maintained that pleasure is our highest good, God is to be loved as a means to that end: we are commanded to live a difficult life of Christian virtue and honesty (*honestas*), but also to live a hedonist (Epicurean) life of joyful freedom and sensual pleasure.

The Author and Scholar

Valla's works reveal the contradictory nature of their author. His likes and dislikes are clearly established. He did not wholly depart from scholasticism in his admiration for Aristotle, but he departed from scholasticism in his employment of dialogue and informal presentation of ideas. Moreover, scholastics had no interest in philology, or linguistic and textual criticism. Such interests were a genuine innovation of Valla, backed only by a handful of humanists from later in his century such as Poliziano, Barbaro and (in the sixteenth century) Erasmus. Thus Valla drew most heavily upon the linguistic and rhetorical skills of classical antiquity. He despised the ancient Egyptian schools of philosophy, and approved of the Athenian Epicurus with his emphasis upon the rights of people to enjoy earthly pleasures. He showed no interest in reviving Stoic philosophy, as other humanists did, and no interest in Neoplatonism, or indeed Plato himself. The most contradictory side of his thought is in relation to Church authority. At times he is very critical of the papacy and of monks, denouncing the Pope as a fraud and those who lead the religious life as corrupt. But on the other hand he was not anti-Christian, as he also drew heavily upon works of patristic thought rather than pagan authors. Moreover, he harboured a lifelong ambition to be a papal secretary; having spent most of his life denouncing the Pope's temporal claims, he nonetheless ingratiated himself to the papal court when the fulfilment of his ambition was in sight, eventually becoming a papal secretary shortly before his death.[21] In his works he contrasted faith and reason, philosophy and theology, paganism and Christianity, arguing that revealed wisdom (from the divine) was always superior to human opinion, a view that Luther would later adopt. Nevertheless, he succeeded in achieving a synthesis between pagan and Christian thought. So, despite his agnosticism, one might see him as a forerunner of the great Christian humanists, such as Colet, Erasmus and More, who were prepared to accept classical, non-Christian literature, albeit in Christianized form, as useful to a reform programme.

How does this breadth of interest demonstrate itself in Valla's works? His hostility towards Aristotle and the scholastics is evident in his *Dialectice Laurentii libri*;[22] philological and historical criticism was largely (but not exclusively) the basis for his *De Falso Credita*; his love of philology blossomed into one of the greatest humanist works on the subject, *De Elegantiae Linguae Latinae*;[23] his love of dialogue is evident in most of his works, especially his treatise on the free will;[24] his condemnation of the ancient schools of philosophy and lack of interest in Platonism or Neoplatonism can be seen in his *De Voluptate ac Vero Bono Libri Tres*;[25] his affirmation of patristic thought became evident in his *Encomium Sancti Thomae Aquinatis*.[26]

Trinkaus rightly locates Valla firmly in the Christian camp, citing his treatise on Free Will as an example of Valla's placement of theology over and above philosophy, especially in his opening words to Bishop Garsia of Lerida:

I would prefer, O Garsia, most learned and best of bish-ops, that other Christians and, indeed, those who are called theologians would not depend so much on philosophy or devote so much energy to it, making it an equal sister (I do not say patron) of theology. For it seems to me that they have a poor opinion of our religion if they think it needs the protection of philosophy.[27]

Unlike Pico and Ficino, Valla rejected the notion of humanity's goal being that of hierarchical ascent to God, in order to become one with the Divine. Rather, Valla emphasized the difference in nature between the human and the divine, thus breaking with the scholastic ideas of Aquinas. As Trinkaus observes, this can be demonstrated by the simple juxtaposition of a passage of Aquinas's work with that of Valla's treatise on free will. Aquinas wrote:

Now the last end of every creature is to attain God's likeness … It would therefore be inconsistent with divine providence if anything were deprived of that whereby it attains to a likeness of God. But the voluntary agent attains to God's likeness in that he acts freely: for we have proved that there is free will in God. Therefore providence does not deprive the will of liberty.[28]

Upon the subject of free will, however, Valla stresses the unknowability of God by human beings, based upon St. Paul's letter to the Romans 11: 33:

'O the depth of the riches both of the wisdom and knowledge of God! How unsearchable his judgements, and his ways past finding out!' For if that vessel of election who, snatched up even to the third heaven, heard the secret words which man is not permitted to speak, nevertheless was unable to say or even to perceive them, who at length would hope that he could search out and comprehend?[29]

Thus Valla denied the scholastic view that free will and divine providence could be reconciled and was suspicious of any attempt to understand God in rational terms.

More evidence of Valla's break with scholastic rationalism can be perceived in some of his other works: in De Voluptate (On Pleasure and True Good) he denied the efficacy of good works as a means of obtaining Christian salvation; in De Professione Religiosorum (On the Profession of the Religious) he denied that those who led the religious, or monastic, life had more claim to the divine than those who practiced spontaneous virtue; and in 'The Donation of Constantine' he attacked the Pope's claim to temporal authority on the grounds that the supposed gift by Constantine of the Western Empire to the Church was a fraudulent document.[30] Even in his sermon 'In praise of St. Thomas Aquinas' Valla could not help stating his distaste for Thomas's use of dialectic, preferring the works of Paul and the early Church fathers: Augustine, Ambrose (c. 337–397), Origen (185–254), Gregory the Great (540–604) and Jerome (c. 342–420).[31]

The Legacy

Valla made an enormous impact upon the humanist world, although he was not widely read during his own lifetime, apart from his *Elegantiae*. His philological approach was developed by subsequent generations of humanists, most notably Angelo Poliziano (1454–1494). Valla's *Elegantiae* was printed many times, although his publications were much less widely read that those of Bruni. Nevertheless, a copy of Valla's annotations on the New Testament was found by Erasmus, who published it. Although Valla was not a theologian, Luther referred to Valla's dialogue on free will and, although Valla's critique of Aristotelianism and scholasticism found favour with humanists, many found Valla's style too aggressive. Some humanists, such as Juan Luis Vives (1492–1540) and Johann Eck (1486–1543) noted Valla's lack of philosophical knowledge, but admired his critique of scholasticism, which was partly responsible for the transition, in Italy, from the Middle Ages to the Renaissance. Valla's influence upon subsequent reformers was mixed. Erasmus, for example, praised his achievements as a philologist, but considered Valla to be a poor theologian:

> From Apostolic times to this day there was no writer hitherto who totally denied the force of free will save Manichaeus and John Wyclif alone. For Lorenzo Valla, who almost seems to agree with them, has little authority among theologians of weight.[32]

Luther, however, saw Valla's ideas as entirely in line with his own: 'Lorenzo Valla is the best Italian that I have seen or discovered. He disputes ably on free will. He sought simplicity in piety and letters at the same time. Erasmus seeks him as much in letters as he condemns him in piety'.[33]

Calvin seemed to stand somewhere in the middle. He agreed that Valla had little theological authority, but argued that he was nonetheless correct concerning free will and foreknowledge:

> But Valla, a man otherwise not much versed in theology, appears to me to have discovered superior acuteness and

judiciousness by showing that this controversy is unnecessary, because both life and death are acts of God's will rather than of his foreknowledge.[34]

Therefore, as Barozzi rightly asserts, Valla paves the way for the philological, critical and linguistic work of Erasmus, and his ideas on free will and the foreknowledge of God look forward to the theological developments of Luther and Calvin.[35]

Valla made a huge contribution to historical, classical, and biblical scholarship by acknowledging, for the first time, the significance of historical and cultural context for the understanding of a manuscript. When considered alongside his criticisms of the scholastic past – however aggressively expressed and sometimes badly argued – his work both insisted upon and accentuated the historical break between the medieval past and the Renaissance, a project that Petrarch had begun and Lorenzo Valla continued during his short life. Neoplatonist humanism would subsequently arrive in the work of Marsilio Ficino and Pico della Mirandola.

Valla: Dates and Events

1406/7: born in Rome.

1429–31: moves to Pavia, and takes up the chair of *Eloquentia* (eloquence) at the university.

1431: ordained Priest.

1433: flees Pavia after attacking the jurists' authority, particularly that of Bartolus Sassoferrato (1313–1357). Writes *De Voluptate* (revised 1435). Moves to Naples, Court of Alfonso V of Aragon (1396–1458).

1437: secretary to Alfonso of Aragon.

1439–40: writes *De Falso Credita et Ementita Constantini Donatione Declamatio* (On the Forged and Mendacious Donation of Constantine); *De Libero Arbitrio*; *Dialecticae Disputationes*.

1441: *Elegantiae Linguae Latinae* finished: for correct use of Latin vocabulary and syntax.

1442: *De Professione Religiosorum* (not printed until 1869).

1443: Alfonso makes peace with the Pope. *Symbolum Apostolicum* (Apostle's Creed): Valla's denial of Pope's apostolic origin, questioning the composition of the Creed by the Apostles.

1444: attacked by Poggio Bracciolini for his works. Returns to Rome but flees for his life to Barcelona then to Naples.

February 1447: Death of Pope Eugenius IV.
1448: Valla returns to Rome, welcomed by Pope Nicholas V as apostolic *scriptor* (scribe) and subsequently retained by Pope Caliztus III.
1455: revises *Rapastinato*; Valla made papal secretary, a lifelong ambition, and professor at the university.
1 August 1457: dies in Rome.
1517: *Donatio* eventually published.
1535: 'Donation of Constantine' published for Thomas Cromwell.

Valla's Key Works

1431: *De Voluptate*: published in 1431, this work was an eloquent examination of Stoic, Epicurean, and hedonistic ethics. Valla argued for the right of humans to indulge in natural pleasures.
1439–40: *De Falso Credita et Ementita Constantini Donatione Declamatio*: demonstrated that the 'Donation of Constantine' document was a forgery and that, therefore, the basis of papal temporal rule was false. Valla argued that, due to the anachronistic Latin of the text, the 'Donation' could not have been written in the era of Constantine I (4th century). The 'Donation' suggested that Constantine donated the whole of the Western Empire to the Roman Church in thanks for the cure of leprosy provided by Pope Sylvester I. Valla's motivation for writing was partly to serve his employer Alfonso, who was in dispute with the Pope over papal states (land).
1439: *De Libero Arbitrio*: on free will. Valla concedes that God's foreknowledge of events (given His omniscience), is not incompatible with free will, for our minds are unable to comprehend the mystery of God's power.
1439–40: *Disputationis (Dialectic disputations)*: strongly opposes Aristotle and the Scholastics, more on the grounds of their use (or misuse) of language than of their philosophical tenets. Made little contribution to philosophy, but helped discredit scholasticism.
1441: *De Elegantia Linguae Latinae*: Latin grammar and syntax. A Latin composition based on analysis and

reason that moved the language away from post-classical and medieval Christian Latin and helped to form a humanist style. It was reprinted nearly sixty times between 1471 and 1536.

1442: *De Professione Religiosorum*: a critique of the monastic lifestyle and a denial that the religious life was the most perfect.

1443: *Symbolum Apostolicum* (Apostle's Creed): resulted in a row with Fra Antonio da Bitonto, and Valla's eventual trial for heresy by the Curia at Naples, for which Valla wrote a self-defence (and later an 'Apology'), and had to be rescued by the king.

1444: *Invectivarum Libri Sex*: written in response to the vicious accusations of Poggio Bracciolini. The *Annotationes*: discussed the Latin used in the New Testament.

1445: *Apologia ad Eugenio IV*: an attempt to pacify the Vatican by tempering some of Valla's previous statements, especially in his *Invenctarium libri sex*.

1451: *revised edition of Repastinatio Dialectice et Philosophie*: Valla attacked scholastic and Aristotelian philosophy. *Repastinatio meant a* 're-ploughing' or 'weeding out' of Aristotelian and scholastic logic, to be re-planted with rhetoric and grammar.

1540 and 1592: collected, but not quite complete, editions of Valla's works were published at Basel in 1540, and at Venice in 1592.

3

MARSILIO FICINO (1433–1499)
The Florentine Platonist

Ficino was one of the greatest philosophers of the Italian Renaissance. Although he was educated as a physician and lamented his inability to write truly classical Latin like his humanist contemporaries, he mastered Greek and his mixture of pagan and Christian allegiances, along with his interest in and mastery of the arts and astrology, and his revival of Neoplatonism demonstrate the breadth of his influence. He was an inspiration for Botticelli, Michelangelo, Raphael and Titian. His followers in philosophy and literature included Cosimo and Lorenzo de' Medici, Poliziano and Pico della Mirandola. His output was considerable, including translations of Plato's works and the *Hermetic Corpus* (Hermes Trismegistos from the second or third century) as well as his commentaries on Plato's *Dialogues* and his prolific philosophical writings and letters; combined with his dedication to Christianity as a priest and canon of Florence Cathedral, these represent his life's work. Ficino believed that the works of Plato and the Neoplatonists contained the secret of human knowledge, that is, union with the Divine.[1] These views were attractive to some but considered dangerously heretical by others.

Introduction

Ficino has been described as the chief influence in the transmission of 'esoteric' knowledge, namely:

> a tradition of religious philosophy which embodies an *initiatic* mode of teaching – a promise of access to hidden meanings deep within the fabric of the world which will eventually lead the searcher to a condition of *gnosis* [divine knowledge] or unity with the source of all being.[2]

Although Ficino and his contemporaries considered this tradition to have started with the Persian Zoroaster and the Egyptian Hermes Trismegistus and passed on to Pythagoras, Orpheus and Plato, it mainly developed in the early Christian era in Graeco-Egyptian Alexandria.[3]

Ficino was responsible for the continuation of classical learning in Italy. During his lifetime he was known by his writings from Naples to Rome, Milan to Venice, as well as throughout Europe, including in Spain, Hungary, Poland, and especially in Britain and the Low Countries.[4] Ficino, along with Pico, has been described as a 'humanist theologian'.[5]

However, his revival of pagan ritual in spiritual matters, along with Pico della Mirandola, was denounced by the Dominican Florentine reformer Girolamo Savonarola (1452–98). Ficino was only saved from an accusation of heresy, in 1489, by the intervention of Archbishop Rinaldo Orsini. Apart from his translations, Ficino's key works are his *Theologia Platonica* (*Platonic Theology or Immorality of the Soul*) and *De Vita* (*Three Books of Life*).[6] In Florence, where he lived and ended his days, Ficino became a magnet for intellectuals and humanists from all over Europe, who appreciated his love, wisdom and understanding.[7] For instance, it is evident that John Colet became infatuated with the works of Ficino and, at some point, entered into correspondence with him.[8] Colet and Ficino never met, but the correspondence took place once Colet had returned to England in 1496 with a copy of Ficino's *Epistolae*, published the previous year, in his possession.[9] Colet also knew Ficino's *Theologia Platonica* (1482) as well as his translations of Plato and Plotinus and the *Corpus Hermeticum*. Likewise, the French humanist Lefèvre d'Étaples was influenced by Ficino, Pseudo-Dionysius and the Fathers, and sought reform in order to recapture the purity of the gospel and the early Church.[10] Travelling from his native France in 1491–2, he visited Italy and made contact with Ficino and Pico. Later, however, Lefèvre expressed reservations about Ficino's opinions, abandoning Platonism as a system in favour of Aristotelian philosophy, and devoting himself thereafter to humanistic textual scholarship, editing and commenting on Aristotle, the Hermetic corpus[11] and Pseudo-Dionysius.

Thus, from his Florentine base, Ficino championed Pseudo-Dionysian thought; his Platonic approach to the Church is particularly evident in his *Theologia Platonica*.[12] Ficino firmly believed the author of the Pseudo-Dionysian texts to be the Dionysius the Areopagite mentioned in the Book of Acts (17:34), a disciple of St. Paul and therefore an author of first-century authority. In fact the texts are closer to the sixth century, possibly Syrian. Nevertheless, in his commentaries on the *Divine Names* and *The Mystical Theology* of Pseudo-Dionysius, printed in 1492, Ficino expounded this mixture of Platonic and Christian thought with a resulting emphasis upon the primacy of the intellect, as pure and refined will, over love, which is secondary, and upon the stages of ascent to union with God.[13]

One of Ficino's great champions in the twentieth century, Paul Oskar Kristeller, wrote: '[Ficino's] doctrine of spiritual love in Plato's sense, for which he coined the term Platonic love, became one of the most popular concepts of later Renaissance literature'.[14] Ficino's Commentary on Plato's *Symposium* (1469), entitled *De Amore*, 'initiated a new genre of literature, the love treatise, which was in vogue in Europe for at least the next two hundred years'.[15] This was first apparent in Italy, with Leone Ebreo's *Dialighi d'Amore* (1535) and Baldassare Castiglione's *Il Cortegiano* (1528). France and Spain were quick to absorb Platonic works, with England eventually responding positively in the works of the Elizabethan poets Philip Sidney, George Chapman and Edmund Spenser.[16]

Life

Ficino was born on 19 October 1433 at Figline Valdarno, about twenty-five kilometeres south-east of Florence. His father, Diotifeci Figline (d. 1478) was a prominent physician and doctor of arts and medicine. Indeed, he was doctor to Cosimo de' Medici (1381–1464) and Antoninus, Archbishop of Florence and apparently particularly renowned for treating the plague.[17] The family did not enjoy great riches as Diotefeci was not strict about payment, a characteristic inherited by Marsilio. Little is known about Marsilio's mother, Alessandra, except that she died in old age only a couple of years before Marsilio himself. In fact, Marsilio looked after both his parents in old age.[18]

Diotifeci and Alessandra's second-eldest son, Marsilio, was probably named after the famous physician Marsilio da S. Sofia, and was expected, no doubt, to follow his father's profession. Indeed, Marsilio was a student of philosophy and medicine at the University of Florence. Although he was to become the most illustrious philosopher of fifteenth-century Tuscany, humanism formed only one aspect of his education. The focus on grammar, rhetoric, poetry, history and moral philosophy of the *studia humanitatis* was combined with a curriculum including Aristotelian natural philosophy and metaphysics.[19]

As a boy, Marsilio's training in the humanities began with Luca da San Gimignano and Comando Comandi.[20] He learned Latin grammar and was familiar with the major Latin authors. He became deeply interested in the works of Dante Alighieri (*c.* 1265–1321), Giovanni del Virgilio (late thirteenth century to 1327) and Poggio (1380–1459). At university he studied with Florence's most illustrious physician, Niccolò' Tignosi (1402–1474). From the age of eighteen he studied the logic of Paul of Venice (Paulus Venetus, 1368–1428) and the ethics of Aristotle. It was clear from a relatively early age that he was more interested in being a philosopher than a rhetorician, especially since his study of medicine required him to read Aristotelian natural philosophy.[21]

Ficino's earliest works began in around 1454. A letter to Antonio Serafico da San Miniato, dated 13 September, contains the first of several tracts on natural philosophy, which are very scholastic in style, but contain the theme of the 'unity of love', which would become a characteristic of Ficino's work. Ficino's first major work, *Institutiones ad Platonicam Disciplinam*, was written in 1456. Although this work has not survived, Ficino's letters of the same period demonstrate his conviction that philosophy played a crucial role in leading humanity towards perfection and unity with the divine.[22]

When the Greek emperor, John Palaeologus (1392–1448), called the great Church Council of 1439, with the aim of reconciling Eastern and Western Churches, a great many scholars and churchmen descended upon Ferrara. Cosimo de' Medici, seeing that the resources at Ferrara were inadequate for such a large gathering, suggested the council move to Florence instead. The council ultimately failed in its objective of ecclesiastical union.[23] However, one of the consequences was the arrival in Florence of the Neoplatonic philosopher, George Gemisthos Plethon (*c.* 1355–1452/4), who had already established a Platonic Academy in Mistra, near ancient Sparta in Greece. Plethon became famous in Florence in the 1450s with Marsilio hailing him as a 'second Plato' due to his lectures on Plato and the Alexandrian Mystics. Corsi recalled that:

[Gemisthos] was called by Marsilio a second Plato, and acclaimed equally for his eloquence and scholarship. When Cosimo heard him frequently discoursing before the scholars and winning their highest applause and administration, it is said that he was set ablaze with an extraordinary desire to recall to Italy as soon as possible, the philosophy of Plato, as of ancient right.[24]

Ficino himself began to learn Greek at the age of twenty-three (1456). The Greek influence in Florence continued with the arrival of John Argyropoulos (1415–1487), a noted Aristotelian, in 1459, who lectured on Greek literature and became Marsilio's tutor.

Marisilo never received a doctorate and had to survive by tutoring. He was, for a time, tutor in the house of Piero de' Pazzi[25] and, by the 1460s, Ficino had begun translating into Latin the works of Hermes Trismegistus, a task he completed in 1463. Hermes, or Thoth as he was known in Egypt, was believed to be a contemporary of Moses, as is demonstrated by a picture, dating from around 1488, on the floor of the entrance to Siena Cathedral, which depicts Hermes handing a book of wisdom to two people, one from the East and one from the West.[26] Hermes' works were, in fact, 'products of late ancient syncretism not far removed from the time of Plotinus'.[27]

However, a significant turning point in events came in 1462/3, when Cosimo de' Medici gave Ficino the annual profits from a farm near the Medici villa at Careggi along with the Greek texts of Plato's works. The Medicis desired that the fourth-century Athenian Platonic Academy should in some way be emulated in Florence.[28] This wish was not fulfilled, but Ficino embodied the so-called Academy in Florence, as it had no institutional form, taught no students and held no regular meetings. It took the form, therefore, of a loose association of scholars and fashionable aristocrats, patronized by Lorenzo and some of them personally supported by him. Ficino was its central figure, and the group met occasionally to discuss the ideas and discoveries resulting from his translations, but, as a body, they issued no publications and took no formal actions:

Rather than leading a regular gathering in a specific place, Ficino preferred to teach Florence's elite youth when he could and, as a Socratic, philosophical friend, to try as best he might to draw out of his associates the better part of their natures in conversation.[29]

Exactly what constituted an 'academy', therefore, is open to debate. As Celenza acknowledges, Plato's *Dialogues*, for instance, could be called an 'academy', as they were 'rich with precious teachings'.[30]

Nevertheless, Ficino was in need of employment and welcomed the Medici patronage. He became tutor to Cosimo's grandson, Lorenzo, and completed one of his greatest tasks, the translation of all Plato's known works into Latin for the first time. They were published in 1484. Ficino's philosophical leanings, however, did not prevent him from pursuing his vocation as a Christian. He was a lifelong believer in the idea that Christian theology should combine with Platonic philosophy to create a harmonious road to self-improvement, by which a human soul might aspire to become perfect and at one with the divine. He was ordained a priest in 1473 and held several benefices, most notably becoming a Canon of Florence Cathedral. He also lectured on St. Paul's letter to the Romans in the Church of S. Maria dei Angeli.

By 1492 he had translated the complete works of Plotinus and, by 1497, the works of Porphyry (232/4–305), Iamblichus (250–325), Proclus (410–485) and others. Thus, these great Greek philosophers became as accessible to Latin readers as Aristotle. Although the translations are not without error, had Ficino achieved nothing else they alone would have secured his name among the great intellectuals of his age.[31]

Uncharacteristically for a humanist, Ficino never travelled, but his prolific output of translations, philosophy and correspondence assured his place as one of the great intellects of the Renaissance. He died at Careggi on 1 October 1499.

The Humanist Author

Ficino wrote no Latin poetry, a few fables (*apologi*) and some dialogues (such as his commentary of Plato's *Symposium*). The largest part of his output consists of the translations (*Hermetic Corpus* and Plato) and his letters, published as works of literature even during his own lifetime.[32] His works are characterized by his eclectic interests and, despite his own tendency to be melancholic, by the command to be happy. His interests ranged from Christian and patristic humanism, vernacular humanism, philosophy, cosmology, astrology and magic, to the arts, and the 'doctrines' of love, beauty, the dignity of man and the immortality of the soul.[33]

His Christian or patristic humanism was influenced by the Italian theologian and Hellenist Ambrogio Taversari (1386–1439), who had made an early humanist study of the Bible as well as the Greek and Latin fathers, translating works by Athenagoras (133–190), Synesius (d. 414) and the Pseudo-Dionysius (sixth century). Although Ficino was more of a philosopher than theologian he was committed to the notion that philosophy and religion were a harmonious combination, especially Christian religion and Platonic philosophy.

Vernacular humanism (*umanesimo volgare*) catered for merchants, artisans and those who had an interest in humanist texts or ideas but no Latin, particularly women. Ficino wrote several vernacular treatises in the Tuscan tongue, and translated Dante's *Monarchia* from Latin to Tuscan.[34]

Ficino's main work of philosophy is his *Theologia Platonica*, which contains scholastic and humanist thought, as well as Platonic and Neoplatonic philosophy. Ficino admired Plato's insistence on the divine within the human soul – a soul, moreover which was immortal, free and most fulfilled in God – a philosophy which he expressed in the preface to his *Platonic Theology*:

> Since [Plato] holds the soul to be a kind of mirror in which the image of the divine countenance is easily reflected, his scrupulous step by step search for God continually prompts him to turn towards the beauty of the soul, understanding the famous oracle 'Know thyself!' to mean above all that whoever desires to know God should first know himself. For this reason everyone who reads Plato's writings...with the care that they deserve will derive from them every conceivable benefit, but above all these two most important principles: the pious worship of a known God and the divinity of souls. These form the basis for all understanding of things, for every disposition of one's life and for all aspects of happiness.[35]

Ficino was undoubtedly the greatest Renaissance Platonist, providing authoritative translations and commentaries, and relating everything in Plato to the divine:

> Plato, the father of all philosophers...considered it just and pious that, as the human mind receives everything from God, so it should restore everything to God...Whatever subject he deals with, be it ethics, dialectic, mathematics or physics, he quickly brings it round, in a spirit of utmost piety, to the contemplation and worship of God.[36]

Indeed, Celenza recognizes that to understand Ficino's Platonism one needs to remember that Ficino was the son of a medical doctor, and was himself a physician, but also that, 'at least from 1473 onwards, he was an ordained Catholic priest, who considered everything he did to be in the service of Christianity'.[37]

Ficino did not confine his interest in Greek philosophy to Plato alone. He was the first western scholar to cite the Greek physician and philosopher Galen of Pergamum (c. 129–200), who was previously unknown.[38]

Another great work by Ficino is his translation of the *Corpus Hermeticum*, which consists of many texts attributed to Hermes, in which creation myth mixes with astrology and theology, resulting in a philosophy of divine humanity that becomes subject to the rule of the stars by taking an earthly physical form. Of Hermes, Ficino wrote:

> Among philosophers he first turned from physical and math-
> ematical topics to contemplation of things divine, and he was
> the first to discuss with great wisdom the majesty of God, the
> order of demons, and the transformation of souls.[39]

The secret knowledge of humanity's original divine status can be known through the spiritual teachings of the present, by means of the mind's ascent through reason to the divine: 'All men suffer what has been ordained, but those with reason, who are led by *Nous*, do not suffer as others do.'[40] The *nous* is the highest part of the human soul and thus humans can be freed from earthly physical restraints by self-realization and by the ascent of intellect and will, soul, or *nous*, to the divine, described by Iamblichus as 'sacred theurgy'[41]:

> Now every living creature is immortal by virtue of *nous*; man
> above all, for he can receive God and he shares God's essence.
> God communicates with this creature alone: through dreams
> by night and through signs by day. Through all these he fore-
> tells to man the future: through birds, entrails, inspiration,
> and the sacred oak. Thus man proclaims that he knows the
> past, present and future.[42]

The ascent of the soul to the divine, or theurgy, in the Egyptian writings, which Ficino translated, is remarkably similar to the Platonic ascent of the soul to The One.

> Our soul by means of the intellect and will, as by those twin
> Platonic wings, flies towards God, since by means of them it
> flies towards all things. By means of the intellect it attaches
> all things to itself, by means of the will, it attaches itself to
> all things. Thus the soul desires, endeavours, and begins to
> become God, and makes progress every day. Every move-
> ment directed towards a definite end first begins, then pro-
> ceeds, then gradually increases and makes progress, and is

finally perfected. It is increased through the same power through which it was begun: it makes progress through the same power through which it was increased; and finally, it is perfected through the same power through which it made progress. Hence our soul will sometime be able to become in a sense all things, and even to become God.[43]

Thus, Ficino's journey from the works of Hermes to Plato in close succession in the 1460s helped to secure the notion of the divinity of the human soul in his thinking.

Ficino's doctrinal influence can chiefly be recognized in his promotion of the historical concept of the Platonic tradition and its place within the Christian tradition. The *Prisca Theologia* (from Hermes Trismegistus), Zoroaster (*c.* 1000 B.C.) and Pythagoras (*c.* 569–475 B.C.) were used by Ficino to extend the origins of Plato back to the time of Moses and the Hebrew prophets. Thus, he considered philosophy, including Aristotle, and religion to be of equal value, being equally ancient in authority. Cosmology, based on Aristotle and Ptolomy (*c.* 121–151), also played a significant part in this framework. For Ficino, the celestial and the elementary spheres are all animated and the visible cosmos dominated by a World Soul. That which is visible is only a part of the universe, which consists of a metaphysical hierarchy from God, to the angels, to the rational soul.[44] Thus God is the ultimate goal of the mind and will.[45] After his ordination, Ficino wrote a treatise, in Tuscan and Latin, defending Christianity against the religions of Judaism and Islam. Nevertheless, this work also demonstrates that Ficino believed religion to be a universal good, with each particular religion perfect in itself and contributing to the whole.[46]

> Philosophy is defined by everyone as love of truth and devotion to wisdom. But truth, and wisdom itself, are God alone, so it follows that lawful philosophy is no different from true religion, and lawful religion exactly the same as true philosophy. If the properties of words derive partly from the properties of things and partly from those of ideas, as Plato, Aristotle, Varro, and Saint Augustine have shown in great detail; then certainly philosophy, the explorer and discoverer of the conception of things, brought forth grammar, the measure of correct speech and writing.[47]

This leaning towards religious tolerance and the doctrine of the universality of religion was later to be used by the Deists in arguing against the sanctification of religious texts, such as the Bible or the Koran, seeing them as human interpretations or responses to the divine creator.

Although Ficino had written a long treatise in condemnation of astrology in 1477, later in life he became increasingly fascinated with astrology and magic, as can be seen in the third volume of *De Vita* (1489), which contains mild references to occultist doctrines, but without promoting sinister rituals. The mild nature of Ficino's interest in magic saved him from condemnation before Pope Innocent VIII in 1489, unlike his unfortunate pupil Pico.

Ficino believed in a perfectly structured cosmos, as set out in Plato's *Timaeus*.[48] The Neoplatonists developed this into a hierarchy of emanations, which can be pictured as a pyramid with The One, divine, at the apex, from which varying levels of being are derived, each with a divine nature, but which decreases in intensity the lower it descends, with human beings retaining a divine trace but pure matter being devoid of divine essence.[49]

However, in his *Disputatio Contra Iudicium Astrologorum* (*Disputation Against the Judgement of Astrologers*) Ficino was quick to point out the limitations of astrology, especially in comparison to theology:

> These astrologers, in declaring that every single thing is necessarily brought to pass by the stars, are themselves involved in three highly pernicious errors, and they involve the public in them too. For insofar as they are able, they take away from God, Almighty and Supreme, his own providence and his absolute sovereignty over the universe. Next, they deny the justice of the angels; for according to them, the angels move the celestial bodies in such a way that from thence come forth all the crimes of men, all evil events for good men, and all good events for evil men. Lastly, they take away from men their free will and deprive them of all peace of mind, for it seems to the astrologers that men, no less than beasts, are driven hither and thither.[50]

Ficino was clear that neither divine law, nor religion, nor Christianity itself arises from the stars, although it may be indicated by them. The Christian religion, ultimately pre-eminent over both philosophy and astrology, depends on God alone.

In the arts, Ficino had a passion for music, and extolled its positive effect on the mind. He played the 'orphic lyre' (lute). He was also a music theorist and one of the first to treat the interval of a third and a sixth as consonant.[51] Unlike Plato, Ficino praised poetry and poets. Although he wrote little if any poetry, he often alluded to classical mythology in his works, which he always interpreted allegorically in order to conform to his Christian beliefs, and he clearly admired the works of Dante and Guido Cavalcanti (c. 1259–1300). Ficino's doctrine of a spiritual love based on the love of God influenced many sixteenth-century writers on love, including Bembo (1470–1547), Castiglione (1478–1529), and Bruno (1548–1600). Ficino also knew the artist brothers Antonio and Piero Pollaiuolo. Marsilio's own portrait was painted by Niccolò Fiorentino and on the walls of Ficino's study was a depiction of the world with a crying Heraclitus (c. 500 B.C.) and a laughing Democritus (c. 460–375 B.C.) on either side, a scene taken from Seneca and other ancient sources.[52] Ficino believed beauty to be goal divine in itself which, through art, philosophy and religion, could transform humanity. At a time when he felt particularly optimistic about the change effected through humanism, he wrote to Paul of Middelburg in 1492:

> Our century brought to light the liberal arts which had been almost extinct, that is, grammar, poetry, oratory, painting, sculpture, architecture, music and the ancient recital of poems accompanied by the Orphic Lyre, and all this in Florence. Wisdom is combined with eloquence, prudence with the military art. Also, astronomy has been revived. The Platonic doctrine has been brought back to light in Florence, and in Germany the art of printing and the clock have been invented.[53]

On music in particular, a letter to Domenico Benivieni, 'a master musician', illustrates Ficino's esteem of the art, which derives from his knowledge of Plato and Hermes Trismegistus:

> Plato thinks that true music is nothing other than harmony of mind: natural, insofar as its powers are consonant with the powers of mind, and acquired, insofar as its motions are consonant with the motions of the mind...Hermes Trismegistus says that both have been assigned to us by God, so that through the former we may continually imitate God Himself in our reflections and dispositions and through the latter we may regularly honour the name of God in hymns and sounds.[54]

In attempting to explain the physical and astronomical causes of harmony, Ficino created a complicated diagram in his letter, showing the correspondence between musical intervals and zodiacal aspects, as he understood them.[55]

The Legacy

Ficino was the most influential Italian philosopher of his time, who brought Platonic and Neoplatonic thought back into the consciousness

of Italian culture and, by extension, to Northern European humanism. Ficino's philosophy emphasized the dignity of man, a favourite
theme for humanists from Petrarch to Pico seeking to extol humanity's
scientific and political capacities and achievements, but Ficino added a
cosmological and metaphysical aspect, particularly by his insistence,
following Plato, on the immortality of souls, which became an extension of the dignity doctrine.

> It was not for small things but for great that God created men,
> who, knowing the great, are not satisfied with small things.
> Indeed, it was for the limitless alone that He created men,
> who are the only beings on earth to have rediscovered their
> infinite nature and who are not fully satisfied by anything
> limited, however great that thing may be.[56]

Ficino's 'enormous treatise, *Platonic Theology, On the Immortality
of Souls*…rehashed the entire question in terms of Aristotelian and
Neoplatonic methods and directly addressed Epicureanism and
Averroism as the ultimate enemies of true Christian thought'.[57] This
polemic against the Averroists focused heavily on immortality, of which
Ficino was an impassioned defender, unlike many university-based philosophers who (except for the mendicant) denied the doctrine.[58]

Although Ficino insisted upon the goal of happiness, he also valued the subjectivity and introspection of melancholy as a way to be
closer to the divine. Developing a Pseudo-Aristotelian doctrine, Ficino
linked intellect with melancholy and, taking the 'mystical' elements of
Plotinus and the Neoplatonists, advocated turning away from external
passion and perceptions, in order to make an interior ascent towards
pure contemplation, towards a direct knowledge of God and of the
intelligible world. In turn this would provide a firm ethical attitude and
the foundation of our moral opinion and action.[59] In a letter to fellow
philosophers, he pleaded:

> Let us, I beg you, nourish and increase the spirit with spiritual
> food, so that it may at length become mighty and have small
> regard for physical things, as though they were worth very
> little. Then may no part of the spirit shift from its own seat
> through the assaults of the flesh.
>   Let us climb into the high watchtower of the mind, leav-
> ing the dust of the body below; then we will gaze more closely
> at the divine and view the mortal from a distance. The former
> will seem greater than usual, and the latter smaller. So, cher-
> ishing the divine, and disregarding the mortal, we will no
> longer be foolish or miserable, but indeed wise and happy.[60]

As in all of his works, it is the divine element that is paramount in love, as in all creation and heaven. Although human love may be weak and full of anxious fear, divine love is a different matter. In a letter to Girolamo Amazzi, Ficino explained:

> Divine love... kindled by the flames of the virtues and growing strong from celestial rays, seeks to return to the sublime heights of heaven that no fear of earthly ills can ever trouble. Of such a kind is our mutual love, Amazzi. Therefore, as you are sure of your love toward me, so be just as sure of my love towards you. Far be it from us that one human heart should fail to respond to another that is always calling. Even strings seem to respond to strings that are similarly tuned, and one lyre resounds in answer to another; indeed a solid wall may echo to one who calls.[61]

Ficino's emphasis upon divine love, through his combination of Platonic and Neoplatonic thought with theology, made him an attractive intellectual for many travellers from other parts of Europe. Through his letters and personal contacts, he helped spread his philosophy throughout Europe.

Ficino: Dates and Events

19 October 1433:	born in Figline (Valdarno) near Florence. Named Marsilio de Figline.
1439:	moves to Ferrara.
c. **1445:**	begins studies with Luca di san Gimignano amongst others.
1451–58:	studies with Niccolò Tignosi da Foligno at Florence University.
1456:	takes the name Ficino and begins to learn Greek.
1456:	writes *Instututiones ad Platonicam Disciplinam* (not extant).
1450s-60s:	member of religious community in Florence.
1450s	George Gemisthos (c.1355–1452/4) teaching in Florence.
1457:	writes commentaries on Lucretius, later destroyed. Religious crisis and internal struggle over supremacy of Aristotle or Plato.
1459:	John Argyropoulos lectures on Greek in Florence and becomes Ficino's tutor.
1459–62:	studies Medicine.

1462:	translates *Hymns of Orpheus* and *The Sayings of Zoroaster* from Greek into Latin. Receives the patronage of Cosimo de' Medici to translate the *Corpus Hermeticum* and complete works of Plato.
1462:	Cosimo gives Ficino annual profits of a farm near Careggi.
1463:	*Corpus Hermeticum* completed. Begins to translate Plato.
1 August 1464:	Cosimo dies.
1468:	translates Dante's *De Monarchia*, writes *De Amore* and commentary on Plato's *Symposium*.
1469:	finishes translation of Plato's works. Begins *Platonic Theology*.
1473:	ordained Priest.
1474:	writes *De Christiana Religione*.
1474–94:	many letters written.
1482:	*Theologia Platonica* published.
1484:	complete works of Plato published. Pico arrives in Florence.
1484–92:	translations of Plotinus, Porphyry and Proclus.
1486:	public Lectures on Plotinus in S. Maria degli Angeli.
1489:	accused of heresy and saved by Archbishop Rinaldo Orsini. Writes *Apology* and *De Triplici Vita*.
1491:	translates works of Dionysius the Areopagite (Pseudo-Dionysius).
1491–2:	writes *De Sole* and *De Lumine*.
1492:	completes translation of Plotinus, Porphyry, Iamblichus and Proclus.
1494:	death of Pico and poet Poliziano.
1495:	letters published in Venice.
1496:	incomplete Platonic commentaries published.
1497:	translation of *Iamlichus* published. Last work on St. Paul's letter to the Romans unfinished.
October 1499:	dies at Careggi.

Ficno's Key Works

1456:	*Institutiones ad Platonicam Disciplinam* (Ficino's first major work).

Although this work is no longer extant, Ficino's letters of the same period show his conviction that philosophy has a crucial role to play in leading humanity towards perfection, and unity with the divine.

1463: Translation of the *Corpus Hermeticum* consists of many texts attributed to Hermes, in which creation myth mixes with astrology and theology, resulting in a philosophy of divine humanity that becomes subject to the rule of the stars by taking an earthly physical form. The secret knowledge of humanity's original divine status can be known through the spiritual teachings of the present, by means of the mind's ascent through reason to the divine.

1469: *De Amore.* Ficino's Commentary on Plato's *Symposium*, entitled *De Amore*, 'initiated a new genre of literature, the love treatise, which was in vogue in Europe for at least the next two hundred years'.[62]

1477: *Disputatio Contra Iudicium Astrologorum (Disputation Against the Judgement of Astrologers)*, in which Ficino was quick to point out the limitations of astrology, especially in comparison to theology.

1482: *Theologia Platonica de Immortalitate Animae.* Ficino's treatise on the immortality of the soul. Controversial in its use of astrology, the *Theologia Platonica* contains scholastic and humanist thought, as well as Platonic and Neoplatonic philosophy, including Plato's insistence on the divine within the human soul – a soul, moreover, which was immortal, free, and, for Ficino the Christian, most fulfilled in God.

1489: *De Vita Libri Tres* contains much on medicine and astrology, including the view that the world is in some way integrated with the human soul. The third volume of *De Vita* (1489) contains mild references to occultist doctrines, but without promoting sinister rituals.

1492: Commentaries on the *Divine Names* and *The Mystical Theology* of Pseudo-Dionysius, in which Ficino expounds a mixture of Platonic and Christian thought with an emphasis upon the primacy of intellect over love and the stages of ascent to union with God.

1495: Ficino's *Epistolae* published in Venice. On his travels to Italy, John Colet purchased a copy of the work and brought it back to England. The copy (now in All Souls' College, Oxford) contains 4000 words of Colet's marginalia and copies of correspondence between Colet and Ficino, showing Colet's admiration for Ficino's Christian Neoplatonism.

4

GIOVANNI PICO DELLA MIRANDOLA
(1463–1494)
The Italian Cabalist

Count Giovanni Pico della Mirandola (February 24, 1463–
November 17, 1494) ranks among the greatest and most
notorious of Italian Renaissance humanist philosophers. The
most famous work of his brief life is his *Oratio* (*Oration*), written
when he was twenty-three, which has become a standard Renaissance
text, but was originally written as a prelude to his *900 Conclusiones*
(*Theses*) of 1486 – an exercise intended to challenge anyone to public
debate on any one of 900 subjects, covering religion and philosophy.
More controversial than Ficino and unable to escape a papal heresy
charge, he was influential throughout Europe, especially in the sixteenth century.[1]

Introduction

The acknowledgement of Pico's importance for our intellectual heritage, as Dougherty has noted, has not always been universal. Assessments of his work have ranged from Lynn Thorndike's opinion, in the 1930s, that 'one cannot but feel that the importance of Pico della Mirandola in the history of thought has often been grossly exaggerated' to Frances Yates's evaluation, thirty years later (although not widely shared) that 'the profound significance of Pico della Mirandola in the history of humanity can hardly be over-estimated'.[2] Since the 1960s there has been a huge increase in scholarship concerning Pico, not least in the early twenty-first century,[3] with the result that his status as a major influence on western philosophy has risen and it is now universally accepted that he made a significant impact upon the philosophers and theologians of his own day, as well as later writers such as Voltaire and John Milton.[4] Pico's works stand as testament to this lasting importance: his *Oratio* and *Conclusiones* are two of the finest humanist texts of the Renaissance; and his *Apologia*, *De Ente de Uno* (of Being and Unity) and *Heptaplus* (On the Seven days of Creation), all demonstrate his mastery of Neoplatonic philosophy, metaphysics, rhetoric and logic, as well as his association and familiarity with humanists such as Ficino and Poliziano.

A famous letter concerning rhetoric and philosophy written to Pico in 1485, by his humanist contemporary Ermolao Barbaro (1454–93), demonstrates Pico's intellectual standing during his lifetime. Barbaro described him as a 'brilliant and quite divine talent' in the field of Aristotelian and Platonic philosophy, and predicted that he would become an 'outstanding poet' and 'most eminent orator'.[5]

Life

Pico lived an extraordinary and intriguing life. He was born to the aristocratic Franceso I, Lord of Mirandola and Count of Concordia, and his wife Giulia, daughter of the Count of Scandiano. Mirandola was a small region of Emilia-Romagna near Ferrara and legend suggests that, at the time of Pico's birth in the castle there, a 'circle of fire appeared for a split second over his mother's bed'.[6] He had two elder brothers, Count Galeotto I and Antoni, as well as two sisters, Caterina, who married Lionello Pio da Carpi in 1473, and Lucrezia, who married Pino Oderlaffi da Forli in 1475.

Pico was a child prodigy with an amazingly retentive memory. His education included Latin and Greek and, at the age of fourteen, he was sent to Bologna to study canon law, apparently destined for a life in the Church. However with the sudden death of his mother, Giulia, in

August 1478, Pico gave up canon law and moved to Ferrara to study philosophy, during which time he continued to study Latin literature and became friends with Poliziano and Savonarola. A year later he moved again, this time to Padua, one of the greatest universities at the time and, of course, a centre of Aristotelian scholasticism. Here Pico studied Hebrew and Arabic with the Jewish Averroist (follower of the Islamic philosopher Averroës) Elia del Medigo (c. 1458–1493), who considered Aristotle 'the father of all philosophers' and Averroës 'his truest commentator'.[7] Elia also introduced Pico to the Cabala, 'an intellectual movement of Jewish gnosis influenced by Neoplatonism', which would be a great influence in Pico's life and work.[8]

Pico seems to have spent much of his time at home between 1482 and 1485, although he also travelled to centres of humanist learning in Italy. He spent the summer of 1482 in Mirandola, travelling to Pavia in the autumn and was, at this time, corresponding with Poliziano and Lorenzo de' Medici on poetry and also with Ficino, requesting a copy of his *Theologia Platonica*.

Following the division of his parents' estate in 1483, Giovanni became one of the richest men in Italy. In May of that year, having sent some of his work to Poliziano, he was invited to Florence, which signified an important stage in Pico's life. Thus, in November 1484, he travelled to Florence and met Lorenzo de' Medici for the first time, on the same day that Ficino published his complete translation of Plato's works. Along with the attention of Lorenzo, Pico quickly attracted the interest of 'physicians and Jewish philosophers, Aristotelians, Platonists and poets, [and] scholars of Dante and Petrarch'.[9] Pico was keen to acquire knowledge of Hebrew in order to study the Old Testament, and he learned it from Guglielmo Raimondo de Moncada, known as Flavius Mithridates.[10] Lorenzo would go on to support Pico until 1492, when Lorenzo died. It is important to remember that Pico's education was broad and that his intellectual outlook was developed by means of engagement with several diverse schools of thought:

> Pico's formation was not limited to the literary humanism of Ferrara and the Platonism of Florence; it likewise included the lay Aristotelianism of Padua and the scholastic theology of Paris. To these elements must also be added the rabbinical theology and the cabalistic speculation that he knew through his quite thorough study of Hebrew.[11]

Thus Pico had mastered humanist techniques, whilst refusing to reject scholastic thought and expression. This was demonstrated in 1485, when Pico wrote a celebrated letter to Ermolao Barbaro, his Aristotelian teacher in Padua.[12] Barbaro had scolded Pico for scorning rhetoric as a means of philosophical expression in a letter dated 5 April 1485. The subject under discussion, therefore, was what style of writing or oratory was appropriate for philosophers to use. Pico's reply of June 1485, which is considered to be 'one of the greatest examples of Renaissance rhetoric', was written as a response to Barbaro's argument that philosophy should not be encumbered by technical language.[13] Pico reposted, in his letter *De Genere Decendi Philosophorum*, that 'philosophical research need not conform to a single, harmonious style if this impeded the pursuit of truth'.[14] Pico advocated giving up Latin in favour of Greek, but nevertheless insisted that the language of philosophy must prioritize the useful over the ornate. His reply to Barbaro is teasing and not without irony; even as he defends his thesis that philosophy is distinct from rhetoric, he does so 'by means of a highly eloquent rhetorical style'.[15] Pico's point appears to be that different styles of writing and expression are appropriate to different subjects and literary forms. The epistolary calls for eloquence and beauty of expression in a manner that a philosophical treatise does not. The letter was used by Pico to show the interrelation between form, style and content: what was required by the art of letter writing was not suitable for that of metaphysical philosophy, but this point had to be made in a manner appropriate to the former (beauty and rhetoric in order to convince and persuade, something philosophy had to do by its claims to a different standard of truth). Thus, 'his letter proves that he knew how to compose in the best literary tradition'.[16] Although Pico admitted that he had 'lost in Thomas, John Scotus, Albert, and Averroës, the best years of my life',[17] nevertheless, he remained certain that philosophy did not need great rhetoric:

> We search after the what of writing, we do not search after the how – that the style be without flourish and without flower. We do not want our style delightful, adorned, and graceful; we want it useful, grave, something to be respected; we would have it attain majesty through rudeness (*horror*) rather than charm through delicateness (*mollitudo*)...Unless you first plaster, you cannot put paint on the walls of a marble house; in either case you would diminish its dignity and beauty. Nor otherwise is it with wisdom and philosophers' teachings; they are not brightened but obscured by word-painting...The most inarticulate wisdom can be of use. Unwise eloquence, like a sword in a madman's hand, cannot but be most dangerous.[18]

It seems that Pico was not against the use of eloquence *per se*, in fact he was a master of the humanist art himself, but those readers of philosophy who rejected scholasticism in favour of fashionable eloquence in philosophy (he called them 'grammaticasters') turned his stomach: 'They say, We do not want these philosophers of yours. Well, small wonder. Neither do dogs care for Falernian'.[19] The Falernian wine would seem to refer to the refined beauty of true (simple, useful) philosophy, which 'dogs' are incapable of appreciating.

The influence of this exchange was felt well into the sixteenth century. Melanchthon, in Germany, had followed the correspondence and sought to improve upon Barbaro's answer, long after Pico and Barbaro were both dead (he published in 1558), arguing that wisdom and eloquence needed each other and were, together, the highest virtues of man: 'for clearly there is no use for wisdom unless we can communicate to others the things we have with wisdom deliberated and thought upon'.[20]

In the summer of 1485, Pico travelled to Paris, the greatest university north of the Alps, and another haven of Aristotelian scholasticism, a subject with which the first 115 theses of Pico's *900 Conclusiones* (begun at this time) were concerned. He was determined to travel to Rome to publish his eclectic collection of theses from various sources, and to provoke public debate in the capital of Christendom.

1486 would become the most extraordinary year of his life. In March of that year Pico returned to Florence, staying with Ficino, Poliziano and Girolamo Benivieni. He left for Rome on 8 May, stopping at Arrezzo two days later, and entered into a love affair with a cousin of Lorenzo de' Medici, Margherita, attempting to abduct her. Pico was caught by her husband, Giuliano Mariotto de' Medici, and imprisoned. Once released, he recovered from his ordeal in Perugia, having to move to Fratta because of the plague. Pico repented of his behaviour and, recovering from his shame, wrote a commentary on a *Canzone* by Benivieni.[21] He also began to read the authors who would become influential in his eclectic brand of humanism: Zoroaster, Melchior, works of the Cabala and Hermes Trismegistus. These and other writers, including Aristotle and the scholastics, were to be as influential as Plato in Pico's humanistic thought. Indeed, it is important to emphasize that humanist philosophers, such as Pico and Ficino, were not in a separate intellectual category to scholastic theologians or even preachers such as Savonarola. As Edelheit rightly observes:

> The distinction between humanist philosophers like Marsilio Ficino and Giovanni Pico della Mirandola, a professional scholastic theologian like Giovanni Caroli, and a preacher like Girolamo Savonarola, is far from being clear-cut in the realities of late fifteenth-century Florence.[22]

As we shall see below, Savonarola was as important an influence in Pico's intellectual development as Ficino, and Pico's interests extended beyond the humanist arts of rhetoric and eloquence until the end of his life.

Pico was ready to debate his collected *900 Conclusiones* by the end of 1486 and published them in December of that year, along with the introductory *Oratio* (later given the title *Oration on the Dignity of Man*), before Pope Innocent VIII could object. Pico's objective was to debate in the apostolic senate before the College of Cardinals, set for January 1487, and with the Pope as supreme judge.[23] However, the Pope intervened and halted any possibility of debate: following an investigation of the *Conclusiones* in March 1487, at which Pico was present for five of the twelve days, thirteen theses were contested and Pico was ordered to retract them. Examples of those chosen as unorthodox were:

1. Christ did not truly and in respect to his real presence descend into hell as Thomas [Aquinas] and the common way propose, but only in effect.
   Wrong, erroneous, heretical.

2. Neither the Cross of Christ, nor any image, should be adored with the adoration of veneration, even in that way that Thomas proposes.
   Outrageous, offensive to pious ears, and unaccustomed in the Universal Church.[24]

Although Pico obliged the Pope by retracting the thirteen offending theses, he added a further insult to orthodoxy by writing a defence of the theses, *Apologia*, published on 31 May 1487. As a result the whole *900 Conclusiones* were condemned by papal bull (*Et Si Injuncto Nobis*) on 4 August 1487 and Pico was forced to flee to France, where he was arrested in 1488, between Grenoble and Lyon, by Philip II of Savoy, and briefly imprisoned at Vincennes castle. Lorenzo de' Medici sent princes to plead Pico's case and Emperor Charles VIII of France released him. Pico returned to Florence in April 1488, although he would not be free of papal condemnation until Pope Innocent's death in 1493.

In 1488, still only twenty-five years of age, Pico settled in Fiesole, near Florence, where he wrote, in 1489, his *Heptaplus*, a commentary on the first twenty-six verses of Genesis, and *De Ente et Uno* (Of Being and Unity) in 1491. The first work was dedicated to Lorenzo de' Medici, the latter to Poliziano. He also composed his *Disputationes Adversus Astrologiam Divinatricem* – a treatise against astrology, which was not published during his lifetime.

By 1491 Pico was increasingly under the influence of the revolutionary preacher Savonarola, and more determined to rid himself of his youthful riotous living in order to live ascetically and become a monk. In this year, he transferred the income he received from the family estate to his nephew, Gianfrancesco. The following year Lorenzo de' Medici died and Pico moved back to Ferrara. He continued to rid himself of earthly possessions, under Savonarola's guidance, and renounced the Egyptian and Chaldean texts that had so captured his imagination in his younger days. Following his absolution by Pope Alexander VI for his 'erroneous' theses in 1493, Pico died in mysterious circumstances on 17 November 1494, with legend suggesting that his secretary poisoned him. Pico was buried in San Marco in Florence, where Savonarola, who had been at his deathbed, preached at his funeral.

The Humanist

In his short but eventful life Pico della Mirandola was, like every other intellectual of the time, an heir of scholasticism. In 1485–6, when he had already corresponded with Barbaro on the subjects of rhetoric and philosophy, Pico was studying in Paris, focussing on scholastic philosophy and theology. When, later in 1486, he was preparing his *900 Conclusiones* in Rome, he still concerned himself with scholastic philosophers for the first 115 theses, ranging from Albertus Magnus (1193/1206–1280), and Thomas Aquinas (1225–1274) to Duns Scotus (*c.* 1265–1308) and Henry of Ghent (*c.* 1217–1293).[25] From the Vatican library, in preparation for his theses, he had borrowed Aquinas's *De Ente et Essential*, astrological writings by Roger Bacon (*c.* 1214–1294), and the *Speculum Naturalium* of Henry Bate (*c.* 1246–1310).[26]

However, in the realm of theology, Pico was dangerous to himself. In a letter to Lorenzo de' Medici, written on 2 October 1489, Pope Innocent VIII warned Lorenzo of Pico's lack of theological expertize:

> If you like him, have him write poetry rather than theological stuff, for that suits him better, since the Count lacks the foundations and hasn't seen as much as is needed for someone who writes on theology.[27]

According to Gianfrancesco's biography of Pico, after the delivery of his *900 Conclusiones* in Rome in 1486 envious enemies had viewed him with suspicion. Even whilst he was preparing the theses, Pico himself realised that his relative youth as well as theological inexperience provided his critics with powerful ammunition against him. 'Some', he wrote,

> do not approve of this whole method of disputation and of this institution of publicly debating on learning [more precisely,

on letters]...[Others] in no wise approve it in me because I, born I admit but twenty-four years ago, should have dared at my age to offer a disputation concerning the lofty mysteries of Christian theology...in so famous a city.[28]

Of course, worse was to come, with the enquiry and subsequent accusations of heterodoxy following the condemnation of his *900 Conclusiones*. The thirteen theses that were questioned as erroneous concerned Christ's descent to hell, mortal sin, God's omnipotence, free will, salvation, the divinity of Christ, the Eucharist (three times), miracles, God's intellect and the soul. These theological issues raised the question of Pico's piety. In his *Apologia*, defending himself soon after the accusations, Pico made liberal use of medieval scholastic theologians to substantiate his claims, and made a cryptic defence of his theses:

Those who hate me should not read what is our opinion, and those who like me, equally should not read that, because from what is mine they may come to think much of what is not ours.[29]

That is to say, Pico meant to take common opinion ('ours') and alien teachings and bridge the gap by way of his own thoughts. Thus, his work should be seen as dialectical.[30] Although there was nothing new in the dialectical form (dialectical reasoning had been practised in medieval universities since the twelfth century) Pico also argued that, given the limits of human knowledge and the constraints of discourse, philosophical and theological differences were inevitable and should not, therefore, be made illegal.[31] Even Thomas Aquinas, he argued, held contradictory theological views, asserting 'one opinion in one place, another in another'.[32] Furthermore, Pico cited St. Augustine as an authority who allowed for differing theologies, for Augustine held that correctly detecting heresy was a very difficult task. For Pico, the Church fathers were not infallible, as their teaching was 'not of so firm an authority and immobility that one may not contradict them...where we gain no certain truth nor doubtless belief, there we give assent with doubt and fear of error'.[33]

However, as Blum observes, the key to Pico's escape from the accusation of unorthodoxy lay in his use of primary Christian sources: the Bible and the divine speech that is apparent in the scriptures. Pico was adept at scriptural exegesis (he had already produced a commentary on the book of Genesis) and, as for the manifestation of the divine, Pico had recognized the importance of the Cabala: Pico was 'the first in the Latin world to mention the Cabala', and to argue that it ought to be taken seriously as part of the Christian heritage:[34]

> The true Cabala was revealed by God to Moses and transmitted from Moses to further wise men by way of succession, so it is properly called 'tradition', which is the meaning of the word *Cabala*. Against this true Cabala Pico distinguishes another one, for the term can be used simply to denote any secret and occult knowledge. The reason for the synonym is that, of course, every sapiential practice lives on occult tradition of combinatoric art, which is said to be analogous to that of Raymond Lull and, again, to magic. Although these are – as was the claim of the indicted thesis – helpful for understanding Christ as God, they are only in a metaphorical sense (transumptive) to be named Cabala.[35]

Pico's faith in the worlds of philosophy, theology and religion can be summarized in his assertion that 'philosophy seeks the truth, theology finds it, and religion possesses it'.[36] In his *Oratio*, Pico explored the relationship between philosophy, theology and religion, arguing that philosophy has been prized by Judaism, Christianity and the ancient Greek world, but that, ultimately, philosophy, even moral philosophy, is only a preparation for the enlightenment of theology, that is, 'the knowledge of divine things ... theological piety and most sacred worship of God'.[37] Michael Suddoth succinctly summarizes Pico's attitude to philosophy and faith:

> That the human person's end is supernatural is not a truth derived from philosophy but an implication of Pico's theological beliefs. Consequently, his view of the value and place of philosophy in relation to theology is ultimately based on his fundamental commitment to Christian supernaturalism. [This demonstrates] an important continuity between Pico and his medieval predecessors, who undertook philosophical inquiry in the larger context of their religious beliefs. Pico does not pretend to stand outside the realm of faith and examine religious belief from a purported neutral perspective. He is a thinker who approaches rational reflection on theological claims within the context of his faith, specifically the Catholic faith, as it existed in fifteenth-century Europe.[38]

Pico's approach to the various strands of philosophical knowledge and theological belief was to try to create a synthesis, or syncretism, of diverse ideas.[39] For instance, in his *Oratio*, Pico finds a parallel between

Moses' laws governing worship and his own progress through moral, dialectic and natural philosophy to illumination and purification:

> Moses gives us these distinct commands, and in giving them he advises us, arouses us, urges us to make ready our way through philosophy to future celestial glory, while we can.[40]

Likewise, in his *Heptaplus* (1489), Pico's interpretation of the creation myth in the book of Genesis makes use of the Cabala, Plato's *Timaeus* and Zoroastrianism, as well as perceiving the seeds of Neoplatonism evident in Moses' work: 'he [Moses] buried the treasures of all true philosophy as in a field... and philosophizes on the emanation of all things from God'.[41] Pico also suggested that, in Moses' work, there is hidden the work of Christ.

Aristotelianism and Platonism were syncretized in Pico's *De Ente et Uno* (1491), in which Pico attempted to reconcile Aristotle's notion that the One and Being are the same with Plato's idea that the One is before Being.[42] His *900 Conclusiones* are replete with attempts to reconcile Judaism and Christianity, Aristotle and Plato, Christian and pagan thought, conflicts within scholastic theology, and the Cabala to Christianity.[43] In order to achieve this end Pico had to emphasize, or find, a hidden meaning in texts that is not immediately apparent. Thus the truth, or mystery, of any text must be uncovered by means of allegorical interpretation.[44] Therefore, 'Moses had to speak with a veiled face, lest those whom he was undertaking to enlighten be blinded by so much light' and 'Plato himself concealed his doctrines beneath coverings of allegory, veils of myth, mathematical images, and unintelligible signs of fugitive reasoning'.[45]

As Suddoth points out, Pico's synthesis of ideas is ultimately Christian: 'Christ is the focal point of a historically situated redemptive plan, explicitly revealed in the Christian revelation'.[46] This redemption, Pico suggested, was available to those who lived before the birth of Christ:

> Then after the ineffable sacrifice performed on the altar of the cross, when Christ had come down to them, he swept them to freedom like the moving power of a whirlwind and carried them up to the level of highest felicity.[47]

In his lifelong exploration of various philosophical and religious traditions, Pico kept his Christian faith as a fixed reference point.[48] Thus, as in the works of Ficino and other humanists, Christian ideas became Platonized and, beyond the limits of philosophy, Christ became a Platonic symbol: the ultimate destination for those who seek illumination and perfection with the divine.

The Author and Scholar

As has been intimated above, it was not until Pico returned from his study in Paris and put his love affairs and imprisonment behind him that his real work began. His idea to hold a conference in Rome, challenging the greatest theologians and philosophers of the time to debate, was typical of the audacity of his character and indicative of his self-confidence regarding his intellectual prowess and rhetorical skills. Although the venture may appear to modern eyes as egocentric— a publicity-hungry public intellectual challenging others to a televised debate, it nevertheless produced two remarkable, if highly controversial documents: the *Conclusiones* and the *Oratio*. Pico's theses were collected from a wide variety of sources: Neoplatonists, such as Proclus and Plotinus, as well as from the Jewish Cabala and his own mind.

Pico's pronouncement at the end of the 1486 edition of his *900 Conclusiones* demonstrates the parameters of his task clearly:

> The Conclusions will not be disputed until the Epiphany [6 January]. In the meantime they will be published in all Italian universities. And if any philosopher or theologian, even from the ends of Italy, wishes to come to Rome for the sake of debating, his lord the disputer promises to pay the travel expenses from his own funds.[49]

The scope of the theses covered the widest range of subject matter ever compiled in a single work until that time: Greek, Arabic, and Hebrew learning; Latin scholasticism; Renaissance Neoplatonism; classicism; humanism; magic; numerology; the Cabala, and many other topics. Pico ostentatiously promised a discussion of 'everything knowable' (*de omni re scibili*).[50] The book became the first printed work ever to be 'banned universally by the Church'.[51]

For Pico, ancient Hebrew texts and their transmission were vitally important for Renaissance reasoning. Of the 900 theses, seventy-two are dedicated to the subject of the Cabala. One such thesis deals with the cabbalistic science of the nomenclature for God:

> Whatever other Cabalists say, I divide the speculative part of the Cabala [the science of names] four ways, corresponding to the four divisions of philosophy that I generally make. The first is what I call the science of the revolution of the alphabet, corresponding to the part of philosophy that I call universal philosophy. The second, third, and fourth constitute the threefold *merkabah* [chariot], corresponding to the three

parts of particular philosophy, concerning divine, middle, and sensible natures.[52]

Thus, as Blum observes:

> Here we are offered a new hierarchy of philosophy, composed of (1) Cabala as the speculation of letters and thus universal philosophy (*philosophia catholica*); (2) philosophical theology; (3) philosophy of the median realm, which obviously encompasses the intellects; and (4) philosophy of visible nature, or physics.[53]

In 1486, Pico published his *Oratio*. In the sixteenth century, an editor of the text changed the title to 'Oration of the Dignity of Man'.[54] However, only part of the work deals with this subject. As such, the *Oratio* is not so much about humanity itself, but is rather a treatise exploring the nature of Platonic theology and philosophy. As with Ficino, his tutor, Pico's ambition for humanity was an ascent to God, and a return to 'the One'. Philosophy was one key to this journey, but was in itself insufficient. Theology was the crucial discipline for humanity, to which philosophy could only point:

> Natural philosophy, therefore, cannot assure us a true and unshakable peace. To bestow such peace is rather the privilege and office of the queen of sciences, most holy theology. Natural philosophy will at best point out the way to theology and even accompany us along the path, while theology, seeing us from afar hastening to draw close to her, will call out: 'Come unto me you who are spent in Labour and I will restore you; come to me and I will give you the peace which the world and nature cannot give.'[55]

Pico was immensely widely read and, throughout his works, sought to reconcile apparently conflicting ideas from history, finding their hidden mysterious meaning by means of allegorical interpretation. Therefore 'truth' has to be found, and this can only be achieved, in Pico's experience, through a dialectical engagement with a diverse range of perspectives:

> Further, if there is a school which attacks truer doctrines and ridicules with calumny the good causes of thought, it strengthens rather than weakens truth, and as by motion it excites the flame rather than extinguishing it. Moved by this reasoning, I have wishes to bring into view the things taught not merely

according to one doctrine (as some would desire), but things taught according to every sort of doctrine, that by this comparison of very many sects and by the discussion of manifold philosophy, that radiance of truth which Plato mentions in his *Letters* might shine more clearly upon our minds, like the sun rising from the deep.[56]

Following the inevitable papal condemnation upon the publication of his work, Pico's 1487 *Apologia* argued that faith was not to be confused with opinion, a form of academic scepticism practised in the Athenian Academy from the first to the third century B.C.E. and 'transmitted to the West largely by Cicero'.[57] Pico was at pains to point out, in rather technical language, that his opinion was credible:

But which of the two opinions on the way of being in a place of separated substances would be truer, i.e., that of the Scotists, or rather the opinion of those which I follow, I do not determine. I am only saying that my opinion was both creditable and held as most true by so many Catholic teachers and Doctors most celebrated both in learning and in sanctity; that those who dare to decide between opinions of such approved Doctors which opinion is heretical or smacks of heresy should by far be considered more rash than me, who prefer the authority of those ancient theologians to the conclusions of recent theologians.[58]

Thus, Pico argued, the Parisian Articles of 1277, drawn up by Bishop Stefan Tempier, merely represented the opinion of one theological school. As Edelheit asserts, 'They are not binding on Christians as the Scriptures and the Apostolic Creed are':[59]

Wherefore though my conclusion is against the article, let those who condemned me remember that they were entirely mistaken in my condemnation, because they said that my conclusion was against the Apostles' Creed, when they should have said that my conclusion was against the Parisian creed...[60]

Thus, fundamental faith (*fides*) and the reasoning of any given opinion (*opinio*) at any given time must not be confused. Edelheit, although in a minority among scholars, has argued that:

The humanist theology of Pico can be understood as an endeavour to establish a new relationship between *opinio* and *fides*, in response to both the Thomists and the Scotists... This relationship was founded on a new method of theology and drew on texts and notions which were almost completely unknown to scholastic theologians.[61]

In our introduction we saw how problematic the notion of 'humanist theology' is, given Kristeller's plausible definition of humanism as fundamentally separate from philosophy and theology.[62] Nevertheless, Edelheit's idea highlights how philosophers like Pico were able to choose humanist tools as part of their intellectual equipment and use them, alongside scholastic methods, in the pursuit of theological and philosophical truth.

In 1489, Pico produced his *Heptaplus*, in which he argued that God's work in the seven days of creation contained all the wisdom, knowledge and secrets of the universe, further revealed by the Mosaic books of the Old Testament but obscured through the centuries. Thus, Pico attempted to interpret all human knowledge through the seven layers of truth expressed in the creation myth.[63]

Happiness, or felicity, as Pico called it, was to be found in humanity's return to God: 'the return of each thing to its beginning…the end of all things is the same as the beginning of all: one God, omnipotent, and blessed'.[64] However, within this process, there is a natural, innate happiness which pertains to all things:

> Since each nature has God within it in some way, since it has as much of God as it has goodness (and all things which God made are good), it remains for it, when it has perfected its own nature in all parts and has attained its potential, to attain God also within itself; and if the attainment of God is felicity, as we have shown, it is in some way happy in itself. This is the natural felicity, of which more or less is allotted to different things according to their natures.[65]

The *Heptaplus* explores an immense wealth of thought, but it is ultimately, like all of Pico's works, Christocentric: 'surely if all things agree with the truth, as Aristotle says, all things ought to agree with Christ, who is the truth himself'.[66]

One of Pico's last works was his *De Ente et Uno* of 1491, which was prompted by Poliziano's request that Pico arbitrate in the debate between Platonists, such as Ficino and Lorenzo de' Medici, and Aristotelians, such as Poliziano himself. Pico chose to write on harmony in public life. The result was a 'sophisticated project to read Plato not only through Plotinus and Proclus but also through Aristotle and medieval theologians'.[67]

In his last years Pico also produced his *Disputationes*. Composed when he was a follower of Savonarola and confined to his villa in

Fiesole, the *Disputationes* is a rebuttal of astrology in three parts: first, Pico argued that astrology is not a form of divination and should be distinguished from the more mathematical science of astronomy; second, that astrology is deceitful, given that predictions are often wrong; and, third, Pico examined astrology scientifically, arguing that 'if heaven was a universal cause, that is, remote, how could one derive from it – as if from a secondary cause – the events of the world?'.[68]

Pico: Dates and Events

24 February 1463:	born to Franceso I, Lord of Mirandola.
1477:	sent to Bologna to read canon law.
1479:	August: mother dies.
1479:	studies philosophy at Ferrara with Battista Guarini. Meets Poliziano and Savonarola.
1480–82:	University of Padua, studies Hebrew and Arabic with Elia del Medigo.
Summer 1482:	in Mirandola.
1482:	corresponds with Poliziano and Lorenzo de' Medici.
Autumn 1482:	travels to Pavia.
1483:	division of his parents' estate. Pico becomes one of the richest men in Italy.
1482–85:	at home and travelling to humanist centres.
May 1483:	in Florence.
1484:	corresponds with Lorenzo and Poliziano.
Nov 1484:	meets Lorenzo in Florence; publishes complete Plato (translated by Ficino).
1485:	at the University of Paris (sometime before 1487). Composes celebrated letter to Ermolao Barbaro.
1485:	writes the *Conclusiones* (900 Theses).
March 1486:	in Florence. Stays with Poliziano, Ficino and Girolamo Benivieni.
8 May 1486:	leaves for Rome. Stops at Arrezzo, and has love affair with Margherita in Arrezzo. He is caught and briefly imprisoned.
Dec 1486:	*Oratio* and *Conclusiones* published.
January 1487:	date set for public debate in Rome of the *Conclusiones*.
February 1487:	orthodoxy of *Conclusiones* questioned by Pope Innocent VIII.
March 1487:	public investigation into the theses with Pico present.

31 May 1487: *Apologia* in defence of theses published.

4 August 1487: Pico condemned and flees to France.

1487/8: arrested between Grenoble and Lyon by Philip II of Savoy and imprisoned at Vincennes Castle.

1488: released with the help of Emperor Charles VIII of France.

April 1488: Pico back in Florence and Fiesole.

1489: writes *Heptaplus*, dedicated to Lorenzo de' Medici.

1491/2: *De Ente et Uno*, dedicated to Poliziano.

1491: under the instruction of Savonarola, Pico gives away income to his nephew Gianfrancesco and begins to rid himself of his possessions.

1492: Lorenzo de' Medici dies. Pico moves to Ferrara and begins *Disputationes*. He renounces Egyptian and Chaldean texts.

1493: Pico pardoned by Pope Alexander VI.

17 November 1494: Pico dies, possibly poisoned. Buried in St. Marco Church in Florence.

1496: nephew, Gianfrancesco, publishes a collection of Pico's works (*Commentationes*).

Pico's Key Works

1485: *Conclusiones* (900 Theses): an eclectic collection of arguments (many scholastic in nature as well as Neoplatonic) on philosophy, theology, astrology and the Cabala, amongst other topics. He intended them to be used as the basis for a great public debate in Rome, in the apostolic senate before the College of Cardinals, but the theses were investigated and condemned by Pope Innocent VIII. Pico had to flee to France as a result.

June 1485: letter to Ermolao Barbaro on the merits of Rhetoric and its uses for philosophy, *De Genere Decendi Philosophia*. Written in perfect humanist style, Pico rejected rhetoric as a necessary tool for philosophical expression.

1486: *Oratio*: later called *Oration on the Dignity of Man* in the sixteenth century. Written as an introduction to the *Conclusiones* and published with them in 1486, the *Oratio* extols the nobility of disciplined reason and imagination, human nature as redeemed by Christ, and the uplifting of humanity through the exercise of the soul and mind, in both philosophy and theology.

1487: *Apologia*: published on 31 May 1487, Pico defended his *Conclusiones* on the grounds that faith was not the same as opinion and that, therefore, his reasoning should not be confused with heresy.

1489: *Heptaplus*: Pico's interpretation of the creation myth of Genesis. Pico argued that God's creation in seven days contained all the wisdom, knowledge and secrets of the universe. Thus, all truth can be found in the seven layers of wisdom encapsulated in the creation myth.

1491: *De Ente et Uno*: prompted by a request from Angelo Poliziano, Pico was asked to arbitrate between Platonists (like Ficino) and Aristotelians (such as Poliziano). Pico wrote on harmony in public life.

1492: *Disputationes adversus Astrologiam Divinatricem* (published 1496). A treatise against astrology. Under the influence of Savonarola, this work argued, in three sections, that astrology is inferior to astronomy, that it is deceitful, and that it is unscientific.

THE LOW COUNTRIES

5

RUDOLPH AGRICOLA (1442/3–1485)
Father of Northern European Humanism

Erasmus once wrote: 'It was Rudolph Agricola who first brought with him from Italy some gleam of a better literature...He could have been the first in Italy, had he not preferred Germany better'.[1] Whilst the latter part of this commendation cannot be true in a chronological sense, given that Petrarch and his predecessors had already cultivated the *studia humanitatis* in Italy long before the fifteenth century, Erasmus meant that Agricola could have been among the foremost Italian humanists of his day. Nevertheless, Agricola was one of the first to bring humanism from Italy to Northern Europe, specifically to Germany and what we now know as the Netherlands.[2] He never reached high office, or wrote many works, but Agricola's legacy survives because of his insistence upon the revival of classical literature, philology and the languages of Greek, Latin and Hebrew in the

Northern European universities and schools, so that the considerable educational, religious and cultural benefits of humanism would not be confined to Italy. He wrote:

> I have the brightest hope that we one day shall wrest from haughty Italy the reputation for classical expression which it has nearly monopolized, so to speak, and lay claim to it ourselves, and free ourselves from the reproach of ignorance and being called unlearned and inarticulate barbarians; and that our Germany will be so cultured and literate that Latium will not know Latin any better.[3]

There were others who had preceded Agricola in bringing classical learning from Italy to Germany, such as Peter Luder (1415–72), who spent nearly twenty years in Italy before returning to lecture at several universities on the *studia humanitatis*. However, Agricola was the first of those who spread humanism in Germany to be acknowledged as an intellectual giant by his contemporaries and successors.[4] His greatest work, *De Inventione Dialectica* (*On Dialectical Invention*), was a key resource for those who later sought to reform dialectic in the sphere of education.

Life[5]

Rudolph Agricola was born Roel of Huesman, on 17 February 1444 in Baflo, near Groningen in Frisia in the Low Countries. His father, Hendrik Vries, was a leading clergyman, who had studied theology at Cologne and who, in 1444, was elected abbot of a Benedictine nunnery at Selward (Siloe), outside Groningen. Roel's mother, Zycka Huesman, was from a peasant background and, although Rudolph was not gentry, his family were affluent enough for him to be sent to university. Agricola was first educated at St. Maarten's School in Groningen and then went to the University at Erfurt, gaining his B.A. in 1458. After Erfurt, Agricola proceeded to Louvain, becoming M.A. (*magister artium*) in 1465 and here in the Low Countries he became renowned for his skill in Latin, studying Cicero and Quintilian, and for his mastery of French and Greek. After a brief spell in Paris, where he first met Johannes Reuchlin, Agricola moved to Pavia, in 1468, in order to study law.

During this period (around 1470), Rudolph achieved the most remarkable success: he not only taught a deaf child how to communicate orally and in writing, but used this experience to create a new theory of dialectic, rhetoric and logic. The result was his *De Inventione Dialectica*, which assimilated rhetoric and dialectic and broadened the range of authorities upon which a scholar might draw, in order to create a wider range of possible conclusions on any given subject than had heretofore been allowed by the scholastics. It would become Agricola's greatest work and proved immensely popular.

From 1475 to 1479 Rudolph studied the humanities, especially Greek, at Ferrara, where he was a pupil of Giovanni Battista Guarneri. Agricola was also an organist at the Ducal Chapel: he was an exceptional musician and the Chapel was one of the foremost musical establishments in Europe. In the late 1470s Agricola returned to the North in order to take up an appointment as secretary to the city of Groningen: his post was that of *scriba et orator* (secretary and travelling ambassador), which he held from 1480–84. However, this period was not always as productive as Agricola would have hoped, and his studies seem to have fallen off and his enthusiasm waned into a kind of depressed apathy. A letter from Groningen to his pupil Alexander Hegius (1433–1498), dated 20 September 1480, demonstrates his lack of intellectual stimulation:

> It is hard to explain to you how dissatisfied I am with my entire situation and, above all, with myself. Each day, a bit of my love of studying dies – or should I say my practice of it? Well, certainly my practice, and therefore perhaps my love for it slowly too... The main reason for this is one which is particularly applicable to me, though I believe it is also important for others: I am not being spurred on to study strongly enough; I lack someone to supervize it, a companion to share things with, someone in whose ears I can deposit things while he in turn deposits in mine anything he has thought up, put into writing, learnt by reading, or anything he thinks deserves some praise or a keen opinion.[6]

Upon his return to Germany, however, opportunities to exercise his philological art seem to have increased as he spent time in Dilligen, where he corresponded with humanist friends and colleagues throughout Europe, promoting the *studia humanitatis*. He remained an independent scholar, unattached to a university or religious establishment; an independence reminiscent of Italian humanist scholars.

In 1481, Agricola spent six months in Brussels at the court of Archduke Maximilian. Friends attempted to dissuade him from accepting the archduke's patronage, afraid that the archduke's influence would undermine his philosophical ideals. Thus, in 1482, Agricola accepted the invitation of John of Dahlberg (1445–1503), the Bishop of Worms, to lecture at the University of Heidelberg. The two men had met in Pavia, and they became close friends in Heidelberg, the bishop being a generous benefactor of learning. At this time Agricola began studying Hebrew in earnest, and published a translation of the Psalms, but he would soon accompany Dahlberg on an embassy to the Pope (Innocent VIII) in Rome. On their return journey, Agricola fell gravely ill and died shortly after their return to Heidelberg, on 27 October 1485.

The Humanist

Agricola was the pioneer of 'Italianized' humanism in Northern Europe, aided by the wealth of the populous towns of the Low Countries and those oriented towards the East: to Westphalia, the Rhineland and those towns of the Hanseatic league. It was in the 1470s and 80s that a new Latin prose was developed in the works of Rudolph and his friends Vrye and Von Langen (1439–1519).[7] The propitious arrival of the first printing presses along the Ijssel river, at Deventer (1477), Zwolle (1477), Nijmegen (1479) and Hasselt near Zwolle (1480), facilitated the dissemination of new Latin and translations of classical texts. Moreover, manuscript books were produced in Zwolle and Selward, where Rudolph's father was abbot. At the Abbey of Aduard, Sanctus Bernadus (founded in 1193), a humanist 'academy' developed and held regular meetings. It was the richest monastic foundation near Groningen and, from 1449–1485, Abbot Hendrik van Rees gathered learned men there. The Aduard circle was a group of diverse personalities, invited to Aduard by the abbot for weeks at a time, in order to pursue learning.

It was at Heidelberg that Agricola wanted to learn Hebrew to add to his Greek, inspired by Wessel Gansfort (1419–1489) and Alexander Hegius (1433–1498), who knew both languages. A letter written from Dilligen to Adolf Occo (1447–1488), a doctor of arts and medicine, dated 24 August 1479, demonstrates his desire to study Hebrew:

> Well, as I have told you on so many occasions, I want to add Hebrew to my studies. I see the Holy Writ as being the most honourable study for my old age, and you know how helpful Hebrew can be to me in this respect. Unless I am simply being too self-indulgent, it will perhaps be the right thing for me to engage in theology in a more sophisticated way, and better equipped with letters than the common run of people over here. No sooner have they mastered the bare rudiments of this discipline than they are shipwrecked on it as on a rock.[8]

Thus Agricola not only introduced Greek and Hebrew studies to Germany and the Low Countries, but also the authors of late antiquity, the art of rhetoric and a new Latin style. Although he left only one major work (*De Inventione Dialectica*), he wrote many speeches, poems, a Life of Petrarch, a few translations of Greek dialogues, and some comments on Seneca, Boethius' *De Consolatione Philosophiae*, and on Cicero's *De Lege Manilia*. He wrote many letters, over fifty of which survive. Indeed, letter writing was key to refining the art of the *studia humanitatis* and to its dissemination:

> Letter writing was the humanists' chief form of communication, not only in east central Europe but all over the continent. Because these scholars were geographically spread out, constant correspondence was necessary for building and maintaining networks. We may recall Erasmus's remark that he devoted half his day to the reading and writing of letters, and his claim that on some days he wrote sixty or ninety letters. Letter writing conveyed information about one's scholarly projects and career plans at the individual level, and disseminated the cult of antiquity and humanist pedagogical and literary norms at the collective level. Underlying all the epistolary activity, though, was the humanist notion that letter writing was an exercise in persuasion.[9]

Indeed one such letter by Agricola provides ample evidence of his humanist outlook. Written to Jacob Barbireau (1455–1491) on 7 June 1484, whilst Agricola was living and teaching in Heidelberg, in some respects it reads more like a pedagogical treatise than an item of correspondence. The letter first sets out Agricola's notions of how to write clearly and eloquently, a necessity for a humanist wishing to communicate effectively:

> Whatever you write, force yourself to express it in as straightforward a way as possible, in no more than correct Latin at first. Saying it in a more elaborate way is something you do later; you certainly will not be able to do this unless a text is sound and unimpaired. An eloquent style is like a body: if not all its members are arranged in their correct position, if they are twisted out of shape, if they have grown bigger than they should be, all the finery you surround it with will to be of no avail. The body will clash with ornaments, and the beauty of the externals will make its ugliness all the more conspicuous by comparison.[10]

Next, Agricola explained that reading demands more than a superficial knowledge of a text; it requires a deep understanding of the hidden matter:

> When we read, we must above all try to understand as best we can what it is we are reading, and be completely clear about it. We should not simply try to get the gist of the matter in question, but also to perceive the significance of the words as they are used by skilful authors, their proper meaning and rhetorical arrangement, what the beauty, what the strength is of the statements, how great the power of explaining hidden matters and putting them into words, dragging them into the light before our eyes, as it were.[11]

Agricola's final point is that, once a text has been assimilated, it must be combined with the mind of the reader, and engaged with, in order to create something original; a dialectical form of reading and encounter that is quintessentially humanist:

> My third point... is how we can create and reproduce original ideas from what we have acquired through learning... The topic is really comprised of two things, either of which in itself merits great praise... The first of these is that we must have our knowledge readily available for use and at our disposal wherever the situation so demands... The second thing is that from what we have learned, we must be capable of discovering and accomplishing something of our own that goes beyond this, something to claim for ourselves, something that we can positively call our own.[12]

The whole point of this exercise was fundamentally an ethical one for Agricola. He instructs that:

> You must not only look to what philosophers have written on this subject (philosophers such as Aristotle, Cicero, Seneca, or any others that either wrote in Latin or were translated into acceptable Latin.) You must also seek it from historians and poets and orators. They do not actually teach, but by praising good deeds and criticizing wrongdoing, they do so in effect, and most effectively: the examples they present mirror what is right or wrong.[13]

However, Agricola, as Erasmus would also do, proclaimed scripture as the true authority for ethical knowledge. As Van Ruler has asserted, 'one of the most basic assumptions of all humanist thought was that classical examples might merge with the example of Christ'.[14] In developing the idea of a *Philosophia Christi*, Agricola stressed that morality must be taken 'a step further, and look at Holy Writ', since '[everything] handed down by others contains mistaken ideas of one kind or another'.[15] As we have seen, this was also a concern of Pico's, whose defence in his *Apologia* made the similar point that tradition as represented in the scriptures was free from error, but that man-made productions from subsequent centuries – including Church councils etc – were certainly not, and merely represented 'opinion' rather than necessary 'truth').

Agricola's humanist credentials are also demonstrated by other items of his correspondence. A letter from none other than Johannes Reuchlin, in 1484, shows the respect that Reuchlin had for him, although it takes the form of a rather abrupt request:

> Johann Reuchlin of Pforzheim sends many greetings to his highly respected friend Rudolph Agricola.
> I am not quite sure whether my most recent letter to you has been delivered. In it, I urgently asked you to write to me at length, giving your opinion on the following controversial issue. When it is said in Psalm 54 (I think): 'O Lord, by your name save me', by which or what kind of name should we implore that we receive salvation? Is it Yohoshua or YHWH? About the first one is written: 'For there is no other name given among men by which we must be saved.' Concerning the second one, the following is written: 'Happy is the man to whom the name of the Lord (YHWH) is his trust.' I implore you to explain why these writings contradict each other. Goodbye.[16]

Agricola's letter to Reuchlin in response to this request, sent from Heidelberg on 9 November 1484, is less than gracious and he refused to comply, predicting that Reuchlin would judge him too harshly in the matter:

> You demand from me, very learned sir, that I write a letter to you, and you demand it almost reproachfully. I, on the other hand, am somewhat reluctant to write. As both of us know very well, you prefer trusting your own judgement rather than other people's commendation of my studies, whatever these amount to, and for my part, I think I should by no means be so reckless as to expose myself to your judgement, you who

bear the distinction of being acquainted with so many different disciplines and languages.[17]

Agricola's reply perhaps serves to show how his humanism did not necessarily lead to religious heterodoxy or doubts. His refusal to answer
signifies a refusal to involve himself in debates about questions that cannot be resolved: the internal inconsistencies of the scriptures or patristic writings. Agricola sought to avoid these kind of debates because of
his relative scepticism regarding the limits of textual criticism (as well
as the limits of human knowledge more broadly. Indeed, it appears that
Agricola's relationship with Reuchlin was a strained one at times. In
congratulating him on his marriage, in a letter from Heidelberg dated
4 February 1485, Agricola includes a subtext that emphasizes the fool-
ishness of getting married:

> I hear that you have married. I include you in all my prayers,
> and hope that it may bring you happiness and good fortune ... It
> is therefore my opinion that you are brave and blessed because
> you have taken such an initiative. As for the future, if I ever
> wished anything for myself, my very learned sir, my very kind
> sir, for you I hope (and I always will) that your happiness will
> be in proportion to your bravery.[18]

Whatever the turbulence of their correspondence, Reuchlin's ultimate
respect for Agricola was demonstrated after Agricola's death, as he
allegedly delivered the address at his friend's funeral.

The Author and Scholar

Of all Agricola's works, his *De Inventione Dialectica* (*On Dialectical
Invention*) is by far the most significant. After the posthumous first
edition of 1515, it was used extensively by educationalists seeking to
teach dialectic. By extolling Cicero and Quintilian above Aristotle as
authorities on dialectic, the work emphasized the 'probable argument
and persuasion rather than absolutely certain conclusions as the kind
of reasoning most useful in everyday living'[19], and thus offered the
humanists a perspective on learning akin to Pico's distinction between
(probable) 'opinion' and (certain) 'knowledge', which broke with the
scholastic tradition of seeking absolute conclusions. Agricola's manual
was very popular and his novel ideas altered the intellectual landscape,
although the medieval *Summulae Logicales* by Peter of Spain remained
the most widely used dialectic textbook in the Renaissance with more
than one hundred and fifty pre-1600 editions. Agricola's logic, with
just seventy-six editions, was still less widely distributed.[20] Agricola's

De Inventione Dialectica demanded the unification of the three arts of language:

> All language has as its object that someone should make someone else share in his thoughts. Therefore, it is apparent that there should be three things in every speech: the speaker, the hearer and the subject matter. Consequently, three points should be observed when speaking: that what the speaker intends should be understood; that the person addressed should listen avidly; and that what is said should be plausible and should be believed. Grammar, which deals with the method of speaking correctly and clearly, teaches us how to achieve the first goal. The second is taught by rhetoric, which provides us with linguistic embellishment and elegance of language, along with all the baits for capturing ears. Dialectic will lay claim to what remains, that is, to speak convincingly on whatever matter is included in a speech.[21]

Nauta has rightly observed that 'Agricola may be said to have completed what Valla initiated: the writing of a dialectical manual based on real language'.[22] For Agricola, dialectic played the role of organizing material prior to making a judgement concerning the subject matter. As such, it is the crucial stage in the linguistic process between the grammar of the words and the final expression of argument in rhetoric.[23] However, Agricola differed from Valla in several ways:

> His aim is not to demolish the Aristotelian metaphysical edifice – he seems, for instance, to accept the basic structure of the categories – nor does he seem to endorse Valla's ideal orator. Far from downplaying (as Valla did) the role of dialectic as an easy and almost puerile activity, defined as a mere part of invention and hence of rhetoric, Agricola makes dialectic the core of the linguistic arts, allotting to rhetoric the modest task of decoration and to grammar the care of correct usage.[24]

Agricola's treatise on dialectical invention was new, in that he created a synthesis of dialectic and rhetoric, taking traditional methods of practising dialectic and adding parts of rhetorical theory to them, such as status and how to handle one's emotions.[25] He considered dialectic to be fundamentally about teaching, 'speaking convincingly (*probabiliter*) on all subjects', based on Aristotle, Cicero, Quintilian and Boethius, but also 'moving beyond these authorities'.[26]

As such, Agricola surpassed Lorenzo Valla's *Repastinatio Dialecticae et Philosophie* (*Reworking of Dialectic and Philosophy*) of the 1430s. Valla's attack on Aristotelian metaphysics prioritized rhetoric as the most important of the three arts of language, describing dialectic as 'simple, quick to learn and useful to everyone'.[27] Whilst Valla relied heavily on Quintilian's *Institutio Oratoria* for his evidence, Agricola created a 'new and extensive' treatment of the subject.[28] In the second book of *De Inventione* Agricola taught that any question must be carefully analysed in order to identify its actual nature, what other questions are raised by implication, and, only then, what the answer may be.[29] In this process, there are two types of discourse: first, the exposition of the problem; and second, the argument which resolves the problem.[30] Using examples from Virgil and Cicero, Agricola examined different ways of making the persuasive argument.

In the third book of the treatise, Agricola investigated emotional persuasion in greater depth than had hitherto been achieved in manuals on rhetoric. For this task, he used Cicero's *De Oratore* (On Rhetoric) and, instead of accepting the traditional four-part structure for oratory, Agricola expanded the old model to include many new configurations: a writer must determine the organization of a work in the light of his subject and objectives, as well as the reaction of his listeners.[31] In addition to using literary examples, Agricola expounded a new dialectical method of reading and oratory that helped to tease out the argumentative structure of the work, as demonstrated in his commentary on Cicero's oration *Pro Lege Manilia*.[32]

The originality of Agricola's *De Inventione Dialectica* and its usefulness to humanist students made it immensely popular, with no fewer than forty-four reprints in the sixteenth century and thirty-two additional editions of epitomes. Some of his ideas permeated the later textbooks of Erasmus and Melanchthon, for instance in Erasmus's *De Copia* and Melanchthon's *De Rhetorica Libri Tres* (*Three Books on Rhetoric*, 1519), his *Compendiaria Dialectices Ratio* (*A Short Course in Dialectic*, 1520) and his *Institutiones Rhetoricae* (*Rhetorical Instruction*, 1521).[33]

Agricola's *De Inventione Dialectica* was especially popular in England. Thomas Elyot's (1490–1546) pedagogical treatise and handbook *The Boke Named the Gouernour* (1531), which offered advice and an education programme for young scholars to follow, recommended Agricola's work as part of the curriculum. The intention of Elyot's work was 'the lernynge and studie wherby noble men may attayne to be worthy to have authorite in a publicke weale'.[34] Amongst his other recommendations for his young students, which included Homer, Virgil and Ovid, Elyot noted that by the time a man reaches fourteen, he should begin to study logic from Cicero's *Topica* (Topics) and Agricola's *De*

Inventione Dialectica which, he says, 'prepareth inuention, tellynge the places from whens an argument for the profe of any mater may be taken with little studie'.[35]

Apart from the educational influence of his *De Inventione Dialectica* in the realm of logic, rhetorical studies and dialectic, Agricola's influence was enhanced by the admiration Erasmus had for him, as reflected in his *Adagia*. For Erasmus, Agricola was a father and a teacher in the art of humanism, although they probably never met. Alexander Hegius, one of Erasmus's teachers in Deventer, was a pupil of Agricola. Hegius wrote: 'It is from my teacher, Agricola, that I have learned all that I know, or that people think I know.'

Agricola: Dates and Events

1444: born at Baflo, near Groningen.

1450s: educated first by the celebrated school of St. Maarten in Groningen.

1458: B.A. from the University of Erfurt.

1465: M.A. from Louvain.

1460s: travels to Italy, where he associated with humanist masters and statesmen.

1468(?)–1475: studies civil law at the University of Pavia.

1470: teaches a deaf child how to communicate orally and in writing inspiring his great work *De Inventione Dialectica*.

1475–77: studies at Ferrara and became the protégé of Prince d'Este and pupil of Giovanni Battista Guarini.

1473–4: composes *Vita Petrarchae*. 1475–7?: employed as the organist to the ducal chapel.

c. 1477: returns to the North. Secretary to the city of Groningen.

1479: in Dilligen, Germany. Completes *De Inventione Dialectica (On Dialectical Invention)*.

1481: spends six months in Brussels at the court of Archduke Maximilian (later Maximilian I, the Holy Roman Emperor).

1482: Agricola accepts the invitation of John of Dahlberg, the Bishop of Worms, to lecture at the University of Heidelberg. Begins to study Hebrew.

7 June 1484: writes *De Formando Studiis*, letter/treatise to Jacob Barbireau.

1485: Agricola dies on his journey back from Rome.

Agricola's Key Works

1479: *De Inventione Dialectica (On Dialectical Invention)*: this is the work for which Agricola is particularly known after its first posthumous edition of 1515. The significance of *De Inventione Dialectica* for the history of argumentation is that it assimilated the art of dialectic to that of rhetoric. Argumentation focused not on truth but on what might be said with reason. Accordingly, Agricola focused on the *Topics* rather than the *Analytics* of Aristotle and Cicero but also the writings of historians, poets and orators. Thus, for Agricola, dialectic was an open field; the art of finding 'whatever can be said with any degree of probability on any subject.'

1477–1485: *Letters*: the letters of Agricola, of which fifty-one survive, offer an interesting insight into the humanist circles to which he belonged.

1483: A *Life of Petrarch*: a tribute to the man from whom Agricola took inspiration and whose ideas Agricola took to Northern Europe.

7 June 1484: *De Formando Studiis*: a letter to his friend, the musician and choirmaster Jacobus Barbireau of Antwerp, from Heidelberg. An influential pedagogical work defending humanistic studies.

December 1484: *De Nativitate Sive Immensa Natalis Diei Iesu Christi Leatitia*: demonstrates that Agricola's humanism was deeply embedded in his Christian faith. Written in his later years when he had turned to the study of theology, it is a pious work.
His minor works include some speeches, poems, translations of Greek dialogues and commentaries on works by Seneca, Boethius and Cicero.

1539: A collected edition of his works (letters, treatises, translations, poems, and discourses) appeared in two quarto volumes (Cologne, 1539), under the title *Rudolphi Agricolae Lucubrationes Aliquot Lectu Dignissimae in Hunc Usque Diem Nusquam Prius Editae, per Alardum Amstelodamum.*

6

DESIDERIUS ERASMUS (1467–1536)[1]
Prince of Humanists

E rasmus has been labelled the 'Prince of Humanists' because of his unrivalled fame and influence throughout late-medieval and Reformation Europe. He inherited four intellectual traits that characterized his life and thought: humanism, devotion, scholasticism, and biblical scholarship. He was an itinerant thinker who left his mark upon various European countries, but was often in conflict with Lutheran and Catholic theologians alike. He produced many works which influenced the European Reformations and his ideas were aided in their distribution by the timely introduction, and use of, the printing press.

Introduction

The single most influential intellect of the late-medieval and early-modern period, it is remarkable that Erasmus of Rotterdam held no long-lasting ecclesiastical, political or administrative office, possessed no great wealth and, for most of his adult life, was of no fixed abode. Superficially, one could describe him as a freelance itinerant writer who relied upon the hospitality and generosity of others to subsidize his projects, not unlike many other humanist authors, who depended upon patrons. Another point of view would suggest that he was so admired for his prolific literary output, correspondence, and his contribution to theological, philosophical and political debate that the Catholic Church, monarchs and wealthy individuals were only too happy to patronize his important works. Erasmus, therefore, is a figure who, even at first glance, reveals a significant truth about late-medieval Europe: that it was an environment in which a great thinker, regardless of his personal circumstances, could travel and flourish to the extent of making a lasting contribution to large-scale institutional reform.[2]

However, Erasmus was not without his enemies, provoking attack from Catholic traditionalists in both Louvain and Paris, as well as a significant dispute with Luther in the 1520s. During his career, both Lutherans and Catholics criticized him: he was encouraged to write against Luther by no fewer than three Popes. Although he remained a Catholic to the end of his life, he ultimately found no comfortable theological place to sit, caught as he was by his inspirational humanist reform ideals, between Luther and the established Church.

His best-known works are his satirical *Praise of Folly*, his critical edition of the New Testament (*Novum Testamentum*), his *Colloquies*, and the *Enchiridion Militis Christiani* (*Handbook of the Christian Soldier*). In his work, he emphasized the importance of the inner life, rather than outward ceremony, and the critical use of language in comprehending both God and human existence.

Early Life and Education

Erasmus was, perhaps, always destined to be an outsider. Given his later fame, his beginnings were extraordinary, for he was illegitimate. Not only that but he was born to parents who inhabited two of the most respected professions: his father, Gerard of Gouda, became a priest and his mother, Margaretha Rogers, was the daughter of a physician. Whether or not his illegitimacy was publicly acknowledged, and despite his unorthodox start, he was nevertheless given the privilege of a noble education. He began his schooling, along with his brother, in the town of his birth, Gouda, and subsequently found himself at Deventer in 1477, from the age of nine. His mother died when he was thirteen and his father shortly afterwards. Thus, there is something of the orphan about Erasmus's early life.

There is a myth that Erasmus first learned his humanism at Deventer with the Brethren of the Common Life, a non-monastic community with no binding vows, but who emphasized simplicity of life and mind, rather than the complexity and relative impenetrability of university scholasticism. However, R.R. Post was correct in his rejection of that fantasy. In fact the Brethren were not a major factor in the rise of humanism or in the educational shaping of Erasmus. They did not control the school at Deventer, though a few of them were employed for wages as teachers there. Erasmus's accomplishments can hardly be attributed to anything the Brethren could offer.[3]

In later life he rather cruelly disparaged his time with the Brethren, claiming that his education there was too scholastic in its Latin methods and not humanist enough in its outlook. Likewise, at his subsequent residence in 's-Hertogenbosch (1485–7), Erasmus was disparaging of the brothers: 'one of the teachers...was the most stupid and self-satisfied man Erasmus had ever met'.[4] Indeed, 'Erasmus had completed, or nearly completed, in Deventer all the classes which the school in 's-Hertogenbosch had to offer'.[5] Although many of Erasmus's personal memories should be taken with a pinch of salt, in this case his criticisms were made with the benefit of hindsight and at a time when humanism had taken hold in Europe, and not with dispassionate objectivity.[6] However, it also seems that Erasmus was ahead of his teachers in his early schooling. In Deventer, at least, Erasmus was able to develop his humanist education, not only in the form of the writings of classical literature, but by virtue of the influence of Agricola on the curriculum taught at Deventer, who was a friend of the School's headmaster, or Rector, Hegius.[7]

Transferring to a genuine monastic company, Erasmus moved, in 1487, to Steyn, to live and study with the Augustinian canons who shared his love of writing, rhetoric and classical literature. In Steyn, Erasmus acquired 'a knowledge of the Greek language which was outstanding for his lifetime' and here he 'felt free to make his own choice between the exegesis of the Greek and Latin fathers', having a preference for Origin and Jerome.[8] Some of his Latin epistles testify that Erasmus devoured Valla's writings, particularly his *Elegantiae* (work on Latin grammar). Erasmus admired Valla's linguistic facility, critical intellect and the philological technique he brought to bear on texts. At Steyn Erasmus took permanently binding vows as a canon and, in 1491, was officially and legally dispensed from his obligation to reside there, first by the bishop and then by papal bulls. Thus, he left the monastery to become secretary to the Bishop of Cambrai on a visit to Italy, although he always remained in theory a canon of the Augustinian community at Steyn, detached on special leave for education and study. The journey to Italy was never made, but the bishop ordained Erasmus as a priest in 1492 and the humanist remained in the service of the bishop, who, in 1496, sent him to Paris to complete his studies. The specific purpose of this trip to Paris was to earn a doctorate in theology and, with a little luck and 'networking' skill, Erasmus worked hard to improve his own abilities and found pastures new at the University of Paris, with the blessing of the Augustinians and the financial patronage of the Bishop.

Erasmus's early university education was critical to his entire working life. For it was in Paris that the humanist nature of his self-taught education came into conflict with the scholasticism he found at the university. So the pattern of intellectual confrontation and conflict began, for Erasmus took an instant dislike, even hatred, of the schoolmen's ideas. Nevertheless, Paris afforded Erasmus the opportunity to expand his list of contacts. His nurture of patrons in order to fund his work was to be a lifelong pursuit, and a necessary one if he were to finance his studies and travel – and travel he did. Without completing his doctorate, he took himself to England in 1499, where he was to meet, amongst others, the humanist and cleric John Colet. Erasmus heard Colet's lectures on St. Paul's epistles in Oxford and received the austere hospitality of the future Dean of St. Paul's Cathedral. Although Colet's biblical exegesis was, in some ways, new, he never learned Greek and was hostile to pagan authors throughout his life. Erasmus, on the other hand, would take biblical scholarship into a whole new realm with his emphasis upon and critical study of New Testament Greek. However, before examining his skill as a biblical translator, interpreter and commentator, it is necessary to investigate how Christian humanism became the essential component and driving force behind his work.

The Christian Humanist

The *studia humanitatis* provided Erasmus with a way of approaching the ultimate text, the Bible, with a critical philological technique. It is hardly surprising that Erasmus's attitude to the scriptures should have been heavily influenced by humanism, given his education and friendship with Colet and Thomas More. However, it was nevertheless a departure from scholastic thought. For Erasmus, Christian humanism meant being able to delight in the skill and eloquence of classical pagan authors, as well as using their tools to interpret the Bible, without being seduced by their pagan beliefs. Many other theologians were to acknowledge the usefulness of the classical world, particularly when so many European clergy and nobility travelled to Italy in the late-fifteenth century. However, none was to put their humanist studies to such powerful and influential use as Erasmus. His intention was to bring about a transformation of human existence through language. From his time at Paris, he had found the scholastic Latin to be clumsy and misleading at best. For Erasmus, authors from ancient Greece and Rome had the power to unlock the caged mind and provide a language that could best express both the goodness and truth of the Christian message.

It is understandable that many scholars had discarded classical pagan writing as pre-Christian and therefore superseded by the superior message of the gospel. But Erasmus argued that clarity of expression was essential to the reception of the message and since the language of the day, Latin, was inherited from the classical world, then that was the world from which to gain mastery of the tongue. Not only this, but it was Erasmus's contention that the pre-Christian pagan world of letters existed primarily as a preparation for Christ's coming, in order that the Christian message might be transmitted in the most eloquent Latin and Greek possible to transform people's hearts and minds. As such, in the Christian tradition, Erasmus preferred the eloquence of Jerome to the theology of Augustine.[9]

The largely self-motivated study of classical literature that Erasmus had conducted in his youth was to shape his attitude towards biblical study for the rest of his life. Although his personal circumstances were frequently to change during adulthood, his opinions were steadfast: classical study and biblical scholarship were omnipresent and symbiotic features of his thought. He believed that it was dangerous to approach the scriptures without first developing a competence in the language in which it was to be read. Thus, Erasmus tended to encourage an allegorical interpretation of scripture, admonishing the scholastics for their literal interpretations.[10] Reading the Bible, for Erasmus, unlocked the mysteries of the divine for humanity, so that body, mind and spirit could be transformed by the love of Christ. In fact, so important is the encounter with Christ through the written word that it is superior to the experience of those who encountered Jesus in his physical manifestation on earth. The power of Christ, once revealed by the philological techniques of Christian Humanism, is the Word.

In repudiating scholastic philosophy as taught in the universities, Erasmus developed an alternative view, namely his *philosophia Christi*. This concept swept away all other complicated theories, stating that the only real philosophy is the philosophy of Christ. It is a strongly Christocentric idea, which emphasizes the inner life. Thus, 'in this kind of philosophy, located as it is more truly in the disposition of the mind than in syllogisms, life means more than debate, inspiration is preferable to erudition, and transformation is a more important matter than intellectual comprehension'.[11] In this sense it is important that the transformation is more than just a moral goodness; it is more of a spiritual renewal. Although Erasmus was fundamentally positive about humanity's capacity to rise beyond the physical and reach a spiritually divine existence, he never, like the Platonists, thought that humanity could rise to a spiritual peak without the aid of divine grace, freely granted.

In terms of his Christology, Erasmus was extremely incarnational. In the *Disputantiuncula* of 1499, the dispute with John Colet over Christ's agony in the garden of Gethsemane before his trial, Colet argued that Jesus was not feeling real human fear, but was merely reticent about allowing the Jews to commit the ultimate crime; Erasmus had no such problem with Jesus' humanity. The passage in Matthew 14:36 clearly expressed, for Erasmus, the natural and understandable terror of a man who was about to be tortured and crucified. Christ as a human being, Erasmus argued, shows us a humility that stands against worldly values of pride.[12]

The Author and Biblical Scholar

Erasmus' major works were written between 1500 and 1518. In 1500 he wrote the first edition of his *Adages,* which were a series of short classical sayings. This first attempt comprised over 800 entries, but by the 1508 version, Erasmus had compiled over 3000 texts. In this early period he also showed his reverence for classical literature by translating Euripides's *Hecuba* and *Iphigenia in Aulis* in addition to translations of Galen, Ptolemy and Aristotle. He considered Plato to be an honorary Christian, although his enthusiasm for Neoplatonism did not last long and left little trace in his mature religious thought.[13] He was a shrewd enough judge of texts to know that most of the Hermetic and Neoplatonic texts were either forgeries or at least later writings contaminated by non-Christian sources. However, he never, it seems, found time or inclination to develop a systematic refutation of these pseudo-Christian sources. His early trips to London were seminal for him, as well as for those whom he met. In 1501 he stayed with Thomas More, who was later to be influential in Erasmus's *Colloquies* and *The Praise of Folly.*

In 1503 Erasmus's *Enchiridion* was published. It asserted that classical antiquity could stimulate understanding of the Bible. Humanity, suggested Erasmus, was of a dual nature, consisting of the body and the soul, but there was another crucial component of existence, and particularly Christian existence, which was the spirit. Much of this theology was derived from Origen, with whom Erasmus was passionately obsessed. In the *Enchiridion*, Erasmus explained that the soul exists between the body and spirit. This is an essential image for our understanding of Erasmus's view of human free will, which was to lead to so much trouble with Luther in 1524-5. The body and spirit are fixed, but the soul can move either towards the spiritual (divine) or towards the body (beastly). It is the sensitive and impressionable soul that makes us truly human and which represents our ability to contribute, in however small a way, to our life with Christ. Not every action is predestined, but we have free will to choose between the earthly and heavenly life. It was paramount to Erasmus, therefore, to feed the soul with the truth of the scriptures and the gospels.

In terms of output, Erasmus's Italian travels between 1506 and 1509 were relatively fruitless. However, on his return to England in 1509, the year of Henry VIII's accession to the throne, Erasmus revisited his friend Thomas More, only to be struck down with kidney pains. As he recuperated in More's house, Erasmus drafted *Praise of Folly* or *Moriae Encomium* in a week. The satirical work is a half-comic, half-serious, stab at the establishment of Church and State. It contains ridicule and anti-clericalism; it attacks the cult of saints, pilgrimage, Marian devotion and sermons:

> [Praise of Folly] is one of the most amazing books of its time. It deals in great detail with the whole scale of critical attitudes that the humanists developed toward the state, the Church, the universities – in fact, toward every value and taboo that had been revered in the past...In its relegation of all moral, political and religious decisions to the discretion of the individual's free human will, it was a challenging document of the desire for change at the height of German humanism.[14]

Lawyers, philosophers, theologians, monks and priests all came in for criticism from Erasmus's pen. For example, on preachers, saints and congregations, Erasmus wrote:

> ...if the preacher starts to rant (pardon me, *orate*) on some old wives' tale as they often do, his audience sits up and takes notice, open-mouthed. Again, if there's some legendary saint somewhat celebrated in fable (you can put George or Christopher or Barbara in that category if you need an example) you'll see that he receives far more devout attention than Peter or Paul or even Christ himself.[15]

Likewise, in laughing at the exploits of humanity, Erasmus also includes the grammarians:

> This class of men would be more calamitous, miserable, and more detestable to the gods than any other if I had not mitigated the suffering of that most wretched profession with a

certain pleasant sort of madness. For they are subject, not
only to the five curses, as the Greek epigram has it, but to six
hundred.[16]

Of Erasmus's other major works his *Education of a Christian Prince*
and *The Complaint of Peace* were published in 1516 and 1517
respectively. However, it was in the realm of biblical scholarship that
Erasmus's written work was to have its most significant and enduring
effect.

Scripture was paramount for Erasmus in how he viewed the world
and how one ought to be educated in it. In his *Enchiridion* Erasmus
had emphasized the importance of sole reliance upon the scriptures:
'Be convinced that there is not a single item contained in Holy Writ that
does not pertain to your salvation.':[17]

> The way to virtue, Erasmus says in his *Enchiridion Militis
> Christiani* of 1504, depends on two things: first, to 'know
> yourself'; secondly, to act 'not according to the passions, but
> the dictates of reason'. Nothing is harder, Erasmus agrees, but
> then 'no reward is greater'. For it was with a view to higher
> pleasures ahead that actual hardships should be surmounted.
> As Plato has written 'whatever is excellent is also hard'.[18]

His most significant contribution to biblical scholarship was the
publication of his own edition of the New Testament. It comprises
of the Greek text, a Latin translation and annotations. It paved the
way for modern biblical exegesis by means of providing, from the
earliest manuscripts available to him, the original text in its original
language, his own translation and occasional comment. The result
was that any reader could, from this single book, examine the source
material from which the Bible was constructed and agree, or disagree,
with Erasmus's translation and interpretation. Thus, Erasmus provided an alternative to the Vulgate (St. Jerome's universally used Latin
translation), which, Erasmus believed, contained mistranslations due
to scribal errors.[19]

The book underwent five editions in his lifetime: 1516, 1519,
1522, 1529 and 1535. The forerunner of the work was, of course,
Lorenzo Valla's *Collatio Novi Testamenti*. After all, Erasmus was the
first to discover, publish and appreciate Valla's *Annotationes in Novum
Testamentum*. The first edition of Erasmus's work in 1516 was called
Novum Instrumentum and was dedicated to Pope Leo X. Subsequent
editions were entitled the *Novum Testamentum*. There followed a
German edition in 1523, a Czech one in 1533 and an English edition in

1538. It was Erasmus's great desire that the scriptures should be available to all in their purest and most accessible form. In the *Paraclesis*, or introduction, Erasmus wrote:

> I would that even the lowliest women read the Gospels and the Pauline Epistles. And I would that they were translated into all languages, so that they could be read and understood not only by Scots and Irish but also by Turks and Saracens.[20]

Thus, even though Tyndale had already translated the Bible into English, Erasmus was instrumental in encouraging new translations of the Bible into all conceivable languages, so that ordinary people could gain access to the life-giving scriptures.

With regard to his other works, by 1518 Erasmus had published, in nine volumes, the works of Jerome, to whom he felt especially drawn. His edition of Hilary of Poitiers appeared in 1523; in 1526 that of Irenaeus; in 1527, Ambrose; in 1528, St. Augustine; in 1529 the edition of Epiphanius; in 1530, Chrysostom; his edition of Origen was left unfinished. In the same period he issued the theological and pedagogical treatises: *Ecclesiastes sive Concionator Evangelicus* (1535), on preaching; *Modus Confitendi* (1525), a guide to confession; *Modus Orandi Deum; Vidua Christiana; De Civilitate Morum Puerilium; De Præparatione ad Mortem* and many other guides.

Besides Erasmus's undoubted influence as a published author, accelerated by the development of the printing press and the dissemination of his works throughout Europe, it must never be forgotten that Erasmus's correspondence was a major contributory factor in the pre-Reformation debates. As we shall now see, in examining his relationship with Luther and other theologians, princes and prelates, letters were the means by which reform ideas were transported. They also provide a means by which we can learn of humanism and pre-Reformation thought today.

The Reformer

The story of Erasmus's involvement with reformation ideas and proponents of change can be seen in the series of events that led up to his great debate with Luther (1483-1546) in 1524-5, in the consequences of that conflict, and in its subsequent influence upon the Radical Reformers of the sixteenth century. The best evidence available to us is in the form of Erasmus's correspondence. I shall begin by examining how Erasmus's ideas first came under attack.

In a letter of 4 September 1524 to John Fisher (1469-1535), Bishop of Rochester, Erasmus complained that he was under siege, facing a:

> Threefold struggle – with those pagans of Rome, who wretch-edly envy me; with certain theologians and monks who leave no stone unturned to ruin me; with certain rabid Lutherans, who rage at me as alone, so they say, delaying their triumph.[21]

However, as early as December 1516, there was evidence that Erasmus's views on human free will were not acceptable to Luther. George Spalatin (1484–1545), secretary to Luther's protector Duke Frederick, wrote to Erasmus warning that an 'Augustinian Priest' (Luther) had reservations about Erasmus's interpretation of St. Paul, especially regarding 'justification by works'.[22] The debate concerning whether one gains salvation by works or faith had been played out many centuries before in the Pelagian controversy, in which the theo-logian Pelagius suggested that human beings could contribute to their own salvation in some way by their own behaviour and by deserving the merit of divine grace and salvation. His argument was condemned as heresy by Augustine, who claimed that humanity could in no way merit divine grace but that it must be the free gift of God bestowed on those predestined to receive it.

By March 1517, Luther was becoming increasingly concerned that Erasmus was espousing a Pelagian view (the heresy that Christ was not fully divine), writing that 'human things weigh more with him than the divine.'[23] By August of 1521 Erasmus complained that 'Luther's party sometimes attack me in their public lectures and call me a Pelagian'.[24]

So much for Luther's concerns about Erasmus's orthodoxy, but in the years leading up to 1524, Erasmus had his own worries about being too closely connected with Lutheran ideas, partly because he was uneasy with Luther's doctrinal certainty, and partly because he found Luther's forceful manner a distasteful way of discussing theology. In a letter dated 30 May 1519, Erasmus wrote to Luther:

> No words of mine could describe the storm raised here by your books, [including] the most groundless suspicions that your work is written with assistance from me [as] a standard-bearer of this new movement.[25]

Erasmus's answer to Luther's hot-headed approach was to advise mod-eration. In 1520 Erasmus wrote to Spalatin that Luther needed treat-ment for his radical approach: 'it must at least be more civilized to cure him than to snuff him out'.[26] Nevertheless, in November 1520, Erasmus defended Luther in his *Axiomata* written for Duke Frederick, calling once again for moderate debate. This plea was in vain, given that, in the previous month, Luther had published his inflammatory *De Captivitate Babylonia* (*On the Babylonian Captivity of the Church*), which condemned the Roman Church and the papacy.[27]

During this period Erasmus became the subject of open criticism by Lutheran supporters. His friend and supporter at this point, Wolfgang Capito (1478–1541), urged Erasmus in April 1519 to ignore the Louvain theologians and support Luther, for it is 'better to make enemies of all the theologians than of his supporters, who include several princes and leading churchmen in Germany, where Erasmus is still revered'.[28]

Erasmus became dismayed as humanists began to join the Lutheran camp. In a letter to Justus Jonas of 1521, containing his biographical sketch of John Colet, he deplores defection and admires the conservative humanism of men like the Dean of St. Paul's.[29] But Capito had little comfort to offer in October of that year when he wrote to Erasmus that the Lutherans 'are now crazier and more insolent and more self-assertive in everything... such is their contempt for all brains except their own'.[30]

It is clear that in the following two years the main site of conflict remained the doctrine of human free will. Not only did Erasmus complain to Pirckheimer that the Lutherans 'tear me to pieces as a Pelagian because they think I give more weight than they do to free will', but also that he considered the problems of free will and predestination to be insoluble, therefore, 'I would rather teach the doctrines that encourage us to try for the best in every way we can'.[31]

Erasmus's view of humanity was founded upon a fundamental (epistemological, rather than religious or philosophical) pessimism seemingly common to many Christian humanists (not least Pico and Agricola): that debates over doctrines such as free will were insoluble (all uncertain). Therefore responsible and learned (not to mention influential) men had a responsibility not to attach more importance to them than they could bear. These elements of scepticism, in contrast to the 'enthusiasm' that lay behind the doctrinal dogmatism of Luther and his followers, demanded that doctrines ought to be measured by their tendency to encourage order and virtue in practice, rather than their supposed truth in philosophical-religious terms.

Erasmus's stance created a doctrinal and personal conflict that would reverberate through Europe for centuries. In September 1524, Erasmus wrote *De Libero Arbitrio* (*On the Free Will*), intending for it to excite great uproar. He sent despatches of it to his friends including Aleander, Duke George, Warham and Tunstall. In the opening *Diatribe* on the free will he attacks Luther's Wycliffite and simplistic

understanding of human and Godly nature, writing that even if there
is some truth

> in the doctrine which Wycliffe taught and Luther asserted,
> that whatever is done by us is done not by free choice but by
> sheer necessity, what a window to impiety would the public
> avowal of such an opinion open.[32]

In other words, if every action of ours is not only constricted by predestination but also useless as a means of moving towards God or salvation,
then we might as well sin as much as we like all the time. Erasmus claimed
that our actions are free and do contribute towards our spiritual well-
being: 'by free choice...we mean a power of the human will by which a
man can apply himself to the things which lead to salvation, or turn away
from them.' For otherwise, 'what does the parable of the labourers in the
vineyard mean? What kind of labourers are they who do nothing?'.[33]

Luther's first reaction to Erasmus's treatise was irritation: 'it is irk-
some for me to have to reply to such an educated man about such an
uneducated book'.[34] However his considered reply was a treatise four
times as long as Erasmus's original. *De Servo Arbitrio* (*On the Bound
Will*) was published in December 1525 and was less of a contribution
to the debate than a dogmatic assertion of truth. For Luther, the idea of
achieving the merit of grace and salvation through free action was blas-
phemy.[35] As for Erasmus's argument that Luther's doctrine opens a win-
dow to impiety: 'let it be so; such people belong to the...leprosy of evil'.[36]

Scholars disagree as to who was misinterpreting whom. It has been
noted that Luther oversimplified Erasmus's subtle and moderate arguments, whilst some have argued that Erasmus's outlook may well have
contained aspects of Pelagian thought.[37]

Although Erasmus received a positive response to his *De Libero
Arbitrio* from people such as Henry VIII and Melanchthon, there was
still an element of misunderstanding (intentional or otherwise) in the
debate, prompting Erasmus to declare that 'I laid a poultry egg, Luther
hatched a very different bird'.[38]

Through 1525 and 1526 the exchanges became more personal and
angry. By February 1526 Erasmus had written part I of *Hyperaspistes*
(*The Protective Shield*): *Diatribe Adversus Servum Abirtrium Martini
Lutheri*, which was published in June of that year. The second part
came in September 1527. Through these works two important points
are emphasized that continued to distinguish Erasmus from Luther.
First:

> God is supremely just and good. If he is just, he does not pun-
> ish for eternity those who sin, not through their guilt but from

inevitable necessity, nor ordains punishment by reason of the wickedness, which he himself operates in man.

And second: 'I have never been an apostate from the Catholic Church'.[39] Erasmus's refusal to adhere to the doctrine of predestination or the bondage of the will, combined with his continued loyalty to the papacy and the Roman Church, drove a wedge between himself and Luther and marked an end to all cordial relations between the two of them, to the point where Luther spat this venom: 'I consider Erasmus to be the greatest enemy Christ has had these thousand years past'.[40] In return Erasmus was dismayed, in March 1529, with the rise of 'paganism' and the end it had brought to sacramental theology and worship as well as monastic orders in many cities that had adopted Lutheran values.[41] Erasmus fled Basel when it became infected with Luther's doctrine, making his way to the appropriately named Freiburg for his final years.

How then was Erasmus a reformer? It is surely difficult to argue that he was an institutional reformer at all: he did not contribute to any of Luther's reforms, and instead sought to argue for continued Christian unity within the institutional parameters of the Roman Church. Although he was not of Thomas More's persuasion that the only route to salvation was through the sacraments, nor was he persuaded by justification by faith alone or predestination. He found the extremes in turn mechanical and irrational, the former requiring merely the consumption of bread and wine, and the latter imposing a 'doctrinal strait-jacket' on believers.[42] All this made Erasmus unpopular with those who held to the two doctrinal extremes. During his lifetime, Catholic conservatives attempted to push Erasmus out of the Church and, after his death, they soon destroyed his reputation amongst most Catholics.

However, Erasmus was always concerned with the reform of the individual through a knowledge of the scriptures and an understanding the gospel in their own language. Although his fight with Luther produced disappointing results for both Protestants and Catholics, it was his biblical scholarship and Christocentricity that would be taken up and used by the reformers of the sixteenth century. With humanism, biblical criticism and translation, and his emphasis upon the transformation of the human soul, Erasmus provided the tools for a transformed Europe.

The Legacy

The first key point to remember in any summary of Erasmus's achievements is that his literary output – and the dissemination of those works – was enormous. Thanks to his prolific writing and the timely expansion of the printing press, Erasmus's works were read in the Low Countries, France, the Rhineland, South Germany and England among others. Although Erasmus never sought a strong political or religious base from which to wield power, he provided the tools with which the Reformation could take place. However, as Dickens and Jones rightly suggest, Erasmus's aims were rather more concerned with the individual's engagement with the scriptures, using humanistic techniques to reach God:

> [Erasmus] sought to rediscover the Christ of the Gospels, to clarify and then expound the written record of Christ's message. This done, by means of a vigorous and scholarly approach to the scriptures themselves, he was then prepared to evaluate Church and Society not only in terms of doctrinal, ritual and organizational issues, but also in those of individual Christian conduct.[43]

Erasmus's way was a *via media* between the brashness of the Protestant reformers and the inflexibility of the Catholic Church. For him the essential message of the gospel was that, through Christ, human beings could be saved and that their souls could move away from the earthly sinful world towards the spiritual and Godly heavens. In this sense our way of living is to nurture, through knowledge and the practice of Holy Scripture (understood in our own language), the innate aspects of our humanity that are pleasing to God. Thus, in Erasmus's *Philosophia Christi*, there is room for some contribution, however small, by humans to please God by doing his will and to earn some merit of grace towards our own salvation.

In his own time he saw no reason to abandon his own Catholic Church: 'I bear with this Church, until I shall see a better, and it cannot help bearing with me, until I shall myself be better. And he does not sail badly who steers between two evils'.[44] However, it is doubtful that the Catholic Church was much moved by Erasmus's efforts in terms of ecclesiastical reform. By the 1560s the last of Erasmus's contemporaries had passed away and the last session of the Council of Trent in 1562–3 abandoned, in effect, any Erasmian ideals.

Today, perhaps, we could learn from Erasmus's use of intellect, good literature, education, high ideals, and desire to move the soul from bad to good; to live a godly life without extremism or the need for condemnation. Perhaps Erasmus could guide today's Church, by his middle way, through the stormy waters of conflicting doctrinal matters. In today's Europe, perhaps Erasmus would have been pleased with his own achievement in the realm of biblical translation and exegesis. What would he think of a world where the Bible is read and understood in every language and the impact that that has had on the world for good and evil?

Erasmus's ultimate influence was on the personal, spiritual life of the religious man or woman: his interest in the individual's journey with God and the soul's journey between body and spirit. He was interested in personal relationships, not just for the sake of securing patronage, but for encouraging debate, scholarship and judging all ideas by the humanist standards of classical eloquence, literature and scriptural wisdom. His personal contacts throughout Europe, as well as his correspondence and his publications, ensured his fame. From Henry VIII, Colet, More, Luther, Melanchthon, Bucer, Zwingli and Reuchlin, to Lefèvre and many others, his ideas were wrestled with during his lifetime. But it was the Protestant Reformers of the sixteenth century that would be most attracted to his biblical techniques and Christocentricity and build upon them a reform program beyond the scope of Erasmus's boundaries.

Erasmus: Dates and Events

1467: born in Gouda, The Low Countries.
1467–1487: educated at Gouda, Deventer and 's-Hertogenbosch.
1487: joins the Augustinian order at Steyn.
1487–1494: self-education in classical literature, reads the Italian Humanist Lorenzo Valla's *Elegantiae*.
1488: takes his vows. Starts writing *Antibarbarorum Liber.*
1492: ordained priest.
1493: Secretary to the Bishop of Cambrai.
1495: given legal dispensation to study theology at the University of Paris under the patronage of the Bishop of Cambrai.
1495–1499: Doctoral Studies (not completed, but later given a doctorate from the University of Turin in 1506).
1497: tutor to William Blount, Baron of Mountjoy.
1497–8: *Encomium Matrimonii* written.
1499: travels to England for eight months. Meets John Colet and hears his Oxford lectures on St. Paul's Epistles.
1499: dispute (*Disputianticula*) with Colet over Christ's agony in the garden.
1500: *Adagia* first published. Writes *Enchiridion Militis Christiani*. Begins critical edition of Jerome.
1501: leaves Paris for St. Omer.

1502: moves to Louvain.

1503: *Enchiridion* published.

1504: returns to Paris. Travels widely and begins the *Enchiridon* in The Netherlands.

1505: second visit to England until June 1506.

1506: travels to Italy for three years. Awarded doctorate from Turin University.

1507–9: Bologna, Venice, Padua and Rome.

1508: revised edition of *Adagia* published.

1509: returns to England for Coronation of Henry VIII. Starts writing *Praise of Folly.*

1509–1515: develops his program for religious reform: *philosophia Christi.*

1511: April to August out of England. *In Praise of Folly* published.

1512: Professor of Theology at Cambridge for two-and-a-half years.

1514: leaves Cambridge for London and then the Rhineland.

1515: Basel, then returns to England in the Spring.

1516: another visit to England. *Novum Instrumentum, Paraclesis, Apologia* and *Methodus* published, and an edition of Jerome.

1517: papal dispensation, England, then Antwerp, Anderlicht and Louvain.

1518: stays in Louvain until November 1521. First edition of *Colloquies* published. *Encomium Matrimonii* published.

1519: second edition of his New Testament. The *Methodus* re-named *Ratio Verae Theologiae.*

1520: debate with Luther begins with letter to Frans van Cranvelt. Attended Coronation of Charles V. *Antibarbari* first published.

1521: leaves Louvain to live in Basel until 1529.

January 1521: Pope Leo X encourages Erasmus to write against Luther.

1522: third edition of his New Testament. *The Godly Feast* Colloquy published.

February 1524: Erasmus publicly circulating his *De Libro Arbitrio* against Luther.

April 1524: Luther writes to Erasmus to warn him not to engage him in dispute.

1527: fourth edition of his New Testament.

1529: *Epistola contra Pseudevangelicos* written.

Spring 1529: leaves Basel and settles in Freiburg. He remains there for the rest of his life.

August 1530: *Epistola ad Fratres Germaniae Inferioris* written in rebuttal of Bucer's *Epistola Apologetica* of March that year.

1535: fifth edition of his New Testament published. Moves to Basel again.

12 July 1536: dies.

Erasmus's Key Works

1488: early Draft of the *Antibarbari*: his defence of classical literature as a means of helping biblical study. It was revised and eventually published in 1520.

1497–8: *Encomium Matrimonii* written. Erasmus placed a high value on marriage. Published in 1518. Erasmus did not consider marriage to be second rate in comparison with celibacy, mainly due to the assumption that being single did not equate with celibacy. This was made clear in his colloquy called "The Girl with no Interest in Marriage".

1499: *Disputianticula*: a dispute with John Colet, the Oxford scholar who was later to become Dean of St. Paul's Cathedral. It concerned Christ's agony in the garden of Gethsemane in the hours before his arrest and crucifixion. Christ's attitude to the impending torture is interpreted by Erasmus as human fear. Colet, not wishing to allow Jesus such negative emotions, due to His divine knowledge of the outcome, explains that Christ's prayer for deliverance is merely an outward show to fulfil scriptural prophecies.

1500: *Adagia* first published in Paris – a compilation of classical texts and evidence of Erasmus's breadth of classical knowledge. There are 818 entries in the first edition, but 3,260 in the revised edition of 1508, published by the Aldine Press in Venice. In 1515, a further edition of the *Adagia* was published by the Froben Press in Basel with several commentaries included.

1503: *Enchiridion Militis Christiani* published: pagan authors can 'invigorate' the understanding of the divine scriptures. Human beings consist of a dual nature, body and soul (physical and divine). However, he also suggests an alternative: body, soul (mind) and spirit. This follows Origen, another of Erasmus's favourite Church Fathers. The soul exists between the body and spirit. Body and spirit, fixed by the soul, can move either towards the spiritual (divine) or towards the body (beastly). It is impressionable and makes us truly human. Thus, it is important to feed the soul with the right food, i.e. the language of scripture and the gospel.

1509: writes *Praise of Folly*: a satirical look at society, written on Erasmus's return to England for Henry VIII's coronation. Erasmus fell ill and, whilst recovering at Thomas More's house, wrote his satire on the Church, politics and manners.

1516: edition of the New Testament published. *Novum Testamentum* with *Paraclesis, Apologia,* and *Methodus.* The *Paraclesis* (introduction) emphasizes a Christocentric inner life that regenerates human existence. In the *Ratio Verae Theologicae,* the introduction to the 1519 edition of the *Novum Testamentum*, Erasmus writes: 'This is your first and only goal; perform this vow, this one thing: that you be changed, that you be seized, that you weep and be transformed into those teachings which you learn'. It is not enough to have an intellectual comprehension of the gospel, but it must be felt to change the inner life, rather like St. Paul's message in Romans 12.2, quoted in Colet's sermon to Convocation in 1512: 'Be ye transformed by the renewal of your mind'.

1516: Edition of Jerome published.

1522: *The Godly Feast* Colloquy published.

GERMANY

7

JOHANNES REUCHLIN (1455–1522)
The Great German Hebraist

Johannes Reuchlin, also known in the Greek form 'Capnion' (Καπνίων), a nickname given to him by his Italian friends, has rightly been placed alongside Erasmus, Ficino and Pico della Mirandola as a towering figure of the Renaissance. Although he had a long and successful career as a lawyer, he was also the foremost German Christian Hebraist and philologist of the age, advocating not only the study of Greek and Latin for biblical and humanist scholarship, which Valla and Erasmus had already pioneered, but also Hebrew. Although he disagreed with the Jews on matters of religion, he was a defender of Jewish literature and culture on the grounds of the rights of Jews under the law of the Holy Roman Empire and, most of all, he was the greatest Christian exponent of the Cabala (the esoteric Jewish mystical tradition dating from around 1200 B.C.) in history. His legacy includes the classic treatise against anti-Semitism, *Recommendation Whether to Confiscate, Destroy and Burn All Jewish Books*, written in response to the anti-Jewish treatises of Johannes Pfefferkorn (1469-1523), and his *De Arte Cabalistica* (On the Art of the Cabala). Erasmus, in his *Apotheosis of that Incomparable Worthy, John Reuchlin*, attributed to him the achievement of renewing 'to the world the gift of tongues'.[1] Reuchlin's greatest contribution to biblical scholarship was his emphasis on the importance of the Hebrew language, taking the notion further than Pico had, as well as his promotion of philology, following Valla and Erasmus, as an acceptable tool in discussing the meaning of the text. His importance for literature was his preservation of Jewish texts, even if his motivation was ultimately to convert the Jews. His enthusiasm for the Cabala helped establish Hebrew as an essential language for biblical scholars to learn, preserve Jewish literature and increase awareness of the Cabala itself.

Without Reuchlin and the spread of his publications in the German vernacular the study of Hebrew and the Christian Cabala in Europe, as well as the humanist movement itself, would have been very much impoverished.

Introduction

Although Rudolph Agricola was largely responsible for the introduction of Italian humanism into Germany, there were other means by which humanism spread throughout the Germanic states. The fifteenth-century mysticism of writers such as Johann Wesel (1420–1489), Puper von Goch (d. 1475) and Wessel Gansfort was one channel;[2] religious or monastic houses were another. The Cistercian Abbey of Advard, outside Groningen, for instance, was the centre where Alexander Hegius, Rudolph Agricola and Johann Wessel gathered with the humanist Abbot Hendrik van Rees. Moreover, the Benedictine Abbey at Sponheim in Southwest Germany, under Abbot Johannes Trithemius, was another humanist centre.[3]

Italian humanism also reached Germany through an imperial route, via the royal and ecclesiastical courts, as well as the universities of Vienna, Heidelberg, Basel, Erfurt, Wittenberg, Leipzig, Tübingen and Ingolstadt.[4] But humanism arrived in Germany earlier than other Northern European countries due to the trade and cultural ties between Italian and German cities, as well as the migration of Northern students to Italian universities to study (mainly) law.[5]

If men like Agricola were first-generation pioneers of humanism in Germany, then Johannes Reuchlin, along with Willibald Pirckheimer (1470–1530), Jacob Wimpfeling (1450–1528) and Conrad Peutinger, fall into the category of second-generation German humanists: those who had received the tools of classical learning and began to use them creatively.[6]

As a very successful lawyer, Reuchlin spent most of his adult life as Chancellor to the Duke of Württemberg. He twice visited Florence and became obsessed with Ficino's Neoplatonism and Pico della Mirandola's discovery of the Hebrew *Cabala*. Reuchlin became the central figure in a 'battle of the books', and when hostility turned instead to Luther, Reuchlin was grateful to spend his final days teaching at Ingolstadt and Tübingen. His grandnephew Philip Melanchthon would become one of the third generation of German humanists and be directly involved in Lutheran reforms.[7]

Life

Johannes was born in Pforzheim, Baden, twenty-four miles north-west of Stuttgart on 22 February 1455. Reuchlin's father worked for the local Dominican monastery, where Johann first learned Latin. Although he took a brief course at the University of Freiburg-im-Breisgau, matriculating on 19 May 1470, he returned to his home, becoming a chorister and gaining a place in the court of Charles I, Margrave of Baden. He accompanied the Emperor's third son, Frederick, to the University of Paris, where he began to learn Greek. In the summer of 1474, he followed Jean à Lapide, the French realist, to the University of Basel, where Johann gained his B.A. in 1475 and M.A. in 1478.[8] It was in Basel that he began to lecture. Already an Aristotelian, under the tutorage of Andronicus Contoblacas (1455–1522), he came into conflict with the 'sophists'. Here in Basel he composed his Latin lexicon *Vocabularis Breviloquus* (1474), but would soon return to Paris to continue his Greek studies with George Hieronymous. In considering a profession, he chose law and thus, in 1478, he went to the University of Orléans and subsequently to Poitiers, where he gained his legal qualification (licentiate) in 1481. Later that year Reuchlin was recommended to Count Eberhard of Württemberg, who was travelling to Italy and needed an interpreter. They stayed in Italy for a few months in 1482, where Reuchlin came into contact with Ficino at Florence.[9] Around this time Reuchlin apparently married, and he returned to Italy in 1490, where he met Pico della Mirandola. Reuchlin's 'interest in Pythagorean philosophy and the Jewish Cabala can safely be traced to the influence of these two illustrious Italians'.[10] Thereafter, he travelled to Linz in Germany in order to learn Hebrew, and Reuchlin's reputation, both with supporters and opposition, grew with the publication of his *De Verbo Mirifico* (*On the Wondrous Word*), a work on the Cabala, in 1494. This work defended Hebrew from the 'barbarian' scholastics. The Hebrew language, Reuchlin argued, was glorious: 'its speech is simple, pure, uncorrupted, holy, brief and consistent, the language by which God spoke to men and men with angels'.[11]

When Eberhard died in 1496, Reuchlin accepted the invitation extended by Johan von Dalberg (Agricola's employer a decade earlier), Bishop of Worms, to go to Heidelberg, where Reuchlin's work was to make translations from Greek texts, although he was by now recognized as an authority on Hebrew by many pupils. He was also employed by Philip, Count Palatine of the Rhine, who employed him to teach his sons and crucially sent Reuchlin to Rome in 1498, where he continued his Hebrew studies and came back with many Hebrew books. He was now able to return to Stuttgart and his wife. Around 1500–1502 he was appointed as a judge in the Swabian League (a post he held until 1512). In 1506 he published arguably his most enduring work, his *De Rudimentis Hebraicis* (On the rudiments of Hebrew). In 1510 Reuchlin became entangled in the attack against Jewish literature. By arguing against the suppression of Jewish books, Reuchlin became known as 'the humanist who provoked the wrath of the Cologne theologians and thus lent his name to the controversy reputed to be the classic confrontation between humanism and scholasticism'.[12]

Following this exhausting and drawn-out episode, and his resignation from the judiciary in 1512, Reuchlin retired near Stuttgart. He died ten years later in 1522.

The Humanist

Reuchlin can be seen as a successor to Pico della Mirandola, whose early death left the way open for Reuchlin to flourish as the Christian Cabalist in his native Germany. For Pico, who had taken a keen interest in the Cabala and Hebrew studies, there remained a mistrust of Jewish culture, religion and literature, which was no less present in Reuchlin's works. Nevertheless, Reuchlin surpassed Pico in explaining how the Cabala should not be despised but could instead strengthen the Christian faith. In his *Oratio*, Pico wrote:

[The Cabala contains] not so much the Mosaic as the Christian religion. There is the mystery of the Trinity, there the Incarnation of the Word, there the divinity of the Messiah; there I have read about original sin, its expiation through Christ, the heavenly Jerusalem, the fall of the devils, the orders of the angels, purgatory and the punishments of hell, the same things we read daily in Paul and Dionysius, in Jerome and Augustine.[13]

Likewise, Reuchlin's *De Arte Cabalistica* explained:

> God has given to men who walk upon the earth nothing they
> could more desire than this contemplative art...Nothing
> admits more of the search for salvation in this world and
> everlasting life in the next. It is by this means that the mind
> of man, so far as nature allows, achieves that Godlike state
> which is the 'peak' of blessedness...In that state man's life
> lacks nothing.[14]

In all of Reuchlin's reverence for Hebrew language and texts, his defence
of the Jews was always on humanitarian and educational grounds.
He never contemplated subscribing to their religion, which he found
abhorrent. Christian scholars had always rejected Jewish tradition on
the grounds that the Jews had, understandably, failed to allow any
Christological interpretation of the Old Testament. Thus, even though
the Vulgate might be acknowledged as imperfect, Hebrew study was not
perceived as a viable alternative, as the rabbis had 'falsified' the interpretation of Jewish history.[15] Even though Pope Clement V had attempted
to found, in 1311, chairs in Hebrew, Aramaic, Syriac and Greek in the
great universities of Oxford, Paris, Bologna and Salamanca, a decree
revived in 1434 in Basel, Hebrew studies made little impact among
humanists or scholastics in the fifteenth century.[16] Even those Christians
that desired private tutoring in Hebrew encountered problems finding a
sympathetic Jewish teacher.[17] Reuchlin argued that even philosophy and
scholasticism had their limitations in comparison with the Cabala:

> The mind of the Cabalist, in a state of unutterable delight,
> rejoicing in spirit, in the depths of inner silence, driving away
> from itself humdrum earthly matters, is carried away to the
> heavenly and the invisible that lie beyond all human sense.
> Then, though yet a guest of the body, he becomes a fellow
> of the angels, a sojourner in the home above the heavens: his
> frequent intercourse may be recognized as being in heaven.
> When he travels to the higher regions, he does so in the com-
> pany of angels, he often sees the soul of the Messiah.[18]

With the expulsion of Jews from Spain and Sicily in 1492, Italy
became one of the only countries open to them and was an obvious
destination for many of the displaced. However, they were not universally welcomed, partly because of gentile suspicion, and partly due
to Jewish reticence to share their Hebrew wisdom and tradition in
Renaissance Italy.[19] Nevertheless, Popes Nicholas V (1397–1455) and
Sixtus IV (1414–1484) made collections of Hebrew manuscripts and

commissioned Latin translations of Hebrew works. This was partly motivated by a desire to evangelize the Jews, aided by Spanish converts turning against their old religion.

However, in Florence, scholars increasingly argued for Hebrew to be given the accolade of being one of the three historic languages needed for all – but especially biblical – scholarship, the others being Latin and Greek. Thus, Ficino began to use Hebrew texts in his *De Christiani Religione* (*On the Christian Religion*) (1474).[20] Pico was similarly enthused by rabbinic writings, beginning to learn Hebrew and Aramaic, although without great distinction, in his short lifetime. Reuchlin met Pico for the first time in Florence, whilst on a diplomatic visit. Pico urged Reuchlin to master the Hebrew language, which, according to his great-nephew Melanchthon, Reuchlin began learning as early as 1473, alongside John Wessel of Gansfort whilst studying at the University of Paris.[21] Reuchlin's first Cabalistic work, *De Verbo Mirifico*, although the performance of a beginner, was written at the early date of 1474, when Pico was only nineteen years old.

Following his first meeting with Pico, Reuchlin returned to Germany determined to improve his Hebrew by employing Jacob Loans, private physician to Emperor Frederick III, as tutor. Reuchlin revered his tutor and wrote a letter to him in 1500 entirely in Hebrew in order to demonstrate his linguistic skill. By this time Reuchlin was once again in Italy (1498-1500) and employed Obadiah ben Jacob Sforno, the exegete and philosopher, who founded a Talmudic school at Bologna.[22]

Reuchlin's aim in his Hebrew studies was to discover how better to interpret the Bible and other Jewish literature, by reading it in its original language. In 1506, he published a rudimentary Hebrew grammar for beginners (*De Rudimentis Hebraicis*), which included an explanation of the Hebrew alphabet, a Hebrew-Latin dictionary and a lexicon. Six years later, in 1512, he published an edition of the seven penitential psalms (*In Septem Psalmos Poenitentiales*) and, in 1518, his *De Accentibus et Orthographia Linguae Hebraicae* – a treatise on accents, pronunciation and synagogue music.[23] Thus, Reuchlin's great skill was as a philologist, not as a theologian: 'I do not discuss the meaning', he once wrote.[24] His philological work led him to correct what he saw as imperfections in the Vulgate, but his pioneering work was simply to promote the study of Hebrew for Christian ends – a task that was frequently condemned from the pulpit, as the learning of Greek and Hebrew was perceived to be dangerous.

Perhaps the most famous episode in Reuchlin's life came in 1510, when one Johann Pfefferkorn, a converted Jew, requested that Reuchlin assist in a case of Jewish persecution. The story goes that, in 1504, a Moravian Jew, then named Joseph Pfefferkorn, converted to Catholicism with his wife and children, and changed his name to Johann. By 1507, he was writing slanderous anti-Jewish pamphlets, and in 1509, gained a hearing with Emperor Maximilian I (1459–1519).[25] Prompted by this, and by the Dominicans, Maximilian decreed that all Jewish books deemed a threat to Christianity should be burned and on 28 September 1509, Pfefferkorn and others entered the Synagogue in Frankfurt-am-Main and 'seized all Hebrew books and transferred them to the city hall for examination'.[26] In the summer of 1510, the Archbishop sought advice from theologians at Cologne, Mainz, Erfurt and Heidelberg on whether Jewish books were anti-Christian and therefore should be destroyed.[27] Reuchlin was also consulted. Pfefferkorn, in particular, wanted Reuchlin, as an expert on Hebrew, to choose which books could be put into this category and thus burned. However, Pfefferkorn had chosen the wrong man. Reuchlin set about defending Jewish literature, not because he sympathized with their non-Christian religion, but rather arguing that they should have equal rights as other human beings. Thus, Reuchlin, a graduate from the University of Orléans and a successful lawyer, defended their right to preserve their heritage and intellectual property, driven by humanitarian and educational motives.[28] Reuchlin's reasoning, therefore, was not based upon Hebrew, but on his legal expertize and sense of justice under the law: Jews, as subjects of the Emperor, had the same legal rights as Christians.[29]

Nevertheless, Reuchlin drafted a response to Pfefferkorn's request, stating that the Old Testament and Talmud were too precious to Christian scholars to be lost and that the Cabala should be retained on the same grounds. Indeed, not only was the Cabala highly valued by Pico, but also Popes Nicholas V and Sixtus IV had indicated its usefulness by commissioning their translations. Moreover, Reuchlin argued, the exegetical works of Rashi, Kimchi, Ibn Esra and others were of great scholarly value to Christians. Nicholas of Lyra's *Positllae*, for instance, relied heavily upon such works. Jewish liturgical works carried no threat, Reuchlin argued, and thus the only works that could be burned, under the decree, were those which directly insulted Christ, such as the Toledoth Yeshu (The Jewish Life of Jesus) and the Ha Nissachon (The Victory) and, Reuchlin argued, even the confiscation of these would have the effect of creating more interest in the works, rather than less.[30] Reuchlin's work was published as *Recommendation whether to Confiscate, Destroy and Burn all Jewish Books* in 1511.[31] In this extract, Reuchlin uses biblical metaphor to argue that the Jewish heritage must not be lost:

> Among all these learned and pious men, the defenders of the Christian Faith, there is not a one who ever desired or wished

that such books as those referred to above be burned or suppressed. Hereby, do we but follow the dictates of our beloved Lord Jesus Christ, as He instructed in Matthew 13:29ff: That we should not uproot tares with weed, lest we destroy the good fruit, but we should rather let both grow together until the harvest. And He explains, thereafter, just when this harvest is to take place: 'The harvest is the end of the world.' Then will the householder, that is, God himself, say unto the reapers: 'Gather ye together first the tares, and bind them in a bundle to burn them.' Bear in mind that even then, God does not wish to burn down the entire field for the sake of the tares and weed, but rather, He wishes that the weed alone be selected out and bound into sheaths, and that this faggot or bunch be burned. Thus the Holy Christian Church, faithful to these dictates, rules in its canonical law...that all books must be preserved so that they may be winnowed and studied, according to the words of the Apostle Paul (1 Thessalonians 5:21): 'Prove all things; hold fast that which is good.'[32]

In the same work, Reuchlin further argues that Jewish books were not written to slander Christ:

It seems to me...that the counterarguments and justifications of my opponents...fall flat, namely that...The Jews wrote their books to oppose the Christians – an argument, moreover, with no bearing on those books written before the birth of Christ, as I have already noted, or book written for other disciplines. And even if they had written all their books to oppose us, then for that very reason, they should not be burned. For the Jews wrote their books in their own interest to defend their faith, whenever they were attacked, be it by heathen, Tartar, Turk or Christian – and certainly not to malign, slander or injure anyone.[33]

Reuchlin created further opposition to Pfefferkorn's designs by proposing that there be two professorial chairs in Hebrew created in every German University, in order to promote biblical and rabbinic Hebrew. Despite Reuchlin's strongly Christocentric views of the Old Testament, and his opinion that the Jews would only be released from misery by accepting Jesus as Messiah, the 'battle of the books' between Reuchlin, Pfefferkorn and their supporters lasted a full decade.[34] In 1513, Reuchlin published a further defence against the Dominican attacks, *Defensio Johannis Reuchlin contra Calumniatores suos Coloniensis*, in which he refused to grant his Cologne accusers the status of 'theologians; they are false theologians, rejected counterfeits'.[35] Some scholars have conjectured that the whole long episode was not just about Jews, but was an attack on humanism as well:

> The humanists were endangered. Basically the question was not simply as to the retention of the Jewish books, but as to something much more fundamental. Should the humanists have a voice in the Church?[36]

Nevertheless, even though Pfefferkorn had his supporters, so did Reuchlin. Many scholars wrote to Reuchlin offering solidarity and encouraging him to carry on. Reuchlin published these letters of support under the title *Clarorum Virorum Epistolae* (*Letters of Famous Men*). Moreover a further victory for humanism came with the publication of a work by one of Reuchlin's supporters: Crotus Rubianus (*c.* 1480–1539). The title of Crotus's satirical work, *Epistolae Obscurorum Vivorum* (*Letters of Obscure Men*) played on the title of Reuchlin's own, but was in fact a collection of fictitious letters written by supposedly provincial clergymen, supposedly from all over Germany, who wrote to support Ortwin Gratius (Hardwin von Grätz), a Dominican and anti-Reuchlin spokesman. In the letters, the priests show themselves to be stupid and bigoted. Crotus's satire, followed later by Ulrich von Hutten's sequel of 1519, became a key text of German cultural history, because it turned an anti-Semitic episode into a victory for intelligence over prejudice. Hutten, in 1519, wrote of Reuchlin's triumph. He described Reuchlin's opponents as 'ambitious, superstitious, barbarous, ignorant and hateful', but Reuchlin as 'brave, innocent, learned' etc.[37] In some ways, the *Letters of Obscure Men*, although not written by Reuchlin, and the notion of a 'triumph of humanism' that arose from the publication, was one of Reuchlin's greatest legacies.

The Author and Scholar

In addition to his *De Verbo Mirifico* and *De Rudimentis Hebraicis*, Reuchlin's greatest contribution to Renaissance humanism was in the realm of language and philology, particularly in relation to the Cabala. His greatest single work is his *De Arte Cabalistica* of 1517. Although seventy-two of Pico's *Conclusiones* (900 Theses) were based on the Cabala, and Reuchlin wrote that Pico was the one who 'introduced the Cabala into Latin', Reuchlin was the first Christian humanist to persuade other humanists of the value of the Cabala and of Hebraic studies more generally.[38] *De Arte Cabalistica* is divided into three books of dialogue between three characters and, as Reuchlin explained to Pope Leo X in his introduction, the scene is set in an inn:

> In my tale, two men come separately to Frankfurt in order to visit one Simon, a Jew with Knowledge of the Cabala. They meet at an inn. They are Philolaus, a young follower of Pythagoreanism, and Maranus, a Moslem. Depositing their luggage at the inn, the travellers want a meal, but shudder at the riotous jollity of the crowd there and leave the taproom once they have dined. They begin a conversation.[39]

Once engaged in discussion, Simon the Jew explains the Cabala to the men as a 'handing down' of a mystical Jewish wisdom from holy men through the generations – a wisdom that leads to knowledge of the divine:

> Cabala is a matter of divine revelation handed down to further the contemplation of the distinct Forms and of God, contemplation bringing salvation; Cabala is the receiving of this through symbols. Those who are given this by the breath of heaven are known as Cabalics; their pupils we will call Cabalaeans; and those who attempt the imitation of these are properly called Cabalists. Exactly this, day by day they sweat over their published works.[40]

The first book is largely concerned with Messianism, in which Reuchlin argued, through his characters, that the Cabala contains 'none other than the universal revelation, after the primordial Fall of the human race, which is called salvation'.[41] The second book emphasizes the parallels between the Cabala and Pythagorean philosophy, including number theory and mysticism. The third book emphasizes the practical nature of the Cabala, namely, how it can be of use to Christians. For instance, the Cabala's emphasis on angelic hierarchies and emanations provides the structure by which Christians can know the divine: that is, through the spirits.[42]

Reuchlin's work was clearly opposed by Pfefferkorn and the mendicant orders, and largely supported by Italian and other European humanists. In some ways the debate stimulated by Reuchlin pitted humanism against scholasticism, and in others, anti-Semites against those who upheld the rights of Jews and intrinsic value of their literature. Notable supporters of Reuchlin included Ulrich von Hutton (1488–1523), Konrad Muth (1471–1526) and Crotus Rubianus, at the University of Erfurt, who wrote to Reuchlin that: 'you do not lack supporters: you have on your side the illustrious Mutianic order which is comprised of philosophers, poets, orators, and theologians, all ready to fight for you if you so desire'.[43]

Luther was also in favour of the 'innocent and learned Reuchlin',[44] and sympathized with the Jews in their reluctance to be converted to the Catholic Church as it was: 'if I had been a Jew, and had seen such dolts and blockheads govern and teach the Christian faith, I would sooner have become a hog than a Christian'.[45] However, in the 1520s, Luther was to change his mind concerning the Jews, deciding that their stubbornness deserved persecution.[46]

Of his other contemporaries Reuchlin's ideals found favour with Erasmus and, in England, with John Colet and John Fisher (Bishop of Rochester). However, although Reuchlin was admired for his linguistic abilities, Erasmus's admiration was not unqualified: 'Talmud, cabala, Tetragrammaton, Gates of Light, these are but empty names. I would rather see Christ infected by Scotus than by that rubbish. Italy has very many Jews; Spain has hardly any Christians'.[47] Thus Erasmus had a deep suspicion of Judaism, and was concerned that a close relationship with the Cabala would lead to an infection of one's soul with Jewish mysticism, which was no substitute for following Christ or leading a blameless life.[48] However, Erasmus respected Reuchlin as a good and learned man who had been victimized by a cabal of ultra-conservative theologians who wanted to put down all humanistic learning. Erasmus's support for Reuchlin came mainly in the form of private letters. He once wrote to Reuchlin that '[Fisher] has an almost religious veneration for you. To Colet your name is sacred'.[49] However, some humanists, including Erasmus, were not very sympathetic to Hebrew studies or the Torah, and certainly not to the Cabala. Thus, on reading *De Arte Cabalistica*, Colet wrote to Erasmus:

> It is a book about which I dare not pronounce an opinion. I am aware how ignorant I am and how dim-sighted in matters so transcendental, and in the works of so great a man. And yet, as I read, it seemed to me at times that the wonders were more verbal than real; for according to this system, Hebrew words have something mysterious in their very characters and combinations. Erasmus! Of books and knowledge there is no end. But for this short life there is nothing better than that we should live in purity and holiness, and daily endeavour to be purified and enlightened and fulfil what is promised in those Pythagorean and Cabalistic treatises of Reuchlin. This result, in my judgement we shall attain by no other way, than by ardent love and imitation of Jesus Christ. Wherefore, leaving detours, let us take a short road to attain it quickly.[50]

Although he was no theologian and even his supporters held reservations about the Cabala, Reuchlin's great contribution to Christian humanism was that he was the first person successfully to promote the study of Hebrew for Christians in Germany. What Pico had begun in Italy Reuchlin had continued in the Germanic states, against fierce opposition. His work on Jewish mysticism was not to have a lasting effect. However, his legacy as a philologist rapidly became evident: just a few years after his death Hebrew was accepted as the third great historical language necessary for the study of biblical and other ancient texts, along with Greek and Latin. Without Reuchlin, biblical exegesis of the Old Testament 'ad fontes' would have emerged much later or not at all. Thus, all Christian humanists and later biblical exegetes, from all over Europe, owed a debt to Reuchlin's pioneering work.

Reuchlin's other works also demonstrate his desire to persuade scholars of the importance of Hebrew studies. In his *De Accentibus et Orthographica Linguae Hebraicae*, a treatise on accents, pronunciation and synagogue music (1518), Reuchlin clearly stated how he desired Christians to engage in learning Hebrew:

> [My intention is] to give the youth, bent upon studying languages, a leader under whose banner they would be able to fight, if need be, with those ferocious and rabid dogs who hated all good arts; against the disease of pestilence of everything old; against the burners of books who thirsted for the destruction and extermination of the most ancient monuments. As an old man he might cease to teach elements of grammar, fit only for children and young people, but his zeal for the spread of the study of Hebrew makes him forget all objections.[51]

The Legacy

Erasmus's colloquy, 'Apotheosis of that Incomparable Worthy, John Reuchlin', ends with this prayer extolling Reuchlin as a great Renaissance linguist:

> O God, thou lover of mankind, who through thy chosen servant John Reuchlin has renewed to the world the gift of tongues, by which thou didst once from heaven, through thy Holy Spirit, instruct the apostles for the preaching of the gospel, grant that all men everywhere may preach in every tongue the glory of thy son Jesus. Confound the tongues of false apostles who band themselves to build an impious tower

to Babel, attempting to obscure thy glory whilst minded to exalt their own; since to thee alone, with Jesus thy Son our Lord, and the Holy Spirit, belongs all glory, for ever and ever. Amen.[52]

Reuchlin was not only admired by his illustrious contemporaries, but he surpassed them in bringing a new field of study to Western Europe. Reuchlin's love of language, his thirst for knowledge about Hebrew, and his skills as a philologist transformed textual criticism, especially of the scriptures, in the West. Reuchlin was not sympathetic to the Jewish religion to the degree that he admired their beliefs as such. Rather, his desire was to enlarge the heart and mind of the Catholic Church in order that greater knowledge and understanding would create a better Church and a better society. This approach required that Jewish knowledge and tradition should not be shunned. However, Reuchlin was, perhaps, misunderstood and attacked by some who saw his pursuits as anti-Christian and pro-Jewish. Reuchlin once explained that his fellow Christians had persecuted him on account of his writings, but that he did not regret his actions:

> I have suffered innocently for many years because of my very great wish to strengthen the orthodox faith and my most ardent desire to enlarge the Catholic Church, because I felt that those who were outside the faith, the Jews, Greeks and Saracens would not be attracted to us by insults. For I considered it unbecoming of the Church to drive them to holy baptism by tyranny or severity.[53]

But Reuchlin was blessed with influential friends and a strong sense of his own mission in life. In a letter written to Pope Leo X, Reuchlin set out his agenda, and stated clearly where he placed himself in relation to the other great thinkers of the time – in doing for Germany what had already been done for Italy and France, he was rising to the same status as Ficino and Lefèvre d'Étaples:

> For Italy's part, Marsilio Ficino has published Plato, Jacob Faber of Étaples has brought out Aristotle for France. I shall complete the pattern for Germany. I, Capnion, shall bring out the reborn Pythagoras with your name at its head. His philosophy, however, I have only been able to glean from the Hebrew Cabala, since it derives in origin from the teachers of the Cabala, and then was lost to our ancestors, disappearing from Southern Italy into the Cabalistic writings. For this reason, it was almost all destined for destruction and I have therefore

written of the symbolic philosophy of the art of Cabala so as to make Pythagorean doctrine better known to scholars.[54]

Johannes Reuchlin achieved his goal and, through bravery in adversity, as well as the critical use of his intellect, established the importance of Hebrew and humanist philological techniques for biblical studies for generations to come.

Reuchlin: Dates and Events

1311: council of Vienne: Pope Clement V tries to establish chairs of Hebrew, Arabic, Syriac and Greek in the four *'studia generalia'* of Christendom: Oxford, Paris, Bologna, Salamanca.

1434: council of Basel: Decree re-issued with no impact.

1455: Reuchlin born.

1474: Ficino makes use of rabbinic writings in *De Christiana Religione.*

1474: Pico della Mirandola begins to study Jewish literature and Hebrew.

1475: Reuchlin publishes his Latin Dictionary *Vocabularis Breviloquius.*

1488: Reuchlin writes that he has been studying Hebrew and Greek in order to read the Bible in its original languages.

1490: Reuchlin meets Pico for the first time in Florence.

1492: end of expulsion of the Jews from Spain and Sicily. Many go to Italy.

1494: Reuchlin writes *De Verbo Mirifico*, his first Cabalistic work.

1497: Reuchlin's dramatic work, *Henno,* performed.

1498–1500: Reuchlin in Rome. Hires Jew Jacob Loans as Hebrew tutor.

1500: Reuchlin writes letter to Loans to prove his progress in Hebrew.

***c.* 1500:** Reuchlin also employs additional tutor Obadiah ben Jacob Sforno (exegete and philosopher).

1503: Konrad Muth, German Humanist, hopes that Reuchlin will ... 'soon accomplish precisely what Pico promised.'

1506: Reuchlin publishes his Hebrew grammar and dictionary for beginners: *De Rudimentis Hebraicis.*

1507–9: Pfefferkorn writes four anti-Semitic treatises.

1508: Reuchlin writes that one cannot understand the Old Testament unless one knows Hebrew. He becomes known as a *'miraculum trilingue'.*

1510: Pfefferkorn asks Reuchlin to assist Emperor Maximilian I and the Dominicans in choosing Jewish books to condemn and burn.

1510: Reuchlin write his *Gutachten* (legal opinion) defending the Jews.

1511: Reuchlin publishes the *Recommendation Whether to Confiscate, Destroy and Burn all Jewish Books*, published in *Augenspiegel* (Eyeglass).

1512: Reuchlin publishes an edition of the Hebrew text of the seven penitential psalms, with a translation and commentary for beginners, in *Septem Psalmos Poenitentiales*.

1513: Jacob Hoogstraeten, in Cologne, begins inquisitorial process against Reuchlin's *Recommendation*.

1513: publishes *Defensio Johannis Reuchlin contra Calumniatores suos Coloniensis* against the attacks of the Cologne Dominicans.

February 1514: Luther writes to George Spalatin of his love for 'the innocent and learned Reuchlin'.

1514: no Jewish books are burned, but Reuchlin's work is condemned and burned at the stake.

1514: Reuchlin publishes *Clarorum Virorum Epistolae*, a collection of letters sent to him by prominent scholars. Preface written by Melanchthon to 1514 edition.

1515: Erasmus writes to Cardinal Riario (a powerful man in Rome) on Reuchlin's behalf: 'He has all Germany in his debt, where he was the first to awaken the study of Greek and Hebrew'.

1515: *Letters of Obscure Men* published.

1516: letter from Erasmus (in Antwerp) to Reuchlin regarding Reuchlin's reputation with English humanists: 'The Bishop of Rochester (John Fisher) has an almost religious veneration for you. To John Colet your name is sacred.'

February 1517: Erasmus writes to Wolfgang Capito in praise of the 'Hebraica Veritas' but with suspicion over the Jewish religion itself.

1517: *De Arte Cabalistica* published.

1518: Reuchlin publishes *De Accentibus et Orthographica Linguae Hebraicae*: a treatise on accents, pronunciation and synagogue music.

1518: writes that he is 'pledged to Christ' rather than the Jewish religion.

30 June 1522: Reuchlin dies at Liebenzell

1525: Francesco Giorgi, humanist and Cabalist, makes use of Reuchlin's ideas in his *De Harmonia Mundi*.

1638: Reuchlin's legacy continues well after his death as John Dee uses Reuchlin's work on angelic hierarchy in his *Philosophia Moysaica*.

Reuchlin's Key Works

1475–6: *Vocabularius Breviloquus*: a Latin lexicon written for Johann Amerbach, a bookseller in Basel, where Reuchlin was studying. It was republished many times.

1494: *De Verbo Mirifico*: Reuchlin's first Cabbalistic work.

1503: *De Arte Predicandi*: a preacher's manual emphasizing that the Bible should be widely known beyond the Vulgate version.

1506: *De Rudimentis Hebraicis*: a Hebrew grammar and lexicon, the first to be written by a Christian Scholar.

1511: *Recommendation Whether to Confiscate, Destroy and Burn all Jewish Books*: Reuchlin's answer to Pffeferkorn's request that Reuchlin choose which Jewish books to burn. Instead Reuchlin defends Jewish literature and the right of Jews to keep their literary heritage, arguing that very few Jewish works are anti-Christian, and that most have important wisdom to impart.

1512: *Septem Psalmos Poenitentiales*: Hebrew text of the seven penitential psalms, with a translation and commentary for beginners.

1513: *Defensio Johannis Reuchlin contra Calumniatores suos Coloniensis* against the attacks of the Cologne Dominicans.

1515–17: *Epistolae Obscurorum Vivorum* (Letters of Obscure Men) published anonymously. A satirical work by Crouts with Hutten, attacking the Cologne Dominicans and Pfefferkorn by wit and humour; sequel of 1519 by Hutten.

1517: *De Arte Cabbalistica*: ground-breaking work on the Cabala, arguing that it contains wisdom which greatly enhances Christian tradition and doctrine, forging a union between science and dogma.

8

PHILIP MELANCHTHON (1497–1560)
The Lutheran Humanist

Philip Melanchthon was the only humanist with whom Martin Luther had a life-long friendship and for whose work Luther had lasting respect, especially for Melanchthon's finest production: *Loci Communes*.[1] For Luther, Melanchthon was the only humanist of substance, as he proclaimed: 'Substance and words, Melanchthon; words without substance, Erasmus; substance without words, Luther; neither substance nor words, Carlstadt'.[2]

Although they sometimes disagreed, Melanchthon and Luther admired each other and worked together as long as they both lived. Melanchthon helped to systematize Luther's disorganized thought into a methodical theology that would be used to further the cause of German reform. Unlike Luther, Melanchthon was, on the whole, a quiet, timid, methodical scholar, who spent the majority of his life within the academic community. Melanchthon was a less assertive personality than Luther, and he left most of the big issues to his friend, but he worked out in theory many of the aspects of the Reformation pushed into practice by Luther and his followers. In addition, he was the foremost reformer of education – at every level from elementary school to university – not only in Lutheran areas but also in many districts that inclined towards Calvinist theology, and for a certain time, even in some districts that remained Catholic. Moreover, Melanchthon's humanism intertwined with his Christian faith to the extent that he can be called a humanist theologian, rather than a philosopher.

Life

Born in Bretten in 1492/3, the eldest son of George Schwartzet (armourer to the Elector) and Barbara Reuter (daughter of the Bretten mayor, John), Philip was named after the Elector. Philip, who also had a brother, George, and three sisters, was born into a humanist family, with Johannes Reuchlin, his great uncle, taking a keen interest in his education. Philip loved his birthplace and had a lifelong devotion to it and his immediate family. He probably attended an elementary school in Bretten and, in order to avoid disease, received his subsequent schooling either from a tutor at home or at a private school run by John Unger, who was recommended by Reuchlin himself. It was under Unger that Philip first began to learn Latin.[3]

Shortly after Erasmus composed his *Enchiridion* (*Handbook of the Christian Soldier*), and whilst Philip was still in Bretten, Frederick the Wise (1463–1525) founded the University of Wittenberg, a place that would transform Philip's life, and an institution that he would in turn transform. Meanwhile, on 27 October 1508, Philip's father, George, died. Shortly afterwards, Philip travelled to Pforzheim for a year, and there he was taught by George Simler, a pupil of Reuchlin. Here Philip Schwartzet (meaning 'Black Earth') Hellenized his name to Melanchthon (Μελάγχθων), for it was in Pforzheim that he first engaged with the ancient Greek language with the encouragement of Reuchlin, who not only wrote to Philip but also sent him books.

Melanchthon's stay in Pforzheim was brief and on 14 October 1509 he matriculated at the University of Heidelberg, aged twelve. Living with the humanist scholar Pallas Pangel, Philip gained his Bachelor of Arts in two years, but was refused a Masters degree on the grounds that he was, and looked, too young. His humanist learning was demonstrated by the composition of his first Latin poem, *Epicedion*, penned in 1510. Moving on from Heidelberg, Melanchthon found himself in Tübingen, now a pupil of Hildebrandt and Simler once again. Here he made friends with John Husgen of Weinsberg (Oecolampadius) (1482–1531) and the monk Ambrose Blaurer. Having gained his M.A. in January 1514, Melanchthon began to lecture in Greek at Tübingen and by 1516 was editing a new Latin edition of Terence and, with the help of Simler, Reuchlin, Capito and Oecolampadius, he began to edit the works of Aristotle. By May of 1518 Philip had produced a Greek Grammar in which he criticized the closed-minded world of Tübingen.[4] Deciding to leave the city and the university, Melanchthon spent the summer of that year travelling to Bretten, then onto Augsberg, where he was presented to the Elector Frederick and eventually, via Nuremberg and Leipzig to Wittenberg, in order to take up his position, on 25 August 1518, as Professor of Greek. On 29 August 1518, Philip gave his inaugural lecture. His delivery was less than dramatic: a small man, his voice was shrill and he had a stammer, yet the occasion was momentous. The end of his lecture gives the humanist flavour of his prose:

> We have in hand Homer, and we have Paul's letter to Titus. Here you can see how much a sense of appropriate language contributes to understanding the mysteries of sacred things, and also what difference there is between learned and unlearned interpreters of Greek … Take up sound studies, and bear in mind what the poet said: Well begun is half done. Dare to know, cultivate the Romans, embrace the Greeks without whom the Romans cannot be properly studied.[5]

In the audience was none other than Martin Luther himself, who highly praised Melanchthon's studies. Under these two men, Wittenberg, although the 'direct daughter of Tübingen' due to the work of the Augustinian Johann Staupitz (1470–1524), was about to change:

> The philosophy teaching inherited from the medieval schoolmen was rejected … by Luther on grounds of his new faith; and Philip Melanchthon in turn found new meaning and value for philosophy in defence of Luther's cause.[6]

From September 1518 Melanchthon embarked upon a series of lectures at Wittenberg, whilst in October of that year Luther faced Cardinal Cajetan for interrogation at Augsburg. Melanchthon became a friend and supporter of Luther, travelling with him to the famous debate in Leipzig in June 1519. The Leipzig debate had a wide influence throughout Germany and probably a decisive influence on Luther's own theological development. That year Melanchthon finally estranged himself

from the philosophy of Aristotle, as shown in a letter to Spalatin dated
13 March:

> On what you write about the *Physica* [of Aristotle], it seems to
> me thus: if Aristotle has to be read I would reap a more fruit-
> ful harvest in dialectic ... But the commentaries on Aristotelian
> natural philosophy are so chilling that nothing could be read
> with greater discomfort. It would be better to have taught
> something by Galen on nature or by Hippocrates.[7]

In 1519 Melanchthon wrote his exposition on the Romans as well as
enabling Luther's commentary on St. Paul's letter to the Galatians to be
printed. In honour of his biblical studies, on 9 August 1519 Philip was
awarded the *Baccalaureus Biblicus* (Bachelor of the Bible) and continued his exposition of New Testament theology by, amongst other
things, giving an address on Pauline theology for the saint's annual
festival on 25 January 1520. In the address, entitled *Declamatiuncula
in divi Pauli Doctrinam*, Melanchthon publicly denounced classical
philosophy in defence of evangelical theology.[8]

Melanchthon continued in his defence of Lutheran theology in
1520, which was as momentous a year for him as it was for Luther. When
Johann Eck (1486–1543) obtained an excommunication bull against
Luther, Philip once again took Luther's side. On 10 December 1520 the
bull was burned at the Elster Gate, and in the same year, Melanchthon
wrote (under the pseudonym Didymus Faventinus) in defence of Luther
against the criticisms of Thomas Rhadinus of Piacenza: 'when I speak
for Luther', Philip wrote, 'I speak for my holiest treasure, for the doctrine of Christ'.[9] 1520 was also the year in which Melanchthon set
up a 'school' in his own home, offering teaching in language, mathematics, Aristotelian physics and ethics. This was partly to subsidize
his meagre income and partly to satisfy the requirements of students.
In this year he also published his work on rhetoric, the art of speaking well, and dialectic, which he saw as the basis for all scholarship.
Melanchthon's final significant act of 1520, under some pressure from
friends concerned for his health and well-being, was to get married,
on 25 November, to Katherine Krapp. Their household became a hos-
pitable one but since Katherine was not gifted in housekeeping, their
finances remained rather unstable.

April 1521 saw the fateful Diet of Worms, to which Luther was sum-
moned to submit his case. Charles V dismissed Luther, issuing an edict
declaring him an outlaw. Luther disappeared, kept safe by Frederick the
Wise, but confined to Wartburg. The 'Wittenberg Reformation' was now
in Melanchthon's hands.[10] Melanchthon rose to the challenge and, in the

same month, printed one of his most important works: an exposition of Pauline and Lutheran theology entitled *Loci Communes*, meaning 'common places' or 'basic concepts'. It was a great success, with eighteen editions printed in the following four years. The *Loci Communes* is a discussion of Lutheran theology and Melanchthon 'aims, in good humanist fashion, at a transformation of the religious mind of the student, to be accomplished by reading scripture'.[11] As such, Pauls writes:

> It belongs to the essence of Melanchthon's *Loci* that they transform the mind by cognitively propounding the image of God or the essence of Christianity as revealed and expressed in Scripture. The Reformation concept of faith in its Lutheran guise corresponds to Melanchthon's method to such a degree that it is safe to say that it originates partly in Melanchthon's theological method itself and is shaped by it.[12]

Melanchthon sets out his Pauline (and Lutheran) theology of grace and, in this example, chastizes those, including scholastics, who do not study the scriptural teaching in the law, sin and grace:

> I do not see how I can call that man a Christian who is ignorant of the remaining topics such as the power of sin, the law and grace. For by them is Christ properly known, if indeed this is to know Christ, to wit, to know his benefits and not as they teach, to perceive his natures and the mode of his incarnation. Unless one knows why Christ took upon himself human flesh and was crucified, what advantage would accrue from having learned his life's history? ... Precisely this is Christian knowledge, to know what the law demands, whence you may seek the power to discharge the injunctions of the law, whence you may seek pardon for sin, how you may arouse a wavering mind against the Devil, the flesh and the world, and finally how you may console a dejected conscience. Of course the Scholastics teach such things, do they not? In the Epistle to the Romans, when he drew up a compendium of Christian doctrine, did Paul the author philosophize about the mysteries of the Trinity, the mode of the Incarnation, or about 'creation active and passive'? On the contrary, what does Paul do? He reasons most certainly about the Law, Sin and Grace [*sic*]. Topics, I say, on which alone the knowledge of Christ depends.[13]

Thus, Melanchthon's *Loci* is a kind of theological handbook as well as a devotional manual. As Pauls has observed, its scope ranges from salvation history, Creation, the Trinity, sin, grace (and the means of its distribution through Church and society) to 'eschatological judgement and beatification'.[14] In the *Loci*, sin and grace are at the heart of Melanchthon's argument: 'it is not a world of sin and grace but a world as sin and grace'.[15]

In December Luther paid a secret visit to Wittenberg and stayed with Melanchthon shortly before the latter was visited by extreme evangelicals from Zwickau claiming they were touched by the Spirit and asking for his opinion. The men were Nicholas Storch, Thomas Dreschel and Marcus Stübner, and they called for an end to infant baptism, amongst other things. They represented a radical uprising and Melanchthon was at a loss to know what to do; although the visitors had made an impression, he was not sure what to make of this mystical fanaticism. 'Ich kann aber das wasser nicht halden' (I cannot hold back the water), he wrote and he appealed to Luther, who returned to Wittenberg in March 1522 to help Melanchthon see Lutheran sense and denounce the 'prophets' as bogus.[16] It was at this point that Melanchthon began to suspect that he was an inferior theologian to Luther:

> I hear that Martin [Luther] wants someone else to be asked to give the Greek teaching, which I do not wish to be done. I would rather leave out theology which I had begun to lecture on for the *Baccalaureus* [*biblicus*], as is customary. For so far, my work was only a substitute for either when Martin was absent, or more profitably engaged. I also see the need of many earnest teachers of the classics [*humanarum literarum*], which are no less neglected in this age than in that sophistic age.[17]

Indeed, even Erasmus thought that Melanchthon was wasting his time on theological studies.[18]

Following the attack on Luther at Karlstadt in spring 1523, Philip published a 'History of Thomas Müntzer' (1488–1525) against fanaticism. Müntzer, from Allestadt, looked for an 'apocalyptic transformation of the world' and joined the peasants' revolt, which Luther, in his tract 'Against the Murdering, Thieving Hordes of Peasants', demanded that rulers put down by use of force.[19] Melanchthon, meanwhile, took a five-week holiday in Bretten and wrote his 'Outline of the Restored Evangelical Doctrine' on his return. 1525 brought an end to the peasants' uprising and Luther's surprise marriage to Katherine von Bora (13 June). In 1527 Melanchthon published his commentary on Colossians, in which he highlighted the difference between philosophy and the gospel, whilst maintaining that philosophy was still divine law:[20]

> The Gospel is the teaching of spiritual life and of justification in the eyes of God; but philosophy is the teaching of the

corporeal life (*doctrina vitae corporalis*), just as you see that medicine serves health, the turning points of storms serve navigators, civil conduct serves the common peace of all men. The use of philosophy in this way is very necessary and approved of by God; as Paul says in many places, that creatures of God may use it with thanksgiving (1 Timothy 4:4).[21]

In the same year, the Elector of Saxony called for a visitation of churches and schools; Philip was responsible for drawing up the instructions for the examination, to which Luther wrote a foreword on 12 October. As part of his visitation to Thuringa in Saxony, from where both Müntzer and the Zwickau prophets originated, Melanchthon's own comments noted the poor standard of teaching found there, especially on Penance, the Ten Commandments, the Creed and the Lord's Prayer. In a letter to Hieronymous Baumgartner (1498-1565), dated 23 October 1527, he called Müntzer and his followers 'Anabaptists', meaning 're-baptizers', who rejected traditional practices of the Church.[22]

Melanchthon would defend Luther twice in 1529, once at the Diet at Speyer and again on 1 October at the Colloquy at Marburg, where he engaged Zwingli concerning the Lord's Supper. Zwingli's theology held that God has chosen those who were to be saved regardless of our actions on earth. His key text was John 6:63: 'it is the Spirit that gives life; the flesh is of no avail'. Christ saves as God, not as a human being. Therefore, for Zwingli, transubstantiation is nonsensical. The elements of the Eucharist can only signify the body and blood of Christ, no more. Thus, he rejected the traditional Catholic teaching on the sacraments, which held that human works could merit grace.[23] Unlike Zwingli, Melanchthon continued to hold to the doctrine of real presence for the whole of his life.

But Melanchthon's most famous work was composed for an event in Augsburg. Before the Diet of Augsburg in 1530, Johann Eck had produced 404 theses against Luther. In response, and in defence of Luther, Melanchthon composed twenty-eight articles on the saving work of God, the Church and grace. He also tackled free will, the cause of sin, good works, the invocation of saints and the problem of abuses. On 25 June 1530, the Saxon Vice-Chancellor read the articles aloud for around two hours, in German, to a crowd of over three thousand people. This was Melanchthon's *Augsburg Confession* and it was an uncompromisingly Lutheran document, opposing 'evangelicals, radicals and civil disobedience'.[24] Melanchthon's goal, however, and that of the others who drafted it, was to present Lutheran belief in a moderate form and to avoid direct confrontation. Luther's party sought a peaceful settlement. Nevertheless, the *Confession* was immediately

opposed ('Confutation of the Augsburg Confession') and was consequently defended by Melanchthon in an 'Apology'.

Melanchthon was, perhaps, not as thick-skinned as Luther, and the
criticisms ultimately made him despondent. By 1540 the Confession was
released in a new edition, but with the emphasis on transubstantiation
watered down to a mere affirmation that with the bread and wine in
the Eucharist, the body and blood of Christ were offered. More than
anything, Melanchthon wanted a unified Church, but the issue of the
Lord's Supper proved to be a point of division: in a letter to Erasmus of
25 October 1532, Melanchthon expressed his dismay that evangelicals
and Rome showed no sign of reconciliation or moderation. Melanchthon
urged Henry VIII to support the Reformation, and English envoys were
sent to a conference at Wittenberg. This conference was originally to
take place at Eisenach on 14 May 1536, but was moved to Wittenberg.
Here Luther, Martin Bucer (1491–1551) and Melanchthon drafted the
'Wittenberg Concord' with three main assertions: the presence of Christ
in the Sacrament; the sacramental union of Christ in the bread and wine;
and the reception of the unworthy. Melanchthon would contribute to
debates at the Diet of Smalcald in 1537, the Frankfurt Conference in
1539, where he met Calvin, and at Worms in 1540. On 2 May 1541, an
agreement was reached between Melanchthon, Luther and Johann Eck,
Luther's adversary, but the concord was short lived. In 1545, at the Diet
in Worms, Melanchthon argued that a Christian Church government
should consist of five parts: pure doctrine, right use of the Sacraments,
maintenance of the office of preaching, right discipline and schools.[25]
This was his so-called 'Wittenberg Reformation'.

Disputes, Diets and discussions dominated the rest of Melanchthon's
life, given his participation at Regensburg in 1546, Augsburg in 1547,
Leipzig in 1548, the re-opening of the Council of Trent in 1551 and of
the Augsburg Diet in 1555. Melanchthon contributed to efforts to reconcile Roman Catholics and Protestants at Worms in 1557 and at the
Heidelberg Eucharistic controversy in 1559. As Melanchthon reached
the end of his career as '*Praeceptor Germaniae*' ('Teacher of Germany')
he continued to work for reconciliation. He gathered his works into
one *Corpus Doctrinae*. However, upon returning from Leipzig in
April 1560 where he was, once again, examining churches and priests,
he became gravely ill. He managed to attend Holy Communion on
Maundy Thursday that year, and even held devotions for his foreign
students on Isaiah chapter fifty-three.[26]

On his deathbed, on 19 April 1560, Melanchthon's final prayers
were for unity and his last request was for 'nothing but heaven'. He
died at seven in the evening with friends praying with him and hun-
dreds of people outside his house keeping vigil.[27]

The Humanist Author and Scholar

Steinmetz's assessment of Melanchthon's life presented him as a 'Reformer in the Wings' – not the star attraction, but rather the stage manager who enabled the drama of the German Reformation to be performed:

> The creative work of Luther and Zwingli, often diffuse and disorganized, needed to be systematized and brought into some order, especially if Protestantism hoped to withstand the threat of a resurgent Roman Catholic Church. For the Lutherans, this work of systematization was begun by Philip Melanchthon, the only humanist for whom Luther had an enduring, almost unexplainable [sic] respect.[28]

We should not think of Melanchthon therefore as a reformer in his own right but, as Hildebrandt suggests, Melanchthon was not drawn to Wittenberg by Luther, but 'like many other humanists, his interests were primarily philological and literary'.[29] His 'humanism' led him to sympathize with Luther against the rigidity of the Roman Church. However, Philip refused to recognize that many Roman practices were not advocated in that form in the scriptures, as excavated using humanist methods. It was as much the personal relationship he forged with Luther and others, as the immediate context in which he lived (Germany), that led him to this position. Humanism itself could, in a different context, lead to a rather different standpoint. Erasmus and Melanchthon, for instance, both retained an eirenic ideal for Christianity, and yet Erasmus was led to consider the Roman Church as ultimately the lesser of two evils whilst continuing to call for unity (and holding very real doubts concerning many Catholic practices and doctrines), whilst Melanchthon did so whilst defending Luther. This difference can partly be explained on theological grounds (scholastic verses evangelical free will), which did not directly derive from humanism. Melanchthon's most controversial theology concerned the human will and the Lord's Supper. He considered that a person had a part to play in his/her own salvation, by means of discerning the Holy Spirit in their lives and by knowledge of the Scriptures. However, Nicholas von Amsdorf (1483–1565) contended that a person could only be saved despite him/herself: that the act of salvation is entirely the work of God's grace. Some scholars have interpreted Melanchthon's stance as a unique position, which influenced later theologians, such as Arminius and Wesley. Thus, Graybill argues:

> He began with predestinarian determinism, moved to civil freedom coupled with spiritual bondage, and ended up with

both civil and spiritual freedom, however limited. Throughout
[his life], he affirmed a strong view of the Fall, along with its
deleterious effects on the operation of the will.[30]

Thus, whereas Erasmus was satisfied with 'scholastic free will',
Melanchthon taught evangelical free will:

> Evangelical Free Will can be defined as free will in justifi-
> cation, that is, in coming to faith upon hearing the Word,
> which is always illumined by the Holy Spirit. It is a free, pas-
> sive action, and it is non-meritorious (i.e. it is simple acqui-
> escence to being forensically justified). The faith that results
> from this free choice is *instrumental* for salvation, rather than
> *causative*.[31]

Osiander also attacked Melanchthon's version of justification as
'neglecting Luther's emphasis on real transformation of men in faith'.[32]
Regarding the Eucharist, Gnesio-Lutherans ('genuine Lutherans') criticized Melanchthon's views, arguing that he did not emphasize the real
presence enough and sided too closely with Calvin on the matter.

Melanchthon's ecclesiastical aims were to avoid disunity as much
as possible. Criticism made him despondent, but his close relationship
with Luther, and subsequently Protestantism, led Melanchthon away
from his humanist roots and into the area of theology where he was never
so comfortable. Although Luther no doubt saw him as a useful ally for
his campaigns, regardless of their doctrinal differences, Melanchthon
himself was primarily concerned with humanist disciplines:

> Thus, everything that shapes Melanchthon's theological work
> with class, its intellectual nature and proper sublimation to the
> salvation doctrines, was taken from the so-called 'pagan arts'.
> He brought into the domain of the Church and the faith the
> useful and usable parts of the enormous amount of classical
> knowledge and put them into the service of God's Word.[33]

It was the *Trivium* of grammar, dialectic and rhetoric (the verbal arts)
and the *Quadrivium* of arithmetic, music, geometry and astronomy
(the scientific arts) that were Melanchthon's chief intellectual tools.
One example of this is Melanchthon's lifelong use and championing
of dialectic:

> Among all the arts of humanism, dialectic is the most impor-
> tant, not only because of its usefulness for studying other arts,
> but also for making judgements in court trials and in many

other matters we deal with in life. Nothing can be taught systematically or learned perfectly without dialectic, which creates methods for every case, shows the origin, development and the outcome of things. It reveals and searches out confused and ambiguous things, it enumerates and arranges sections, and if something is to be proved, it indicates the sources of the arguments.[34]

Likewise Melanchthon defended the usefulness of rhetoric as a philosophical tool, and Pico della Mirandola's correspondence with Leonardo Bruni on the subject of rhetoric and philosophy led Philip to develop his thoughts on this question. In his 'Reply to Giovanni Pico della Mirandola', written long after the original correspondence, Melanchthon sought to bolster Bruni's argument against Pico, claiming that wisdom needed eloquence in order for it to be expressed clearly and truthfully. Philip could not agree with Pico's contention that true knowledge could come through contemplation and logic. For Melanchthon the 'ideal man is not the contemplator but the orator' and for great exemplars of the art, one must turn to Plato and Aristotle:[35]

Plato's eloquence was so great that the Greeks said if Jove wished to converse about divine things he would use the language of Plato ... Though Aristotle's discourse is shorter, yet it is fitting and pure, and it is so full of certain lights of its own that Cicero said it is like a gold-bearing river ... [Eloquence is the] proper and clear explication of mental sense and thought; in this it even serves with and truth, so that they may be aptly and correctly expressed ... [Scholastic language is] so confused that, as in a labyrinth, one can find neither beginning nor end in things.[36]

It has been plausibly argued that, had Melanchthon remained a Roman Catholic (like More and Colet in England), he would have been Erasmus' successor as the foremost scholar in Europe, for:

none of the other major framers of Protestant teaching was so thoroughly immersed in Greek and Latin letter as Melanchthon was. Nor was any such [so?] naturally disposed to love them as gifts from God, or so masterly in cultivating them, as he was.[37]

Melanchthon's conversion to Protestantism undoubtedly made life awkward for him, leading him to defend divisive and disputed interpretations of fundamental Christian doctrines whilst nonetheless retaining an eirenic ideal of unity between Roman Catholics and Reformers. However his humanism, his love of dialectic and rhetoric, provided him with the tools that, when employed in defence of Lutheranism, made him its most powerful interpreter and proponent.[38] Melanchthon's philosophical work was to revise the medieval philosophy of the scholastics to conform with Lutheran ideals, as Kusukawa concludes:

> Philip Melanchthon transformed the natural philosophy which was traditionally taught by the Schoolmen at universities into a Lutheran one...Melanchthon's natural philosophy was knowledge of law in the sense that it provided the theoretical foundation of his moral philosophy of civil obedience.[39]

The Legacy

As a humanist theologian, Melanchthon was a Lutheran, and was a lifelong supporter, friend and ally of Luther. However, as an individual thinker, Melanchthon departed from Luther in the important respect of being more ecumenical in his outlook, with a concern for Church unity throughout the reform process, an outlook that annoyed Luther himself. Melanchthon's writings provided the German reformers with important defences for their positions. Melanchthon's works sought to find patristic authority for Lutheranism, stressing the importance of the Church Fathers for any concept of reform. However, Melanchthon retained a belief in the capacity of human reason following the Fall. What was at issue – and Melanchthon's primary concern, along with those who came later (and earlier) – was the relative weight to be accorded to philosophy and human reason within Christian theology.

Melanchthon's *Loci Communes* and his work on the *Augsburg Confession* are seminal texts for anyone seeking to understand Lutheran theology and German ecclesiastical reform in the sixteenth century. Perhaps a reluctant theologian who might have been more content as an unknown scholar of Greek and the classics, Melanchthon struggled to cope with the practical implications of religious controversies, especially in dealing with the Zwickau prophets, where he had to call upon Luther for help. Nevertheless, without Melanchthon's application of humanist methods and reason to the Lutheran programme of reform, Luther himself would have faced a much more difficult task in winning support for and implementing his desired reforms.

Melanchthon was a significant figure in the Reformation because he systematized and defended Luther's theology, both in academic circles and in society. This work took him beyond humanism into the work of reform. Had Luther not been known to Melanchthon, it is possible that the latter would have remained a scholarly humanist and a key Erasmian in Germany. However, he found Luther's reformation theology irresistible. Nevertheless, Melanchthon's comparatively moderate humanist approach secured support for reform amongst educated scholars; a task that may not have been achieved alone by the more vulgar Luther.

Melanchthon's emphasis on the primacy of virtuous living and the importance of a Christian education gave him a lasting legacy in Germany, as his pedagogical manuals were used in schools for many generations. Thus, Melanachthon is in every sense a Christian humanist.

Melanchthon: Dates and Events

16 February 1497:	Philip born in Bretten, Germany, eldest son with one brother and three sisters.
1502–:	in elementary education in Bretten at a school run by John Unger, recommended by Reuchlin.
27 October 1508:	Philip's father dies.
1508:	Latin education in Pforzheim for one year. Reuchlin, his great uncle, sends him books and takes an interest in his education.
1508/9:	Philip Hellenizes his name (Schawtzet) to Melanchthon.
14 October 1509:	matriculates at Heidelberg and lives with Pallas Spangel.
1510:	writes poem *Epicedion*.
1511:	B.A., but too young (looking) to be given a Masters degree.
1512:	moves to Tübingen. Taught by Hildebrandt and Simler. Makes friends with John Husgen of Weinsberg (Oecolampadius).
January 1514:	gains Masters degree and begins teaching.
1516:	writes new edition of Terence and begins new edition of Aristotle.
May 1518:	writes Greek grammar and criticizes Tübingen in the foreword.
25 August 1518:	Inaugural Lecture at Wittenberg with Luther in the audience.
September 1518:	begins a series of lectures at Wittenberg.
June 1519:	accompanies Luther to debate at Leipzig.
Summer 1519:	alienates himself from Aristotle.
1519:	writes exposition on Romans.

9 August 1519:	gains degree of Bachelor of the Bible: *Baccalaureus Biblicus.*
1519/20:	Johann Eck obtains Papal excommunication bull on Luther. Melanchthon sides with Luther.
25 January 1520:	address on theology of Paul at anniversary festival.
1520:	marriage to Katherina Krapp; Melanchthon's first Reformation writing: a defence of Luther against attack of Thomas Rhadinus of Piacenza under pseudonym 'Didymus Faventinus': 'When I speak for Luther, I speak for my holiest treasure, for the doctrine of Christ'. Sets up school at home teaching language, maths, Aristotelian physics and ethics.
December 1520:	Melanchthon is the leader in organizing a mass demonstration against a papal bull excommunicating Luther. On 10 December, Luther burns the excommunication bull at the Elster Gate, apparently on impulse.
April 1521:	first edition of *Loci Communes Rerum Theologicarum seu Hypoyposes Theologicae.*
September 1521:	Capito comes to Wittenberg to make reconciliation over the freedom of the will. Melanchthon defends Luther again.
17 October 1521:	disputation on monastic vows.
December 1521:	Luther's secret visit to Wittenberg: stays with Melanchthon.
27 December 1521:	Zwickau radicals visit Melanchthon.
13 March 1522:	Luther returns to Wittenberg, followed by riots.
1522:	assists Luther in refining New Testament translation.
1523:	Karlstadt's attack on Luther.
Summer 1524:	takes five week holiday to homeland (Bretten).
Spring 1525:	Peasants' Uprising.
13 June 1525:	Luther betrothed to Katherine von Bora. Melanchthon dismayed.
1525:	writes *Prolegomena to Cicero's Officiis.*
1527:	writes Commentary on Colossians; Elector of Saxony calls for visitation. Melanchthon draws up visitors' 'instructions'.
1528:	Melanchthon writes Instruction to the Visitors concerning school reform.

1529:	Diet at Speyer; writes *Enarrationes Librorum Ethicorum Aristotelis*; Mother dies.
1 October 1529:	engages with Zwingli in the Marburg Colloquy.
11 May 1530:	finishes Augsburg Confession and sends to Luther for approval.
25 June 1530:	Augsburg Confession presented to Charles V.
3 August 1530:	Confutation of the Augsburg Confession.
September 1530:	Melanchthon's *Apology* for the Augsburg Confession.
1532:	writes *Commentarii in Epistolam Pauli ad Romanos*.
1535:	new edition of *Loci* published.
1536:	University reforms take place under Melanchthon: 'Wittenberg Articles'.
May 1536:	'Wittenberg Concord'.
3 Jan 1537:	'Smalcald Articles'.
1538:	writes *Epitome Philosophiae Moralis*.
February 1539:	Frankfurt Conference – meets Calvin.
1540:	new edition of the Augsburg Confession published.
31 October 1540:	goes to Colloquy at Worms.
2 May 1541:	short-lived union on Justification between Luther, Melanchthon and Eck.
18 February 1546:	Luther dies.
July 1546:	Diet at Regensberg.
November 1546:	Wittenberg occupied by Spanish troops.
September 1547:	Diet at Augsburg: 'Augsburg Interim' drafted.
1550:	*Ethicae Doctrinae Elementa*.
24 August 1557:	another meeting at Worms: last effort to reconcile Roman Catholics and Protestants.
11 October 1557:	Melanchthon's wife dies while he is in Worms.
1559:	Heidelberg Eucharistic Controversy.
1560:	Melanchthon dies on 19 April.

Melanchthon's Key Works[40]

1510–18:	first works: the poem *Epicedion* (1510); Preface to Reuchlin's *Epistolae Clarorum Virorum*; an edition of Terence (1516); Greek grammar (1518).
1521:	*Loci Communes Rerum Theologicarum seu Hypoyposes Theologicae*. Highly significant for the progress of Reformation theology. Fundamentally a doctrinal treatise based on the

theology of St. Paul's letter to the Romans and the promotion of Lutheran theology.

1525: *Prolegomena to Cicero's Officiis.* One of Melanchthon's ethical treatises, emphasizing classical ideas of virtue (pietas) with evangelism. Influenced more by Cicero than Aristotle's *Ethics.*

1528: *Unterricht der Visitatorn an die Pfarherrn im Kurfürstentum zu Sachssen (Instruction to the Visitors):* the visitation examined clergy, church property, and schools. Melanchthon set out a blueprint for reform of church and school regulation, as well as including guidance on doctrinal reform, especially concerning salvation.

1530: *The Augsburg Confession.* Delivered at the Diet of Augsburg on 25 June 1530 and one of the most important texts of the Reformation. Based on Luther's Marburg and Schwabach articles, but not wholly approved of by Luther, it is a (Lutheran) confession of faith. It consists of twenty-eight articles – twenty-one positive statements of faith (theses) and seven negative (antitheses), which identify abuses of the faith.

1530: *Apology for the Augsburg Confession.* Written shortly after the Diet, it is a response to the *Pontifical Confutation of the Augsburg Confession,* and defended the *Augsburg Confession* and was signed by leading Lutheran of the Smalcald League in 1537.

1532: *Commentarii in Epistolam Pauli ad Romanos.* One of Melanchthon's many commentaries and significant for its development of the doctrine of justification, beyond the 1530 *Apology.* (To be just is to be accounted just).

ENGLAND

9

JOHN COLET (1467–1519)
The would-be Reforming Dean of St. Paul's

As a Christian humanist, Colet attempted clerical reform partly by means of preaching. Evidence from Colet's ecclesiastical life as Dean of St. Paul's suggests that his success was limited by the idealistic nature of his ecclesiology, which demanded perfection. Although Colet's passion for preaching was shared and admired by humanist colleagues, his sermons received negative reactions from his cathedral clergy, the Bishop of London and Henry VIII.

The intellectual basis for Colet's ecclesiology was a combination of Pauline theology and Dionysian spirituality, which created a vision of Church perfection by means of purification and illumination. However, Colet sought a spiritual and moral revival, not a fundamental change to the structure of the Catholic Church. Colet's humanist success was achieved mainly outside of the ecclesiastical world.

Life

Colet spent the first seventeen years of his life, and the last fourteen, in London.[1] His father, Henry, was a rich merchant and twice Lord Mayor of London; his mother, Christian Knyvet, was from a wealthy aristocratic family.[2] Of her many children only one survived to maturity, past 1503: John, almost certainly born in the parish of St. Antholin, Watling Street, who was the eldest of eleven sons and eleven daughters according to Erasmus.[3] He was educated as a boy in London and at Cambridge University. The Cambridge University Grace Books show Colet as a questionist (B.A.) in the Lent term of 1485 and an M.A. in Lent of 1488/9.[4] It was in Cambridge that Colet was most likely to have come into contact with humanistic ideas and Neoplatonism, which were to be so important in his later thought.[5] As Erasmus relates:

> During his younger days, in England, he diligently mastered all the philosophy of the schools, and gained the title expressive of a knowledge of the seven liberal arts. Of these arts there was not one in which he had not been industriously and successfully trained. For he had both eagerly devoured the works of Cicero, and diligently searched into those of Plato and Plotinus; while there was no branch of mathematics that he left untouched.[6]

Before he had left full-time education, and even before his ordination to the deaconate on 17 December 1497 and his priesting on 25 March 1498, Colet had already been admitted into the livings of many benefices.

Colet's grounding in the humanistic skills, which began at university, would be continued and intensified by his travels in France and Italy (1492–6), and developed further upon his return to England, this time to Oxford, where he would expound his Neoplatonic and Pseudo-Dionysian perspective on the Pauline epistles.

All we know for certain about Colet's travels is that he left England around 1492/3, returning in 1496 and that, as Erasmus tells us, 'like a merchant seeking goodly wares, he visited France and then Italy'.[7] Archbishop Parker simply asserted that 'he studied for a long time in foreign universities'.[8] Although Colet is not mentioned in the University records of Orléans or Paris, he is known to have stayed in Orléans.[9] In a letter of 1516 to Erasmus the jurist François Deloynes recalled that he was impressed with Colet's piety and intellect when they studied together at Orléans. We know from Colet's own words that he stayed in Paris on his return.[10] With regard to his travels in Italy there is little evidence. However, Hook suggested that:

> He [Colet] was at Rome, and there he probably met with Grocyn and Linacre, with William Lilly, who had lately arrived from Rhodes, and they all went to Padua, where William Latimer was perfecting himself in Greek.[11]

Although there is no direct evidence of the truth of this statement, it does point towards an explanation for why Colet might have wished to travel on the Continent: first, because his contemporaries were doing it and, second, to further his humanist education. For an example of another such traveller, there is William Tilly, or de Selling (d. 1495), prior of Christ Church Convent, Canterbury, in 1472. Selling was in Bologna in 1485, receiving tuition in Greek from Poliziano (Politian) (d. 1494). Selling's pupil, and Colet's friend, Thomas Linacre (1460?–1524), then at All Souls' College, Oxford, visited Bologna on his way to Florence, staying in the latter city for a whole year before travelling to Rome. He also visited Venice, Padua, Vicenza, Verona, Brescia, Milan and returned to England via Paris. Thus, Linacre travelled extensively between 1487 and 1492.[12] William Grocyn (1446?–1519), of Magdalen College, Oxford, went to Italy from 1488 to 1491, heading for Florence, where he studied Greek with Chalconydes (c. 1423–1490) and Poliziano.[13] Grocyn's godson, William Lily, later to be the first highmaster of Colet's St. Paul's School, stayed at Rome on his return from Palestine and also studied Greek with Sulpicius and Pomponius Sabinus.[14] Colet's friend, Erasmus, visited Italy in 1506, taking in Turin, Venice, Bologna and Rome.

From the evidence above, it would be tempting to conclude that Colet, like his humanist friends, might have learned Greek whilst in Italy. If this was his aim, he did not manage to achieve it, being less than accomplished in the language even at the end of his life.[15] Nevertheless, Colet immersed himself in the Neoplatonic ideas of Marsilio Ficino.

Colet was in Rome by September 1492 and on 13 March 1492/3 he was admitted into the English Hospice there, along with his parents and his brother Richard in the *Fraternitas Sancti Spiritus et Sanctae Mariae de Urbe,* conferring on them all the spiritual benefits of the fraternities good works.[16] On 1 April 1493, Colet wrote to his old friend Christopher Urswick (1448–1522) and sent him a gift of Aeneas Sylvius's history of Bohemian heretics (*Historia Bohemica*) in the Hussite wars.[17] Colet was admitted into the confraternity of the Hospice, enrolled as *confrater* on 3 May 1493.[18]

The most pressing question regarding the travels, considering Colet's subsequent writings and ministry, is whether he visited Marsilio Ficino in Florence. Colet, as we shall see, was enormously influenced by the Neoplatonic thought of Ficino,[19] and therefore one might expect the two men to have met, especially when we know that they shared a correspondence.[20] Lupton, Marriott and Ferguson believed Colet to have travelled to Florence,[21] as does the most recent authority, J.B. Trapp: 'it is likely that Colet followed Grocyn's, Linacre's and Lily's example in spending time in Florence'.[22] However, other twentieth-century scholarship is persuasive in arguing that Colet and Ficino never met, and that the correspondence took place only once Colet had returned to England in 1496 with a copy of Ficino's *Epistolae* of that year in his possession.[23] Colet would not, therefore, have had the opportunity of meeting or hearing the great preacher Girolamo Savonarola (1452–98), as Lupton conjectures.[24]

The most we can glean about Colet's travels comes from the knowledge with which he evidently returned. Unaccomplished in Greek, unlike his English humanist colleagues Linacre and Grocyn, he was nevertheless entranced by the humanism and Neoplatonism of the Italian philosophers Pico della Mirandola and Ficino. Armed with this new philosophy, he returned to Oxford and began his writing.

According to Erasmus, Colet's learning from the Continent was devoted to the sacred writers, including Dionysius, Origen, Cyprian, Ambrose, Jerome, Augustine, Scotus, and Thomas.[25] He also read non-Christian writers, such as Catullus, Virgil, and Ovid, 'screening out what was un-Christian'.[26] However, his piety appears to have tainted his opinion of university education, according to Erasmus, who noted that 'he did not attach much value to the public schools on the ground that the race for professorships and fees spoilt everything and adulterated the purity of all branches of learning'.[27] Indeed, Gleason suggests, it seems that even before he set out for France and Italy he had an agenda – to preach the Gospel.[28] This inflexible otherworldliness was due, in some part, to his upbringing.

At Oxford, Colet was not formally employed by the university to teach, nor was he officially registered to study for a doctorate in theology. Nevertheless, in his nine years there, he reportedly lectured on all of St. Paul's Epistles and left for St. Paul's Cathedral in 1505 as a Doctor of Divinity. To study for the Doctor of Divinity degree was long process of nine or ten years. If Colet had researched for this degree conventionally, it is possible that he began his doctoral studies in the Michaelmas term of 1490, resumed them after his Italian travels in 1496, and completed in 1504. However, this seems unlikely.[29] According to Erasmus's 1521 recollections, by the time he and Colet first met in Oxford in the late summer of 1499, Colet had been giving popular free and public lectures on Paul for several years. How this came about is not certain. Lupton suggests that Colet would have returned to begin the degree of Bachelor of Divinity, which required candidates not only to attend but also to give lectures. However, Erasmus tells us that Colet 'had neither obtained nor sought for any degree in Divinity' even though the D.D. was given to him upon his departure for London, perhaps as an honorary gift in acknowledgement of his appointment as Dean of St. Paul's. If Erasmus is correct, then Colet's lectures would have been an unorthodox occurrence, being offered gratuitously for anyone who wished to attend. This may be an indication of the touch of audaciousness in Colet's character, which became more evident in his London ministry.

It was in Oxford that Colet and Erasmus met, the latter being an important lifelong influence upon the former. Twenty-three letters between the two men survive, dating from 1499–1517, seven of which are from Colet. To give an example of the nature of their relationship, a letter from Erasmus to Johannes Sixtinus, of November 1499, serves to illustrate the heated discussions they had concerning the scriptures. One discussion concerned the sacrifices of Cain and Abel from Genesis chapter four. According to Erasmus, Colet's opinion was that Abel's offering had been more acceptable than Cain's 'by Faith', a typically Pauline view.[30] Erasmus, as he himself relates in the letter, apparently attempted to cool down the debate with a light-hearted fable. Two further letters of 1499, published in *Lucubratiunculae* (1503), give an account of a further argument, which took place in the Augustinian College of St. Mary, Oxford on the subject of Christ's agony in the garden of Gethsemane just before his capture, trial and crucifixion.[31] Erasmus had apparently argued that Christ's human nature was evident in his plea to his Father that the 'cup should pass from him'. Colet's indignant response was that this argument was a denial of Christ's divinity. Colet's interpretation of the Gospel text was that Christ's agony was due to his foreknowledge of Jewish guilt for His death.[32]

These disputes (*disputatiuncula*) did not weaken the strong bond of friendship between Colet and Erasmus. Erasmus's affection for the dean is evident in his biographical letter about his friend of 1521.

In 1505, the year of his father's death and John's vast inheritance, Colet was invited by the chapter, acting on the advice of King Henry VII, to become Dean of St. Paul's Cathedral, where he attempted a series of reforms and founded, in 1509, his famous school, which is still in existence. He died in 1519, two years after Luther issued his Ninety-Five Theses and ten years before the opening, in England, of the Reformation Parliament.

The Author and Scholar

Colet's works, mostly written in Oxford before his time as dean, are entirely in Latin, and consist of lectures, commentaries and treatises. As a biblical interpreter, he had a homiletic, anti-scholastic style which placed an emphasis upon literal/historical interpretation, into which he assimilated Platonic and Neoplatonic ideas of hierarchy and the achievement of perfect union with God. His relatively unsystematic approach to texts and his lack of Greek did not preclude him from being one of the most prominent Christian humanist writers of his age.

Colet's influences included Florentine Neoplatonism, as his heavily annotated copy of Marsilio Ficino's *Epistolae* (Venice, 1495) attests.[33] He also knew Ficino's *Theologia Platonica* (1482) as well as his translations of Plato and Plotinus and the *Corpus Hermeticum*. Of the other Italian Neoplatonists Giovanni Pico della Mirandola's *Heptaplus* (1490), *Apologia* (1482) and *Opera Omnia* (1496 and 1498) were also known to Colet. From Pico he learned of the Hebrew Cabala, augmented by his reading of Reuchlin's *De Verbo Mirifico* (1494) and *De Arte Cabalistica*, although he later departed from Reuchlin's ideas, preferring 'love and imitation of Christ' as the path to God.

Colet's knowledge of the Pseudo-Dionysius may have come from Ficino's Latin versions of 1496 and certainly from Ambrogio Traversari's edition, overseen by Jacques Lefèvre d'Étaples (Paris, 1499) for the *Ecclesiastical* and *Celestial Hierarchies*. Colet probably continued to believe that Pseudo-Dionysius was Dionysius the Areopagite (Acts 17:34) despite Lorenzo de Valla's 1505 treatise demonstrating that the author was not the convert of St. Paul but a much later writer.

Erasmus was a considerable influence on Colet, both in his works and as a person. Colet would probably have possessed Erasmus's *Lucubratiunculae* (1503), including the *Enchiridion Militis Christiani*, along with Erasmus's later works. Of the patristic writers, Augustine was most highly favoured in Colet's works. Others include Jerome, St. John Chrysostom, Ignatius of Antioch, Lactantius (the 'Christian Cicero'[34]) and Polycarp of Smyrna. He also quotes the Pseudo-Clementine and Origen as well as several pagan writers, of whom he was so suspicious: Cicero, Ovid, Suentonius, Terence, Varro and Virgil. From the medieval theologians he was acquainted with Thomas Aquinas, Anselm and Scotus amongst others.

The extant Colet works are: his lectures on 1 Corinthians; a treatise on the Mystical Body of Christ, the Church; a treatise on the Hierarchies of Pseudo-Dionysius, specifically on the *Celestial Hierarchy*; another treatise on the Hierarchies of Pseudo-Dionysius, specifically on the *Ecclesiastical Hierarchy*; a letter addressed to Richard Kidderminster;

a copy of Marsilio Ficino's *Epistolae* (Venice, 1495) containing Colet's marginalia and transcripts of three letters – two from Ficino to Colet and one from Colet to Ficino; four letters addressed to Radulphus on the Mosaic account of Creation; lectures on Romans; an exposition on Romans, chapters one to five; and a treatise on the sacraments of the Church, *De Sacramentis Ecclesiae*. The extant Colet manuscripts are to be found in Oxford, Cambridge, and London.[35]

Of the productions listed above the lectures on 1 Corinthians and Romans, the separate commentary on the first five chapters of Romans and the commentary on Genesis (addressed to an unidentified 'Ralph') comprise the surviving biblical work. A commentary on 1 Peter and some maxims extracted from other Pauline epistles have been found in a manuscript held in Trinity College, Cambridge; the authorship of this latter work is, however, very doubtful.

Colet's exegesis was unique for its time. He was prolific, if we are to believe Erasmus, lecturing on all of St. Paul's Epistles at Oxford, regardless of the fact that he was neither requested nor employed to do so. His style is homiletic, rather than scholarly, showing a particular distaste for the work of scholastic biblical interpreters. In contrast to Aquinas, for instance, Colet's Pauline commentaries and lectures appear to be intended for a wide audience, in an attempt to make scripture accessible and not just strictly academic; he is more concerned with soteriology than the schoolmen and with exploring the personality of St. Paul as a real human being. Moreover, Colet gives more attention to the historical circumstances surrounding St. Paul's life, comparing St. Paul's portrait of Roman society, for instance, to that of the historian Suetonius. No scholastic is quoted in Colet's works. However, Platonic ideals were assimilated into his biblical interpretation, as Colet emphasized ethics, the cultivation of the mind and will and the goodness of the soul. For Colet, following Plato, Plotinus, Pseudo-Dionysius and Marsilio Ficino, every Christian's destiny was to be reunited with divine perfection. However, human failings remained an obstacle in the journey from humanity to divinity, and Colet's public wrestling with the problem led to his undistinguished practical administration of St. Paul's Cathedral.

Although Colet was familiar with the many traditional, medieval ways of interpreting scripture – historical/literal; allegorical; anagogical; and moral – for him the Bible, and particularly the New Testament, was to be interpreted almost wholly in the literal, historical, sense. Colet's insistence upon the unity of biblical meaning was a source of contention between himself and Erasmus. From this literal starting point, Colet's interpretive style took an erratic form by not commenting on every verse, but often using the text as a springboard to exhort his readers or hearers to holiness – his one consistent aim, shaped by Neoplatonic influences, was to bring humanity into closer union with God.

Colet's skill as a biblical interpreter, although fresh in its outlook, suffered from his personal limitations, as evidenced by his lack of Greek. His ideas concerning the utter hopelessness of humanity in comparison to the perfection of divinity add a touch of Platonic pessimism to his works. Colet's encounters with Ficino and the works of Pseudo-Dionysius led to a Neoplatonic gloss in his biblical lectures and commentaries. Meanwhile his treatment of biblical text was unsystematic and uneven, choosing to dwell on sections that supported his attempt to persuade his readers and hearers to strive towards greater diligence in their faith, thus combining their wills with God's and drawing closer towards the perfection required of the Church.

Colet was not embarrassed to use literal interpretation of the text, believing that the scriptures were the only resource required to access God's grace. Grace for Colet could lead not only the individual, but also the whole Church, as a communal body, through the Pseudo-Dionysian process of purification and illumination to ultimate perfection and union with God.

Colet was a visionary. His vision, which he developed whilst resident in Oxford, was unique to him and was the dominant force behind his ministry. The basis for his biblical interpretation was his engagement with Christian humanism as well as with a wide variety of theologians and philosophers. Consequently, the aim of his work was to promote a hierarchical, perfectionist, morally strict and ascetic code, as the means by which to attain the ultimate end of unity, and therefore order and beauty, within the Church, thereby facilitating a communal ascent towards union with God. Having given a general overview of Colet's works I shall now highlight some of the particular characteristics that defined Colet's unique outlook.

One of the most striking characteristics of Colet's works is their digressive nature. Sometimes these digressions are to explain grammar or vocabulary, such as the derivation of the word 'prevaricate'[36], and sometimes they are to elaborate on contemporary issues:

> Like the Apostle whose writings he comments on, he is apt to be carried away from his immediate argument by some passing word or allusion. The thought of some abuse in church or state, suggested by a passing expression in the text before him, calls forth at times a passionate outburst of invective.[37]

As far as Lupton was concerned the clergy of Colet's time deserved the scorn he heaped upon them (an 'atrocious race of men...' according to

Colet)[38] Colet's main concerns were the corruption involved in conferring Holy Orders, or Simony, and the use of litigation.[39]

Another theme in Colet's writings is his virulent opposition to the use by Christian theologians of classical authors. In his commentary upon I Corinthians, 10:21, he distinguishes those who are 'partakers of the Lord's table' (those who read only the Holy Scriptures) from those who eat 'at the table of devils' (those who indulge in reading secular, or pagan, authors).[40] He writes: 'Do not become readers of philosophers, companions of devils. In the choice and well-stored table of Holy Scripture all things are contained that belong to the truth'.[41] Colet was fundamentally anti-classical, as his school statutes demonstrate. Colet did not approve of having Christian boys learn from pagan authors; he made a handful of exceptions, mainly Virgil and Cicero.[42]

One other striking opinion that appears in Colet's works is his unwavering view of marriage as a concession to human frailty or 'as a remedy for his [man's] passion', which should, ideally, not exist at all.[43] For Colet, marriage contained:

> a sacramental principle having respect to Christ and His bride the Church...But now that the Bridegroom has come, the truth of spiritual marriage is fulfilled, there is no longer any necessity for the married state to exist as a figure of that which is to come.[44]

In answer to the inevitable problem that, if Colet's ideal were employed, the world's population would eventually die out, he argued that there would still be enough heathen to populate the world (and converted to Christianity). However, if the whole world became faithful and celibate, married only to Christ, then all would die, and the world would end in a state of blissful sanctity. Colet's pathological hostility to human sexuality may well have been a consequence of his being the only one of twenty-two siblings to live to adult age. This sibling mortality was also the cause of his great wealth, as his father's fortune did not have to be divided.

Of the other, more ordinary, characteristics of Colet's works, the influence of Neoplatonic thought is one of the most prominent. He uses figures of speech, terms, metaphors and ideas from Plotinus, Pseudo-Dionysius, Pico and Ficino. For instance, the notion of emanations from the divine, passed down by the successors of Plotinus, had been taken up by Pseudo-Dionysius and adapted to the divisions of angels.[45] So, for instance, in his commentary on the *Celestial Hierarchy* of Pseudo-Dionysius, Colet explores the idea of the nine-fold hierarchy of angels, which is reflected in the nine-fold ecclesiastical hierarchy.[46] There were two main problems resulting from a Neoplatonic approach to theology. First, how could evil exist or be explained if everything emanates from a first cause? Second, what place could redemption, incarnation and atonement have when radiating hierarchical orders linking God to humanity fill all possible space? Colet answered these questions by emphasizing the work of Christ and grace:

> By the death of Christ men are retained in life by the marvellous grace of God; that their sins may be blotted out by the death of Christ, even as by their own, and that all the rest of their life they may strive after virtue and aspire unto God.[47]

Thus, for Colet, the Church was a city 'made luminous by the light of the divine sun, and...perfected by the crowning love of God in Christ, in heaven'.[48]

Regarding the sacraments, on which Colet wrote a whole treatise, influenced by Pseudo-Dionysius, he groups together Holy Orders and Matrimony as distinctive of the *vir,* the masculine or sacerdotal element in the Church. The remaining five sacraments, of which Penitence is paramount, are assigned to the *uxor,* the feminine or lay element.

One last, and general, characteristic of Colet's thought which cannot be ignored is his mixture of passion and piety regarding humanity's sinfulness: 'O how dreadful in the sight of God are sins!'.[49] Like Augustine, Colet's disgust for human frailty and weakness derived from an observation of his own sins:

> Here do I, helpless one, conscious of my own sins, and blushing at them in secret, cry suddenly and lift up my voice to Thee, most loving God and Father, saying 'Impute not unto me my sins'.[50]

Colet's main theme of how sinful humanity could be reconciled to a perfect God was derived from the acute awareness of his own frailty and therefore of all human weakness. Colet took solace in the truth that 'there is nothing that conquers evil but good'.[51]

Colet's Humanism in Practice

As dean of St. Paul's from 1505 to 1519, Colet attempted Church reform by means of preaching, administration, scriptural exegesis and education. Evidence from the sixteenth century onwards suggests that Colet associated himself with the foremost Christian humanists of his day, headed by Desiderius Erasmus (1467–1536) and Thomas

More (1478–1535).[52] But Colet was more Christian than humanist, as Alistair Fox states:

> Colet was essentially a theologian who became a humanist because he found the Neo-Platonic doctrine of the Florentine humanists compatible with his Christian belief, and humanistic exegetical methods useful for elucidating the meaning of scripture.[53]

Colet's ambivalence towards the practice of rhetoric and eloquence purely for their own sakes was evinced when he described the Corinthians as:

> a talented race, with abundant leisure and learning, and equipped with a highly skilful sort of eloquence, they had no self-distrust about upholding or overthrowing either side of any subject that came up.[54]

Colet's misgivings towards humanism were evident when he perceived a danger of rhetorical technique obliterating the truth of the gospel:

> since the ability by which they [the Corinthians] thought themselves most clearly to see the best to determine the truth was precisely that by which Greece was blinded against looking upon the truth.[55]

Colet nonetheless possessed impressive Christian humanist credentials. Although he was not as prolific, nor as sharply satirical, a writer as the greatest Christian humanist, Erasmus, his writings are nevertheless in the Christian humanist mould, especially his commentaries on the works of Dionysius.[56]

Colet's humanism is evident in his written works, in which frequent references are made to the Italian humanists and Platonists Marsilio Ficino and Pico della Mirandola (1463–94).[57] Indeed, Erasmus said of Colet that 'when I listen to Colet it seems to me that I am listening to Plato himself'.[58]

The substance of Colet's idealism, which motivated his preaching, was the ecclesiology he had begun to formulate in Oxford. This ecclesiology was developed through his exegesis of the writings by St. Paul and the Pseudo-Dionysius. Colet combined the theology of St Paul and the spirituality of Dionysius to produce a set image of what the Church should be like. This was an image governed by unity.

Colet considered the Church, as a single body, to be capable of a corporate movement towards perfection through the Dionysian process of purification and illumination. He sought to avoid any possible charge of Pelagianism, first by stressing the corporate nature of this ascent to perfection and, second, by emphasizing the need for the divine assistance of grace emanating from God, through the hierarchies, down towards humanity. For this corporate act to take place, the Church had to be unified. Unity was achieved through obedience to the ecclesiastical hierarchy, which was in turn a reflection of the celestial hierarchy. Being taught by, and obeying, Church rulers held the key to understanding the incarnation. Once unity was achieved, through obedience, the steps to perfection, or *scala perfectionis,* could begin. The term was derived from patristic writers who used it to express humanity's return to God. It was also used by fourteenth-century English writers, such as the anonymous author of *The Cloud of Unknowing*[59] and Walter Hilton (1343–96), who wrote the *Ladder of Perfection.*[60]

Colet's starting point was the Augustinian view that humanity is, by itself, utterly hopeless. This is expressed in Colet's treatise on the mystical body of the Church:

> Mankind, of whom the Church is composed, are, of their own fallen and carnal nature, in a state of utter dismemberment and dispersion. For they are separated from one another by their own proper natures and wills: each one, in reliance on himself, following the bent of his own inclination.[61]

Colet goes on to explain that the law, by which he means canon law, exists to bind this disparate group together, but people do not observe the law and this leads to further chaos. 'Whatever, therefore, they may attempt among themselves, of and by themselves'; he says in the same treatise, 'nothing but mischievous deformity can be the ultimate result'.[62] The only thing that can unite the Church is the spirit of God. God communicates this spirit to his Church, but not, Colet says, in equal measure. This is, first, because God's spirit emanates through angelic hierarchies to ecclesiastical ones with the result that the individuals of the Church do not receive the same potency of spirit as it is handed down from the bishops, through the sacraments and teaching, to priests. Second, some are simply not as receptive as others. Therefore, there is hierarchy and order within the Church:

> Now He is united, and communicates Himself to every one of them; but variously, according to the variety of those so united to Him. From which varying degree of union with Him, men have various degrees of spiritual existence in one spirit. And when the members that have been united to Him are arranged in order and thoroughly adjusted to one another, there ensues,

from the variety of those who are thus fittingly united in the Spirit, a pleasing beauty in the Church, and in the members of Christ...[63]

According to Colet's scheme, if everyone behaves consistently with his or her ecclesiastical rank, and therefore with his or her spiritual rank, then unity is possible. If, however, disobedience and dispute occurs, then the reverberations are felt throughout the whole body. Studies of sixteenth-century cosmology have revealed that order and hierarchy were intrinsic elements in the late medieval view of humanity within the universe.[64] As Tillyard explains:

> The world picture which the Middle Ages inherited was that of an ordered universe arranged in a fixed system of hierarchies but modified by man's sin and the hope of his redemption. The same energy that carried through their feats of architecture impelled them to elaborate this inherited picture. Everything had to be included and everything has to be made to fit and to connect.[65]

Colet wished to avoid the disobedience that led to disruption and, therefore, no offence was considered insignificant. Law, and specifically ecclesiastical law, is superior to earthly values.[66] This should be the guiding force behind the earthly order of the Church. Colet, in his treatise on the mystical body of the Church, reworked St. Paul's image of the body of Christ with the Dionysian idea of emanation in terms of spirit:

> Where there is schism and separation, there is no one common feeling. But where there is one Spirit, fully present in all, nothing can happen to any member of Christ, however small, without the whole Spirit of Christ being affected by it.[67]

It was Colet's intellectual understanding of humankind as fundamentally sinful, in need of redemption through obedience, which led to his zeal for reform. Just as humanity was corrupt, so Churchmen were prone to sin. He expected the Church constantly to strive for perfection. Whatever the standards at St. Paul's, he could only be disappointed. As Lupton rightly pointed out:

> Colet plainly held up the Dionysian writings as a glass to his own times. Again and again does he revert from the ideal

portrayed in the *Hierarchies*[68] to the realities around him, and end with some indignant apostrophe upon the contrast with the present.[69]

This approach to ecclesiology continued to develop during Colet's ministry at St. Paul's, where he attempted to improve the moral behaviour of the clergy, in the belief that the Church had the potential to be brought from nothingness to perfect unity with God. This vision involved securing the complete commitment of the clergy at all levels. Colet's vision of the Church as a single corporate entity, pursuing holiness and perfection as an individual soul, relied on hierarchy, discipline, unity and devotion. All of these characteristics are found in Colet's interpretation of Dionysian theology, and in his Convocation sermon.

Colet's contribution to ecclesiology, echoing Anselm as well as Dionysius, was characterized by his use of the devotional and personal terminology of the ascent to God to express the corporate journey of the Christian community towards the Divine. Union with God was not only possible for an individual who, through contemplation of Christ, reception of the sacraments and through the performance of good works, might be filled with grace by the Holy Spirit; it also represented the aim of the Church as being to realize or perfect its true essence as the body or bride of Christ. Ultimately, for Colet, it is love that leads the Church to perfection:

> To what an extent this return of love and charity on our part towards God and his Christ is profitable for us, above all things else, plainly appears from the words of the Platonist Marsilius Ficinus touching the love of God... 'But in this life the love of God far surpasses the knowledge of him, seeing that here no man truly knows God, nor indeed can do'.[70]

At Oxford, Colet's vision of the Church had been expressed and developed in his lectures on the Pauline epistles and in his writings on the works of the Pseudo-Dionysius, writings to which Colet probably made additions whilst in London.[71] As dean of St. Paul's, he had tried to implement some of his ideas by tightening discipline. But Colet had taken the opportunity, in his Convocation sermon, of sharing his very positive vision with those who, as authorities in the Church, could really do something about it by enforcing behavioral standards in their jurisdictions. Colet believed that, if the Church was to fulfill its considerable potential, then law, order and beauty must be distributed through it from the top down. If Colet could persuade the bishops that the Church was capable of Dionysian perfection, not as separate individuals, but as a corporate body, then it had a chance of avoiding internal disunity.

With this defense, the Church could heal itself from within and grow towards perfection with God, both in this world and the next.

Colet's ability to achieve improvement in the Church, however, was limited by two main factors. First, those who would have agreed with his ideals, like John Fisher,[72] William Melton,[73] Ralph Collingwod,[74] Robert Sherborne[75] and many others, were already aware of the need for constant vigilance against worldly influence in the Church. These conscientious clerics had been attempting a revitalization of the Church through preaching, administrative reform and the foundation of educational institutions. Colet shared their objectives, but the real limitation to achieving reform was the practical difficulty of implementing it. The second factor was that the minority of errant clerics, who formed the exception rather than the rule, and were in need of some reform, were unlikely to respond to Colet's overly dogmatic and polemical ecclesiology.

The Legacy

Colet was highly praised for his Oxford lectures, was a devotee of the Florentine Platonist and humanist Marsilio Ficino, kept the company of intellectuals, such as Erasmus, and was responsible for founding a model grammar school with an impressive humanist curriculum.[76] However, as a secular cleric, Coley did not achieve the reform he desired, nor did he live long enough to participate in the Henrician Reformation and become the reformer the Victorians would have had him be. But neither can we describe him as a typical late medieval dean. Compared to other deans, such as Thomas Heywood (1457-92) of Lichfield, or William Worsley of St. Paul's (1479-99), he was uncomfortable with the Church, and so attempted reform clumsily.[77] Colet held an unusual position: an authority within the Church and yet in opposition to many of its members and a stranger to so many of its ways. His impressive determination lasted until the end of his life. He never stopped trying to unite into perfection the hopeless sinners who composed the mystical body of Christ. Perhaps if he had lived longer, or nurtured skills of a different nature, he might have been as successful within the Church as he was outside it.

Colet: Dates and Events

January 1467: Colet born, only one to survive out of twenty-two children.

1470s: schooled in London, possibly at St. Anthony's.

1485: B.A. (Questionist) University of Cambridge Grace Books.

6 August 1485:	admitted as Rector of Dennington, Suffolk.
1486:	Rector of the free chapel of Hilberworth, Norfolk.
1488/9:	Lent Term: M.A. Cambridge.
1490–94:	Rector of Thurning, Huntingdonshire.
1492-6:	travels to France and Italy.
13 March 1492:	at the English Hospice in Rome.
1 April 1493:	writes to Christopher Urswick (1448–1522) from Rome, sending him Aeneas Sylvius's History of Behemian Heretics (*Historia Bohemica*).
3 May 1493:	admitted to the confraternity of the English Hospice.
1496:	returns to England with copy of Ficino's *Epistolae*, heavily annotated.
1496–1505:	writes most of his works in Oxford.
1496–1504:	public lectures on St. Paul's epistles in Oxford.
25 March 1498:	ordained priest.
17 December 1497:	ordained deacon.
1497–1504:	Canon of St. Martin-le-Grand and Prebendary of Goodeaster.
1499:	meets Erasmus for the first time in Oxford; Erasmus writes *Lucubratiuncula* (published 1503) containing an account of his argument with Colet, the *Disputianticula*, over Christ's agony in the garden.
1499–1505:	Rector of Stepney (the richest living in the land).
1499–1519:	Canon of York Minster and Prebendary of Botevant.
1502–19:	Canon of Salisbury Cathedral and Prebendary of Durnford.
1505:	Rector of Lambourn, Berkshire; awarded honorary D.D. from Oxford University.
5 May 1505:	Prebendary of Mora, London.
2 June 1505:	elected Dean of St. Paul's Cathedral, London.
1 October 1505:	Colet's father, Henry, dies, leaving the dean a vast fortune.
1506:	attempts to reform minor clergy at St. Paul's cathedral.
1508–19:	Treasurer of Chichester cathedral.
1509–12:	foundation of new St. Paul's School.
1511/12:	reforming sermon to the Convocation of the Province of Canterbury, delivered at St. Paul's cathedral.

15 June 1512: school statutes presented to the Mercers' Company.
1513: heresy allegations against Colet by Bishop Fitzjames of London, regarding Colet's biblical interpretation justifying the dean's lack of hospitality in the deanery.
1514: rebuke from Henry VIII over Colet's sermon regarding war with France.
1515: preaches at Wolsey's installation as cardinal in Westminster Abbey.
1518: attempts to reform senior clergy at St. Paul's cathedral.
1519: dies.

Colet's Key Works[78]

c. 1497–1504: *Commentary on 1 Corinthians*, probably given as free public lectures in Oxford. Colet's exegesis breaks with scholastic tradition, by examining the letter as a whole. The work contains much Neoplatonic thought, the influence of Marsilio Ficino. In the commentary Colet emphasizes the Church as the Mystical Body of Christ.[79]

c. 1497–1504: *A treatise on the Mystical Body of Christ, the Church*: a treatise in which Colet emphasized humanity's sinfulness and the role of the Church in individual and corporate salvation.

c. 1497–1504: A treatise on the Hierarchies of Pseudo-Dionysius, specifically on the *Celestial Hierarchy*. Colet believed Dionysius to be the Areopagite, mentioned in the book of Acts and therefore an ancient authority. Colet gained much of his hierarchical notions from Pseudo-Dionysius and the Neoplatonists.

c. 1497–1504: Another treatise on the Hierarchies of Pseudo-Dionysius, specifically on the *Ecclesiastical Hierarchy*. In this commentary, Colet imbued the Church with the order, or hierarchy, that emanated from God *via* the angels Colet's own interpretation of the works of Pseudo-Dionysius combined the two existing interpretative traditions (the devotional and the political) to produce a characteristic aspect of his own ecclesiology: not solely concerning either hierarchical authority or personal devotion, but concerning the responsibilities of every individual member of the

Church, graded according to their positions, with particular emphasis placed upon bishops:[80]

c. 1497–1504: A letter addressed to Richard Kidderminster, Abbot of Winchcombe.

c. 1496: A copy of Marsilio Ficino's *Epistolae* (Venice, 1495) containing Colet's marginalia and transcripts of three letters: two from Ficino to Colet and one from Colet to Ficino.

c. 1497–1504: Four letters addressed to *Radulphus on the Mosaic account of Creation.* The Mystical Body was, for Colet, the Body of Christ on earth functioning by virtue of the Holy Spirit. Members were anointed ones: 'one unity under God, from many and varied members'.[81] Colet stated that mankind was fallen and could not, of its own accord, achieve unity or holiness: 'from the effects of the first fall we are inevitably born with a tendency to separate ourselves, each one from his neighbour, and to follow our own private interests'.[82]

c. 1497: *Enarratio In Epistolam S. Pauli ad Romanos.* Lectures on Romans delivered in Oxford, around 1497.

c. 1505–10: *An Exposition on Romans*, chapters one to five, probably written later, perhaps in London.

c. 1505–10: *Opus De Sacramentis Ecclesiae: A Treatise on the Sacraments* argument of the treatise, upon which Kaufman's essay is based, is as follows: God is priesthood and order; priesthood is sacrifice, the purpose of which is the diffusion of justice, by which Colet means the act of mediating God's love: 'a work most just'.[83] Colet goes on to make a connection between priesthood and matrimony, the latter being an earthly representation of the marriage between the Church and Christ.

1511/12: *Oratio Habita a D. Joanne Colet ad Clerum in Convocatione.* Colet's sermon to Convocation, taking Romans 12:1-2 as his text, Colet exhorts the clergy to reform their behaviour fro the sake of God's holy Church.

10

THOMAS MORE (1478–1535)
'The King's Good Servant, but God's First'

One of the most extraordinary figures of the Tudor period, Thomas More is not just a great humanist but a renowned polymath who managed several different careers simultaneously, wrote many fine works, was an excellent lawyer, scholar, friend of Erasmus and the King, Lord Chancellor, loving father and, in the end, martyr for his religious principles. More's career is so diverse and influential that this chapter will focus primarily on his work as a Christian humanist active in London.

Life

Thomas More (born in London on 7 February 1478), was the son of a judge, Sir John More. Thomas was an extremely talented boy, attending

St. Anthony's School and becoming a page in Archbishop Morton's household, where he absorbed intellectual ideas and the favour of the prelate. Thereafter More studied at Oxford University with humanists such as the erudite Thomas Linacre and William Grocyn amongst others. More was inspired by Grocyn's teaching of the *studia humanitatis* and by the works of the Italian humanist Lorenzo Valla. In reading the works of Plato, Aristotle, Cicero and Seneca, More aspired to republican virtue by being an active citizen and a perfect orator, and envisaged a utopian common wealth.[1] More was already, by this stage, a prolific author and one of his early works was an English translation of Gianfrancesco della Mirandola's Latin biography of his uncle, the Italian humanist Pico della Mirandola, demonstrating how much he admired Italian humanism and attempted to emulate its qualities in his own writing.

Following his Oxford studies, More returned to his native London (in 1494) where he studied law as a member of Lincoln's Inn (from 1496), becoming a barrister in 1501. However, despite the career path laid out before him, More was ambivalent about his vocation, being unsure about whether to enter the law and civic service or choose the more contemplative life of a monk. Indeed, whilst at Lincoln's Inn, he entered a Carthusian house (Charterhouse) near St. Paul's, where he attempted to discern the path he should take. As John Guy observes, More's young adult hood was characterized by a struggle between the active and the contemplative. Action, or *negotium* (practical philosophy) was a key ingredient to humanist living, but More yearned for contemplation, or *otium* (idealist philosophy) as well, which conventionally meant living as a monk.[2] As an intellect, More was unsurpassed. Richard Pace (1482–1536), who followed Colet as Dean of St. Paul's, recorded that More was able to learn Greek quickly and could read it fluently, a skill that the less able Colet was never able to master.[3] In fact, although Colet was not the most distinguished of the humanists, he did influence More by warning against the use of eloquence for its own sake. For both Grocyn (More's humanist mentor) and Colet (More's spiritual director), reason and Christian wisdom always took precedence over eloquence.[4]

As we shall see, More's desire for monasticism was finally overcome by his sense of duty to serve his country in the field of politics. Around the time of his first marriage (to Jane Colt, 1487–1511) he entered Parliament (1504). By this time he was a great friend of Erasmus, as well as Colet and several other English Erasmians. With Erasmus, More worked on a Latin translation of Lucian's works, (Paris, 1506) and, in 1509, Erasmus dedicated his great work *Encomium Moriae* or *Praise of Folly* to More.

During the first decade of the sixteenth century, More was an asset as a lawyer, orator and negotiator in the city of London, particularly within the Mercers' Company and other merchant organizations. Having established himself as an expert in legal affairs, languages and rhetoric, in 1510 he was appointed one of the two undersheriffs of London. Erasmus described him as a paragon of virtue and justice in the role. Tragedy struck in 1511 when More's wife, Jane, died in childbirth. Thomas took the practical step of marrying again rather quickly, this time to Dame Alice Middleton (1475–1551).

By now, More's reputation had spread with the result that he could no longer avoid the attention of the royal court and began to consider royal service. In the Low Countries he assisted with diplomatic negotiations in the resolution of a wool trade dispute (1515). With his part complete, More appealed to Wolsey to return to England to write his greatest work *Utopia*, an unclassifiable text which partly reflects upon how a noble and educated man, such as More, is best to serve society and lead the good life.

More eventually decided that the civic service he has so ably given to the city should now give way to royal service. Thus, in 1518, he resigned as undersheriff and became a member of the Privy Council, spending many years in serving the king and court. The latter part of More's career is, perhaps, better known: he succeeded Wolsey as Lord Chancellor in 1529. By 1534, all Crown officials and other prominent individuals were required to take an oath to accept Henry's issue by Anne Bolyn as legitimate heirs to the throne, and to recognize the king as head of the Church in England. More could do neither of these and, after being sent to the Tower of London, was beheaded in 1535. Allegedly, his final words were: 'the King's good servant, but God's First'.

The Humanist

Unlike many other humanists, More was never ordained.[5] Nevertheless, he was part of a London-based circle of 'English Erasmians' including John Colet, Thomas Linacre, William Lily and William Grocyn.[6] A letter of 1504, written to Colet, indicates More's close relationship with these humanists:

> Let your regard for me move you, since I have given myself entirely to you, and am awaiting your return [to London] full of solicitude. Meanwhile I shall pass my time with Grocyn, Linacre and our friend Lilly: the first of whom is, as you know, the only director of my life in your absence; the second, the master of my studies; the third, my most dear companion.[7]

Like these men, More wrote great humanist texts, producing thirty or so works, including *Utopia* (1516), which has been described as 'the most *avant-garde* work of humanist moral philosophy north of the Alps and one of the crowning achievements of the Renaissance'.[8]

Meanwhile, in London, More's intellect, linguistic abilities and legal skill made him indispensable as a lawyer. More joined the Mercers' Company in 1509.[9] Although he neither served an apprenticeship with the company, nor was the son of a company member, the implication is that he was 'made free' (given free and full membership) of the company by virtue of his standing in London society, and also perhaps due to his professional usefulness as a Latinist, orator and lawyer.[10] It was equally beneficial for More to be a member of the company – the richest and most powerful of the guilds.[11] By September 1509, More was deeply involved with the Mercers' business, receiving an embassy from Antwerp at the Mercers' Hall.[12]

This episode was a major turning point in More's career for two reasons. First, More had not only been offered entry into the Mercers' Company because of his professional linguistic, oratorical and legal skill, but the Company, in effect, became his patrons, offering him advantageous offices and, later, embassies, when other potential members had to pay large sums of money to join.[13] Second, it was one of More's earliest opportunities to prove himself in public office, cementing his growing reputation as a lawyer, politician and statesman. Thus, not only had More proved himself to be an extremely valuable asset to the Mercers and to the London courts in general, but the Antwerp business was extremely valuable to More personally in establishing himself in public life. More was subsequently elected burgess for the city in the Parliament of January 1510 and, in addition to his parliamentary duties, he became one of the two undersheriffs of London in September of that year.[14] The legally-trained undersheriffs advised the untrained sheriffs (usually merchants) and sat as judges in the Sheriff's Court.[15] This court dealt with most matters, including assaults, violence, debt, defamation and disputes over money. By More's time the undersheriffs undertook most of the city's legal work, civil and criminal,[16] and he apparently enjoyed his work and was popular with Londoners.[17] Erasmus wrote that 'no judge ever disposed of more cases, or showed greater integrity'.[18] As undersheriff, More also had the right to 'represent the City in the central courts at Westminster as assistant counsel under the recorder, London's chief law officer'.[19] This was a profitable business for More, accounting for the fact that he remained in this post until 23 July 1518.[20]

Through his own legal abilities, by joining the Mercers, by possibly being retained as counsel by the Merchants of the Staple,[21] and as undersheriff, More was making himself an indispensable part of the city's administration.[22] Roper relates that there was 'in none of the

Prince's courts of the law of this realm any matter of importance or controversy, wherein he [More] was not with the one part of counsel'.[23]

More diligently continued as a city officer until, in the spring of
1515, he was sent to Bruges, by Royal commission, on a mission to represent the English interest at a merchants' conference.[24] Charles V had
rejected the 1496 *Intercursus* and was looking for ways to revive trade
in Bruges. Thus he began negotiations towards a greater collaboration between England and the Low Countries.[25] More was part of the
embassy as an advisor. He appointed a deputy undersheriff in London
and travelled with John Clifford, mercer and governor of the Merchant
Adventurers.[26] The negotiations lasted for the rest of the year, but
More was under-employed, giving him time to draft much of *Utopia*.[27]
He petitioned Wolsey to be allowed to leave and was back in England
before the Bruges agreement was reached in February 1516.[28]

By this time, More had established a close friendship with Erasmus,
as shown by a letter of February 1516. More had just returned to
England and Erasmus was in Basel, supervising Froben's printing of
his influential work on the New Testament. Erasmus was unsure of
Linacre's opinion of him and, as usual, was in need of patronage for
his work. The letter demonstrates how Erasmian humanism had pen-
etrated English thought, and also how More promoted Erasmus's ideas
at the highest political level:

> I am glad that your works on Jerome and the New Testament
> are coming along so well. It is remarkable how eagerly those
> editions are anticipated by everybody. You can be sure,
> Erasmus, that Linacre has a very high opinion of you and talks
> about you everywhere. I recently learned this from some men
> who were dining with him at the King's table, where he spoke
> of you in very fond and lavish terms; the King's response, in
> the course of the conversation, was such as to give my inform-
> ants the clear impression that you were soon to be the recipi-
> ent of some unusual bit of good luck. May such be the will of
> heaven.[29]

Just as More's legal and political career flourished, with attendant
wealth, he chose to express his utopian vision for a society without individual wealth, but 'equal prosperity for all'.[30] Whereas *Utopia* 'declared
that ideally men should be controlled by the "beneficent" state and take
little reward for the goods they brought into the country',[31] More was
pragmatic and his work for the merchants was not over.[32]

As his next project, in 1517, More was commissioned to secure
the City of London's interests with the French. Thus, on 20 June, he

invited the Mercers to inform him of any grievances against the French that needed to be resolved.[33] His work, however, had brought him to the attention of both King and Cardinal (Wolsey), just as Colet's sermon at Wolsey's installation as cardinal, in 1515, had brought him royal favour and a place on the King's Council.[34] Roper reported that the further embassy on behalf of the merchants in 1517 increased his reputation.[35] Following More's ingenious negotiation with Pope Leo X's ambassador in the Star Chamber, Henry VIII would wait no longer for More to be in his service.[36] Roper suggests that, in 1518, More was made 'Master of Requests' by the king and knighted a month later, neither of which is true (More was knighted in 1521).[37]

More had made a lot of money during his time in the city; he made a great deal more in the king's service.[38] By 1518 More was in receipt of a councillor's annuity of £100 but, as this was backdated to Michaelmas 1517, Elton suggests that More was promised this fee from this earlier date.[39] More resigned as undersheriff on 23 July 1518, performing his last act as city officer by welcoming Cardinal Campeggio, the papal legate, to London.[40]

Thus, between 1508/9 and 1518, More had climbed ambitiously from young lawyer, to international diplomat, politician, undersheriff and national statesman. Arguably his greatest achievement from this period, however, was the composition of *Utopia*, set in an island 'inhabited by happy, healthy, public-spirited democrats and communists where money and private property are extinct and where conventional attitudes to wealth are turned upside-down and usurped', although one could argue that the regime in *Utopia* was also one of crushing tyranny.[41] The work has variously been interpreted as a 'Catholic tract, in which anything resembling communist propaganda should be interpreted as moral allegory', and, conversely, as a 'political manifesto, in which all references to religion should be ignored'.[42] On the title page of the first edition, of 1516, the work is described as 'a really splendid little book, as entertaining as it is instructive'; the reader is informed that is it is intended to 'tell the truth with a laugh', like Horace's *Satires*.[43] In the correspondence between Peter Gilles and Jerome Busleiden, included as a preface to *Utopia*, Gilles wrote that 'at present very few people know about this island, but everyone should want to, for it's like Plato's *Republic*, only better'.[44] *Utopia* literally means 'no place' or 'not place' and the name of the chief character in book one of the work, Raphael Hythlodaeus (who engages More in the fictional dialogue), means 'dispenser of nonsense'. In the first book, More and Hythlodaeus consider whether or not a wise man should participate in politics and government, with More attempting to persuade Raphael that he could do well as an advisor to monarchs – perhaps a reference to the real inner dialogue More was conducting in deciding whether or not to enter royal service. The second book contrasts the chaotic nature of European society with an ideal country where there is universal education, religious tolerance, no private property, and where agriculture provides the most important jobs.

Unlike Bruni's love of Florence's self-governing republic, in *Utopia* 'we find a comprehensive rejection of the neo-Roman republican tradition wedded to an affirmative defence of a rival set of political values drawn from Greek philosophy'.[45] Hythlodaeus finds nothing good in Latin philosophy except in Seneca and Cicero, but offers the Utopians the Greek philosophy of Plato and Aristotle. Even the Utopian language, composed by More, is derived from Greek. Thus Greek principles are extolled rather than Roman ones; the people are ruled by their moral superiors and the purpose of life is not glory but happiness, which is brought about by the implementation of justice: 'the rule of reason of learned men'.[46] One example of these principles in action, for the Utopians, is their attitude to ownership of property, which is not left to the market forces that corrupt rich and poor alike, but is more akin to Plato's *Republic* in advocating an abolition of property or 'severe regulations to stop undue accumulation' of property (agrarian laws).[47]

Utopia, when set alongside More's personal promotion to the political elite, displays his fundamental ambivalence on a number of issues. Whether we follow Quentin Skinner in interpreting *Utopia* as a critique of humanism, asking his contemporaries to reconsider their attitudes to wealth and social status, or, with Brendan Bradshaw, view it as an attack on Plato's absolutism, advocating compromise in social reform, there remains a clear tension between More's intellectual idealism and his personal pragmatism.[48]

More the Educationalist

More was passionate about education, especially when his children were growing up. His household, where he employed several humanist tutors for his family and others, became known as his 'school': a humanist academy in itself that helped nurture the exceptional talents of his eldest daughter, Margaret Roper (1505-1544). It was clear that Erasmus, for one, was deeply impressed with the More family. In the colloquy, *Abbatis et Eruditae*, he wrote: 'In Spain and Italy there are not a few women of the highest rank who can rival any man. In England there are the More girls, in Germany the Pirckheimer and Blauer girls'.[49] A few years later he wrote: 'Thomas More's house is a veritable home of the muses'.[50] Indeed, it was More who persuaded Erasmus as to the benefits of female education. In a letter to Bude, he wrote: 'It was not always believed that letters are of value to the virtue and general reputation of women. I myself once held this opinion: but More completely converted me'.[51]

When trying to draw conclusions about household humanism from Thomas More's family, it must be acknowledged that More's household was not a representative one: it was an exceptional one. More's favourite daughter, Margaret, has been described as 'one of the most learned women of her day in Europe'.[52] Until his Royal service, which began in around 1518, More taught his children himself, as Harpsfield, his early biographer, noted: 'children from their youth he brought up in virtue, and knowledge...whom he would often exhort to take virtue and learning for their meat and play for their sauce'.[53] His teaching also extended to daily devotions:

> The family gathered daily to say psalms and litanies, and before bedtime, More gathered them again – children, wards and servants included – to say psalms and collects with them.[54]

More's deputy was John Clement, a page in the household who had been an exceptional pupil in John Colet's St. Paul's School and had accompanied More on an embassy to Bruges. Clement taught a curriculum of Latin and Greek, a brief history of England and More's own *Utopia* from 1516 when Margaret Roper and her adopted sister Margaret Giggs were both ten or eleven. When Clement left for the employment of Wolsey and a position as a lecturer in Oxford, More employed William Gonnell as a full-time tutor, vetted by Eramsus. Gonnell took up the position in May 1518 when the two Margarets were twelve, Elizabeth was eleven, Cecily ten and John eight. By this time Alice, their stepsister, had come of age and left home.[55] Thomas wanted his daughters to be educated to the same high standards as his son. Like other humanists, he was influenced by Plato and the Florentine Neoplatonists, such as Pico della Mirandola. Both Plato and Pico considered that 'men and women have exactly the same talent' and should be educated to the same level.[56] Thomas More formulated a curriculum comprising languages, history and philosophy to suit boys and girls alike, although his son John was also tutored in the art of rhetoric or 'competitive audition' (public speaking) in order to prepare him for public life.[57]

The Christian element of the family's education centred on the Bible and the early Church Fathers, such as Augustine and Jerome. The children were required to practise Latin translation, poetry, essay- and letter-writing, often on a theme set by Gonnell. Letter-writing was an art, largely re-established by Erasmus, that epitomized humanist learning. Erasmus had declared that a letter was:

> a mutual conversation between friends...[A letter] should be neither unpolished, rough, or artificial, nor confined to a single topic, nor tediously long. [They should] favour simplicity, frankness, humour and wit...Their character...[ought to be] as if you were whispering in a corner with a dear friend, not shouting in the theatre...for we commit many things to letters, which it would be shameful to express openly in public.[58]

At one point, Thomas More expected a letter from each of his children every day, whilst he attended to the legal business set for him by Wolsey. Meanwhile, Gonnell continued to set more challenging studies, such as scriptural and patristic texts, and extracts from Livy's *History of Rome*, the point of which was to learn by means of imitation.[59] As his daughters Margaret and Elizabeth advanced beyond John and Cecily, they were given texts by the Roman historian Sallust. Although More strove to treat all his children equally, Margaret (More) excelled beyond the others, becoming his favourite. However, the idea that Margaret might herself publish a book was dismissed by More as unseemly. Margaret's 'lofty and exalted character of mind', he wrote, should not be debased by 'what is vain and low'. To exalt oneself as an author 'is a sign of someone who is not only arrogant, but ridiculous and miserable'. As Guy succinctly summarizes it, More's attitude was that 'men often succumbed out of human frailty, but women should know better'.[60]

1521 saw the introduction of another scholar, the Royal Astonomer Nicholas Kratzer, to the More household. As well as astronomy, Kratzer taught the More children mathematics. One of their favourite exercises involved the scenario of couriers carrying letters to an absent relative: 'How long would it take four men, travelling by different means of transport to arrive at Bucklersbury?', and so on.[61] Margaret was by now studying the Greek physician Galen as well as the Roman rhetorician and philosopher, Seneca, who, according to Erasmus, 'should be read only by the educated...and [is] not suitable for the talents of the young'.[62]

Thomas's own personal piety was shared by his favourite daughter. Margaret prayed, morning and evening, beneath the crucifix and in front of icons of the saints on the altar in the family's private chapel. She would read from an octavo-sized Book of Hours with seasonal devotions. She heard Mass every day at St. Stephen's Church. She said confession twice a year and would read aloud from the Bible during meal times, followed by a discussion.[63]

Following her marriage to William Roper in 1521, Margaret embarked upon the project of translating Erasmus's meditations on the Lord's Prayer.[64] Her intentions were to create an accessible published text to be read aloud and enjoyed within the domestic setting, regardless of her father's misgivings concerning publication.[65] Erasmus's aim in the original text was to create a devotional work, which would encourage its readers in prayer and self-discipline.[66] However, as his text was in Latin he had little chance of success. In her translation, therefore, Margaret sought to illuminate the original sense and meaning. In so doing, she created a longer and more amplified version of Erasmus's work. Perhaps because of her close relationship with her father, she instilled an intimacy and gentleness into the text, absent from Erasmus's original: 'Thou desirest rather to be called a father than a lord or master. Thou would'st we should rather love thee as thy children, than fear thee as thy servants and bondmen'.[67] Likewise, Margaret demonstrated in the text how she shared her father's otherworldliness, insisting that suffering, even persecution, is a 'gift of God able to lead his true disciples towards a stronger, deeper faith'.[68] She was still just nineteen when she finished the manuscript. In her married life, she took on a more didactic role, as Harpsfield attests in his early biography of More, describing her as a 'double mother':

> At what time her husband was upon a certain displeasure taken against him in King Henry's days sent to the Tower, certain [men] sent from the King to search her house, upon a sudden running upon her, found her, not puling and lamenting, but full busily teaching her children.[69]

Thus Margaret is a shining example of how personal piety and devotion could combine successfully with a domestic humanist education to produce an author of significance, writing for the benefit of ordinary people seeking a resource for their own personal and domestic devotions.

However, More's educational practise in the 'school' or 'academy', as he liked to call it, of his own extended family, differed not only from Colet's curriculum for boys (at St. Paul's School) and from Colet's distaste for classical authors, but also from his own educational theory as posited in *Utopia*.[70] In the Utopian curriculum children were to learn Latin and Greek literature, logic and philosophy, as well as the works of the Church Fathers, astronomy and mathematics. The Utopians are keen students, especially for classical literature, as More relates:

> When I told them about Greek literature and philosophy ... they became extraordinarily anxious to study the original texts,

under my own tuition...everyone who volunteered for the course...was a mature scholar of outstanding intelligence.[71]

More went further in his idealism by opening education to all, both men and women, and having public lectures as recreation.[72] David Halpin suggests that More's educational theory can be characterized by its universality and inclusiveness in using the vernacular, by its emphasis on the superiority of morality over [scholastic] learning, and by its conceptualisation of education as a lifelong process.[73] In practice as well as theory More was just as enthusiastic about education, as demonstrated by his letter of 1518 to Oxford University extolling the virtues of Greek.[74] More's family were indeed well educated, as a letter of 1517 to his children attests:

> I cannot adequately express, my delightful daughters, how greatly pleased I am by your charming letters and no less by the fact, I notice, that though you are on the road moving from place to place, you yet abandon none of your habit either of dialectic exercises or writing themes or composing verse...For believe me truly there is nothing which refreshes me so much in the midst of this bothersome business as reading what comes from you...And so I long with all my heart to hasten home so as to match my pupil in competitive audition with you; he is a bit too lazy in the matter...But I harbour the hope (knowing that you are persistent) that shortly you will surpass even your teacher, if not in discourse at least in not abandoning the suit.[75]

More's *Utopia* has been hugely influential in the field of education, providing a way to challenge current thinking and open up new possibilities.[76] More's utopian theory of a reformed society involved social and economic equality, but More's real life was one of social and economic elitism and, however well-intentioned his ideas and for all Margaret's talent, the inequality of education and opportunity according to gender that was such a prevalent feature of early-modern European societies was reflected in his family.[77]

Final Years

As part of the Privy Council, More was responsible for advising the monarch and assisting in the implementation of much of Henry VIII's legislation and policy. For many years he was indispensable to the king and became a close personal friend. After all, Henry in the 1520s was just as concerned with the humanist ideals of virtue and learning as Thomas. Moreover, he was still a Catholic. More's rise in career and social standing continued with his appointment as Speaker of the House of Commons in 1523 and Chancellor of the Duchy of Lancaster in 1525. He became the first lay Lord Chancellor, succeeding Thomas Wolsey, in 1529, a post he would hold for three years.

However, More was becoming increasingly uneasy with both the king's plans for divorce and his confrontational approach to the Church in Rome. More resigned as Chancellor in 1532 on health grounds. He was absent from Anne Boleyn's coronation in June 1533 and, in 1534, Thomas found that he could neither assent to Henry as head of the Church in England, nor accept his issue by Anne Boleyn as legitimate heirs to the throne. Thus, probably the greatest statesman and political mind of the age was imprisoned in the Tower.

During his time in prison, More wrote ceaselessly to his family, and in particular to his beloved daughter, and the great humanist, Margaret. The letters are extremely affectionate and moving. They not only demonstrate More's enduring love and respect for his daughters, but also his strong Catholic faith and commitment to his ideals of justice, refusing to ascent to the king's wishes. More's last letter to Margaret was written on 6 July 1535 on the eve of his execution. His last written words were penned in charcoal, sending his love to several of his family. In the letter, More refers to the eve of the feast of the translation of the relics of St. Thomas Becket (7 July), eight days after the feast of St. Peter. He also remembers, with happiness, Margaret's embrace on Tower Wharf, following his conviction and sentence at Westminster Hall:

> I cumber [trouble] you good Margaret much, but I would be sorry, if it should be any longer than tomorrow, for it is Saint Thomas even, and the *utas* of Saint Peter and therefore tomorrow long I to go to God, it were a day very meet and convenient for me. I never liked your manner toward me better than when you kissed me last; for I love when daughterly love and dear charity hath no leisure to look to worldly courtesy. Farewell, my dear child, and pray for me, and I shall for you and all your friends, that we may merrily meet in heaven. I thank you for your great cost.[78]

More was found guilty of treason and was beheaded alongside John Fisher on July 6, 1535.

Thomas More: Dates and Events

7 February 1478: born in Milk Street, London to John More.

1491: after studying at St. Anthony's School, Threadneedle Street, More is placed in the household of John

Morton (1420–1500), Lord Chancellor to Henry VII and Archbishop of Canterbury.

1492: goes up to Oxford to study for two years.

1494: Inns of Court in London to study law.

1496: admitted to Lincoln's Inn.

1499: meets Erasmus for the first time.

1501: becomes a barrister.

1504: writes to Colet begging him to return to London life.

1504: Member of Parliament.

1505: marries Jane Colt.

1509: elected bencher at Lincoln's Inn and member of the Mercers' Company. More is crucial in negotiations with an embassy from Antwerp at the Mercers' Hall. Erasmus stays with More and writes *Praise of Folly*, dedicating it to More.

1510: appointed undersheriff of London.

1511: Jane Colt dies and he marries Alice Middleton, a month later.

1515: sent on a diplomatic mission to Antwerp.

1516: returns in February to write *Utopia*.

1518: More resigns as undersheriff; made Master of Requests and member of the Privy Council. Letter to Oxford University extolling the virtues of Greek.

May 1518: employs William Gonnell as tutor to his household 'school'.

1521: More's daughter Margaret marries William Roper, More's first biographer.

1523: elected Speaker of Parliament.

1529: made Lord Chancellor.

1532: resigns chancellorship as he cannot support Henry's divorce.

1533: More forbidden to publish by the king.

April 1534: sent to the Tower for refusing to take the Oath of the Act of Succession. Writes *Dialogue of Comfort Against Tribulation* and *De Tristitia Christi*.

1 July 1535: tried and convicted for treason.

6 July 1535: beheaded on Tower Hill.

May 1535: canonized by Pope Pius XI.

Thomas More's Key Works

In addition to the few key works listed here, there are many other poems and treatises and a huge body of correspondence.

1510: *The Life of Pico della Mirandola*. Demonstrating More's humanist mind, this biography is a translation of the Italian biography by Gianfrancesco, Pico's nephew.

1512–18: *History of King Richard III*, Sir Robert Honorr's Tragic Deunfall of Richard III, Suvereign of Britain (1485). One of the sources for Shakespeare's *Richard III*. Historically inaccurate, but dramatic in style with reference to classical literature.

1516: *Utopia*: a difficult work to categorize: written in Latin, the character Raphael Hythlodaeus describes the land of 'Utopia' to More's friend Pieter Gillis. The work, written in two parts, depicts an island of communal ownership with no private property, universal education, sexual equality and religious toleration *Utopia* is an enigmatic text that is hardly an attempt to create a blueprint for a better society, and yet More implies criticism of contemporaneous society and of humanism itself. More did not live by the ideals espoused in the work. This portrait of a perfect society, taking its inspiration from Platonic and Aristotelian models, became enormously influential in the fields of education and sociology.

1523: *Responsio ad Lutherum*: More's response to Luther's 1520 treatises, in which he defends traditional Catholic teaching regarding the papacy and the sacraments.

1528: *A Dialogue Concerning Heresies*: this work reaffirms the CatholicChurchastheonetrueandapostolicChurch,condemning Luther and the reformers as heretics.

1529: *The Supplication of Souls*: another treatise on orthodoxy in response to the reformist work *Supplication for the Beggars* by Simon Fish.

1531: *Confutation of Tyndale's Answer*: an enormous work writteninresponsetoWilliamTyndale's*AnAnsweruntoSirThomas More'sDialogue[ConcerningHeresies]*.IttakestheformofadialoguebetweenTyndaleandMore,asMoretackleseachofTyndale's points in turn.

1534/5: *A Dialogue of Comfort Against Tribulation* and *De Tristitia Christi* (*The Sadness of Christ*). Apart from his many letters, these were his last works, written whilst imprisoned in the Tower of London.

11

THE ENGLISH ERASMIANS
Thomas Linacre, William Grocyn and Thomas Lupset

Thomas Linacre

The lives of English humanists were intertwined by geography, friendship and intellectual thought. Thomas Linacre (*c.* 1460–1524), William Grocyn (1446–1519), and slightly later, Thomas Lupset (*c.* 1495–1530), were closely linked to each other by their associations with Oxford and its university, London and their travels in Italy.[1] They were also humanist colleagues of Colet and More, as well as being highly influenced, and praised by, the greatest humanist of the age: Erasmus. But most importantly they were, individually and as a group, responsible for the continued progress of Christian humanism in England, bringing their knowledge and experience of Italian humanism to bear in their professional lives: Grocyn was a great linguist and teacher; Linacre brought Italian humanism and educational methods to the forefront of English medical science by his teaching, the foundation of the Royal College of Physicians and the establishment of lectureships in Oxford; and Lupset continued their vision, by facilitating the work of Erasmus and, as Colet's disciple, continuing the cause of the humanist project in England, especially in his *Exhortation to Young Men*. Their lives are portrayed together below, in order to demonstrate their intersecting journeys and their mutual aims.

Thomas Linacre (*c.* 1460–1524)[2]

Thomas Linacre was a classic humanist in the mould of Colet, More, Grocyn and Erasmus and a good friend of them all. Like them, he had close associations with London and Oxford, and travelled extensively throughout Italy, gaining an essential education in his chosen speciality of medicine as well as learning Greek and the humanities in Florence and Rome. He was an accomplished linguist, which enabled him to publish ancient medical texts, and he translated many works of the Greek physician Galen into Latin. He also established the Royal College of Physicians in London, and was its first president, as well as the Royal physician and the founder of lectureships in medicine at both Oxford and Cambridge.

Linacre was possibly born in the diocese of Canterbury, and was educated at the cathedral school there for a time, although nothing is known of his parentage. He was elected a fellow of All Souls' College in 1484.[3] Hence, from the terms of the fellowship, he must have been in Oxford from 1481 (i.e. three years in residence).[4] However, the relevant university register (of congregation 1464–1504) has been lost and so we know nothing of Linacre's humanist studies in Oxford. C.H. Clough has noted that a study of Linacre's intellectual progress in his early years in Italy would give some indication of his achievements in Oxford.[5] Clough also speculates that Linacre's teacher in Oxford might have been the Italian humanist Cornelio Vitelli (*c.* 1450–*c.* 1525).[6] Grocyn was certainly in Oxford with Linacre, as a reader in theology at Magdalen College from 1483–7, and they studied together in Italy.[7]

Linacre left, in 1487, for Italy, as many other humanists did, to further his learning. He probably travelled with William Sellyng (*c.* 1448–94), prior of Christ Church, Canterbury, as well as with other envoys sent to Rome to meet Pope Innocent VIII for the purpose of obtaining a dispensation for the marriage of Henry VII to Elizabeth of

York.[8] Sellyng reached Rome on 8 May 1487, but nothing is mentioned of Linacre's stay there.[9]

Linacre spent two years in Florence, studying Greek with Poliziano (Politian) and Chalcondyles, alongside his Oxford colleague, Grocyn. William Latimer (c. 1467–1545) wrote that Grocyn studied with Poliziano and Chalcondyles for two years and Linacre studied with them 'for the same number of years or even longer' (totidem aut etiam plures annos).[10] From Poliziano, Linacre would have learned rhetoric and Latin poetry, Homer, the Iliad and the Odyssey, and the Historia naturalis of Pliny.[11] He would have been studying under Poliziano at the same time as Giovanni de' Medici (1475–1521), who would later become Pope Leo X. Linacre and Giovanni were friends and the Englishman dedicated a translation of Galen to him in 1521.[12] Much less is known about Linacre's studies with Chalcondyles, but his mastery of Greek can be said to date from this period. Moreover:

> Chalcondyles' interest in the Greek medical corpus may have a significant bearing on the development of Greek studies at Padua, for the university's Greek Renaissance began with his appointment to the first chair in Greek there in 1463.[13]

Linacre was still in Florence by the end of 1489 as the Will of John Morer (dated 16 November 1489) attests.[14]

By November 1490 Linacre was in Rome and admitted to the English Hospice (4 November) and named 'a custos' (Warden) on 3 May 1491, a position he held for a year.[15] The Hospice of Saint Thomas had been a college for English travellers to Rome since its foundation in 1362. Those English humanists who stayed at the Hospice shortly after Linacre included Colet, William Latimer, Richard Pace (c. 1482–1536), Cardinal Pole (1500–1558), and John Fisher.[16]

In 1492 or 1493 Thomas travelled to Padua in order to undertake his medical studies, and although we do not know when and how he attempted to gain a medical degree, several others from All Souls' College had done the same.[17] At Padua, medicine was not taught in a separate faculty of arts (as in Northern European universities), although some arts subjects were taught within the faculty of medicine. He obtained his degree in medicine in the summer of 1496.[18] Although some scholars have considered the label 'humanist' to have been applied too liberally to English scholars at this time 'by an excessive, and sometimes exclusive, reliance on extrinsic rather than intrinsic evidence', and even Linacre has been thought of as 'overrated', yet 'Linacre was probably the only Englishman up to the 1520s to have attained a level of classical erudition which is comparable to his Italian contemporaries'.[19] Furthermore:

> it was an applied erudition, not merely existing for example, in a reputation forged through friendship with Erasmus: he was responsible for new translations of Galen which reached a considerable European audience and which had a major role in the sixteenth-century transformation of European medicine.[20]

Linacre, along with Latimer, was still in the Bursar's Book at All Souls' College in 1495, which lists the charges for rent, meals etc. However, it appears that Linacre was not in Oxford during this year, but retained as a fellow whilst continuing his studies in Padua.[21] In order to obtain a degree in medicine at Padua, Linacre was required, by the university statutes, to study for three years, in contrast to a degree *in artibus*, which required five years' study.[22] Linacre arrived with considerable experience and learning, and may well have been exempt from the foundation studies in logic and natural philosophy. There were four professorships in medicine. The professor of theoretical medicine taught in a three-year cycle: the first book of Avicenna's *Canon medicinae* in year one, Hippocrates' *Aphorisms* with Galen's commentary Hippocrates' *Liber Prognosticorum* in year two and Galen's *Ars Parva* and parts of the fourth book of Avicenna's *Canon* in year three.[23] Practical medicine was also taught on a three-year cycle, mainly on Avicenna's *Canon*. The third professor was to concentrate on the third book of the *Canon*, which covered the 'symptoms, diagnosis and treatment of specific diseases'.[24] The fourth Chair was in anatomy and surgery. As Schmitt plausibly asserts:

> Padua in the 1490s was a mixture of medieval tradition and Renaissance novelty ... Thus Linacre left Padua having supplemented his earlier training in classical languages and literature with what was probably the best medical education the Continent had to offer.[25]

It was here in Northern Italy, especially in Venice, that he began to follow the work of Aldus Manutius (1449/50–1515) and the Νεακαδημία (Neakademia), a 'new academy' of humanists promoting the study of Greek. Linacre's friendship with Aldus is attested by a letter of February 1498, from Aldus to Alberto Pio, Prince of Carpi (1475–1531), in which he cites Linacre as one of those who verified the accuracy of Aldus's *edition princeps* of Aristotle. Also William Latimer confirmed that Linacre was in Venice in a letter to Aldus dated 4 November 1498.[26]

The meetings of the 'Aldine' academy were held in Greek and the group attracted some of the greatest Northern European scholars, including Linacre and Alberto Pio, who recalled, thirty years later, having met Linacre in Aldus's Venetian house.[27] Linacre collected many Greek texts, several of which he used for his later translations of Galen.

Linacre returned to London on 27 August 1499, and became tutor to the young Prince Arthur (1486-1502), to whom he dedicated his first published work, a translation of the *Sphaera* attributed to Proclus.[28] In London, Linacre offered a Latin grammar for Colet's School, which the dean rejected; he taught Thomas More Greek; and became executor of Grocyn's estate. In 1509 he became a physician to the new King, Henry VIII. Five years later he was also made personal physician to Princess Mary and accompanied her to Paris, coming into contact with the French humanist Guillaume Budé (1467–1540) in the process. However, little else is know about his work as a physician.

As he was ordained subdeacon in 1515 and deacon in 1520, and he received several lucrative benefices from his royal service, in Kent, the Isle of Wight, Devon, and Wigan, as well as Prebends in York and Westminster.

Linacre's lasting legacy is the Royal College of Physicians. Concerned about the lack of expertize amongst English physicians, in 1518 Linacre, along with the physicians John Chambre, Ferdinand de Victoria, Nicholas Halswell, John Francis and Robert Yaxley, as well as Cardinal Wolsey no less, petitioned the King for royal support for the foundation of such a college in London.[29] The college was to be a regulatory body, licensing learned physicians working in the London area; an organization that was hitherto lacking in England, although other European countries, such as Italy, had long had a controlling and supervizing college. Linacre was its first president, a position he held until his death in 1524, and he shaped the original statutes, framed 'with regard to their [the college's] own dignity, the good of the people, and in particular honour of the universities'.[30] The initial meetings were held in Linacre's own home, the Stone House in Knight Rider Street.[31] The eighteenth-century historian John Freind encapsulated Linacre's vision:

> His scheme without doubt, was not only to create a good understanding and unanimity among his own Profession, which itself was an excellent thought, but to make them more useful to the publick: and he imagin'd, that by separating them from the vulgar Empiricks, and setting them upon such a reputable foot of distinction, there wou'd always arise a

spirit of emulation among men liberally educated which wou'd animate them in pursuing their inquiries into the Nature of Diseases and Methods of Cure, for the benefit of mankind.[32]

The foundation was an unashamedly humanist one, attempting to build upon the new humanist learning from those physicians, like Linacre himself, who had trained in Italy, and to dispel some of the mistakes and misconceptions in medicine of the previous few decades. As Webster puts it:

Linacre was a characteristic advocate of the civic humanism of the More circle, and his classical learning, cosmopolitan associations, and active involvement in London affairs provided a range of experience which was essential for the success of his plan.[33]

The King granted letters patent for the establishment on 23 September 1518, incorporating the President and College.[34] Their incorporation ranked them alongside the merchant companies, establishing them as 'unum corpus et communitas perpetua sive Collegium perpetuum, having perpetual succession, the right to a common seal and to the possession of lands to the value of £12'.[35] The Charter was ratified by an Act of Parliament in 1523. However, the college was small with only six original fellows, although this number had increased to twelve by the time Linacre died in 1524, and eighteen by 1537.[36] There were eight electores (elects), who were to be doctors of medicine and of English nationality. From this elite group the president and pro-president were elected. The regular membership was limited to twenty and increased to thirty in 1590.[37]

Early evidence concerning the history of the college is scant given that annals were only begun by John Caius (1510–1573) in 1555, the first year of his presidency. Along with Edward Wotton and John Clement, Caius continued the humanist tradition of the college.

A further contribution by Linacre to medicine and learning was his establishment of lectureships in Oxford and Cambridge. Linacre may have been encouraged by the recent establishment of other endowments for lectureships at these universities: Bishop Richard Fox (1448–1528), the founder of Corpus Christi College, Oxford in 1517, provided for three lectureships in Latin, Greek and theology. In 1518 Cardinal Wolsey also declared his intention to fund lecturers at Oxford and Lady Margaret Beaufort (1443–1509) had already established the lectureships in theology at both Oxford and Cambridge in 1502 and the re-foundation of St. John's Hospital as St. John's College was completed after Margaret's death by John Fisher.[38]

From his ecclesiastical livings and property transactions, Linacre was a wealthy man and desired that Oxford should have two lectureships devoted to the work of Galen. The lectures, given over nearly three years, would provide a complete medical history – a reflection of the three-year lecture cycle that Linacre would have received in his studies in Padua. The best source of information regarding Linacre's wishes is his final will, dated 18 October 1524, just two days before he died.[39] With regard to the Cambridge lectureship, Linacre expressly stated that he had bequeathed money to St. John's College:

> to the entent that they ther with schall founde, erecte, and stablische oon substanciall lecture of physick in the seid universite of Cambridge...made and redde by oon graduate persone off the seyd universite of Cambridge being master of arte at the lest...And I will that the tyme of the seyd reyng be not spent in suche questions as Gallyan callyth logycall, but onely twoche suche questions as be litterall soo that he may in II yeeris and a halfe make an ende off the sayd books are at the farthest in III yeris.[40]

There were to be two lecturers in Oxford, a *lectio superior* and a *lectio inferior*. The senior lecturer was to receive an annual stipend of twenty marks.[41] The texts to be taught were largely Linacre's own translations of Galen and the standard medical works from his own Italian education. The senior lecturer was to read:

> a dowble lecture of Galyen and noon other in forme folowyng, that ys to say six books of Galyen De Sanitate Tuenda for his ordynary, and for his afture lecture three books of Galyen De Alimentis, also for his ordynary lecture XIII books of Galyen De Methodo Medendi, and for his after lecture the V first books of Galien De Simplicibus Medicamentis.[42]

The junior lecturer was to receive £6. 13s. 4d. annually:

> And I will that the sayd persone apoyntyd and lymyted to be the other reder of the sayd II lectures, and having the VI li. XIIIs. IIIId. For his labur, schall rede for his ordynary leccion three books of Galyen De Temperamentis, three books of Galien De Naturalibus Potentiis, and six books De Morbis et Simtomatis and the II books De Differentiis Febrium, and for his aftur lecture six books of Galien De Locis Affectis, and these doon, Pronostica Hipocratis with Galiens comment.[43]

Again, Linacre exhorts the lecturer not to deal with such questions as Galen calls 'logical', but only those he terms 'literal'.[44]

Like Colet's St. Paul's School, the future of the lectureships was not given to the university, nor to Linacre's executors, but to the Mercers' Company, an institution that was often at the centre of humanist endeavours in the early modern period. The first occupant of the position of Cambridge lecturer seems to have been a Christopher Jackson,[45] as a brass plaque in the chapel of St. John's College, Cambridge suggests:

> Christophorus Iacsonus, socius huiuscollegii et artium ac medicae lectionis a doctore Linacro institutae professor, e sudore Britannico adhuc iuvenis moritur atque hic sepelitur anno 1528° die 2° Iulii.[46]

At Oxford, however, progress on the implementation of Linacre's will was halted when the Mercers' Company refused to endow the lectureships, although documents relating to the endowment were held with the Mercers' from September 1532.[47] The precise reason for their refusal is not known, although it is plausible that by the 1530s the trading company may not have wished to have been involved with academic affairs, which had become a politically sensitive area during the Reformation.[48] With Thomas More executed and Stokesley dead, the last executor of Linacre's will, Cuthbert Tunstall (1474–1559), Bishop of Durham, negotiated with the Principal of Brasenose College and Warden of All Souls' College to have lecturers appointed, but with two key differences from Linacre's will: the control of the lectureships was no longer to be with the Mercers, and the estates to pay for the stipends were handed to the Colleges.

However, even these plans were abandoned, perhaps unfinished, due to Tunstall's intense diplomatic activity elsewhere. But on 25 September 1542, Tunstall requested that he be given the 'cheste of evidence of doctor Lynackors' which had been kept by the company for eleven years. Tunstall now turned to the Warden of Merton College, John Chambre (Warden from 1525–44), who had been one of the original members of the Royal College of Physicians. Eventually, in 1549, Tunstal agreed with Chambre's successor, Thomas Reynold, to establish the lectureships, now worth £12 and £6 respectively; however the 'double lecture' a day scheme was rejected, in favour of both lecturers reading for one hour and a quarter each day.[49]

One of Tunstall's last acts was to oversee the appointment of the first Linacre Lecturer in Oxford, although Tunstall died just six days before the appointment of George James was formally made, as recorded in the Merton College register records, on 24 November 1559.[50] Thus it was thirty-five years after Linacre's last will that the first lecturer took up office. Although Linacre's wishes had not been carried out exactly as he requested, his wish to improve, if not transform, university medical education had some success for well over a century:

> Between 1560 and 1690 the lectureships, according to the eclectic, widely read, practical, and far from insular standards of English medicine of the day, were a useful institution, held by a variety of able men.[51]

After 1690, however, the lectureships went into decline. At Oxford, 'only a few men of distinction have held the lectureship...There is too much truth in what Henderson says in the history of the college [Merton]: "The happy interior of the Linacre bequest received his money gladly and made no pretence of work" '.[52] Moreover, the Cambridge bequest 'was mismanaged and the stipends were regarded as nothing more than a welcome addition to the income of the fellow, who treated the appointment more or less as a sinecure'.[53]

William Grocyn (*c.* 1449–1519)

Grocyn was born at Colerne in Wiltshire, and grew up in Bristol, in the parish of St. Nicholas.[54] The son of a tenant of Winchester College, William became a scholar there on 26 September 1463, taking the statutory oath on 17 January 1465. Thereafter, he progressed to another educational institution founded by William of Wyckham (1320/24–1404): New College, Oxford, where he was admitted as a scholar on 7 September 1465 and soon after was promoted to a fellowship in 1467, becoming tutor to the future Archbishop of Canterbury, William Warham (*c.* 1450–1532), who also became Grocyn's patron. Granted his M.A. by 1474, he was in employment as a teacher in 1477, when he was paid 40s by Lincoln College (he received his B.Th. much later, in June 1491).

William resigned his fellowship in March 1481 in order to take up the living of Newton Longville, Buckinghamshire. Like many other English humanist clerics, he held many other benefices during his life, including a prebend of South Scarle in Lincolnshire (1485–1514); Rector of Debden, Essex (1492–1493); Rector of Shepperton, Middlesex (from 1504–1513); and Rector of East Peckham, Kent (1511–1517). More significantly, he held the living of St. Lawrence Jewry in the City of London from 1496 to 1517, and was Master of the College of All Saints in Maidstone, Kent from 1506 until his death in 1519.

Though he had resigned from New College, Grocyn remained as divinity reader at Magdalen College in 1483, where, on 25 July, he took part in a theological debate with Master John Taylor that was attended by the college's founder, William Waynflete (c. 1398–1486) and King Richard III (1452–1485), for which he received financial reward. Clearly established as a talented scholar in Oxford and admired by the highest of dignitaries, nevertheless, like many of his intellectual colleagues, Grocyn succumbed to the temptation of travel to Italy. He resigned his readership in 1488 and set out for the Continent, in order to improve his linguistics skills in Greek and Latin (already begun, as he had signed his name in Greek characters in the university letter-book in 1476) and to broaden his humanist education.

Once in Italy, Grocyn studied with Poliziano and Chalcondyles for two years, alongside Linacre in Florence. Here, he also came into contact with humanists Girolamo Aleandro (1480–1542) and Aldus Manutius, as well as Johannes Reuchlin through correspondence. Grocyn wrote a letter to Aldus from London, dated 27 August, in which he thanked Aldus for his generosity to Linacre. This letter became Grocyn's only published work when it was used as a preface to Linacre's translation of Pseudo-Proclus's *De Sphaera in Astronomici Veteres* (Venice, 1499).

Grocyn returned to England in June 1491, where he resided at Exeter College, Oxford until the Trinity Term of 1493. Whilst in Oxford, he gave public lectures on Greek literature. In Oxford Grocyn continued his association with Linacre and Colet, who returned from his Italian travels in 1496 to lecture on St. Paul's letter to the Romans and write on the works of Pseudo-Dionysius, a writer whom Grocyn also studied. Thus Erasmus encountered a closely-knit group of active humanists on his first visit to England in 1499, and the learning of Grocyn, Colet and More astounded him.

Grocyn gave a series of lectures on the Celestial Hierarchy of Pseudo-Dionysius at St. Paul's Cathedral in 1501. By this time he was settled in London and, in 1506, Erasmus stayed with him on one of his visits. Grocyn introduced Erasmus to William Warham, and Erasmus dedicated his translation of Euripides' *Hecuba* to Warham. When Erasmus was appointed to Cambridge in 1511, he had Grocyn's copy of St. Basil on Isaiah with him.

Although Grocyn was highly praised by Erasmus, as were many other humanists, he was allegedly very modest and he wrote, or at least published, very little, which may have been due to his very bad eyesight and a terrible paralyzing disability in his later years. He ended his days in Maidstone, as Master of All Saints College and, having suffered a stroke in 1518, he died there in 1519, in the same year as John Colet's death.

Grocyn's legacy lay in his considerable aptitude for and his lectures on linguistics, as well as his collection of books and manuscripts.

He owned works such as Petrarch's *Rerum memorandarum libri*, as well as Lorenzo Valla's annotations on the New Testament and the Psalms and his *Elegantiae*. He also owned works by Francesco Filelfo (1398–1481), Ermolao Barbaro (1453/4–1493), Ficino and several other Italian humanists. As well as humanist works, he owned many writings by patristic, classical Greek and Latin and Neoplatonic authors.

Thomas Lupset (*c.* 1495–1530)

By the time Thomas Luspet was born, Grocyn and Linacre had already studied with Poliziano and Chalcondyles in Italy and returned to Oxford to help establish humanism in England. Lupset belongs, therefore, to the next generation of English humanists. Just as Boccaccio, Salutati and Bruni promoted Petrarchan ideas in Italy, so Lupset, disciple of the first-generation humanists Colet, More, Linacre and Grocyn, paved the way for later English humanists, such as Thomas Elyot (1490–1546) and John Cheke (1514–1557), who advanced humanist techniques and philosophy into the Elizabethan era.

Thomas Lupset was born in the City of London to Thomas Lupset, senior, and Alice, probably in St. Mildred's Parish. His father was a member of the Goldsmith's Company. Even at the young age of thirteen (in 1508), when he became a member of Colet's household and the dean's protégé, Lupset was in receipt of his first living: St. Margaret's Church, Hilborough in Norfolk. Being Colet's pupil also meant that Lupset gained the supervision of William Lily in Latin and Greek.

Lupset was in Cambridge by 1513, probably at Pembroke College, and assisted Erasmus in editing his New Testament. Little is known about the next three years of his life, but by 1516 Lupset was back in London, again in contact with Erasmus, particularly over some concerns about the authorship of a work entitled *Julius Exclusus*, thought to be by Erasmus and in Lupset's possession. Lupset possessed several other manuscripts by Erasmus, which he gave to Thomas More, an acquaintance by this time.

In early 1517 Lupset travelled to Paris to supervize, with Budé, the publication of Linacre's translation of Galen's *De Sanitate Tuenda*, before overseeing the publication of More's *Utopia*. Erasmus communicated to Lupset that he wanted a copy of Lincare's *De Sanitate*. On a visit to Louvain, Lupset became engaged in Edward Lee's attack on Erasmus's New Testament, a work that Lupset defended.[55]

Although Lupset travelled like Linacre he never shared his interest in medicine, preferring 'the fields of education, classical scholarship, moral philosophy, and patristic theology'.[56] Lupset returned to England in 1519, shortly before Colet's death. Colet left many books to Lupset in his Will and Erasmus turned to Lupset for information about Colet's life in order to write his short biography of the dean in his letter to Justus Jonas in 1521. In 1520 Lupset took up the post of lecturer in rhetoric and humanity at Corpus Christi College, Oxford, as Wolsey's appointee. Among his students was the translator Gentian Hervet. Lupset did not stay in the post for long, being succeeded by the Spanish humanist, Juan Luis Vives.

Lupset received his M.A. on 9 July 1521 and, on 31 January 1522, a royal grant of a pension from the Abbot of St. Mary's, York, as well as the living of Ashton, Derbyshire a little later. He left for Padua in Italy soon afterwards, probably with Thomas Starkey (c. 1495–1538). There Lupset met Reginald Pole (1500–1558), and both received tuition from Niccolò Leonico Tomeo (d. 1497), whose *Dialogi* Lupset helped prepare for publication in 1524. By 1525 Lupset was in Venice, keeping in touch with Leonico over the impending battle of Pavia, and here he renewed his acquaintance with Richard Pace, ambassador to Venice and later Dean of St. Paul's Cathedral. Lupset had known Pace from around 1517 or 1518 when Lupset wrote to him from Paris.[57] In fact, Pace's diplomatic missions of the 1520s, and his renewed intimacy with Leonico, were 'underscored on the one hand by the arrival in Padua of Leonico's new English students Pole and Lupset, and on the other by Leonico's revived contact with Tunstall and Latimer in England'.[58]

Later in 1525, Lupset introduced Pole to Erasmus in a letter dated 23 August 1525. Lupset was one of four English humanists to prepare the Aldine edition of Galen for publication, which appeared in five volumes in the same year (1525).

After a brief visit to Paris in 1526, Lupset returned to Padua and then back to England in the company of Pole, where Wolsey made Thomas tutor to his illegitimate son Thomas Winter. Lupset travelled to Paris with Winter in February 1528, before Wolsey recalled him to England in 1529.

In 1529, whilst residing with Thomas Wolsey, Lupset wrote his *Exhortacion to Young Men*, which has been described as 'one of the most polished pieces of English prose written to this time.'[59] The work, which was first printed in August 1529, is addressed to an Edmund Withypoll, one of Lupset's ex-pupils, who was son of a London alderman. Lupset exhorts the young student to prioritize his life: first, his soul; his body next; and material wealth and pleasures thereafter. It also offers suggested reading for the serious-minded scholar. This list is a classic Christian humanist curriculum: the New Testament, read according to the interpretation of the Church fathers Chrysostom and Jerome; Aristotle's Ethics; Plato, Cicero and Seneca; Erasmus's Enchiridion; Galen, and Aristotle's Politics.

Around this time Lupset also wrote *A Treatise on Charitie*, published in 1533 and written for a nun. In this work, Lupset equates charity with all of Christianity, along with the Stoic notion that the goal of charity was a stillness of the mind.[60] Thus, Lupset disliked (as did Thomas More) Tyndale's translation of the Greek '*charitas*' as 'love'.

Lupset also inspired works of literature by other scholars, such as Starkey's *Dialogue between Pole and Lupset*, in which Lupset is portrayed as attempting to persuade Pole to undertake civic duties for the commonwealth in the service of the king, a position adopted by Thomas More after the composition of his *Utopia*. Moreover, in Lupset's *A Compendious Treatise of...Dieyng Well*, finished in 1530 and directed towards Pole's servant, John Walker, he expresses his admiration and high expectation of Pole within the realms of public service. Nevertheless Lupset exhibited a traditional tension between the active and the contemplative, between Christian and Roman republican notions of virtue. His admiration for Pole's active role in public service was in contrast to his thesis that 'a good death required contempt of this life'.[61] Evidence for the validity of this idea, Lupset argued, could be found in both classical and Christian tradition, for instance the death of Canius at the hands of the Emperor Caligula and the Christian martyrs.

Unlike Thomas More, Lupset was able to separate his ideal of royal service from that of royal policy itself and, as such, persuaded Pole to support the king's divorce, acting as a messenger between Pole and the king himself on the matter. For this, he received his reward: Lupset was given 100 crowns in April 1530 and another £10 in May.[62] In addition to the many benefices he had already accrued, Thomas was given the rectory of Cheriton, Hampshire, on 1 August 1530, and a canonry at Salisbury Cathedral along with the prebend of Ruscombe Southbury, almost certainly from royal patronage. However, at the same time, Lupset was also writing a work, no longer extant, critical of the king, which was burnt in 1538.

Lupset returned to England in 1530, dying of tuberculosis in his mother's house on 27 December of that year. The inscription on his tomb in St. Alfege Cripplegate read: 'Here lies Thomas Lupset, a man most learned in Greek and Latin, as well as in theology', an effigy that any Christian humanist would have been proud to have.[63] His death grieved the king greatly, and his works were first published in a collected edition in 1546 and again in 1560.

Linacre: Dates and Events

c. 1460:	born, possibly near Canterbury.
1481:	studies at Oxford.
1484:	Fellow of All Souls' College, Oxford.
c. April 1487:	leaves for Italy with William Sellyng with envoys to Pope Innocent VIII.
1489–90:	Linacre and Grocyn have two years study in Florence.
4 November 1490:	Linacre admitted to English Hospital in Rome.
3 May 1491:	named *a custos* of the English Hospital.
c. 1492:	leaves for Venetian Republic.
1496:	receives degree in medicine from Padua.
November 1498:	in Venice.
1499:	returns to London; tutor to Prince Arthur (1486–1502).
15 October 1499:	publishes translation of pseudo-Proclus, *De Sphaera*.
5 November 1499:	Linacre, Colet and Grocyn acquainted with Erasmus.
c. 1500:	Linacre studies Greek with More, and possibly Grocyn, in London.
1503:	witness to Reginald Bray's Will, Lord High Treasurer.
1509:	appointed a physician to King Henry VIII.
14 December 1509:	Prebendary of Wells.
c. 1510:	delivers 'Shaglyng' lecture at Oxford.
1511:	admitted to living of Hawkshurst, Kent.
Pre 13 Sept. 1511:	composes Latin Grammar for St. Paul's School: rejected by Colet.
1514:	Linacre in service of Mary of France (1496–1533). September travels to Paris and meets Guillaume Budé.
c. 1515:	Linacre publishes *Progymnasmata Grammatices Vulgaria*.
22 December 1515:	ordained subdeacon.
23 September 1518:	Linacre's Foundation of Royal College of Physicians.
June 1519:	publication of *Methodus Medendi*.
1520:	Linacre executor of Grocyn's Will and catalogues Grocyn's books.
7 April 1520:	Linacre Ordained Deacon.
1521:	publishes *De Temperamentis* and *De Inaequali Intemperie*.

1522:	publishes *De Pulsuum Usu*; preface to Galen, *De Motu Musculorum*.
1523:	Linacre publishes *Rudimenta Grammatices*. Charter of College of Physicians ratified by Act of Parliament; publishes translation of *De Naturalibus Facultatibus*; tutor to future Queen Mary I (aged 7).
14 June 1524:	Linacre agrees to lecture on physic in Cambridge.
19 June 1524:	Linacre's Will.
12 October 1524:	royal consent for Mercers' Co. to pass Linacre's estate into mortmain, for foundation of lectureships Oxford and Cambridge.
20 October 1524:	Linacre dies.
1524:	publication of *De Symptomatum Differentiis* and *De Symptomatum Causis*.
December 1524:	publication of *De Emendata Structura Latani Sermonis*.
1526:	publication of Linacre's translation of Paulus Aegineta, *De Victus Ratione Quolibet Anni Tempore Utili*.
1528:	appointment of Linacre Lecturer in Cambridge (Christopher Jackson).
December 1528:	publication of Linacre's translation of Paulus Aeginata, *De Diebus Criticis*.
24 November 1559:	first Linacre Lecturer appointed in Oxford (George James).

Grocyn: Dates and Events

c. **1449:**	born in Colerne, Wilshire.
26 September 1463:	scholar at Winchester College.
17 January 1465:	takes statutory oath at Winchester.
7 September 1465:	scholar at New College, Oxford.
1467:	elected fellow at New College.
1474:	M.A. at Oxford; signs Oxford letter-book in Greek characters.
1477:	paid 40*s*. by Lincoln College, Oxford.
19 February 1481:	receives living at Newton Longville.
March 1481:	resigns his Fellowship at New College.
1483:	achieves Divinity readership at Magdalen College, Oxford.
25 July 1483:	public theological debate with John Taylor.
1488:	Grocyn leaves for Italy.

1491: admitted B.Th. at Oxford.

1491–1493: at Exeter College, Greek lectures in Oxford.

26 December 1496: enters living of St. Lawrence Jewry.

October 1491: Grovyn's letter to Aldus published in Linacre's *De Sphaera* translation.

1501: lectures on Pseudo-Dionysius at St. Paul's.

17 April 1506: Grocyn admitted to Mastership of All Saints College, Maidstone, Kent.

1504: Erasmus names Grocyn sole guide of his life in the absence of Colet.

1506: Erasmus stays with Grocyn in London; Master of All Saints College, Maidstone.

1518: suffers a stroke.

1519: Grocyn dies in Maidstone.

Lupset: Dates and Events

c. 1495: born in London.

1508: Lupset joins Colet's household becoming his protégé.

1513: Lupset at Pembroke College, Cambridge for three years.

1516: in London.

1517: in Paris. Supervising publication of Linacre's translation of Galen's *De Sanitate*.

1519: books left to Lupset by Colet in his Will.

1520: Lupset lecturer in rhetoric at Oxford.

9 July 1521: M.A. at Oxford.

31 January 1522: receives a pension for York, St. Mary's.

1522: in Padua.

1525: in Venice. Introduces Pole to Erasmus.

February 1528: Lupset in Paris with pupil Winter.

1529: recalled to England by Wolsey.

August 1529: Lupset publishes *Exhortacion to Yonge Men*.

1530: finishes *Diyng Well* and supports the king's divorce.

1530: Lupset dies.

1533: Lupset's *Treatise on Charitie* published.

Key Works by Linacre, Grocyn and Lupset[64]

Linacre

1499: Linacre's first publication was part of a series of astronomical texts published by Aldus Manutius in Venice. Linacre translated *De Sphaera*, ascribed to Proclus (410-85): *Iulii Firmici Astronomicorum libri octo integri, et emendati, ex Scythicis oris ad nos nuper allati... (Venetiis cura, et diligentia Aldi Ro. Mense octob. MID)*. This work was immediately popular and reprinted in various countries.

1511–24: Linacre also published three works on Latin Grammar: *Progymnasmata Grammatices Vulgaria* (London, *c.* 1515). This work was possibly submitted as an elementary grammar for Colet's St. Paul's School, but Erasmus's letter to Colet of 13 September 1511 seems to suggest that it was rejected.[65] Also *Rudimenta Grammatices* (London, 1523) and *De Emendata Structura Latini sermonis* (London, Dec. 1524).

1517–24: Linacre's great contribution to literature was his translation of Galen's work from Greek to Latin. He translated these works:

De Sanitate Tuenda (Paris, 1517): dedicated to Henry VIII. *Methodus Medendi* (Paris, 1519): dedicated to Henry VIII.
De Temperamentis et de Inaequali Intemperie (Cambridge, 1521): dedicated to Pope Leo X.
De Naturalibus Facultatibus (London, 1523): dedicated to William Warham, Archbishop of Canterbury.
De Symptomatum Differentiis et Causis (London, 1524).
De pulsuum Usu (London, 1523/4): dedicated to Cardinal Wolsey.

1526–9: Linacre's other works included translations of Paul of Aegina, *De Victus Ratione* (Cologne, 1526); Paul of Aegina, *De Crisi* and *De Diebus Criticis* (Paris, 1529).

Grocyn

1499: His only published work is his epistle to Aldus commending him for his care of Linacre, published in the preface to Linacre's translation of Pseudo-Proclus's *De Sphaera* in *Astronomici Veteres* (Venice, October, 1499).

Lupset

1529: *Exhortacion to Young Men*, called 'one of the most polished pieces of English prose written to this time'.[66] First printed in 1529 and addressed to an Edmund Withypoll.

Lupset exhorts the young student to prioritize his life: soul, body and wealth and pleasures thereafter. It also offers suggested reading for the serious-minded scholar.

1533: *A Treatise on Charitie*, written for a nun. Lupset equates charity with all of Christianity, along with the Stoic notion that the goal of charity was a stillness of the mind.[67] Thus, Lupset disliked (as did Thomas More) Tyndale's translation of the Greek *'charitas'* as 'love'.

1529–31: Lupset inspired Starkey's *Dialgue between Pole and Lupset*, in which Lupset is portrayed as attempting to persuade Pole to undertake civic service for the commonwealth in the service of the king, a position adopted by Thomas More after the composition of his *Utopia*.

1530: *A Compendious Treatise of…Dieyng Well*, finished in 1530, expresses Lupset's high regard and expectation of Reginald Pole within the realms of public service.

FRANCE

12

JACQUES LEFÈVRE D'ÉTAPLES
(*c.* 1460–1536)
The Great French Humanist

Jacques Lefèvre, also known by his Latin name Faber Stapulensis, was a priest, theologian, exegete, dogmatician and moralist who was at the forefront of French humanism on the eve of the European Reformation. Through his work on philosophy, spirituality, patristics and scripture he pointed to a middle way between the fanaticism of Germanic evangelical reformers and the rigidity of conservative Roman Catholics. His insistence upon '*ad fontes*' and his biblical translations, prefaces and commentaries had a dramatic effect upon his contemporaries, creating a school of disciples wherever he went, be it Paris, Meaux or Strasbourg. The assimilation of his work into the European consciousness was enabled by the publication of his works from the early sixteenth century by the first Parisian printers.

His, sometimes controversial, Christocentric theology attracted criticism from the Paris Theology Faculty as well as Erasmus. However, there is no doubt that his translation of the Bible into French and his commentaries on the Psalms were a contributory factor in the development within late-medieval thought that would lead to calls for religious reform.

This chapter offers an outline of Lefèvre's life and work, but also focuses on one particularly controversial battle he fought, concerning the identity of the three characters called Mary in the Gospels. His scriptural interpretation earned him condemnation in Paris and resulted in his exile.

Life

Lefèvre was born in Étaples in Picardy. He was educated at the Collège du Cardinal-Lemoine in Paris becoming a professor there himself. Like his English humanist contemporary, John Colet, he travelled to Italy in 1492. There he met Barbaro, Ficino and Pico della Mirandola:

> In the years that followed, his scholarly production moved across the philosophical spectrum of Aristotelianism and Platonism where Pico had aspired to forge a harmony that more critical minds would deem impossible.[1]

Lefève's *De Magica Naturali* (*On Natural Magic*) of the early 1490s, is dedicated to his patron Germain de Gauay (d. 1520), at that time a canon of Notre Dame in Paris and a correspondent of Ficino: the first book is based upon Ficino's *De Vita* (*Three Books of Life*), as well as his *Theologia Platonica* (*Platonic Theology*) and *De Amore* (*On Love*).[2]

Lefèvre returned to France a confirmed Aristotelian, annotating his entire works and embracing the ideas of the Neoplatonists Pseudo-Dionysius, Richard of St. Victor, Ramon Lull, Ruysbroeck and Hildegard of Bingen. He became a brilliant and renowned teacher and was extolled for his restoration of genuine Aristotelian works and ideas in the faculty of arts. In Paris he produced his preface to Ramon Lull's *Contemplations*. Editing and translating became characteristic of his quiet scholarly endeavours, culminating in his three volumes of the works of Nicholas of Cusa (1401–1464) in 1514. However, Lefèvre gradually withdrew from philosophical concerns to biblical ones, becoming, in turn, a commentator, translator and preacher on the Holy Scriptures.[3]

In 1509 Lefèvre was called by Guillaume Briçonnet (c. 1472–1534) to the Abbey of St. Germain-des-Prés in Paris. Here he composed his five Latin versions of the Psalter, the *Quincuplex Psalterium*, which was used by both Luther and Zwingli.[4] The *Quincuplex* was re-published by Henri Estienne in 1513. In 1512, Lefèvre published his commentary on the Pauline Epistles, the second edition of which included a response to Erasmus's criticisms of Lefèvre in the *Annotationes* to his 1516 *Novum Instrumentum*.[5] The conflict, which we shall consider shortly, concerned Hebrews 2:7. Soon after this, Lefèvre left St. Germain to travel, once again at the invitation of Briçonnet, to Meaux.[6]

In Meaux, Lefèvre became Briçonnet's Episcopal vicar and wrote his commentary on the four gospels. Characteristically, Lefèvre soon established a band of followers who have been described as a 'laboratory of preaching'.[7] They included François Vatable (a notable Hebraist), Gerárd Rousell, Michel d'Arande and Guillaume Farel (1489–1565), who was born in the same region as Lefèvre (Étaples). Here, too, Lefèvre began his translation of the Bible into French. By 1523, he had acquired the new disciples Sauvie and Pauvan, but Lefèvre was under attack from the Paris Theology Faculty. Despite Briçonnet's edict which banned priests from possessing Luther's works, there is evidence that Lefèvre was not wholly opposed to Luther's theology. In two letters from Lefèvre to Guillaume Farel (now in Basel), Lefèvre expressed his admiration for 'that which comes from Germany'.[8]

Until this point Lefèvre had been protected by King Francis I, but with the King's imprisonment after his defeat at the battle of Pavia on 24 February 1525, Lefèvre left for Strasbourg where, in October 1525 he wrote his commentary on the 'Catholic Epistles', published in 1527. The character of Martin Bucer, who had arrived there in May 1523, having left his Dominican order and married, dominated Strasbourg at this time. But Lefèvre's circle of disciples and colleagues included Matthias Zell (b. 1477), Wolfgang Capito (from Basel), François Lambert of Avignon and Caspar Hedio. He continued translating the (Vulgate) Bible into French, which was eventually published in Antwerp in 1530. This important work inspired other translations, such as that by Pierre Olivetan and those undertaken at Louvain. With Francis I released from prison, Lefèvre was called back to France, in April 1526, to Nérac. Lefèvre was enthusiastic about the exegetical school of thinkers in Strasbourg but failed to translate that enthusiasm into reform in France. In Nérac he became tutor to King Francis I's children and the Royal Librarian, and was still in post by May 1530.[9] This was, in effect, his retirement from controversy and public life. He stayed in Nérac until his death in 1536, effectively silent on Church reform.

The Christian Humanist

Lefèvre's theology encompassed the apostolic fathers, Pseudo-Dionysius, the Christian Cabala, mysticism, Nicholas of Cusa, and the 'Catholic concordance'. There is evidence, in the 1524/5 letters to Farel, that he admired Oecolampadius and Zwingli, and he mentions positively the work of Melanchthon. But, ultimately, there is no evidence that he desired a break with Rome.

Scholarship has generally been divided into two camps regarding Lefèvre: those who have regarded him as the principal French Catholic humanist, and those who have considered him to be a proto-reformer. These two categories of opinion divided chronologically in the same way: nineteenth-century and early twentieth-century scholars tending towards the proto-Protestant theory, and later revisionist ideas reclaiming Lefèvre for the conservative Catholic camp.[10]

Lefèvre's 'prefaces' to scripture were essentially Christocentric, a humanist characteristic: the *Quincuplex* (1509) hermeneutic was based upon a combination of a literal and spiritual interpretation to create a 'true sense' of scripture. Lefèvre wrote: 'we call literal the sense that agrees with Spirit and that the Holy Spirit reveals to us'.[11] Thus he rejected the traditional medieval four-fold interpretation of scripture (literal, allegorical, anagogical and tropolgical):

> Thus the literal sense and the spiritual sense coincide [so that the true sense is] not that which is called allegorical or tropological, but that which the Holy Spirit certifies speaking through the prophets.[12]

Lefèvre has a claim to originality regarding his biblical hermeneutic of the literal and spiritual interpretations combined, because it creates a strictly Christological view of scripture as a whole. In his 1524 preface to the Latin Psalter he wrote: 'Christ is the Spirit of the entire scripture. And scripture without Christ is only writing and the letter that kills'.[13] Unfortunately, as we shall see, this also produced the side-effect of a narrow interpretation which led to the controversy with Erasmus.

Lefèvre enjoyed the techniques of the Christian Cabala, which combined philology and theology.[14] He desired the unity, or concord, of the scriptures, noting that 'it is the accord, the concord of Scriptures, with which we are concerned, which guides us'.[15] However, Lefèvre found himself at odds with Erasmus over scriptural interpretation. One example of their conflict arose over the interpretation of Hebrews 2:7 ('You have made them for a little while lower than the angels; You have crowned them with glory and honour' (NRSV)) which serves to show their differences. Lefèvre was more concerned with defending his

Christological vision than with being a thorough exegete in the mould of Erasmus. Citing Psalm 8:6 ('You have given them dominion over the works of your hands; you have put all things under their feet' (NRSV)), Lefèvre preferred 'You have made him a little less than a God' (*minuisti eum paulominus a Deo*) to 'You have placed him below the level of the angels' (*minuisti... ab angelis*), because his Christological interpretation of the scriptures would not allow him to place Christ below an angel. Erasmus criticized Lefèvre for this in 1516 and Lefèvre retaliated by charging Erasmus with impiety. The consequence of this was an assertion of Erasmus's intellectual and theological superiority in his *Apologia ad Fabrum Stapulensem* of 1517. Erasmus, deeply hurt by the accusation of heresy, lashed out at Lefèvre's weaknesses: his naivety, his relatively poor Greek (in comparison to Erasmus), the gaps in his patristic interpretation and knowledge, and his alleged monophysitism. Erasmus explained that Christ was below the angels in the sense that his humiliation and abasement on the cross and his death brought salvation.[16]

The themes of Justification, Faith and Works were present in Lefèvre's thought by the time of his 1512 Commentary on Paul, long before Luther expounded upon the same ideas. Lefèvre held that there were two justifications: in 1512, commenting on Romans 3:19–20, he wrote that the just work of the law was favoured by philosophy; but that justification from faith, which was grace, was favoured by the Gospel. Likewise in 1522, commenting on John 1:29, he distinguished two justifications, as distinct from one another as heat is from light.

However, Lefèvre's thought was not the precursor of Luther's ideas. For Lefèvre, works were necessary for the preparation, retention and augmentation of justification; whereas Luther clearly saw and embraced the consequences of the doctrine, realizing that they made many religious practices untenable. Thus, in a letter to Spalatin of 19 October 1516, Luther wrote:

Even Stapulensis, a man otherwise spiritual and most sound – God knows – lacks spiritual understanding in the interpretation of divine scripture; yet he definitely shows so much of it in the conduct of his own life and the encouragement of others.[17]

From Romans 3:28 we learn that without works we lose the grace of justification. But from James 2:18, we hear that works outside of faith are not good. Lefèvre's hermeneutic found both of these justifications in the New Testament. Faith and works are, as it were, symbiotic. In the end it is neither faith nor works that are crucial, only God (Romans 4:2).[18]

Regarding the sacraments, Lefèvre called baptism the *Lavacrum Regeneratis* (the bath of regeneration). It brought pardon of sins and adoption into the family of Christ (2 Corinthians 5:18). Thus the Church was the 'communion of the regenerate' who had undergone a second birth (Psalm 132). A baptism with triple immersion was preferable as it symbolized the Trinity, Christ's three days in the tomb and the three-fold purification, justification and sanctification espoused in Romans 6:4, Matthew 3:16–17 and in the later works of the Pseudo-Dionysius.

The Eucharist, for Lefèvre, was *viaticum vitae aeternae* (provision for eternal life, Psalm 4:8). It was a 'memorial of redemption' (Psalm 110) and *memoria et recordation* (a memorial and remembrance, Hebrews 5). Lefèvre also described it as a 'new sacrifice' (Psalm 49:15, similar to Zwingli's 'commemorative sacramental theology').[19] Lefèvre believed that confession, penitence and absolution were made to God in faith (James 5:16). Nevertheless, Lefèvre laid a heavy stress upon the role of purgatory, as in Matthew 5:22–3, 18:23 and Luke 16: 19–31. Divine unction for the dying was accepted by Lefèvre (James 5:15), but not by Luther. Moreover, in 1525, Lefèvre stressed that the faith of the one praying over the dying person was more important than the anointing with oil. Lefèvre called for reforms in the sacrament of unction, claiming that the presence of oil was unnecessary. This was rejected by the Council of Trent in 1547.[20]

Lefèvre's homilies, published as *Epitres et Evangiles pour lec Cinquante et Deux Semaines de l'an* and printed by Simon du Bois in Paris in 1525/6, are some of his best writings. One homily, entitled 'Exhortation', is one of the finest texts of its time. He spoke of the search for the 'secrets of God' and the need for a spiritual intelligence, with a rejection of human interpretations of scripture. The door to scripture was the word of God itself: 'to each Christian full authority and irrevocable power is given to judge all human decrees and statutes, to determine of they conform to the Word of God or not'.[21]

The Christian Church, Lefèvre argued, is composed of saints of the elect who proclaim the secrets of the word, which is Christ in the flesh, the redeemer. As such, we are sanctified by the imitation of Christ, not only in his life, but also by the imitation of his death in that we deny sin within ourselves.[22] Thus Lefèvre's idea of conformity to Christ, or 'Christoformity' (Galatians 4:19) echoed that of Pseudo-Dionysius, Nicholas of Cusa and John Colet in England. Mortification, Lefèvre argued, aided interior Christoformity (Collosians 3:12): 'Let us go then to Jesus Christ in complete confidence', he wrote from Meaux on 6 November 1523, 'He must be our thought, our speech, our life and salvation, and our all'.[23]

The Three Marys Controversy

Until very recently it had been forty years since the last serious scholarly work on the controversy surrounding Lefèvre d'Étaples' biblical exegesis, in particular his views on Mary Magdalen. Much scholarship about Lefèvre has been published in the meantime, not least a new edition of Lefèvre's own treatise on the subject with an extensive introduction to the debate.[24]

The controversy over Mary Magdalen ran from November 1517 until the Spring of 1520, directly coinciding with Luther's first confrontation with Rome. The debate went to the heart of pre-Reformation religious controversy, focussing on scripture and its authority in the light of Patristic tradition, as well as on Church practise and the status of popular, if ill-founded, beliefs. Lefèvre's works can roughly be put into three categories: his editions of Aristotle; his editions of medieval and mystical texts; and his biblical works. His work on Mary Magdalen, however, requires its own category as a statement of opinion and this category itself can be subdivided into three parts: his work on the three Marys, not one Mary Magdalen; his work on St. Anne and the popular belief that Jesus's Mother, Mary, had two sisters, their mother, Anne, having married three times; and his work on the belief that these three Marys were the three Marys of the Gospels. The third part is his treatise on the *triduum*, or the three days and nights of Christ's entombment ending in his resurrection.[25]

The first edition of Lefèvre's *De Maria Magdalena* was published in 1517. There were some stirrings of anger concerning this work, but no published attack. The second edition of Lefèvre's treatise came in 1518 and included a preface by Josse Clichtove (1472–1543). The work contained Lefèvre's ideas on St. Anne, the *trinubium* on the three marriages of Anne and his pamphlet on Christ's three days in the tomb, *De Triduo*. This second, expanded, edition provoked a published response in the form of Marc de Grandval's *Apologia* in September 1518. Lefèvre's final word was his *Disceptatio Secunda* of 1519. The publication of John Fisher's rebuttal of Lefèvre, his *Libri Tres* (three books), marked the end of the first phase of the controversy.[26]

The second phase saw a number of other scholars taking part in the attack on Lefèvre, including Thierry Martens, a humanist of Louvain, who in 1519 published his *Eversio Munitionis* (Overturning the Bulwark) against Clichtove and followed this with his *Confutatio* on 3 September 1519 aimed against Lefèvre's *Disceptatio*. Noel Beda's (1470–1537) own contribution, *Apologia pro Filiabus*, marked the end of the second phase, whilst the denunciation of the idea of three Marys by the Faculty of Theology saw the end of the third phase. By this time Grandval was dead, Lefèvre had acceded to the urging of Bishop Briçonnet to go to Meaux, in order to help in a project of diocesan reform, and Clichtove had repented to the Faculty in Paris and changed his mind to save his skin.

According to Cameron, there were three attacks on Lefèvre's orthodoxy and his biblical work: an attack on his handling of the vulgate; one on his suggestion that there were three characters called Mary in the gospels that had subsequently been amalgamated into Mary Magdalen in Christian tradition; and, later, accusations of Lutheranism made by the faculty of Theology and Beda.[27] Up until 1514, Cameron argued in 1969, Lefèvre had lived a relatively placid and uneventful career as a writer and teacher: his 1509 *Quincuplex Psalterium* was used by both Cardinal Ximenes at Alcala and Luther in Wittenburg, as was his 1512 translation of St. Paul's epistles. The argument that it was the German Cabalist Johannes Reuchlin's invitation to Lefèvre, in 1514, asking for support against his Dominican attackers, which precipitated Lefèvre's troubles is a plausible one, given that Reuchlin was himself under investigation for his work *Letters of Obscure Men*, and that therefore Lefèvre's teaching would naturally be scrutinized as potentially suspect.[28]

Lefèvre's first treatise to argue that the Mary Magdalen of tradition was, in fact, an amalgam of three separate scriptural figures was his *De Maria Magdalena* of 1517 – followed by the second treatise *De Tribus et Unica ... Disceptatio* that appeared in 1518.[29] Lefèvre's arguments drew on Origen and other early Greek Fathers. The three Marys in question are the prostitute mentioned in Luke 7: 36–50; Mary Magdalen, from whom seven devils are cast out in Luke 8:2 and John 22:11–18; and Martha and Lazarus's sister of John 11: 19, John 12: 1–8 and Luke 10: 38–42.[30] Lefèvre was writing in order to answer a question posed by his friend François de Rochefort who, in his attempt to write a life of Mary Magdalen, had become uneasy about the conflicting biblical texts. The publication of the second edition of Lefèvre's *Disceptatio* in 1518, with the foreword by Clichtove and the attack on the legend of St. Anne, the mother of the Virgin Mary, provoked almost immediate retaliation.[31]

By the late-medieval period, the above verses of scripture were popularly believed to refer to a single woman, Mary Magdalen. She had become widely venerated as a saint partly as a consequence of the preaching of Anselm (1033–1109), and in France through the writings of Olivier Maillard in the fifteenth century and Michel Menot in the sixteenth.[32] The homiletic theme was usually that of a repentant sinner who is converted by the love of Christ. Various churches were dedicated to the Magdalen, including Vézelay and La Sainte-Baume.[33]

Lefèvre begins his thesis thus:

> You asked me, most celebrated Francois, what I thought
> about whether Mary Magdalen was one woman or several
> women ... in my opinion three women were usually celebrated
> under the name of Mary Magdalen, and that the attributes
> which belonged to each one individually were usually given
> to all three.[34]

The first attack upon Lefèvre's ideas came from Marc de Grandval, an
Augustinian Canon of St. Victor, in his 1518 treatise.[35] In *Ecclesiae
Catholicae no tres Magdalenas*, Grandval declared himself outraged at
Lefèvre's presumption:

> Even though Lefèvre cites Ambrose, Origen, Chrysostom and
> Jerome, those who hold to this opinion shall hardly escape
> the suspicion of heresy. Now it remains to praise a reunited
> Magdalen and to the praise the glory of Christ's life in the
> hymn which follows: *Lauda Mater Ecclesia* ...[36]

It is interesting that much of the ensuing debate was left to Lefèvre's
disciple Josse Clichtove, who made the official repost to Grandval's
conservative theology in his preface to the second edition of the
Disceptatio, which emphasized Lefèvre's theological coherence.
Clichtove wrote:

> [Grandval states that] 'the Church admits one [Magdalen], not
> three.' But did the Church not exist in the time of Irenaeus,
> Origen, Eusebius, Chrysostom, Jerome, Ambrose? Yet at
> that time the Church admitted several. Is it now another
> Church?[37]

Clichtove even suggested that a true understanding of the three Marys
would increase popular piety, not undermine it.[38] Grandval took his
argument further in his subsequent treatise, entitled 'Shield and Anchor
of the Apology or Defense of the Catholic Church's custom of paying
reverence to a single, not three, Mary Magdalenes'.[39] In Lefèvre's treatise, *Disceptatio Secunda*, which again focussed on '*ad fontes*' biblical
exegesis for his argument of refuting tradition and myth,[40] Lefèvre's
method was outlined clearly:

> This is the method of inquiry: to draw conclusions from no
> other source than the gospel. If any other elements are intro-
> duced, I will not draw the principal arguments from them.
> And I will proceed in the manner of dialecticians: by setting

down certain propositions which I will attempt to prove from the light of the gospel alone, aided by the laws of reason.[41]

For Lefèvre, the direct truth of the original text outweighed later Christian writers' claims throughout the Christian tradition: 'the gospel is stronger than any number of authors', he wrote.[42] Truth was the crucial factor for Lefèvre and the Church must attain the truth, through reform if necessary:

> If I am being faithful to the truth, this truth should not be obstructed by a custom of thinking otherwise, however ancient and familiar that custom may be. Such a situation would be contrary to the Church, for the Church is wherever the truth is to be found.[43]

This idea that the Church was to be purged from moral weakness and purified into a perfected ideal Church is resonant of Colet's attempt to reform the clergy in London around the same time. The problem with Lefèvre's idealism was that it assumed that the truth of the gospel was abundantly clear to any reader at face value, an issue clearly recognized by Erasmus, hence why he sought to discourage debates on questions of doctrine that he considered to be insoluble.

Meanwhile, in Metz, the humanist Henry Cornelius Agrippa of Nettesheim (1486–1535) was preaching in defence of Lefèvre against attacks from Franciscans and Dominicans.[44] Similarly a humanist physician of Lyons, Symphorien Champier (1471–1538), wrote a treatise supporting the thesis that the sinner Mary must be distinguished from the sister of Martha, whilst also, incidentally, making some scathing attacks on Grandval as a scholastic.[45]

The argument over whether it was scripture that revealed only one Mary Magdalen, or whether that was a development of tradition, became so heated that Bishop Etienne Poncher of Paris (d. 1519), Bishop of Sens from 1519, requested that another Christian humanist, John Fisher, Bishop of Rochester and Chancellor of Cambridge University, intervene in the feud.[46] Having examined the New Testament Greek and Lefèvre's work, Fisher condemned Lefèvre for his bad translation, his refutation of tradition, his contempt of his contemporaries, and for his neglect of the Church Fathers and Thomas Aquinas on the subject:[47]

> I immediately thought of how many difficulties would confront the whole Church if Lefèvre's opinion were ever accepted. How many authors would have to be rejected, how many books would have to be changed...![48]

Fisher also made the important point that not everybody was capable of an intelligent, or rational, reading of scripture, and that tradition was necessary to assist them to interpret the text. Erasmus agreed with Fisher, stating that their humanist friend Lefèvre had great tenacity in defending his reputation on this one subject for so long.[49] By the end of 1519 there were a number of tracts and letters making reference to the debate, which eventually ended with Grandval's death (by natural causes) and Lefèvre's flight to Meaux.

A year later, in 1521, the Paris Faculty of Theology brought a close to the whole episode by issuing an edict which, though it did not mention Lefèvre by name, condemned his views and led Clichtove to retract his support openly to the faculty.[50] The Faculty declared that Church tradition must not be called into question, or nothing would be safe: tradition is 'defined, decreed and determined' and anything to the contrary is forbidden, either in books or from the pulpit.[51] Erasmus, as was his wont, satirized the whole affair in a letter to John Merliberch of Diest in 1520, including a poem to Mary Magdalen which parodies the style that Lefèvre and Clichtove criticized so heavily.[52] Erasmus's ability to stand back from current events, to assess them so acutely, and then parody them is one of his most endearing qualities as a humanist. His letter also suggests that humanists should perhaps understand the limits of their art and not try to take on popular devotion – a powerful force.

The Legacy

Lefèvre possessed a unified vision of scripture as spiritual and Christological. Unlike the German Reformers and Conservative Roman Catholics, he sought some modest reforms that would improve the life of the Church without leading to schism and, as such, he was a leader in the evangelical movement. He believed that, as he wrote, 'a renewed and unified reading of the Bible ought to be enough for the needed reformation of the Church'.[53]

The controversy surrounding the three Marys highlights the importance of the early-modern debate on scripture, patristic authority, Church tradition and popular piety. Although Lefèvre was eventually silenced, hounded and exiled for his views, his ideas were nevertheless kept alive in treatises, polemic and sermons by his followers. Thus, like Colet, More, Erasmus and many other great Christian humanists at work on the eve of the European Reformation, Lefèvre did not relinquish his Catholicism, nor did he condemn it or seek its downfall or replacement. He did, however, wish to reform traditional attitudes to the scriptures and Church tradition. Although many intellectual churchmen were humanists of some sort in the early sixteenth century, not all humanists were quite so influential in the realm of theology, hermeneutics, homiletics and evangelism.

Without Lefèvre d'Étaples, the development of humanist theology and values in Europe on the eve of the Reformation would have been greatly impaired. He was a spectacularly talented teacher of undergraduates and widely admired, even by those who had no interest in humanism, as the restorer of genuine Aristotelian texts and ideas in the university faculty of arts. The main sadness is that he failed to collaborate and be inspired by his association with Erasmus, choosing rather to fall out over the interpretation of a verse of the letter to the Hebrews. Nevertheless, he was a towering figure who provoked debate with the most important of thinkers, including Erasmus, Luther and many others. His works on the scriptures and their interpretation, as well as his French translation of the Bible, constitute his lasting legacy. They show us the quality of theology evident in the late-medieval Church.

Lefèvre: Key Dates and Events

c. 1455:	born in Étaples, Picardy.
1460s:	educated at the Collège du Cardinal-Lemoine in Paris.
Before 1486:	travelled to Italy to hear lectures of Argyopoulos in Florence.
1492:	travelled to Italy again, studying in Florence, Rome and Venice.
1507:	resident at Abbey of St. Germain des Prés, where he knew Guillaume Briçonnet, later Bishop of Meaux.
1509:	wrote *Quintuplex Psalterium: Gallicum, Romanum, Hebraicum, Vetus, Conciliatum.*
1512:	wrote *S. Pauli Epistolae xiv. ex Vulgata Editione, Adjecta Intelligentia ex Graeco cum Commentariis.*
1517:	wrote *De Maria Magdalena et Triduo Christi*, arguing that the three Marys (the sister of Lazarus, Mary Magdalene and the penitent woman who anointed Christ's feet) were different people. Condemned by the Paris Faculty of Theology and John Fisher in 1521.
1518:	*De Tribus et Unica Magdalena Disceptatio Secunda.*
1520:	flees Paris, moves to Meaux (with Briçonnet).
1 May 1523:	appointed Vicar-General to Bishop Briçonnet.
1523:	publishes French version of the New Testament, which was used in the diocese and which has been the basis of all subsequent French translations.
February 1525:	protected by Francis I and Marguerite d'Angouleme.

1525: Lefèvre was condemned by Parlement. Quashed by return of Francis I.

1525: publishes *Le Psautier de David*.

1526: appointed Royal Librarian at Blois.

1528: publishes a version of the Pentateuch (the first five books of the Old Testament).

1530: publishes complete version of the Bible in French, based on the vulgate.

1531: Marguerite (now Queen of Navarre) takes Lefèvre into refuge at Nerac.

1534: publication of new edition of the Bible based on the Hebrew and the Greek.

1536/7: dies.

Lefèvre's Key Works

1492–1506: Aristotelian works. In his early years, Lefèvre wrote editions and introductions to Aristotle, including his 1492 *Paraphrases of the Whole of Aristotle's Natural Philosophy*, published by Johannes Higman, in Paris; *Introduction to the Metaphysics* and *Introduction to the Nicomachean Ethics* in 1494; *Logical Introductions* in 1496, and Aristotle's *Politics* in 1506.

1509: *Quincuplex Psalterium; Gallicum, Romanum, Hebraicum, Vêtus, Conciliatum*, republished in 1515. Five Latin versions of the Psalter, used by both Luther and Zwingli. The *Quincuplex* (1509) hermeneutic was based upon a combination of a literal and spiritual interpretation to create a 'true sense' of scripture.

1512: *Commentaires sur Saint Paul, avec une Nouvelle Traduction Latine*, Paris. Republished in 1531, Lefèvre's commentary on the Pauline Epistles, the second edition of which included a response to Erasmus's criticisms of Lefèvre in the *Annotationes* to his 1516 *Novum Instrumentum*.[54] Erasmus criticized Lefèvre's section on grammar. Noel Beda criticized its theology.

1517: *De Maria Magdalena*, followed by another entitled *De tribus et unica Magdalena*. The controversy over Mary Magdalen ran from November 1517 until the spring of 1520, directly coinciding with Luther's first confrontation with Rome. The debate went to the heart of Pre-Reformation reform, focussing on scripture and its authority in the light of patristic tradition, as well as Church practice and the status of popular belief.

1523: *Traduction Française du Nouveau Testament*, Paris. Lefèvre's French edition of the New Testament, from the Vulgate, intended for liturgical use. However, Lefèvre was even attacked in Meaux for his work from the Vulgate because he intended it for the use of the faithful. It appeared again in his complete version of the Bible, Antwerp, 1528 onwards.

1525: *Commentaires sur les Évangiles*. Written in Meaux, Lefèvre's doctrine was orthodox, although criticized by Beda again.

1525: *Commentaires sur les Épitres Canoniques*. Written in Meaux, this was another controversial commentary, provoking an inquisition by Pope Innocent VIII.

1525: *Épitres et Evangiles pour les Cinquante et Deux Semaines de L'an*, published by Simon du Bois of Paris in 1525/6. One homily, called 'Exhortation' is one of the finest texts of its time. He spoke of the search for the 'secrets of God' and the need for a spiritual intelligence with a rejection of human interpretations of scripture.

SPAIN

13

JUAN LUIS VIVES (1493–1540)
The Spanish Erasmian

Foremost among Spanish humanists, Vives emerged from a persecuted family of Jewish descent to become a prominent humanist voice in Europe on the eve of the Reformation. Like humanists in other countries, including Petrarch himself, Vives's humanist programme contained a particularly Christian dimension. His desire to reconcile classicism and Christianity resulted in a Christian humanism that would prove especially influential in the movements for reform in both Protestant and Catholic Churches. From the moment that he met Erasmus in 1514, Vives was a devoted Erasmian. If the quiet German Melanchthon was a humanist theologian, then Vives, by contrast, was an Erasmian Christian philosopher and philologist. This is most clearly seen in the emphasis he placed upon '*pietas erudita*', the combination of devoted study with pro-found and intense religious feeling. Like Erasmus, and following the legacy of Lorenzo Valla in Italy, Vives perceived the need for a closer bond in the minds of intellectuals between religion, philosophy and education.

Introduction[1]

Vives's parents were Jewish cloth merchants who had converted to Christianity. Thus, during the time of the Inqusition (introduced to Valencia in 1484), their lives were blighted by suspicion of their religious heritage. Juan Luis's father, Llúis Vives Valeriola (1453–1524) and mother Blanquina (Blanca) March (1473–1508) had both been suspected of practising Judaism, Llúis being prosecuted in 1477 and Blanca, as a child, in 1480. Llúis was again prosecuted in 1522 and burned at the stake in 1524. Blanca died in 1508 of the plague but her bones were exhumed in 1528 and burned in front of Valencia Cathedral.[2] Such were the social, religious and political circumstances of Vives's birth: his heritage was that of the caste of *Judeo-Conversos* (new Christians) or '*Marranos*', and this had a life-long impact upon his work.[3] On the one hand, many of the *Marranos* remained Jewish at heart: 'In race, belief, and largely in practice, they remained as they were before the conversion. They were Jews in all but name, and Christians in nothing but form'.[4] On the other hand, the Jews of the *Conversos* seem to have quickly turned against Judaism in favour of Christianity, and continued to do so through the fifteenth century, and as a result were viewed as pagans by Jews.[5]

Following the persecution of his family Vives went into exile. His parents' fate may explain why he turned down a valuable professorship in Spain's most famous university (Salamanca) and lived in the Netherlands instead. His works reflect not only his development as a scholastic philosopher and humanist, therefore, but one whose family 'caste' had been persecuted to extinction.[6] Although Vives was a disciple of Erasmus, the latter was deeply suspicious of the *Marranos*, expressing, in a letter of 1517 to Willibald Pirckheimer, contempt that the court of the future Charles V was overrun by them.[7] Meanwhile, as Gonzalez has noted, 'far from avoiding persecution, Vives's family was entirely decimated by the Inquistion, a slow process which Juan Luis helplessly witnessed, first in Valencia and subsequently in exile in the Low Countries'.[8] Vives spent his life attempting to bridge the polarity of his Christian faith and the persecution of his family by means of a kind of irenicism, advocating peace and conciliation through the use of reason.

Life

Juan Luis Vives, born on 6 March 1493, was the eldest of five children, three girls and another boy. He lived for the first sixteen or seventeen years of his life in Valencia and was initially educated there at the *Estudi General*, the new university, from 1507. However, this education cannot be considered either particularly scholastic in nature, or humanist, as González notes, with reference to Joan Roìs de Corella, a Valencian writer of Catalan works:

> Joan Roís de Corella's prose compositions with classical pretensions... are the best proof of how far humanism was from Valencia in the first quarter of the sixteenth century. At the same time, [the] lack of a local university throughout the whole Middle Ages precluded the creation of a solid academic tradition conducive to disciplines favoured by scholasticism, such as dialectic, natural philosophy and theology. Books on these disciplines were indeed very rarely printed in Valencia at the time. Not even the foundation of the *estudi general* in 1502 effected any improvement during its first years.[9]

It may have been the absence of scholastic academic tradition in his early training that later led Vives to question it once he had come into contact with it. Moreover, Vives's early education was not so much influenced by the intellectual climate of humanism and the revival of ancient learning from Greece and Rome, as had been the case for many an Italian humanist. Rather, it was the social and political changes, and how they were imparted, that affected him most profoundly in his early years.[10]

In 1509, Vives moved to Paris to begin his studies at the Collège de Lisieux, where Juan Dolz had just started a triennial course, but soon moved to the Collège de Beauvais, where he attended the lectures of Jan Dullaert (d. 1513). It is notable that, unlike many of the other humanists we have considered, Vives never travelled to the spiritual homeland of humanism – Italy – nor seems to have expressed a desire to do so.[11]

In contrast to the rather conventional education he had received in Valencia, in Paris Vives was introduced to newer currents of European thought, scholastic and humanist, which widened his intellectual horizons. He devoted his time to scholasticism, as Erasmus related, although he failed to obtain a bachelor degree, preferring to spend his time studying non-curricular humanist writings, as well as spending recreational time drinking and playing games.[12]

By the Autumn of 1512, Vives was immersed in humanist learning, attending lectures by the Aragonese Gaspar Lax (1487–1560) at the

Collège de Montaigu, and meeting Nicholas Bérault (*c*. 1470–*c*. 1545), a colleague and friend of the French humanist Guillaume Budé (1467–1540). González notes that the intellectual atmosphere in Paris at this time, and the teaching that he received, resulted in Vives taking a stance between scholasticim and humanism, with a distinct emphasis upon his Christian heritage, and an attempt to Christianize the moral philosophy of the ancients:

> In the Paris prior to the controversial publication of Erasmus's *Novum instrumentum* and the scandal of Luther's theses, scholastics and humanists lived side by side with no great tensions. It is hardly surprising that the names of the logicians Dullaert and Lax…occur in harmony with the names of of humanist Bérault in Vives's Parisian writings when he was midway between the two movements. It is certain that the letters, dialogues and declamations were genres beloved of humanists, and that Vives sought to express himself in a Latin worthy of a 'Roman citizen'. Nevertheless, these writings still reveal an obsessive desire to Christianize to the letter the classical world, whose 'otherness' was still not very clear to Vives.[13]

In 1514 Vives travelled to the Low Countries, settling in Bruges, and it was here that he first came into contact with Erasmus. Erasmus's distinctive effort to marry classicism and Christianity seems to have brought Vives's own concerns – perhaps informed by his own background – into clearer focus and thus encouraged his subsequent intellectual development. Although Vives had first interacted with currents of humanist thought in Paris, he took his philosophy from Erasmus, especially the notion of *pietas erudita*, that union of learning and religious faith.[14]

With a move to Louvain at end of 1514,[15] Vives became a friend of Hadrianus Barlandus (1486–1538), professor of the Faculty of Arts at Louvain:

> No one, I think, will doubt that in some sense Vives was and always remained an 'Erasmian'…As a humanist, Vives shared Erasmus' admiration for classical culture but was much more severe in his moral judgements of it. Erasmus' enthusiasm for Eurpides, Arstophanes, Terence, Lucian, and Ovid did not find lasting favour with Vives. Mastery of Latin and Greek was for Vives a mean to learn ancient wisdom rather than a tool to read the Greek New Testament or to improve Saint Jerome's Vulgate Latin translation.[16]

Vives was introduced to the Brussels court, and also appointed tutor to the Flemish nobleman Guillaume de Croy. From 1517 until Croy's premature death in 1521, Vives lived in Louvain and taught at the Collegium Trilingue, a humanist foundation based on Erasmian educational principles. As has already been suggested, those principles emphasized the importance of a closer proximity between education, philosophy and religion.[17]

> How long Vives was a member of the royal court is not exactly known, although he was well qualified, as he possessed excellent humanist talents, with a good knowledge of Latin, French, Spanish and Dutch. In November 1516, Vives was a 'resident and member of the royal court' for there is evidence that he received a commission from the city of Valencia at that time.[18]

In March 1517 Vives was in Cambrai writing speeches for peace negotiations between Spain and France. The diplomacy culminated in the Peace at Cambrai, a document signed on 11 March 1517.[19]

Works from this period include *Fabula de Homine* (*A Fable about Man*, 1518), on the nature of humanity. In this work, one can see a '... radical reversal of the medieval interpretation of metaphysics and a renunciation of the primacy of all speculation about nature, a discovery of every form of *a priori* or formal thinking'.[20] The Fable attempted to reveal 'the truth in disguise': an eternal unchanging meaning to reality.[21] In this period Vives also wrote *De Initiis, Sectis et Laudibus Philosophiae* (*On the Origins, Schools and Merits of Philosophy*, 1518), a short essay on the history of philosophy; *In Pseudodialecticos* (*Against the Pseudo-Dialecticians*, 1520) as well as, with Erasmus's encouragement, an edition of Augustine's *De Civitate Dei* (*City of God*, 1522) with a commentary.

It is clear that Vives made an alliance with England after Croy's death, for, in 1521, he was in receipt of a small pension from Catherine of Aragon and, in 1522, dedicated his edition of *De Civiate Dei* to Henry VIII. Moreover, in April 1523, he presented a manuscript copy of the *De Institutione Feminae Christianae* to Queen Catherine. Of course, as a Spanish princess, it was only natural for Catherine to attract a circle of Spaniards into her service.

Between 1523 and 1528, Vives visited England six times, attending the court of Henry VIII and Catherine of Aragon. Vives was tutor to their daughter, Mary, and was appointed as lecturer at Corpus Christi, the Oxford college that had recently been founded by the humanist Richard Fox.[22] It was in both London and Oxford that he came into contact with the humanists Thomas More and Thomas Linacre.

Publications from this time include *De Institutione Feminae Christianae* (*The Education of a Christian Woman*, 1524); *Introductio ad Sapientiam* (*Introduction to Wisdom*, 1524), an ethical guide based upon a combination of Stoic philosophy and Christian doctrine, and *De Subventione Pauperum* (*On Assistance to the Poor*, 1526), dedicated to the magistrates of Bruges. Meanwhile, Vives's notion of a utopian society governed by its citizens' was expounded in the voluminous *De Concordia et Disconcordia in Humano Genere (1529).*[23] In 1528 he lost the favour of Henry VIII by siding with his fellow countrywoman Catherine of Aragon, and fellow humanist, Thomas More, in the matter of the king's divorce. After being arrested and released, he fled back to Bruges, where he had married Margarita Valldaura in 1524. Vives was most prolific in the last decade of his life, producing his most mature works:

> The promising young man, whose declamations and invectives had been praised by Erasmus, Thomas More and Guillaume Budé, soon became the prolific author of an encyclopaedic range of philosophical and critical works, schoolbooks, and texts which display a deep interest in the social, political and religious conflicts of his time.[24]

Works include the anti-war treatise *De Concordia et Discordia in Humano Genere* (*On Concord and Discord in Humankind*, 1529); *De Disciplinis* (*On the Disciplines*, 1531), on educational renewal; *De Anima et Vita* (*On the Soul and Life*, 1538), on the souls and emotions, and finally *De Veritate Fidei Christianae* (*On the Truth of the Christian Faith*), published posthumously in 1543. *De Veritate*, the longest of all Vives's works, and the one most explicitly engaging with the vexed question of man's capacity for religious knowledge, has provoked debate amongst scholars as to whether Vives's response reflected an ingrained scepticism, possibly allied with a hostility towards Judaism.[25]

As with the writings of many of the Christian humanists we have considered, however, such suggestions of scepticism miss the crucial point that men like Vives were indeed engaged with the most pressing (and, from a Christian perspective, threatening) questions of their time, but nonetheless determined to show the truth of Christianity and to reconcile it with ancient philosophy (in Vives's case, particularly with Stoicism). *De Veritate* is, therefore, better understood as a defence of Christianity, which, in its five books, also emphasizes the essential unity of all humankind, echoing St. Paul's theology that in Christ there is no Jew or Gentile:

> For in His law Christ conjoins and bonds men together, however different, in good will, teaching them to be brothers

among themselves, for they are children of the self-same God.[26]

As Colish points out, 'with respect to the Old Christians and New Christians of Vives' Spain, this ideal, and this vision, were not to be realized'.[27] Indeed, as we have seen, in the 1520s Vives's father had been imprisoned by the Inqusition and then burned at the stake and his mother's bones were exhumed and publicly burned. Vives himself remained at risk because of his family background. He wrote to Erasmus in 1534: 'These are difficult times. We can neither keep silent nor speak up without risk to ourselves'.[28] The irenic vision of his final work none-theless reveals a conviction that relations between Christians and Jews in Spain could be – and according to St. Paul and truly Christian policy, should be – harmonious.

He also had other difficulties. Around this time two of his friends died, Linacre in 1524 and Maarten van Dorp, at Louvain, in 1525. Moreover, when he returned to England in 1526, his lectureship at Oxford had been discontinued by Wolsey. Eventually he was appointed preceptor to Princess Mary in October 1527, but England was becom-ing increasingly uncomfortable for Vives, as Wolsey was suspicious of him. At the end of February 1528 Vives was even placed under house arrest for thirty-eight days. As a result, Vives took Queen Catherine's advice and left England after his release, only to return in November with Cardinal Campeggio to examine to royal marriage:

> Vives advised the queen not to take oath in the trial. Catherine interpreted Vives' advice as a sign of weakness and was 'furi-ous' at him. A few days later Vives left England for the last time. He returned to Bruges embittered and impoverished but also better prepared to carry out the most ambitious and pro-found explorations of his intellectual journey.[29]

Nevertheless, Vives produced an amazing range of high-quality human-ist texts, which were widely disseminated by the best printers and pub-lishers of the day:

> Like Thomas More, Vives was an individual who believed in the legitimacy of honest pleasures, and friendship in par-ticular. He was a connoisseur of food and drink and enjoyed painting, neither an ascetic nor a killjoy, in short, a man of the Renaissance.[30]

He died in Bruges on May 6, 1540.

The Legacy

Vives was not only a prolific author in his short life, and a promoter of Erasmian ideas throughout Europe, he was also widely quoted in the works of others, both during his lifetime and afterwards. For instance, Mario Nizolio (1488–1567) cites Vives numerous times in *De Veris Principiis et Vera Ratione Philosophandi Contra Pseudophilosophos* (*On the True Principles and True Method of Philosophizing against the Pseudo-Philosophers*, 1553) and G. W. Leibniz (1646–1716) considered Vives's works to be worth editing more than a hundred years later.

In *Quod Nihil Scitur* (*That Nothing is Known*, 1581), one of the most systematic expositions of philosophical skepticism produced during the sixteenth century, the Portuguese philosopher and medical writer Francisco Sanches displays a familiarity with *De Disciplinis*, and there are indications that he might also have been acquainted with *In Pseudodialecticos*.

In *Exercitationes Paradoxicae Adversus Aristoteleos* (*Paradoxical Exercises against the Aristotelians*, 1624), a sceptical attack on Aristotelianism, Pierre Gassendi wrote that reading Vives gave him courage and helped him to free himself from the dogmatism of Peripatetic philosophy. Moreover, Philip Melanchthon recommended *De anima et vita* in the prefatory letter to his *Commentarius de Anima* (*Commentary on the Soul*, 1540).

Vives's influence on the naturalistic pedagogy of the Spaniard Juan Huarte de San Juan (*c.* 1529–1588), in his celebrated *El Examen de Ingenios para las Ciencias* (*The Examination of Men's Wits*, 1575) is undeniable and, in his discussion of the passions of the soul, the Jesuit Francisco Suárez (1548–1617) counted Vives among his authorities, pointing out that the study of the emotions belongs to natural philosophy and medicine as well as to moral philosophy. Vives's work was also an important source of inspiration for Robert Burton (1577–1640), who, in *The Anatomy of Melancholy* (1621), repeatedly quotes from *De Anima et Vita*.

The reference to Vives by René Descartes (1596–1650) in *Les Passions de L'âme* (1649) suggests that he had read the humanist's work, and William Hamilton (1788–1856) praised Vives's insights on memory and the laws of association. In his *Contributions Towards a History of the Doctrine of Mental Suggestion or Association*, he quoted extensive portions of Vives's account of memory and maintained that the observations of 'the Spanish Aristotelian' comprise 'nearly all of principal moment that has been said upon this subject, either before or since'.

Vives's *Dialectices Libri Quatuor* (1550) provided one of the primary sources for Thomas Reid (1710–1796) in his *A Brief Account of Aristotle's Logic* (1774) and Vives's work was also cited by authors such as Ernest Renan (1823–1892), Friedrich Albert Lange (1828–1875), Wilhelm Dilthey (1833–1911), Pierre Duhem (1861–1916), Ernst Cassirer (1874–1945), and José Ortega y Gasset (1883–1955). Lange, for instance, regarded Vives as one of the most important reformers of philosophy of his time and a precursor of both Bacon and Descartes.

Vives: Dates and Events

1477–1516:	reign of King Ferdinand of Aragon.
1480:	Vives's mother (to be), Blanca, questioned by the Inquisition.
1492:	Vives's parents, Lluis and Blanca, marry.
1493:	Juan Luis Vives born on March 6, eldest of five children.
1502:	University of Valencia founded.
1507–9:	Vives studies at Valencia.
1508:	Blanca dies of the plague.
1509–12:	studies at the Collège de Lisieux in Paris with Fleming Jan Dullaert (active 1487–1514) and the Aragonese Gaspar Lax (1487–1560).
1512:	Vives moves to the Low Countries, Bruges and Louvain.
1514:	Parisian writings published: four prefatory epistles and nine short pieces, including two colloquies, a dialogue and an oratorical text.1515: Prefatory letter in praise of Homer.
1515–19:	Vives withdraws from publishing.
November 1516:	Vives resident and member of the royal court at Valencia.
1517:	at the Court of Brussels.
March 1517:	Vives in Cambrai for peace negotiations between Spain and France.
11 March 1517:	Peace of Cambrai.
1519:	break with scholasticism in *Pseudodialecticos*.
April 1519:	*Opuscula Varia*.
1519–20:	Germanias insurrection in Valencia.
1520:	Erasmus charges Vives with the task of a new edition of Augustine's *De Civitas*.; Two Declamations; at the English Court. Friend of More, Corpus Christi College.

1521: receives small pension from Catherine of Aragon.
1522: Vives's father's final trial.
July 1522: edition of *De Civitas* published.
April 1523: *De Institutione* dedicated to Catherine of Aragon.
1524: *De Institutione* published.
1524: Father burnt at the stake.
1524: marries Margarita Valladura.
1526: *De Subventione Pauperum.*
1528: Vives leaves England; his mother's bones exhumed and burned in front of Valencia Cathedral.
1529: Blanca posthumously accused on Jewish practises in 1500; *De Concordia et Disconcordia.*
1531: *De Disciplinis.*
1540: dies in Bruges.

Vives's Key Works

1520: *In Pseudodialecticos (1520)*: a break with scholastic logic.
1524: *De Institutione Feminae*: divided into three books: on the young girl, the married woman and on the widow. Unlike Erasmus and other humanists, Vives espoused the benefits of marriage, not purely in terms of procreation, but in terms of community. As Fantazzi observes:

> The primary goal of marriage, according to Vives, is not so much the production of offspring as community of life and indissoluble companionship (*communionem quandam vitae et indisociabilem societatem*). This view is in sharp contrast with the teachings of the church fathers, who consistently cite procreation as the primary goal. Erasmus in his *Christiani Matrimonii Institutio* (The Institution of Christian Matrimony) defines marriage in a very legalistic fashion as 'a lawful and perpetual union between a man and a woman, entered into for the purpose of begetting offspring and involving an indivisible partnership of life and propoerty.'[31]

De Institutione Feminae also addressed the issue of the validity of non-Christian, classical writers. Like John Colet, who denounced 'pagan' authors whilst also including their works in his school curriculum, so Vives, whilst warning against the dangers of ancient texts, used them in his teaching:

> Although Vives professes in the opening of his address to the Queen to eschew the merely exhortatory precepts of such writers as Tertullian, Cyprian, Jerome, Ambrose, Augustine, and Fulgentius, he paradoxically cites these very authors as the *De Institutione* unfolds.[32]

1524: *Satellitium Animi (The Soul's Escort)*. A collection of sayings dedicated to Princess Mary. In the work, Vives points out that 'man knows as far as he can make'. Vives wrote: 'human inquiry comes to conjectural conclusions, for we do not deserve certain knowledge (*scientia*), stained by sin as we are and hence burdened with the great weight of the body; nor do we need it, for we see that man is ordained lord and master of everything in the sublunary world'.

1531: *De Disciplinis*: 'I think there can be little doubt that the *De Disciplinis* is the most complete and most important philosophical text of Vives.'[33] The work is divided into three parts: *De Causis Corruptarum Artium (On the Causes of the Corruption of the Arts)*, seven books analysing the origins of education; *De Tradendis Disciplinis (On Handing Down the Disciplines)*, five books in which Vives outlines his program for educational reform; and five shorter treatises *De Artibus (On the Arts)*, dealing mainly with logic and metaphysics:

> *De Prima Philosophia (On First Philosophy)*
> *De Censura Veri (On the Assessment of Truth)*
> *De Explanatione Cuiusque Essentiae (On the Explanation of Each Essence)*
> *De Instrumento Probabilitatis (On the Instrument of Probability)*
> *De Disputatione (On Disputation)*

1538: *De Anima et Vita*, published in 1538, is divided into three books: the first book addresses the functions of the vegetative soul and the cogitative soul. The second book examines the functions of the rational soul and its three faculties (mind, will, and memory), as well as topics stemming from Aristotle's *Parva Naturalia*. The third book concerns the emotions. Vives saw the soul as 'the principal agent inhabiting a body adapted to life' (*agens praecipuum, habitans in corpore apto ad vitam*).

1538: *Censura de Aristotelis Operibus (Assessment of Aristotle's Works, 1538)*. Vives's appraisal of the Aristotelian corpus.

1550: *Dialectices Libri Quatuor* (*Four Books of Dialectic*). Published posthumously, this work concerns the supremacy of the *sermo communis* (ordinary discourse) over the abstract language of metaphysics. Philosophy, Vives argued, ought not to invent the language and subject of its own specific investigation.

APPENDICES

APPENDIX I
OTHER NOTABLE HUMANISTS

Agrippa, Heinrich Cornelius (Agrippa von Nettesheim) (1486–1535) German author. Born in Cologne he taught at the Univeristy of Dole in France on Reuchlin's *De Verbo Mirifico*. Author of *De Occulta Philosophia Libri Tres* on the occult. He worked for some time for Maximilian I and was persecuted for his occult beliefs.

Alberti, Leon Battista (1404–72) Florentine Humanist, art theroist and architect employed mainly at the papal court. He composed many treatises, including *Della Famiglia* (on the family), which describes the world as a struggle between virtue and fortune; *Della Pittura* on humanism and the visual arts; and *De Re Aedificatoria* (on architecture).

Argyropoulos, John (*c*. 1415–87) Greek (Byzantine) lecturer, philosopher and humanist who revived classical learning in the fifteenth century. Translator of theology and philosophy from ancient Greek into Latin as well as a theologian and orator in his own right. His career spanned the Roman and the Byzantine world.

Ariosto, Lodovico (1474–1533) From Ferrara, highly imaginative writer of comic plays for the Ferarrese court and author of the poem *Orlando Furioso*, an adaptation of the Romance legend.

Ascham, Roger (1515–68) English Elizabethan humanist, tutor and author with a style that promoted the use of vernacular language. His fame led to his appointment as tutor to the young Elizabeth, in Greek and Latin, finding royal favour also throughout the reigns of Edward VI, Mary I and Elizabeth I.

Bacon, Francis (1561–1626) English philosopher, statesman, scientist, lawyer and author. Attorney General and Lord Chancellor of England;

philosophical advocate and practitioner of the scientific revolution. Established the 'Baconian method' or 'scientific method' moulding a rhetorical and theoretical framework for science.

Bembo, Pietro (1470-1547) Venetian humanist, poet and cleric who helped develop Italian as a language for literature, particularly Tuscan, following Dante. He was partly responsible for promoting the work of Petrarch in the sixteenth century.

Boccaccio, Giovanni (1314–75) Venetian humanist and vernacular author of the *Decameron* and *On Famous Women*. Devotee of Petrarch and noted for his dialogue. Influential in establishing Petrarchan humanism in Florence.

Brant, Sebastian (1458–1521) Born in Strassbourg; a leading exponent of humanism; educated at Basel in law; author of the *Ship of Fools* (1494), a satirical poem that bridged traditional wisdom and morality from classical, biblical and medieval sources with new concepts of society and spiritual life.

Bracciolini, Poggio (1380–1459) Florentine humanist employed mostly at the papal court. Great collector and copier of Latin manuscripts and wrote Latin dialogues on avarice and hypocrisy.

Bruni, Leonardo (1370–1444) Born in Arezzo. Austere Florentine humanist, writer of state documents, Secretary to the papal court and, from 1427, Chancellor of Florence. Author of a *History of the Florentine People*, which glorified the Roman republic and developed from the ideas of Cicero and Livy. A Greek scholar, he translated works by Aristotle and Plato.

Bruno, Giordano (1548–1600) Born in Nola, Southern Italy. Philospher, mathematician and astronomer best known as a proponent of heliocentricism and the infinity of the universe.

Budé, Guillaume (1467–1540) Son of a wealthy Parisian magistrate, Budé was a philologist and humanist and the greatest French Hellenist of his time. Author of *Annotationes in Quattuor et Virgini Pandectarum Libros*, which applied philological and historical methods to the science of jurisprudence. He invented, or rather rediscovered, the term *encyclopaedia* and, in his work, *De Philologia*, argued that philology was the basis for all education.

Capito, Wolfgang (c. 1478–1541) Born in Haguenau, educated at Pforzheim and graduated from University of Freiburg. Could not reconcile the new religion with the old, and from 1524 was one of the leaders of the reformed faith in Strasbourg.

Castiglione, Baldassare (1478–1529) From near Mantua. Diplomat and author who popularized humanist ideas. Employed by courts of Mantua and Urbino. Author of *The Courtier*, on how gentlemen should behave, adapting humanist ideas for the context of courtly society, thus moving the ideas outside the arena in which they arose.

Cavalcanti, Giovanni (1444–1509) Italian Florentine poet and aquaintance of Ficino. He lived for many years with Ficino at his villa, and Marsilio dedicated his essay *De Amore* (1484) to Cavalcanti. Ficino addressed him as '*Giovanni amico mio perfettisimo*' ('Giovanni my most perfect friend').

Celtis, Conrad (1459–1508) German humanist and poet; author of *Ars Versificandi et Carminum* (The Art of Writing Verses and Poems, 1486). Lectured on the works of classical writers in Vienna and, in 1502, founded the *Collegium Poetarum*, a college for poets there.

Chalcondyles, Demetrius (*c.* 1423–90) Byzantine Greek Athenian scholar. Taught by Plethon. Author of *Proofs of Histories* in ten volumes.

Cheke, John (1514–57) English classical scholar and statesman, notable as the first regius Professor of Greek at Cambridge; tutor to Edward VI.

Clichtove, Josse (1472–1543) Born in Flanders, he was a champion of reform in philosophical and theological studies during the earlier part of his life, he devoted himself later to combating the doctrines of Luther. He defended the work of Lefèvre d'Étaples, especially during the Three Marys controversy.

Contarini, Gasparo (1483–1542) The greatest of the Catholic Reformers who incorporated Aristotelian and humanist ideals into his work as diplomat (in Venice) and cardinal. Advocate of *renovatio ecclesiae* (Church reform). His Christian humanism fostered Catholic reform and pre-figured the structural changes of the Council of Trent.

Elyot, Thomas (1490–1546) English diplomat, lexicrographer and scholar. In 1531 he produced *The Boke Named the Gouernour*, dedicated to Henry VIII. Tried to persuade Charles V to take a more favourable view of Henry's proposed divorce from Catherine of Aragon. His *Image of Governance, Compiled of the Actes and Sentences notable of the most noble Emperor Alexander Severus* (1540) was supposedly a translation from a Greek manuscript of the emperor's secretary Encolpius.

Fisher, John (1469–1535) Bishop of Rochester, cardinal and martyr. Humanist who condemned Lefèvre's work on the Three Marys. Fisher was executed by order of Henry VIII, like Thomas More, for refusing to accept the King as Head of the Church in England.

Fox(e), Richard (1448–1528) English churchman and humanist, Bishop of Exeter, Bath and Wells, Durham and Winchester. Lord Privy Seal, and founder of Corpus Christi College, Cambridge.

Froben, Johann (1460–1527) Famous printer in Basel who published many influential works including Erasmus's 1516 *Novum Testamentum*.

Geremia da Montagnone (1255–1321) Along with Lovato dei Lovati, Albertino Mussato and Rolando da Piazzola, he was one of the earliest to develop humanist ideas in Italy.

Huarte, Juan (de San Juan) (*c*. 1529–88) Spanish humanist and author of *El examen de ingenios para las ciencas (The Examination of Men's Wits*, (1575).

Hutton, Ulrich von (1488–1523) Humanist and reformer, born in Hesse. An ally of Erasmus and then Luther during the Reformation. He wrote invectives against the clergy and appeals to the nation; produced a sequel to *Letters of Obscure Men* (1519), which was a triumph for humanism following the Reuchlin affair over Jewish books.

Isabella d'Este (1474–1539) From Ferrara and moved to Mantua, a female humanist who was patron of painters and humanists such as Castiglione.

Landino, Cristoforo (1424–98) Florentine humanist and friend of Ficino; tutor to Lorenzo de' Medici and his brother Giuliano. Chancellor of the Guelf party (1467) and later Scriptor of public letters for the Signoria.

Latimer, William (*c*. 1467–1545) English priest and Greek scholar. Tutor to Cardinal Pole and advisor to Henry VIII on the theological issues surrounding his divorce from Catherine of Aragon.

Lax, Gaspar (1487–1560) Aragonese humanist and teacher at the Collège de Montaigu, Paris. Taught Juan Luis Vives in Paris, *c*. 1512–14.

Lily, William (*c*. 1468–1522) English classical grammarian and scholar. He was an author of the most widely used Latin grammar textbook in England and was the first highmaster of John Colet's St. Paul's School.

Lovato dei Lovati (*c*. 1240–1309) Early Italian humanist and lawyer from Padua; originator of 'secular' Italian humanism and a forerunner of Petrarch.

Maarten van Dorp (1485–1525) Louvain theologian and humanist. Published a dozen books between 1488 and 1519 thereafter retiring from public life due to a battle with the theological faculty regarding his anti-scholastic oration *Oratio in Praelectionem Epistolarum Divi Pauli,* delivered in 1516 and published in 1519.

Machiavelli, Niccolò (1469–1527) Florentine philosopher/writer, considered one of the main founders of modern politics. His key role in public life was as a civil servant to the republic in Florence, exercising great skill in diplomacy. He became Second Chancellor to the Signoria and Secretary to the Dieci di Balìa in 1498. Author of *The Prince* (1513) published in 1532 and *The Art of War* (1521), about high-military science.

Manutius, Aldus (1449/50–1515), called Teobaldo Mannucci in Italian. Born near Rome. Humanist printer and publisher founder of the Aldine Press at Venice. Inventor of italic type and introduced small inexpensive vellum books.

Martens, Dierik (1446–1534) Dutch printer, humanist and friend of Erasmus. Published editions of Church Fathers and the first in the Low Countries to print texts in Greek.

Mussato, Albertino (1261–1329) Paduan lawyer, politician, poet, dramatist and one of the first Italian humanists who provided the impetus for the revival of ancient Latin and culture.

Niccoli, Niccolò (1364–1437) Florentine humanist who studied ancient languages, manuscripts, as well as buildings, sculpture and engraved gems.

Nicholas of Kues (1401–64) Also known as Nicolaus Cusanus or Nicholas of Cusa. German Cardinal, philosopher, mathematician, astronomer and polymath. He made significant scientific and political contributions in Europe, including mystical or spiritual writings.

Nogarola, Isotta (1418–66) One of the first generation of Quattrocento women humanists. Perhaps the most famous and accomplished learned woman of the century. She learned Latin and Greek at an early age, studying with Martino Rizzoni, a pupil of Guarino of Verona (1374–1460). Through Rizzoni, perhaps, Isotta, as well as her sister Ginevra (1417–1461/8), became known to the circle around Guarino.

Oecolampadius, Johannes (1482–1531) German Protestant reformer and humanist, preacher, and patristic scholar who, as a close friend of Zwingli, led the Reformation in Basel.

Pio, Alberto (*c.* 1475–1531) Prince of Carpi. One of the most intellectually renowned humanist princes of the Renaissance and friend to the Medici Popes; he blamed Erasmus as the cause of the Lutheran heresy.

Pirckheimer, Willibald (1470–1530) German Renaissance lawyer, author and Erasmian humanist who made a significant contribution to civic life in Nurenberg. He edited Ptolomy's *Geographica* for publication in 1525.

Plethon, George Gemisthos (c. 1355–1452/54) Byzantine scholar of Neoplatonic philosophy, who assisted in the reintroduction of Plato's thought to the West.

Poliziano, Angelo Ambrogini (1454–94) Born in Montepulciano. Also known as Politian. Humanist Latin poet and translator, including an edition of the *Iliad* (books II-V), completed when he was a teenager, and later translations of the works of Hippocrates, Galen, Plutarch and Plato. Also author of a series of essays on philology entitled *Miscallanea* (1489) and the poem *Manto* (1480s).

Pomponazzi, Pietro (1462–1525) Mantuan Aristotelian philosopher. His greatest work is his 1516 *De Immortalitate Animae* (On the Immortality of the Soul).

Rhenanus, Beatus (1485–1547) Alsatian humanist, historian, translator and textual critic.

Rolando de Piazzola (d. 1325) Paduan, fourteenth-century, 'secualar' humanist.

Salutati, Coluccio (1331–1406) Italian humanist and intellectual heir of Petrarch; responsible for the growth of civic humanism and republicanism in Florence. Invited the Greek scholar Manuel Chrysolorus to be Professor of Greek in Florence, 1397–1400. Author of *De Tyranno* 1400. He collected over 800 books and manuscripts, including Cicero's lost *Letters to his Friends* (*Epistulae ad Familiares*). He promoted the work of Braciolini, Bruni and Poggio.

Scrovegni, Maddalena (1356–1429) From a noble Paduan family; one of the first women humanists. Lombardo della Seta, humanist and companion of Petrarch, dedicated to her a work on famous women (now lost) in which he praised her learning.

Traversari, Ambrogio or Ambrose the Camaldulian (1386–1439) Italian humanist, hellenist and theologian. Born in Portico di Romagna near Forlì, at fourteen he entered the Camaldulian monastry of Santa Maria degli Angeli in Florence and became general of the order in 1431; he translated many Greek works into Latin, attended the Council of Basel as legate of Pope Eugenius IV and helped draft the decree of union between the Greek and Latin Churches in 1439. He died soon afterwards.

Tunstall, Cuthbert (1474–1559) English Church leader, diplomat, administrator and royal adviser. He served as Bishop of Durham from the reign of Henry VIII to Elizabeth I.

Varano, Costanza (1428–47) From Pesaro, she became an accomplished Latinist; wrote several letters, orations, and poems that are preserved. In 1444 she married Alessandro Sforza, lord of Pesaro, which ended her studies. Her daughter Battista later married Federico da Montefeltro.

Vergil, Polydore (1470–1555) historian and humanist, born in Urbino, Italy. He studied at Bologna and Padua, served as secretary to the Duke of Urbino, was Chamberlain to Pope Alexander VI, and was sent to England as Subcollector of Peter's Pence in 1501 or 1502. He secured the patronage of Henry VII, held many ecclesiastical preferments, and became an English subject in 1510. In 1515 he was briefly imprisoned for his criticism of Thomas Wolsey. Vergil remained largely aloof from the religious controversies of the time. He returned to Italy a few years before his death. His chief work was his *Anglica Historia* [26 books of English history] (1534). This work is the first critical history of England and the first interpretive study of Henry VII.

Wimpfeling, Jacob (1450–1528) German humanist and theologian, born in Alsace. Author of *Elegantiarum Medulla* (1493), a version of Valla's *Elegantiae*; the anti-scholastic *Isidoneus Germanicus* (1496); and the pedagogical and ethical work *Adolescentia* (1500), which consist of twenty laws for young men to live by.

APPENDIX II
GLOSSARY OF TERMS AND OTHER NOTABLE FIGURES

Pietro d'Abano (*c.* 1250–*c.* 1316) Professor of Medicine at Padua, who combined Arab and Greek medicine and natural philosophy.

Albertus Magnus (1193/1206–80) Scholastic Dominican and follower of Aquinas who studied at Paris and Regensburg Universities. Attempted to join Aristotelianism and Christianity.

all' antica in the style of ancient Greek or Latin (literature or art).

Ambrose, St. (337/9–397) Early Medieval Church father who, along with Augustine, Jerome and Gregory the Great, became one of the four great authorities in theology, particularly with regard to orthodoxy in scriptural exegesis.

Aquinas, Thomas (1225–74) Theologian whose works gained great authority after the Council of Trent. Often criticized harshly by late-medieval writers, he was a Dominican, whose theology was set out in his life's work, *Summa Theologicae* (in several volumes). It contains a strong Aristotelian element. His theology was the basis for Roman Catholic teaching and doctrine.

Archimedes (287–212 B.C.) Born in Sicily and raised in Alexandria, famous as the greatest inventor, scientist and mathematician from antiquity.

Aristotle (384–322 B.C.) One of the greatest of Greek philosophers and Plato's pupil at the Athenian Academy for twenty-one years. Thereafter he became a teacher and, notably, tutor to Alexander the Great. He established the Lyceum school and became famous for his writings on natural sciences, ethics and logic.

Augustine, St. (354–430) Bishop of Hippo, philosopher and theologian, Latin Church Father and one of the most important figures in the development of Christianity in the West. Following his conversion and baptism in 387, he believed that the grace of Christ was necessary for human salvation and developed the concepts of original sin and just war.

Averroës (Abu al-Walid Muhammad ibn Ahmad, 1126–98) Influential polymath, Aristotelian philosopher, physician and astronomer from Islamic Spain. Born in Córdoba, Andalucia, his most important original philosophical work was *The Incoherence of the Incoherence* (*Tahafut al-tahafut*), in which he defended Aristotelian philosophy against al-Ghazali's claims in *The Incoherence of Philosophers* (*Tahafut al-falasifa*).

Basil, St (*c.* 330–79) Greek Church Father of Caesarea and Mazaca in Cappadocia, Asia Minor. Supporter of the Nicene faction opposing Arianism and Apollinaris of Laodicea.

Bassarion (1403–72) Cardinal who introduced Italians to Greek philosophy and whose books were used to start the library at St. Mark at Venice.

Boethius (*c.* 480–*c.*524) Roman philosopher and Christian theologian. Consul of Rome in 510.

Botticelli, Sandro (1445–1510) Florentine artist, famous for his *Birth of Venus*, who painted rooms for the Medicis influenced by Ficino's interpretation of classical mythology, which marked a digrerssion from religious imagery in this period.

Cabala, or Cabbala, meaning 'receiving'. A School of thought concerned with Jewish mysticism and a set of esoteric teachings, the aim of which is to understand the mystery of humanity's mortality with an infinite and immutable God. As such, the Cabala examines essential questions surrounding revealed religion and existence. It was the focus of study for Pico della Mirandola and Johannes Reuchlin.

Careggi, Villa Medici One of the first Medici Villas, situated outside Florence. Cosimo de' Medici died at the villa in 1464.

Cato, Marcus Porcius (234–149 B.C.) Roman author of *De Re Rustica* on agriculture and condemning the pursuit of wealth and pleasure.

Chalcidius (*c.* 300) Neoplatonist and grammarian. Translated Plato's *Timaeus*.

Christine de Pisan (*c.* 1363–1431) Venetian-born author who strongly challenged misogyny and stereotypes prevalent in the male-dominated realm of the arts. As a poet, she was well known and highly regarded in her own day. Gave public orations in Padua and Venice.

Cicero (106–43 B.C.) Roman orator, stateman and philosopher. One of Rome's greatest figures. He introduced Greek philosophy to Rome and created a Latin philosophical vocabulary. A prolific writer and influence upon the classical world and the Renaissance.

Constantine (*c.* 272–337) Roman Emperor Caesar Flavius Valerius Annelius or Constantine the Great. Roman Emperor from 306 until his death. The first Christian Emperor. He reversed the persecutions ordered by his predecessor Diocletian. Issued the Edict of Milan in 313 encouraging religious tolerance.

Council of Ferrara/Florence (1438–45) Council for Eastern and Western Churches begun in 1431 in Basel, but transferred to Ferrara by Pope Eugenius IV in 1438 and then to Florence in 1439 due to the danger of plague at Ferrara. The Council brought very brief agreement between East and West Churches but soon failed.

Dante Alighieri (*c.* 1265–1321) Italian poet of the Middle Ages. His work *Commedia* was later nicknamed *Divina* by Bocaccio, *Divine Comedy*, and is often considered the greatest literary work composed in Italian. The work is in three parts: hell, purgatory and paradise.

Deism/Deists The idea that God does not intervene with the natural world that he created. God is transcendent. For Deists, God can only be known by means of reason and observation of nature but not by revelation.

Democritus (*c.* 460–*c.* 375 B.C.) Astronomer, theologian and natural philosopher influenced by Pythagoras. Expanded the atomic theory of Leucippus.

Demosthenes (384–322 B.C.) Athenian orator and statesman. His rhetoric made a significant contribution to the development of Athenian intellectual life and provides an insight into Greek culture during the fourth century B.C.

Diadochus, Proclus (410–485) Author of *On Sacrifice and Magic*, translated by Ficino. Athenian head of Neo-Platonic school.

Dionysius the Areopagite (*c.* 500) See Pseudo-Dionysius.

Epicurus (341–270 B.C.) Greek philosopher and founder of Epicureanism, which espoused that there was a direct correlation between goodness and pleasure and, correspondingly, evil with pain. Although little remains of Epicurus' prodigious output, much of his thought has been related by later Epicureans, who believed that peace and happiness were to be found in sensual and aesthetic experiences in this life, without the need to fear the afterlife or divine punishment.

Eugenius IV, Pope (*c.* 1383–1447) Gabriele Condulmer, Venetian Pope who presided at the Council of Florence.

Eusebius (Third Century A.D.) Author of *History of the Church*, one of the earliest Church histories with quotations from early Christian writers.

Figline Valdarno Ficino's birthplace, 25 km southeast of Florence.

Galen (131–201) Highly influential Greek Physician and follower of Plato. His Hippocratic medicine influenced humanist physicians well into the Renaissance, including Italian university curricula and physicians such as Thomas Linacre.

Gregory Nazianzen, St. (329–89) Greek Church Father and Bishop of Nazianzus Archbishop of Constantinople. The best rhetorician of the patristic age and a notable Trinitarian theologian.

Gregory the Great (540–604) Author of a commentary on Job in thirty-five books – *Moralia in Iob*, and four Homilies on the Gospel and rules for pastors. One of the four great Fathers of the Church. He was the first Pope to come from a monastic background.

Heraclitus (*c.* 500 B.C.) Greek sage famous for his riddles.

Hippocrates (460–377 B.C.) The greatest physician of his age and founder of the medical school on the Greek island of Cos. The first to develop medical theories upon observation and rational explanation.

Historiography The study of the means by which historians write history and the influences that come to bear upon them.

Homer Author of the *Iliad* and *Odyssey*. The greatest and most famous Greek poet to this day.

Humphrey, Duke of Gloucester (1391–1447) Patron of learning and humanism and benefactor to Oxford University.

Iamblichus of Chalcis (*c.* 250–325) Neoplatonist author of *On the mysteries of the Egyptians* translated by Ficino.

Irenaeus, St. (*c.* 130–*c.* 200) Latin Church Father and Bishop of Lyons. His writings were formative in the early development of Christian Theology. A disciple of Polycarp.

Jerome, St. (*c.* 342–420) Latin Church Father and translator of the Bible.

Lateran Council, Fifth Convened by Pope Julius II (1443–1513), it met on May 1513 at St. John Lateran Basilica in Rome. Pope Leo X continued the council after Julius's death; the last session was held on 16 March 1517.

Leo X, Pope (1475–1521) Giovanni de' Medici, Florentine Pope from 1513 to his death in 1521.

Peter Lombard or **Petrus Lombardus** (*c.* **1100–60)** French scholastic theologian and bishop. Author the *Four Books of Sentences* (from scripture) – the standard textbook of theology for many generations. He was known as *Magister Sententiarum*.

Lorenzo de' Medici (*Lorennzo il Magnifico*) (1449–92) Ruler of the Florentine republic and patron of many humanists, including poets and artists during the early Italian Renaissance. He achieved peace among Italian States which collapsed with his death.

Lucian (*c.* 120) Assyrian comic author and rhetorician who wrote Greek satire.

Macrobius (*c.* 400) Neoplatonist author of *Commentary on the Dream of Scipio* – one of the most influential sources of Platonism in the Renaissance.

Maximilian I (1459–1519) King of the Germans and Holy Roman Emperor from 1508 until his death, having jointly ruled with his father since 1483. He increased the House of Habsburg but lost Austrian lands at the battle of Dornach in 1499 and made treaties with the Swiss.

Cosimo de' Medici (1389–1464), or Cosimo the Elder Florentine statesman and patron of humanism.

Morton, John (*c.* 1420–1500) Archbishop of Canterbury from 1486 and Lord Chancellor from 1487. He took the young Thomas More into his household and was responsible for his early development.

Neoplatonism Religious and mystical philosophy, based upon Plotinus and Plato. The Neoplatonism of Plotinus and his pupil Porphyry was succeeded by that of Iamblichus and Proclus, which included magical practises, intended to assist the soul's return to the 'One'.

Nicholas V, Pope (1447–55) Humanist Pope who aimed to build a library containing all Greek literature available in Latin translation. To this end he employed Valla and Filelfo. He also planned to rebuild Rome in the classical style, for which purpose he employed Alberti and Fra Angelico.

Origen of Alexandria (185–254) Early theologian and highly influenced by Greek philosophy. Author of *On First Principles* and *Against Celsus* – a response to Celsus' attack on Christianity.

Ovid (43 B.C.–c. 17 A.D.) Ovidius Naso Roman poet and author of three major collections of poems: *Heroides*, *Amores* and *Ars Amatoria*, as well as the *Metamorphoses* and many other great works. Along with Virgil and Horace he is one of the canonic Latin poets and hugely influential as a source of classical mythology and elegiac writing for the Renaissance.

Papal nuncio Papal ambassador (to a foreign country or government for example).

Patristics Study of the works of the early Church Fathers and writers, such as Gregory the Great, Augustine of Hippo, Origen and Jerome.

Paul of Venice (1368–1428) Venetian theologian and logician. As a teenager he joined the Augustinians at the Venetian religious house Santo Stefano. Studied at Oxford and Padua. Called to Rome in 1427 by Pope Martin V in order to assess charges brought against Bernardino of Sienna.

Peter of Spain (1210/20–77) Pope John XXI from 1276, Portuguese logician and author of *Tractatus* or *Summulae Logicales Magistri Petri Hispani* (Logical matter of Master Peter of Spain)

Philology The critical study of the content and language of literary texts in order to reveal their true meaning and original intention.

Pius II, Pope (1458–64) (Enea Silvio Piccolomini) Humanist Pope who spent a great deal of money on a monument to his family in Pienza, subsequently converted into classical buildings, which still stand.

Pope Innocent VIII, Giovanni Battista Cybo (1432–92). Pope from 1484.

Plato (c. 429–347 B.C.) The greatest Greek philosopher. He studied with Socrates and the Pythagoreans in Egypt. Founded the famous School of Athens for philosophy.

Platonic Academy Named after the fourth-century Platonic Academy at Athens, the so-called Academy in fifteenth-century Florence was a collection of scholars, patronized by Lorenzo de' Medici, and some of them supported by him, who never had an institutional form. It held no regular meetings and taught no students. The group met occasionally to discuss Ficino's ideas and discoveries arising from his translations of Plato and Neoplatonists.

Plotinus (204–70) Egyptian founder of Neoplatonic philosophy. He studied with Ammonius Saccas in Alexandria before founding his own school of philosophy in Rome. Works include the *Enneads*, edited by his pupil Porphyry.

Podestà A title given to a chief magistrate in Late-medieval Italian States (such as Florence).

Porphyry (232/4–c. 305) Neo-Platonic follower of Plotinus who studied in Athens before settling in Rome, where he edited Plotinus' works and wrote his biography.

Pseudo-Dionysius (c. Sixth Century) Anonymous author of the *Corpus Areopagiticum* (early sixth century) thought to be the Athenian convert mentioned in Acts 17: 34, but probably a fifth or sixth-century Syrian writer. Extant include *Divine Names, Mystical Theology, Celestial Hierarchy* and *Ecclesiastical Hierarchy*, and various letters.

Ptolomy, Claudius (c. 121–51) Alexandrian astonomer, mathematician and astrologer. Author of *Tetrabiblos* and *Centiloquium* both on astrology.

Pythagoras, of Samos (c. 569–c. 475 B.C.) Huge influence on western mathematics and science, although he left no works. Founder of a strict community at Kroton in southern Italy. His ideas were transmitted to the Renaissance *via* generations of Pythagoreans, and his ideas were viewed as the purest form of Platonism.

Quintilian (b. 35/40–c. 100) Marcus Fabius Quintilianus. Roman rhetorician from Hispania much admired in the Renaissance. Author of *Institutia Oratio*, a twelve-volume work on rhetoric.

renovatio Latin for 'renewal' in the context of the Renaissance uncovering of their classical heritage of literature and art.

Rhetoric The art of persuasive, elegant public speaking. An art rediscovered and practised by Renaissance humanists as a means of developing ideas through well-expressed dialogue.

Sallust (86–c. 34 B.C.) Gaius Sallustius Crispus Roman historian and statesman, supporter of Caesar and oppose of Pompey. Author of *De Coniuratione Catilinae* (Conspiracy of Catiline), *Bellum Iugurthinum* (Jugurthine War) and *Historiae*, a history of Rome from 78–67 B.C.

Savonarola, Girolamo (1452–98) Dominican priest from Ferrara. He was known for his outspokenness on the immorality of his age in Florence. He preached against the shortcomings of the clergy, finding opposition from Rodrigo Borgia (Pope Alexander VI) who was responsible for his execution in Florence in 1498.

Scholasticism From the Latin *scholasticus* (belonging to the school). A method of learning taught by *scholastics, school people,* or *schoolmen* in medieval universities *c.* 1100–1500. Originally begun as an attempt to reconcile ancient classical philosophy with medieval Christian theology. Scholasticism was not a philosophy or theology in itself, but rather a tool or method for learning that placed emphasis on the use of reason.

Seneca the Elder (*c.* 55 B.C.–37/41 A.D.) Lucius or Marcus Annaeus Seneca. Roman rhetorician of Spanish birth; author of the ten volumes of *Controversiae*, discussing seventy-four topics from Greek and Roman orators.

Seneca the Younger (*c.* 4/5 B.C.–65 A.D.) Lucius Annaeus Seneca. Son of Seneca the Elder; Roman philosopher admired in works by Dante, Petrarch and even Chaucer. Tutor and advisor to Nero. Author of philosophical essays, letters, tragedies and satires.

Socrates (469–399 B.C.) Controversial Athenian philosopher who was executed for his outspokenness on politics and religion. Tutor to Plato and committed to critical reasoning, truth, virtue and dialectic.

Suetonius (69–*c.* 140) Author of *Lives of Caesars*. Roman biographer and one-time secretary to Emperor Hadrian.

Tacitus (*c.* 55–after 115) Publius (or Gaius) Cornelius Tacitus. Roman historian and senator. Author of the *Annals* and *Histories*, which examine the reigns of Emperors Tiberius, Claudius, Nero and the year of the Four Emperors. The works cover the death of Augustus in 14 A.D. to the death of Domitian in 96 A.D.

Tertullian (*c.* 162–224) Leader of the Carthage Church and theologian, who promoted Latin as the standard ecclesiastical language in the West.

Theurgy From the Greek θεουργία. The practice of magical rituals, intended to invoke the presence of God (or gods), and unite humans with the divine, achieving a perfection of oneself.

Thomists Followers of St. Thomas Aquinas.

Timaeus of Locri Possibly a fictitious character invented by Plato. The 'Pythagorean' was the subject of Plato's great work *Timaeus*.

Trismegistus, Hermes meaning thrice-great Hermes, the name is a combination of the Greek God Hermes and the Egyptiam God Thoth, as the Greeks related the two as one. In the Renaissance, he is believed to have been a contemporary of Moses and the literature attributed to him (proabably from the second and third centuries A.D.), the *Corpus Hermeticum*, covers alchemy, magic, ancient wisdom and philosophy, mainly in the form of dialogue. In the Renaissance, Ficino's Latin edition of the *Corpus Hermeticum* was reprinted several times before 1500.

Virgil (70–19 B.C.) Author of *Eclogues, Georgics* and *Aenead*. The greatest of all Latin poets.

Vulgate Latin version of the Bible ascribed to St. Jerome (*c.* 347–420).

Wolsey, Thomas (*c.* 1471–1530) Virtually the most powerful Tudor statesman and clergyman; patron of humanism; Lord Chancellor; Archbishop of York; made Cardinal in 1515, giving him precedence over the Archbishop of Canterbury.

Xenophon (*c.* 430–*c.*355 B.C.) Another follower of Socrates, Greek historian soldier who helped defeat the Athenians in 394 B.C. and was, thereafter, banished to support Sparta; author of several histories.

Zoroaster (**Zarathushtra**) (*c.* 1000 B.C.) Enigmatic Iranian founder of the Persian religion, Zoroastrianism. Ficino promoted his reputation as a sage and magician as well as one of the chief sources of ancient theology, along with Hermes Trsimegistus.

ABBREVIATIONS

Add.   Additional.
ch.   chapter
ed.   edited by
Ep.   Epistle
fol(s). folio(s).
MS(S)   Manuscript(s).
n.   note.
no.   number.
r.   *recto.*
STC   Pollard, A.W. and Redgrave, G.R., *A Short Title Catalogue of Books Printed in England, Scotland and Ireland and of English Books Printed Abroad, 1475–1640*, first compiled in 1926, second edition revised and enlarged by W.A. Jackson and F.S. Ferguson (1976–86), completed by K.F. Pantzer, The Bibliographical Society, I: A-H; II: I-Z; III: printers and publishers index, indices and appendices (London, 1976–91).
trans. translated by
v.   *verso.*
vol(s). volume(s).

NOTES

Introduction

1. J. Hankins, 'Humanism, Scholasticism, and Renaissance Philosophy' in J. Hankins (ed.), *The Cambridge Companion to Renaissance Philosophy* (Cambridge, 2007) [hereafter *CCRP*], pp. 30–48 [hereafter Hankins, 'Humanism']. Here at pp. 30–31, citing G. Voigt, *Die Wiederbelebung des Classischen Altertums Oder das Erste Jahrhundert des Humanismus* (Berlin, 1859) and V.R. Giustiani, 'Homo, Humanus, and the Meanings of "Humanism" ', *The Journal of the History of Ideas* [hereafter *JHI*], 46 (1985), pp. 167–95.

2. R. Weiss, *The Dawn of Humanism in Italy* (London, 1947), revised and reprinted in *The Bulletin of the Institute of Historical Research*, 42 (1969), pp. 1–16. [hereafter Weiss, 'Dawn of Humanism']. Here at p. 3. Other early humanists included Geri d'Arezzo and Francesco da Barberino in Florence, as well as Paolo da Perugia and Barbato da Sulmona in Naples.

3. R. Witt, 'Coluccio Salutati in the Footsteps of the Ancients', [hereafter Witt, 'Salutati'] in A.A. MacDonald, Z.R.W.M. von Martels and J.R. Veenstra (eds.), *Christian Humanism: Essays in Honour of Arjo Vanderjagt* (Leiden, 2009) [hereafter *Christian Humanism*], pp. 3–12.

4. Attributed to the humanists Crotus Rubeanus (Johannes Jäger) and Ulrich von Hutten, who wrote a sequel (1519). L.W. Spitz, 'The Renaissance: Humanism and Humanism Research', English version of 'Humanismus/ Humanismusforschung' in *Theologische Realenzyklopädie*, 15 (Berlin and New York, 1986), pp. 639–61; reprinted in L.W. Spitz, *Luther and German Humanism*, (Hampshire, 1996), pp. 1–40 [hereafter Spitz, 'Humanism']. Here at pp. 2–3.

5. For this survey, see M. Dowling, *Fisher of Men: A Life of John Fisher, 1469–1535* (Basingstoke, 1999) [hereafter Dowling, *Fisher*], p. 31; N. Mann, 'The Origins of Humanism' in J. Kraye (ed.), *The Cambridge Companion to Renaissance Humanism* (Cambridge, 1996) [hereafter

CCRH], p. 1; A. Hamilton, 'Humanists and the Bible' in *CCRH*, p. 100; N. Mann, 'The Origins of Humanism' in *CCRH*, pp. 1–2.

6. Hankins, 'Humanism', p. 31.

7. *Ibid.*, p. 32.

8. *Ibid.*

9. D. MacCulloch, *Reformation: Europe's House Divided, 1470–1700* (London, 2003) [hereafter MacCulloch, *Reformation*], p. 76; R. Rex, 'The New Learning', *The Journal of Ecclesiastical History* [hereafter *JEH*], 44 (1993), pp. 26–44.

10. Hankins, 'Humanism', p. 46; P.O. Kristeller. 'The Scholar and his Public in the Late Middle-Ages' [hereafter Kristeller, 'Scholar'] in E.P. Mahoney (ed.), *Medieval Aspects of Renaissance Learning: Three Essays by Paul Oskar Kristeller* (Durham, N. Carolina, 1974) [hereafter Kristeller, *Renaissance Learning*], pp. 3–28. Here at p. 10: For the humanists, 'grammatical and historical interpretation for the most part takes the place of dialectical analysis and argumentation, more value is placed on style, and the terminology of scholastic learning is rather avoided.'; on the *Septennium* and liberal arts see S. IJsseling, *Rhetoric and Philosophy in Conflict: A Historical Survey* (The Hague, 1976) [hereafter IJsseling], p. 46.

11. P. Mack, 'Montaigne and Christian Humanism' in *Christian Humanism*, pp. 199–209. Here at p. 199.

12. IJsseling, p. 1. See also Spitz, 'Humanism', pp. 5–7; Weiss, 'Dawn of Humanism', p. 1.

13. Hankins, 'Humanism', p. 39; this point is also noted by R. Witt, *'In the Footsteps of the Ancients': The Origins of Humanism from Lovato to Bruni* (Leiden, 2000), p. 240.

14. Witt, 'Salutati', p. 9.

15. Weiss, 'Dawn of Humanism', p. 14.

16. A. Levi, *Renaissance and Reformation: The Intellectual Genesis* (New Haven, Connecticut and London, 2002) [hereafter Levi], pp. 80–85.

17. F. Petrarch, 'On his Own Ignorance and that of Many Others', trans. H. Nachod in E. Cassirer, P.O. Kristeller and J.H. Randall, Jr. (eds.), *The Renaissance Philosophy of Man* (Chicago, 1948) [hereafter *Renaissance Philosophy of Man*], p. 115.

18. '*Nihil enim est aliud eloquentia nisi copiose loquens sapientia*': Cicero, *De Partitione Oratoria*, p. 79. Also quoted in H.H. Gray, 'Renaissance Humanism: The Pursuit of Eloquence', *The Journal of the History of Ideas* [hereafter *JHI*], 24 (1963), pp. 497–514, quoted on p. 508.

19. Kristeller, 'Scholar', p. 12.

20. *Ibid.*, pp. 16–17.

21. *Ibid.*, pp. 13–14.

22. J.B. Gleason, *John Colet* (Berkeley, 1989) [hereafter Gleason], pp. 46 and 194–5; S. Jayne, *John Colet and Marsilio Ficino* (Oxford, 1963) [hereafter Jayne], pp. 47–55; L. Miles, *John Colet and the Platonic Tradition* (London, 1962) [hereafter Miles], *passim*; L. Miles 'Platonism and Christian Doctrine: The Revival of Interest in John Colet', *Philosophical Forum*, 21 (1964), pp. 87–103 [hereafter Miles, 'Platonism'].

23. E.A. Livingstone (ed.), *The Concise Dictionary of the Christian Church* (Oxford, 1977), pp. 405–6. In the 1960s Garin closely connected philosophy and humanism but Kristeller had already rejected the idea that humanism was a philosophy: E. Garin, *Italian Humanism: Philosophy and Civic Life in the Renaissance*, trans. P. Munz (Oxford, 1965), *passim.*; P.O. Kristeller, 'Florentine Platonism and its Relations with Humanism and Scholasticism', *Church History,* 8 (1939), pp. 201–11 [hereafter Kristeller, 'Florentine Platonism']. However, the connection between philosophy and humanism is upheld, perhaps anachronistically, by A. Edelheit in *Ficino, Pico and Savonarola: The Evolution of Humanist Theology 1461/2–1498* (Leiden, 2008).

24. For instance, in Cambridge University Library [hereafter CUL], MS Gg.iv.26, fol. 34v, John Colet demonstrates how Platonic ideas were employed by a Christian humanist; J. Colet, *Joannis Coleti Enarratio In Epistolam S. Pauli ad Romanos: An Exposition of St. Paul's Epistle to the Romans, delivered as Lectures in the University of Oxford about the year 1497, by John Colet D.D.,* trans. J.H. Lupton (London, 1873) [hereafter *Colet Romans*], p. 74/Latin, p. 186.

25. K.L. Flannery, SJ, 'Plato and Platonism' in A. Hastings, A. Mason and H. Pyper (eds.), *The Oxford Companion to Christian Thought* (Oxford, 2000), pp. 542–4.

26. J.E. Siegel, *Rhetoric and Philosophy in Renaissance Humanism: The Union of Eloquence and Wisdom, Petrarch to Valla* (Princeton, 1968) [hereafter Siegel], p. 258; Kristeller, 'Florentine Platonism', pp. 201ff.

27. Siegel, p. 258. Letter of Pico to Barbaro, June 1485, translated in Q. Breen, 'Giovanni Pico della Mirandola on the Conflict of Philosophy and Rhetoric', *JHI* (1952), pp. 384–412 [hereafter Breen, 'Pico to Barbaro'].

28. For a good survey of humanism's influence in at least parts of Europe, see the articles in N. Scott Amos, A.D.M. Pettegree and H. Van Nierop (eds.), *The Education of a Christian Society: Humanism and the Reformation in Britain and the Netherlands* (Aldershot, 1999) [hereafter Scott Amos], especially, regarding England, Richard Rex's 'The Role of English Humanists in the Reformation up to 1559', pp. 19–40 [hereafter Rex, 'Humanism']: 'Civic humanist assumptions prevailed everywhere from the early sixteenth century to such an extent that it was impossible to attain political or even ecclesiastical office without a humanist formation.', p. 40.

29. Siegel, p. 259.

30. C.G. Nauert, *Humanism and the Culture of the Renaissance* (Cambridge, 1995; second edition, Cambridge, 2006) [hereafter Nauert, *Humanism*], pp. 151–167.

31. Rex, 'Humanism', p. 19.

32. J.M. Kittelson, 'Humanism in the Theological Faculties of Lutheran Universities during the Late Reformation' in M.P. Fleischer (ed.), *The Harvest of Humanism in Central Europe. Essays in Honour of Lewis W. Spitz* (St. Louis, 1992), pp. 139–57. Here at p. 154.

33. H. Baron, *The Crisis of the Early Italian Renaissance: Civic Humanism and Republican Liberty in an Age of Classicism and Tyranny*, 2 vols. (Princeton, 1955) [hereafter Baron, *Crisis*].

34. Rex, 'Humanism', p. 36 and p. 40.

35. MacCulloch, *Reformation*, p. 76.

36. Breen, 'Pico to Barbaro', p. 384.

37. *Ibid.*, p. 385.

38. *Ibid.*, p. 386.

39. *Ibid.*, p. 395.

40. *Ibid.*

41. Q. Breen, 'Melanchthon's Reply to Giovanni Pico della Mirandola', *JHI*, 13 (1952), pp. 413–426.

42. J. Hankins, 'The Significance of Renaissance Philosophy' in *CCRP*, p. 341.

43. *Ibid.*

44. Z. S. Schiffman, *Humanism and the Renaissance* (Boston, 2002) [hereafter Schiffman], p. 1.

45. J. Michelet, *Renaissance* (Paris, 1855).

46. Schiffman, p. 2.

47. *Ibid.*

48. *Ibid.*, p. 3, quoting Michelet. For an excellent assessment of Burckhardt's influence until the mid-twentieth century, see W.K. Ferguson, *The Renaissance in Historical Thought: Five Centuries of Interpretation* (Cambridge, Mass. 1948; reprinted in Toronto, 2006) [hereafter Ferguson], pp. 179–385.

49. J. Huizinga, *The Waning of the Middle Ages: A Study of the Forms of Life, Thought and Art in France and the Netherlands in the XIVth and XVth Centuries* (First Dutch edition, 1919; Second Dutch edition, 1921; English edition, London, 1924); C.H. Haskins, *The Renaissance of the Twelfth Century* (Cambridge, Mass., 1927); E. Panofsky, *Renaissance and Renascenes in Western Art* (London, 1969); Schiffman, p. 3.

50. Baron, *Crisis*; *idem, From Petrarch to Leonardi Bruni* (Chicago, 1968); *idem, In Search of Civic Humanism*, 2 vols. (Princeton, 1988).

51. Baron, *Crisis*; Seigel; Q. Skinner, *The Foundations of Modern Political Thought, Vol. I: The Renaissance* (Cambridge, 1978); A. Grafton, 'Humanism and Political Theory' in J.H. Burns (ed.), *The Cambridge History of Political Thought, 1450–1700* (Cambridge, 1991), pp. 20–29. Schiffman, pp. 5–6; E. Cassirer, 'Giovanni Pico della Mirandola. A Study in the History of Renaissance Ideas', *JHI*, 3 (1942), pp. 123–44 and 319–46; *idem, The Individual and the Cosmos in Renaissance Philosophy*, trans. M. Domandi (New York, 1963).

52. Schiffman, p. 4.

53. A. Edelheit, 'Humanism and Theology in Renaissance Florence: Four Examples (Caroli, Savonarola, Ficino, and Pico)', in *Verbum Analecta Neolatina*, 8 (2006), pp. 271–290 [hereafter Edelheit, 'Humanism and Theology']. Here at p. 272, citing Eugenio Garin, 'Le interpretazioni del pensiero di Giovanni Pico', *L'Opera e il pensiero di Giovanni Pico*

della Mirandola nella storia dell' umanesimo, convegno internaziale (Mirandola, 15–18 Settembre, 1963), 2 vols. (Firenze, 1965), I, pp. 3–33, at pp. 32–33.

54. Kristeller, 'Florentine Platonism', pp. 201–11.

55. P.O. Kristeller, *Renaissance Thought and its Sources*, ed. M. Mooney (Columbia, 1979), p. 23; see also, R. Witt, 'The Humanism of Paul Oskar Kristeller' in J. Monfasani (ed.), *Kristeller Reconsidered. Essays on his Life and Scholarship* (New York, 2006), pp. 257–67, esp. pp. 258–9.

56. E. Garin, 'Ricordando Giovanni e Gianfrabcesco Pico della Mirandola', *Giornale Critico Della Filosofia Italiana*, 74 (1995), pp. 5–19, here at pp. 8–9, cited in F. Borghesi, 'A Life in Works', in M.V. Dougherty (ed.), *Pico della Mirandola: New Essays* (Cambridge, 2008) [hereafter Dougherty, *New Essays*], pp. 202–219 [hereafter Borghesi], p. 203.

57. C. Trinkaus, *In Our Image and Likeness: Humanity and Divinity in Italian Humanist Thought*, 2 vols. (London, 1970) [hereafter Trinkaus, *Image*]; *idem, The Scope of Renaissance Humanism* (Ann Arbor, 1983); J. O' Malley, *Praise and Blame in Renaissance Rome: Rhetoric, Doctrine, and Reform in the Sacred Orators of the Papal Court, c. 1450–1521* (Durham, North Carolina, 1979); J. D'Amico, *Renaissance Humanism in Papal Rome: Humanists and Churchmen of the Eve of the Reformation* (Baltimore, 1983); A. Edelheit, *Ficino, Pico and Savonarola: The Evolution of Humanist Theology, 1461/2–1498* (Leiden, 2008) [hereafter Edelheit, *Humanist Theology*].

58. Trinkaus, *Image*; W.J. Bouwsma, 'The Two Faces of Humanism: Stoicism and Augustinianism in Renaissance Thought,' in H.A. Oberman and T.A. Brady, Jr. (eds.), *Itinerarium Italicum: The Profile of the Italian Renaissance in the Mirror of Its European Transformations* (Leiden, 1975).

59. Edelheit, 'Humanism and Theology', p. 272.

60. *Ibid.*, p. 290.

61. Edelheit, *Christian Humanism*, p. 18.

62. *Ibid.*, p. 464.

63. *Ibid.*, pp. 18–19; quotation, p. 21.

64. *CCRH*; A. Rabil, Jr.,(ed.), *Renaissance Humanism: Foundations, Forms and Legacy*, 3 vols. (Philadelphia, 1988) [hereafter Rabil, *Renaissance Humanism*]; A.E. McGrath, *The Intellectual Origins of the European Reformation* (Oxford, 1987; second edition, Oxford, 2004); L. Kekewich (ed.), *The Renaissance in Europe: A Cultural Enquiry* (New Haven, Connecticut and London, 2000); C.G. Nauert, *Humanism and the Culture of the Renaissance* (Cambridge, 1995; second edition, Cambridge, 2006); A. Goodman and A. Mackay (eds.), *The Impact of Humanism on Western Europe* (London, 1990); Schiffman, *passim*; Levi; J. Brotton, *The Renaissance Bazaar: From the Silk Road to Michelangelo* (Oxford, 2002) [hereafter Brotton, *Renaissance Bazaar*]; R. Black (ed.), *Renaissance Thought: A Reader* (London and New York, 2001).

65. *Christian Humanism, passim*; A. Edelheit, *Humanist Theology*.

66. On women and humanism see M.L. King and A. Rabil Jr., 'The Other Voice in Early Modern Europe: Introduction to the Series', in *The Education of a Christian Woman: A Sixteenth-Century Manual*, ed. and trans. C. Fantazzi (Chicago, 2000) [English translation of *De Institutione Feminae Christianae*, hereafter *De Institutione*], pp. ix-xxviii; M.L. King, 'Book-lined Cells: Women and Humanism in the Early Italian Renaissance', in P.H. Labalme (ed.), *Beyond Their Sex: Learned Women of the European Past* (New York, 1980) [hereafter Labalme], pp. 71–81 [hereafter King, 'Book-lined Cells'], *passim.*; L. Kekewich, 'Women Humanists' in L. Kekewich (ed.), *The Renaissance in Europe: A Cultural Enquiry. The Impact of Humanism* (New Haven, Connecticut and London, 2000) [hereafter Kekewich], pp. 87–90. See also, Brotton, *Renaissance Bazaar*, pp. 73–76; Nauert, pp. 54–59.

67. Kekewich, pp. 87–90; Brotton, *Renaissance Bazaar*, pp. 73–76; Nauert, pp. 54–59.

68. King, 'Book-lined Cells', pp. 71–81. See also M.L. King and A. Rabil (eds.), *Her Immaculate Hand: Selected Works by and about the Women Humanists of Quattrocento Italy* (New York, 1983) [hereafter *Her Immaculate Hand*], *passim.*

69. M.L. King, 'Goddess and Captive: Antonio Loschi's Poetic Tribute to Madalena Scrovegni (1389), Study and Text', *Medievalia et Humanistica*, 10 (1980), pp. 103–27 [hereafter King, 'Goddess and Captive']; *Her Immaculate Hand*, p. 16.

70. *Her Immaculate Hand*, p. 16.

71. Their lives are briefly outlined in *Her Immaculate Hand*, pp. 16–20.

72. *Ibid.*, pp. 21–25.

73. King, 'Book-lined Cells', p. 77, quoted in Schiffman, p. 118.

74. King, 'Goddess and Captive', pp. 103–27 and *Her Immaculate Hand*, p. 11.

75. *Her Immaculate Hand*, p. 13.

76. L. Bruni, *De Studiis et Literis*, trans. by W.H. Woodward in *Vitorino da Feltre and other Humanist Educators* (New York, 1963), pp. 119–33. [hereafter Bruni, *De Studiis*]; *Her Immaculate Hand*, p. 13.

77. Bruni, *De Studiis*, p. 126; *Her Immaculate Hand*, p. 14.

78. Bruni, *De Studiis*, p. 129.

79. *Her Immaculate Hand*, p. 15.

80. King, 'Book-lined Cells', p. 73.

81. King, p. 81, quoted in Schiffman, p. 122.

82. *Her Immaculate Hand*, pp. 25–6.

Chapter 1: Francesco Petrarch

1. For the latest work on Petrarch see B. Reynolds, *Petrarch: The Forgotten Genius* (London, 2011). For two observations on Petrarch's mixed Christian and Pagan heritage, see M. Lorch, 'Petrarch, Cicero and the Classical Pagan Tradition' in Rabil, *Renaissance Humanism*, I, pp. 71–94;

and A. Rabil, 'Petrarch, Augustine and the Classical Christian Tradition' in *idem*, pp. 95–114.

2. F. Petrarch, *Le Traité De Sui Ipsius et Multorum Ignorantia*, ed. L.M. Capelli (Paris, 1906), trans. by H. Nachod [hereafter Capelli], p. 78–9, translation, p. 115; P.O. Kristeller, *Eight Philosophers of the Italian Renaissance* (Stanford, CA, 1964) [hereafter *Eight Philosophers*], p. 17.

3. Spitz, 'Humanism', pp. 5–7.

4. Levi, pp. 80–85.

5. Witt, 'Salutati', p. 3.

6. *Seniles* 17:2 in F. Petrarch, *Francesco Petrarca: Prose*, ed. G. Martellotti, P.G. Ricci, E. Carrara and E. Bianchi (Milan, 1955); Witt, 'Salutati', p. 4.

7. Introduction, pp. 1–4.

8. C. Salutati, *Epistolario di Coluccio Salutati*, ed. F. Novati, 4 vols. (Rome, 1891–1911), vol. 3, p. 84, quoted in Witt, 'Salutati', p. 4.

9. Witt, 'Salutati', p. 27.

10. Introduction, pp. 8–11.

11. P.O. Kristeller and J.H. Randall, Jr, 'General Introduction' *The Renaissance Philosophy of Man*, p. 3.

12. *Eight Philosophers*, p. 18.

13. M. Bishop, *Petrarch and His World* (London, 1964) [hereafter Bishop], p. 13, quoting Petrarch's *Epistle to Posterity*, printed in F. Petrarch, *Epistolae Seniles* (Venice, 2003), XIII, p. 3.

14. Bishop, p. 14. Both White and Black Guelphs were pro-Papal and the Whites had been in power at the end of the thirteenth century.

15. N. Mann, *Petrarch* (Oxford, 1984) [hereafter Mann], p. 11.

16. Levi, p. 81

17. Bishop, p. 71.

18. *Ibid.*, p. 79, quoting Petrarch's *Canzionere*, poem LXXVI.

19. A. Mortimer (ed.), *Petrarch's Canzionere in the English Renaissance* (Revised and enlarged edition, Rodopi, Amsterdam and New York, 2005) contains many works which owe a debt to Petrarch's love poem.

20. Mann, p. 12.

21. Bishop, pp. 68–9: letter from Petrarch to Giacomo di Colonna (1336), *Epistolae Familiares*, II, p. 9.

22. Levi, p. 81.

23. *Ibid.*, p. 82.

24. Bishop, p. 62, quoting some words written by Petrarch on the flyleaf of his copy of Virgil, reprinted in G. Carducci and S. Ferrari (eds.), *Le Rime di Francesco Petrarca* (Florence, 1899), p. 370.

25. Levi, p. 82 and p. 389, n. 10 citing C.N.J. Mann's Rowe Memorial Lecture, 'Petrarch: The Life of Letters', delivered at Oxford on 19 May, 1997. In fact 6 April 1347 was not Good Friday, but a Monday.

26. Nauert, *Humanism*, p. 19.

27. *Ibid.*, p. 19.

28. *Ibid.* p. 20; A.S. Bernado, 'Petrarch, Dante and the Medieval Tradition' in Rabil, *Renaissance Humanism*, I, pp. 115–140.

29. Nauert, *Humanism*, p. 20.

30. Ferguson, pp. 179–385.

31. F. Petrarch, *Epistolae Rerum Familiarium*, in F. Petrarch, *Le Familiari*, ed. V. Rossi and U. Bosco (Florence, 1933–42), Book VI, no. II, pp. 55–60, at p. 55; and *ibid.*, Book XVII, no. I, 221–30, at p. 224, quoted in *Eight Philosophers*, p. 12.

32. *Eight Philosophers*, p. 12.

33. Nauert, *Humanism*, p. 23. John Colet famously condemned pagan authors only to include them in his school's curriculum alongside Christian texts.

34. Quotation from Nauert, *Humanism*, p. 23.

35. F. Petrarca, *Invectives,* ed. and trans. D. Marsh (Cambridge, Mass., 2003) [hereafter Petrarca, *Invectives*].

36. *Eight Philosophers*, p. 6.

37. Bishop, p. 354, quoting Petrarch's *Epistolae Seniles*, V, p. 2.

38. *Eight Philosophers*, p. 7.

39. *Ibid.*

40. Petrarca, *Invectives*, paragraph 110, quoted in Hankins, 'Humanism', p. 44.

41. Petrarca, *Invectives*, paragraph 87, quoted in Hankins, 'Humanism', p. 41.

42. *Eight Philosophers*, p. 8.

43. J. Kraye, 'The Revival of Hellenistic Philosophies' in *CCRP*, pp. 97–111, here at p. 100; F. Petrarca, *Remedies for Fortune Fair and Foul*, trans. and comm. C.H. Rawski, 5 vols. (Bloomington, IN, 1991), III, pp. 267–79.

44. C.S. Celenza, 'The Revival of Platonic Philosophy', in *CCRP*, pp. 72–96, here at p. 73.

45. Capelli, p. 75, trans. Nachod, p. 111. In the same treatise, on ignorance, Petrarch describes Plato as '*Philosophie Principem*', 'Prince of Philosophy', p. 72, trans. Nachod, p. 98, quoted in *Eight Philosophers*, p. 9.

46. *Eight Philosophers*, p. 10.

47. Petrarca, *Invectives, passim*.

48. E.H. Wilkins, *Life of Petrarch* (Chicago, 1961), pp. 123–4.

49. Petrarca, *Invectives*, p. 181.

50. *Secretum*, book II in Petrarch's *Prose*, ed. Martellotti, *et al* (Milan and Naples, 1955), pp. 106–28.

51. Capelli, p. 45; trans. Nachod, p. 80.

52. Capelli, p. 70, trans. Nachod, pp. 105–6.

53. *Eight Philosophers*, p. 17.

54. Capelli, p. 78–9, trans. Nachod, p. 115; *Eight Philosophers*, p. 17.

55. C.L. Stinger, 'Humanism in Florence' in Rabil, *Renaissance Humanism*, pp. 175–208.

56. Nauert, *Humanism*, p. 25.

57. *Ibid.*, p. 26.

58. Witt, 'Salutati', p. 6.

59. *Ibid.*, p. 4.
60. Nauert, *Humanism*, p. 27.
61. Witt, 'Salutati', p. 5.
62. Nauert, *Humanism*, p. 28.
63. Witt, 'Salutati', p. 5.
64. *Ibid.*, p. 12.
65. C. Salutati, letter to Ugolino Orsini in *Epistolario di Coluccio Salutati*, ed. F. Novati, 4 vols. (Rome, 1891–1911), I, p. 110; Witt, 'Salutati', p. 12.
66. Nauert, *Humanism*, p. 30.
67. *Ibid.*, p. 31.
68. Appendix, *CCRP*, p. 347.
69. A. Rabil, 'The Significance of "Civic Humanism" in the Interpretation of the Italian Renaissance' in Rabil, *Renaissance Humanism*, I, pp. 141–175.
70. Nauert *Humanism*, p. 32.
71. Sallust, *Bellum Iugurthinum*, X.6 in Sallust, *Works*, ed. J.C. Rolfe (Cambridge, Mass., 1921), p. 149, quoted by E. Nelson, 'The Problem of the Prince' in *CCRP*, pp. 319–337 [hereafter Nelson], here at p. 326.
72. L. Bruni, *Laudatio Florentinae Urbis*, trans. R.G. Witt in B.G. Kohl and R.G. Witt, *The Earthly Republic: Italian Humanists on Government and Society* (Philadelphia, PA, 1978), p. 149.
73. *Ibid.*, p. 151.
74. Quotation from *ibid.*, p. 173; Nelson, p. 328.

Chapter 2: Lorenzo Valla

1. '*Plures a me libri compluresque emissi sunt in omni fere doctrinarum genere, in quibus quod a nonnullis magnisque et longo iam evo probates auctoribus dissentio…qui non tantum adversus mortuos scribo, sed adversus etiam vivos, nec in unum alterumve, sed in plurimos, nec contra privates modo, verum etiam contra magistrates!*': translation from L. Valla, *On the Donation of Constantine*, trans. G.W. Bowersock (Cambridge, Mass., 2007), pp. 2–3.
2. C.S. Celenza, *The Lost Italian Renaissance: Humanists, Historians, and Latin's Legacy* (Baltimore and London, 2004) [hereafter Celenza, *Lost Renaissance*], p. 85; J. Kraye, 'Lorenzo Valla and Changing Perceptions of Renaissance Humanism', *Comparative Criticism*, 23 (2001), pp. 37–55.
3. L. Nauta, 'Lorenzo Valla and the Rise of Humanist Dialectic', in *CCRP*, pp. 193–210 [hereafter Nauti, 'Valla'], here at p. 195.
4. For a concise biography of Valla, see M. Lorch, 'Lorenzo Valla' in Rabil, *Renaissance Humanism*, I, pp. 332–349.
5. Celenza, *Lost Renaissance*, p. 86; J. Davies, *Florence and its University during the Early Renaissance*, Education and Society in the Middle Ages and Renaissance, 8 (Leiden, 1998).
6. Nauta, 'Valla', p. 204. In Valla's words, '*fictio non quadrat nec sibi constat*': L. Valla, *On Pleasure/De Voluptate*, ed. M. Lorch, trans.

A.K. Hieatt and M. Lorch (New York, 1977) [hereafter Valla, *De Voluptate*], pp. 188–9; U. Langer, 'The Ring of Gyges in Plato, Cicero, and Lorenzo Valla: The Moral Force of Fictional Examples' in *Res et Verba in der Renaissance*, ed. E. Kessler and I. Maclean (Wiesbaden, 2002), pp. 131–45.

7. Valla, *De Voluptate*, p. 49.

8. Nauta, 'Valla', in *CCRP*, pp. 193–4.

9. L. Valla, *De Falso Credita et Ementita Constantini Donatione Declamtio (1440): The Treatise of Lorenzo Valla on the Donation of Constantine*, trans. Christopher B. Coleman (Toronto, 1993, reprinted 2005) [hereafter Valla, *De Falso*], pp. 27 and 29 (Latin, pp. 26 and 28).

10. *Ibid.*, p. 159 (Latin, p.158).

11. Nauta, 'Valla', pp. 195–6. Valla explains this thesis in a letter to Giovanni Tortelli: L. Valla, *Epistole*, ed. O. Besomi and M. Regoliosi (Padua, 1984), pp. 214 and 216.

12. *De Professione Religiosorum* was not published until 1869: *De Professione Religiosorum*, ed. J. Vahlen (*Laurentii Vallae Opuscula Tria*, in 'Sitzungsberichte der Kaiserlichen Akademie der Wissenschaften, Philos. Und Hist. Kl.,' nos. 61 and 62) (Vienna, 1869).

13. L. Nauta, *In Defence of Common Sense : Lorenzo Valla's Humanist Critique of Scholastic Philosophy* (Cambridge, Mass., and London, 2009) [hereafter Nauta, *Common Sense*], pp. 13, 48–9.

14. L. Valla, *Repastinatio Dialectice et Philosophie*, ed. G. Zippel, 2 vols. (Padua, 1982) [hereafter Valla, *Repastinatio*], I, *passim*.

15. Celenza, *Lost Renaissance*, p. 86. See also the Dialogues of Reuchlin and Pico.

16. *Ibid.*, p. 87; N.S. Struever, *The Language of History in the Renaissance: Rhetoric and Historical Consciousness in Florentine Humanism* (Princeton, 1970); R.G. Witt, *In the Footsteps of the Ancients: The Origins of Humanism from Lovato to Bruni* (Leiden, 2000), pp. 432–42; L. Jardine, 'Lorenzo Valla and the Intellectual Origins of Humanist Dialectic', *Journal of the History of Philosophy*, 15 (1977), pp. 143–64.

17. Nauta, 'Valla', p. 202 ; Valla, *Repastinatio*, I, pp. 175–6

18. Valla, *Repastinatio*, I, pp. 175 and 447.

19. Nauta, 'Valla', p. 202, quoting Quintilian, *Institutio Oratoria*, 5.10.8.

20. II Corinthians 12:10: 'There I am content with weaknesses, insults, hardships, persecutions and calamities for the sake of Christ, for when I am weak, then I am strong.' NRSV.

21. For an excellent overview of this contradictory output, see C.E. Trinkaus, 'Lorenzo Valla on Free Will to Garsia, Bishop of Lerida: Introduction' [hereafter Trinkaus, 'Valla'], in *Renaissance Philosophy*, pp. 147–154.

22. L. Valla, *Dialectice Laurentii Vallae libri tres seu ejusdem Reconcinnatio totius dialectice et fundamentorum universalis philosophiae; ubi multa adversus Aristotelem, Boetium, Porphyrium etc.* (Paris, 1509).

23. L. Valla, *De Linguae Latinae Elegantia Libri Sex* (Cambridge, 1588).

24. *Laurentii Vallae De libero Arbitrio Edidit Maria Anfossi* ('Opusculi filosofici: testi e documenti inediti o rari pubblicati da Giovanni Gentile', VI (Florence, 1934) [hereafter *De libero Arbitrio*].

25. L. Valla, *De Voluptate ac Vero Bono Libri Tres* (Basel, 1519).

26. L. Valla, *Encomium sancti Thomae Aquinatis*, later published by Johannes Vahlen in *Vierteljahschrift für Kultur- und Litteraturgeschichte der Renaissance*, I (1886), pp. 387–96.

27. *De Libero Arbitrio*; Trinkaus, 'Valla', p. 155.

28. T. Aquinas, *Summa Contra Gentiles*, III. LXXIII, quoted in Trinkaus, 'Valla', p. 150, n. 13.

29. L. Valla 'Dialogue on Free Will', translated in *Renaissance Philosophy*, p. 176.

30. Trinkaus, 'Valla', pp. 150–51; *De Professione Religiosorum*, ed. J. Vahlen (*Laurentii Vallae Opuscula Tria*, in 'Sitzungsberichte der Kaiserlichen Akademie der Wissenschaften, Philos. Und Hist. Kl.,' nos. 61 and 62 (Vienna, 1869); Valla, *De Falso*.

31. *Encomium Sancti Thomae Aquinatis*, pp. 394–5; Trinkaus, 'Valla', p. 151.

32. D. Erasmus, *De Libro Arbitrio Distriba sive Collatio*, in *Opera Omnia* (Leyden, 1706), IX, columns 1215–48, quoted in Trinkaus, 'Valla', p. 153.

33. M. Luther, *De Servo Arbitrio*, ed. A. Freitag (*Werke*, WA, Band XVIII 1908), pp. 600–787 [here, p. 640]; Trinkaus, 'Valla', p. 153.

34. J. Calvin, *Institutes of the Christian Religion* (sixth edition, Philadelphia, 1932), Book III, chapter 23, section 6, quoted in Trinkaus, 'Valla', p. 153.

35. Luciano Barozzi, *Lorenzo Valla*, printed with Remigio Sabbadini, in *Studi sul Panormita e sul Valla* ('R. Istituto di studi superiori...in Firenze, Sezione di filosofia e filogia, Pubblicazioni', no. 25) (Florence, 1891), especially chapter 7, quoted in Trinkaus, 'Valla', p. 154.

Chapter 3: Marsilio Ficino

1. M. Ficino, *The Letters of Marsilio Ficino*, translated from the Latin by members of the Department of the School of Economic Science, London, 8 vols. (London, 1975–2010) [hereafter Ficino, *Letters*], I, p. 1. On Ficino see also P.O. Kristeller, *Marsilio Ficino and his Work after Five Hundred Years* (Florence, 1987) [hereafter Kristeller, *Five Hundred Years*]; J. Hankins, *Plato in the Italian Renaissance*, 2 vols. (Leiden, 1990); M.J.B. Allen, *Synoptic Art: Marsilio Ficino on the History of Platonic Interpretation* (Florence, 1998); M.J.B. Allen and V. Rees, *Marsilio Ficino: His Theology, his Philosophy, his Legacy* (Leiden, 2002); J. Hankins, *Humanism and Platonism in the Italian Renaissance*, 2 vols. (Rome, 2003–4) [hereafter Hankins, *Humanism and Platonism*], II.

2. A. Voss, (ed.), *Marsilio Ficino* (Berkeley, 2006) [hereafter Voss], p. 1.

3. *Ibid.*

4. Kristeller, *Five Hundred Years*, p. 1.

5. Edelheit, *Ficino, Pico and Savonarola*, pp. 2 and 210–368 *passim*.

6. Voss, p. 1.

7. Ficino, *Letters*, p. 1.

8. Probably on his return to England; Jayne, *passim*; Gleason, p. 45.

9. Jayne, *passim*; Gleason, pp. 47–52. Gleason believes Colet may have been in Florence but missed meeting Ficino, who was then in exile: 'by the time he was settled there [Florence], Ficino was off to a self-imposed exile of indeterminate duration…Thus , there is no need to doubt that Colet passed in Florence at least a good part of the two years or more after he is last heard of in Rome', Gleason, p. 52.

10. G. Bedouelle, 'Jacques Lefèvre d'Étaples (*c.* 1460–1536)' in C. Lindberg, *The Reformation Theologians: An Introduction to Theology in the Early Modern Period* (Oxford, 2002) [hereafter Lindberg], pp. 19–33 [hereafter Bedouelle].

11. Books ascribed to Hermes Trismegistus, *c.* 1st to 3rd centuries.

12. Jayne, pp. 12, 28–9, 36, 43 and 67–8.

13. J.B. Trapp, 'An English Late Medieval Cleric and Italian Thought: The Case of John Colet, Dean of St. Paul's (1467–1519)' in G. Kratzmann and J. Simpson (eds.), *Medieval English Religious and Ethical Literature: Essays in Honour of G. H. Russell* (Cambridge, 1986), pp. 233–50 [hereafter Trapp, 'English Cleric'], pp. 237–8; Jayne, pp. 60–5, 70–75 and 104–9.

14. P.O. Kristeller, *The Classics and Renaissance Thought* (Cambridge, Mass., 1955), p. 59.

15. Voss, p. 49.

16. *Ibid.*

17. A. Field, *The Origins of the Platonic Academy in Florence* (Princeton, 1988) [hereafter Field, *Origins*], p. 177; for Diotifeci's treatment of the plague see Ficino's *Consilio contro la Pestilentia*, cited in C. Salaman, 'Introduction' [hereafter Salaman] in *Meditations of the Soul: Selected Letters of Marsilio Ficino*, translated from the Latin by Members of the Language Department of the School of Economic Science (London, 1996) [hereafter *Meditations*], p. xi.

18. Salaman, p. xi.

19. Kristeller, *Five Hundred Years*, p. 3.

20. Field, *Origins*, p. 178.

21. Kristeller, *Five Hundred Years*, p. 6; S.J. Hough, 'An Early Record of Marsilio Ficino', *Renaissance Quarterly*, 30 (1977), pp. 301–4 [hereafter Hough, 'Early Record'].

22. Field, *Origins*, p. 181.

23. Salaman, p. xii.

24. Quoted in Salaman, p. xii.

25. Hough, 'Early Record', pp. 301–4.

26. Salaman, p. xiv.

27. C. Celenza, 'The Revival of Platonic Philosophy', in *CCRP*, pp. 72–96 [hereafter Celenza, 'Revival'], p. 85 citing B.P. Copenhaver, 'Introduction'

in Hermes Trismegistus (Pseudo), *Hermetica: The Greek Corpus Hermeticum and the Latin Asclepius in a New English Translation with Notes and Introduction*, trans. B.P. Copenhaver (Cambridge, 1992).

28. Field, *Origins*, p. 3.
29. Celenza, 'Revival', p. 83.
30. *Ibid.* See also Hankins, *Humanism and Platonism*, II, pp. 194–210 and 223–5.
31. Kristeller, *Five Hundred Years*, pp. 5–6.
32. *Ibid.*, p. 3.
33. For this brief overview of Ficino's work I am indebted to Kristeller, *Five Hundred Years*, pp. 1–16.
34. *Ibid.*, p. 5.
35. M. Ficino, *Platonic Theology*, trans. and ed. M.J.B. Allen and J. Warden, 6 vols. (Cambridge, Mass., 2001–6) [hereafter Ficino, *Platonic Theology*], I, p. 148, quoted in Voss, pp. 9–10.
36. Ficino, *Platonic Theology*, vol. 1, p. 9.
37. Celenza, 'Revival', pp. 81–2.
38. Voss, p. 221.
39. Celenza, 'Revival', p. 85, quoting M. Ficino, *Opera Omnia*, 2 vols. (Turin, 1959; photo reprint of Basel, 1576 edition), p. 1838, cited and translated in B.P. Copenhaver and C.B. Schmitt, *Renaissance Philosophy* (Oxford, 1992), p. 147.
40. *Corpus Hermeticum*, trans. C. Salaman, D. van Oyen and W. Wharton, in *The Way of Hermes* (London, 1999) [hereafter *Corpus Hermeticum*], Book XII, p. 7.
41. Iamblichus, *On the Mysteries*, trans. E.C. Clarke, J.M. Dillon and J.P. Hershbell (Atlanta, 2003), VIII, p. 4, quoted in Voss, p. 18.
42. *Corpus Hermeticum*, Book 12, p. 19.
43. Ficino, *Platonic Theology*, IV, book 13, p. 3, trans. C. Trinkaus, 'Humanist Themes in Marsilio Ficino's Philosophy' in *idem*, *In Our Image and Likeness* (London, 1970), p. 483, quoted in Voss, pp. 20–21.
44. Kristeller, *Five Hundred Years*, pp. 12–13.
45. For the influence of this aspect of Ficino's thought in England, see the chapter on Colet in this volume and J. Arnold, *Dean John Colet of St. Paul's: Humanism and Reform in Early Tudor England* (London, 2007) [hereafter Arnold, *Dean John Colet*], chapter 2.
46. Kristeller, *Five Hundred Years*, p. 9.
47. *Meditations*, p. 106.
48. Voss, p. 10, citing Plato, *Timaeus*, 29e-39e
49. Voss, p. 11.
50. M. Ficino, *Marslii Ficini Florentini Disputatio Contra Iudicium Astrologorum*, translated by members of the Language Department of the School of Economic Science, *The Letters*, III (London, 1981), no. 37, reprinted in Voss, pp. 67–70, here at p. 67.
51. Voss, p. 10.
52. *Ibid.*, p. 11.

53. Kristeller, *Five Hundred Years*, p. 12, quoting Marsilius Ficinus, *Opera Omnia* (Basel, 1576, reprinted Turin, 1959), translation by P.O. Kristeller.

54. *De Rationibus Musicae*, in Ficino, *Letters*, VII (2003), no. 76, reprinted in Voss, pp. 179–187, here at p. 179.

55. Voss, p. 186.

56. Letter to Giovanni Calvalcanti, *Meditations*, p. 25.

57. P.R. Blum, 'The Immortality of the Soul' in *CCRP*, pp. 211–233. Here at p. 213.

58. P.O. Kristeller, *Renaissance Thought and its Sources* (New York, 1979), pp. 169–81; *idem*, *Five Hundred Years*, p. 14.

59. Kristeller, *Five Hundred Years*, pp. 15–16.

60. Letter to Riccardo Angiolieri of Anghiari, Oliviero Arduini, and Antonio Serafico: *Meditations*, p. 32.

61. Letter to Girolamo Amazzi: *Ibid.*, pp. 175–6.

62. Voss, p. 49.

Chapter 4: Giovanni Pico della Mirandola

1. For instance, see Q. Breen, 'Melanchthon's Reply to Giovanni Pico della Mirandola', *JHI*, 13 (June 1952), pp. 413–426 [hereafter Breen, 'Melanchthon's Reply'].

2. M.V. Dougherty, 'Introduction' in Dougherty, *New Essays*, p. 1 quoting L. Thorndyke, *A History of Experimental Science*, IV, *Fourteenth and Fifteenth Centuries* (New York, 1934), p. 485; and F.A. Yates, *Giordano Bruno and the Hermetic Tradition* (Chicago, 1964), p. 116.

3. For bibliographical details, see Dougherty, *New Essays*, *passim*.

4. Dougherty, 'Introduction', in *Ibid.*, p. 2.

5. J. Kraye, 'Pico on the Relationship of Rhetoric and Philosophy', in Dougherty, *New Essays*, pp. 13–38 [hereafter Kraye, 'Pico'], here p. 17, quoting E. Barbaro, *Epistolae, orations at carmina* I: 85: '*O praeclarum et plane divinum ingenium tuum, Pice...deo te poetam egregium, oratorem eminentissimum vel esse iam vel brevi fore. Animadverto te philosophorum prius aristotelicum, nunc etiam platonicaum esse factum.*'

6. F. Borghesi, 'A Life in Works' [hereafter Borghesi] in Dougherty, *New Essays*, p. 205. The legend was started by the early biography of Pico by his nephew, Gianfrancesco, later translated by Thomas More. See S.E. Lehmberg, 'Sir Thomas More's Life of Pico della Mirandola', *Studies in the Renaissance*, 3 (1956), pp. 61–74.

7. For this quotation and for an account of Pico's life see Borghesi, pp. 202–219. Here at p. 207.

8. *Ibid.*

9. *Ibid.*, p. 208.

10. *Ibid.*

11. P.O. Kristeller, 'Thomism and Italian Thought' in *idem*, *Mediaeval Aspects of Renaissance Learning: Three Essays by Paul Oskar Kristeller*,

ed. and trans. E.P. Mahoney (Durham, N. Carolina, 1974), pp. 29–94. Here at p. 71.

12. On which see introduction, pp. 10–11.
13. Borghesi, p. 210.
14. Borghesi, pp. 210–11.
15. Q. Breen, 'Giovanni Pico della Mirandola on the Conflict of Philosophy and Rhetoric', *JHI*, 13 (June, 1952), pp. 384–412 [hereafter Breen, 'Pico and Barbaro']. Here at p. 386.
16. *Ibid.*, p. 389.
17. *Ibid.*, p. 395.
18. *Ibid.*, pp. 397, 399 and 401. Breen's translation, he writes, is of the 'text found in *Corpus Reformatorum*, IX, pp. 678–87.
19. *Ibid.*, p. 402.
20. Breen, 'Melanchthon's Reply', p. 414.
21. Borghesi, p. 212.
22. Edelheit, 'Humanism and Theology', p. 272.
23. S.A. Farmer, *Syncretism in the West: Pico's 900 Theses (1486): the Evolution of Traditional Religious and Philosophical Systems: with Text, Translation and Commentary* (Tempe, Arizona, 1998) [hereafter Farmer, *Syncretism*], p. x.
24. P.R. Blum, 'Pico, Theology, and the Church', in Dougherty, *New Essays*, [hereafter Blum] p. 40, quoting Pico's *900 Theses* from an English translation in Farmer, *Syncretism* , pp. 62, 92–5 and 105.
25. Kraye, 'Pico', p. 33; Farmer, *Syncreticism*, pp. 212–49 and 294–5.
26. Kraye, 'Pico', p. 34.
27. Blum, p. 37, quoting R.M. Zaccaria, 'Critiche e difesa dell' *Heptaplus*', in *Pico, Poliziano e L'Umanesimo di fine Quattrocento*, ed. Paolo Viti (Florence, 1994), nr. 16, 76–8, quoted on pp. 76–7 from Archivio di Stato, MS. MAP, 58, 96.
28. Giovanni Pico della Mirandola, *Oration on the Dignity of Man*, in *Renaissance Philosophy*, p. 239, quoted in Blum, p. 38.
29. Pico della Mirandola, *Apologia*, in *Opera Omnia* (Turin, Bottega D'Erasmo, 1971), p. 237, quoted in Blum, p. 44.
30. Blum, p. 44.
31. *Ibid.*, pp. 46–7.
32. *Apologia*, p. 134, quoted in Blum p. 47.
33. *Apologia*, p. 143, quoted in Blum, p. 48.
34. Blum, p. 50
35. Blum, p. 52 referring to *Apologia*, pp. 180–181
36. *Opera*, p. 359, quoted in M. Suddoth, 'Pico della Mirandola's Philosophy of Religion' in Dougherty, *New Essays* [hereafter Suddoth], p. 61.
37. Pico, *Oratio*, pp. 9 and 16; Suddoth, p. 64.
38. *Ibid.*, pp. 65–6.
39. *Ibid.*, p. 66.
40. *Oratio*, 13, Suddoth, p. 66.
41. Pico, *Heptaplus*, first proem, 71; Suddoth, p. 67.
42. *Ibid.*, p. 67.

43. *Ibid.*, p. 68.
44. *Ibid.*, p. 69.
45. Pico, *Heptaplus*, second exposition, proem, 94 and first proem, 69.
46. Suddoth, p. 76.
47. Pico, *Heptaplus*, seventh exposition, proem 153.
48. A '*Christosyncretism*', as Suddoth calls it, p. 77.
49. British Library, MS IB 18857, fol. 35v, reprinted in Farmer, *Syncretism*, p. viii.
50. Farmer, *Syncretism*, p. x.
51. *Ibid.*
52. Farmer, *Syncretism*, p. 521, quoted in Blum, p. 53.
53. Blum, pp. 53–4.
54. R. Kirk, 'Introduction' to Pico, *Oration on the Dignity of Man*, trans. A. R. Caponigri (Washington D.C., 1956), p. xvii.
55. Pico, *Oratio*, ed. Paul Miller (Indianapolis: Bobbs-Merrill, 1965), p. 11, quoted in Suddoth, p. 64.
56. Pico, *Oratio*, 23, quoted in Suddoth, p. 73.
57. Edelheit, 'Humanism and Theology', p. 287.
58. Giovanni Pico della Mirandola, *Apologia, Opera Omnia* (Basel, 1557, reprinted Hildesheim: Olms, 1969) [hereafter Pico, *Apologia*], p. 128; quoted in Edelheit, 'Humanism and Theology', p. 288.
59. Edelheit, 'Humanism and Theology', p. 289.
60. Pico, *Apologia*, p. 130; Edelheit, 'Humanism and Theology', p. 289.
61. A. Edelheit, *Ficino, Pico and Savonarola: The Evolution of Humanist Theology, 1461/2–1498* (Leiden, 2008), p. 285.
62. See introduction above, pp. 1–12.
63. Borghesi, p. 217.
64. Giovanni Pico della Mirandola, *Heptaplus*, ed. Paul Miller (Indianapolis, 1998) [hereafter Pico, *Heptaplus*], seventh exposition, proem, p. 148, quoted by Sudduth, p. 64.
65. Pico, *Heptaplus*, seventh exposition, proem, p. 148, quoted by Suddoth, pp. 64–5.
66. Pico, *Heptaplus*, seventh exposition, chap. 5, pp. 165–6; Suddoth, p. 80.
67. Borghesi, p. 218.
68. *Ibid.*, p. 219.

Chapter 5: Rudolph Agricola

1. Spitz, 'Humanism in Germany', p. 210. (Spitz does not give the original reference). See also N.L. Braun, 'Humanism in Germany' in Rabil, *Renaissance Humanism*, II, pp. 123–155.
2. The Netherlands was legally part of Germany at this time, or at least the Holy Roman Empire, headed by the King of Spain as it included, until 1648, the seventeen provinces of the Netherlands as well as the German states.
3. R. Agricola, *Rudolphi Agricolae Phrisii De Inventione Dialectica Libri Omnes et Integri et Recogniti, etc. per Alardum Aemstelradamum*

(Cologne, 1539), II, p. 178, quoted in Spitz, 'Humanism in Germany', p. 210.

4. Nauert, *Humanism*, pp. 110–11.

5. For biographical details, see R. Agricola, *Letters*, ed. and trans. with notes, by Adrie Van Der Laan and Fokke Akkerman (Tempe, Arizona, 2002) [hereafter Agricola, *Letters*], pp. 3–7; C G Leijenhorst. '*Rodolphus Agricola*, 17 February 1444- 27 October 1485' in A-E. Peter G. Bietenholz, Thomas B. Deutsche (eds.), *Contemporaries of Erasmus: A Biographical Register of the Renaissance and Reformation*, I, (Toronto, 1985), pp. 15–17.

6. Agricola, *Letters*, p. 125; Latin, p. 124.

7. Agricola, *Letters*, p. 4; Latin, p. 3, demonstrates his friendship with Vrye and Langen.

8. Agricola, *Letters*, p. 115–117; Latin p. 114 and 116.

9. J.L. Glomski, *Patronage and Humanist Literature in the Age of the Jagiellons: Court and Career in the Writings of Rudolf Agricola Junior, Valentin Eck and Leonard Cox* (Toronto, 2007), p. 49.

10. Agricola, *Letters*, p. 209; Latin p. 208.

11. *Ibid.*, p. 211; Latin, p. 210.

12. *Ibid.*, p. 213; Latin, p.212.

13. R. Agricola, *De Formando Studiis* (letter to Jacob Barbireau of 7 June 1484) in *Lucubrationes Aliquot Lectu Dignissime* (Cologne: Ioannis Gymnicus, 1539), facsimile reprint *Opuscula Orationes Epistolae* (Frankfurt am Main, 1975) [hereafter *De Formando*], p. 194, quoted in Van Ruler, p. 236.

14. H. Van Ruler, 'The *Philosphia Christi*' in *Christian Humanism*, p. 236.

15. *De Formando*, p. 194; *Letters*, pp. 205–7; Van Ruler, p. 237.

16. *Letters*, p. 257; Latin and Greek and Hebrew on p. 256. Written after April 1484 from Stuttgart.

17. *Letters*, p. 228; Latin, p. 227.

18. *Letters*, p. 241; Latin, p. 240.

19. Nauert, *Humanism*, p. 111.

20. *Ibid.*, p. 216.

21. All Souls' College Library, Oxford, MS Gallery g.16.1: R. Agricola, *De Inventione Dialectica*, (Cologne, 1552) [hereafter Agricola, *De Inventione*], p. 192, quoted in P. Mack, 'Humanist Rhetoric and Dialectic' in *CCRH*, pp. 82–99 [hereafter Mack]. Here at p. 86.

22. L. Nauta, 'Lorenzo Valla and the Rise of Humanist Dialectic', in *CCRP*, pp. 193–210 [hereafter Nauta, 'Valla']. Here at p. 205; see also P. Mack, *Renaissance Argument: Valla and Agricola in the Traditions of Rhetoric and Dialectic* (Leiden, 1993), chapter 13.

23. Agricola, *De Inventione Dialectica*, pp. 8, 180–2, 268, 316; Mack, p. 86.

24. Nauta, 'Valla', p. 205.

25. Mack, p. 87.

26. Nauta, 'Valla', p. 205.

27. *Ibid.*, Mack, p. 85; L. Valla, *Repastinatio Dialecticae et Philosophie*, ed. G. Zippel (Padua, 1982), pp. 175–7.

28. Mack, p. 87.

29. Agricola, *De Inventione*, pp. 240–52.

30. *Ibid.*, pp. 258–60; Mack, p. 87.

31. R. Agricola, *De Inventione*, pp. 412–50; Mack, p. 87.

32. R. Agricola, *De Inventione*, pp. 353–63, 461–71.

33. Mack, p. 88; Nauta, 'Valla', p. 207; K. Meerhoff, 'The Significance of Philip Melanchthon's Rhetoric in the Renaissance' in *Renaissance Rhetoric*, ed. P. Mack (London, 1994), pp. 46–62; A. Moss, *Renaissance Truth and the Latin Language* (Oxford, 2003), pp. 153–69 and 247–50.

34. T. Elyot, *The Boke named the Gouernour*, ed. H.H.S. Croft, 2 vols. (London, 1883; reprinted New York, 1967) [hereafter Elyot], I, p. 96, quoted in C. Carroll, 'Humanism and English Literature in the Fifteenth and Sixteenth Centuries', in *CCRH*, pp. 246–268. Here at p. 262.

35. Elyot, I, p. 72.

Chapter 6: Desiderius Erasmus

1. For evidence of Erasmus's birth date as 1467, see J.B. Gleason, 'The Birth Dates of John Colet and Erasmus of Rotterdam: Fresh Documentary Evidence', *Renaissance Quarterly*, 32 (1979) pp. 73–6. Other scholars date his birth to 1469: J.L. Carrington, 'Desiderius Erasmus (1460–1536)' in Lindberg, pp. 34–48 [hereafter Carrington], here at p. 34. This introduction is indebted to Carrington's work on Erasmus (*ibid.*) and A.G. Dickens and W.R.D. Jones, *Erasmus the Reformer* (London, 1994) [hereafter Dickens and Jones], *passim*.

2. A. Rabil, Jr., 'Desiderius Erasmus' in Rabil, *Renaissance Humanism*, II, pp. 216–264.

3. R.R. Post, *The Modern Devotion: Confrontation with Reformation and Humanism* (Leiden, 1968) [hereafter Post], pp. 396–8.

4. Allen, II, no. 447, p. 295.

5. Post, p. 398.

6. Arnold, *Dean John Colet*, p. 4.

7. Carrington, p. 35.

8. C. Burger, 'Erasmus of Rotterdam and Late-Medieval Theologians on the Doctrine of Grace' in *Christian Humanism*, pp. 225–234.

9. Carrington, p. 36.

10. D. Erasmus, *The Collected Works of Erasmus*, trans. and ed. R.A.B. Mynors and D.F.S. Thomson, annotated by P.G. Bietnholz, W.K. Ferguson and J.K. McConica (Toronto, 1974–1988) [hereafter *CWE*]. Here, LXVI, pp. 33–4.

11. D. Erasmus, *Christian Humanism and the Reformation: Selected Writings of Erasmus with The Life of Erasmus by Beatus Rhenanus*, trans. and ed. J.C. Olin (first edition, New York, 1965; second edition, New York, 1975) [hereafter Olin, *Humanism*]. Here at p. 100. Reprinted in Carrington, p. 38.

12. Carrington, p. 39.
13. Dickens and Jones, p. 42.
14. R.P. Becker, *German Humanism and Reformation* (New York, 1982) [hereafter Becker, *German Humanism*], p. 49.
15. D. Erasmus, *Praise of Folly*, trans. B. Radice (Harmondswoth, 1971), pp. 135–6.
16. Quoted in Becker, *German Humanism*, p. 97.
17. *Enchiridion*, ed. R. Hemelick, p.75 and Dickens and Jones, p. 52.
18. D. Erasmus Roterodamus, *Enchiridion Militis Christiani* in *Ausgewählte Werke*, ed. H. and A. Holborn, I (Munich, second edition, 1964), p. 46. Translation from *The Enchiridion of Erasmus*, ed. and trans. R. Himelick (Bloomington, 1963), pp. 70–71; quoted in H. Van Ruler, 'The *Philosophia Christi*, its Echoes and its Repercussions on Virtue and Nobility' in *Christian Humanism*, pp. 235–263. Here at p. 235.
19. Carrington, p. 41.
20. Dickens and Jones, p. 61 quoting Olin's translation, p. 96.
21. D. Erasmus, *Opus Epistolarum Desiderii Erasmi Roterdami*, I-IV, ed. P.S. Allen and H.M. Allen (Oxford, 1906–22) [hereafter Allen], IV, Ep. 1489; Dickens and Jones, p. 115.
22. *CWE*, 4, no. 501; *Luther's Works*, ed. J. Pelikan, 56 vols. (St. Louis, 1955–1986) [hereafter *Luther's Works*], XLVIII, pp. 23–6.
23. *Luther's Works*, XLVIII, p. 40; Dickens and Jones, p. 117.
24. *CWE*, VIII, no. 1225.
25. *CWE*, VI, no. 980.
26. *CWE*, VI, no. 872.
27. Dickens and Jones, p. 119.
28. *CWE*, VI, no. 938; Dickens and Jones, p. 122.
29. Allen, IV, pp. 502–28.
30. *CWE*, VIII, no. 1241; Dickens and Jones, p. 123.
31. *CWE*, IX, nos. 1259 and 1342: letters to Pirckheimer and Marcus Lauvinus; Dickens and Jones, p. 124.
32. *De Libero Arbitrio*, trans. and ed. G. Rupp, pp. 36–7, 41.
33. *Ibid.*, pp. 43 and 60; Dickens and Jones, p. 133.
34. W. von Loewenich, *Martin Luther: The Man and his Work*, trans. L.W. Denef (Minneapolis, 1986), p.263; Dickens and Jones, p. 136.
35. Dickens and Jones, p. 136.
36. M. Luther, *De Servo Arbitrio*, translated as *The Bondage of the Will*, by P. Watson and B. Drewery in *Luther's Works*, XXXIII, p. 295.
37. A.G. Dickens, *Martin Luther and the Reformation* (London, 1967), pp. 83–6; P.S. Watson, *Luther and Erasmus: Free Will and Salvation*, pp. 113–7; Dickens and Jones, p. 137.
38. Allen, IV, Ep. 1528, December 1524.
39. D. Erasmus, *Hyperaspistes: Diatribe Adversus Servum Abirtrium Martini Lutheri*, (Basel, 1526), X, p. 1423 B-C; also in J. Huizinga, *Erasmus and the Age of Reformation* (New York, 1957), p. 165.
40. A. G. Dickens, *Martin Luther and the Reformation* (London, 1967), p. 86, and source of Luther's quote.

41. Allen, VIII, Ep. 2134.
42. Dickens and Jones, p. 146.
43. Dickens and Jones, p. 290.
44. M. Luther, *Hyperaspistes: Diatribe Adversus Servum Abirtrium Martini Lutheri*, LB, X, 1423 B-C; also in J. Huizinga, *Erasmus and the Age of Reformation*, p. 165; Dickens and Jones, p. 139.

Chapter 7: Johannes Reuchlin

1. *The Colloquies of Erasmus*, English Translation by C.R. Thompson (Chicago, 1965)[hereafter Erasmus, *Colloquies*], p. 86, quoted in G. Lloyd Jones, 'Introduction', pp. 7–32 [hereafter Lloyd Jones] in J. Reuchlin, *De Arte Cabalistica: On the Art of the Cabala*, trans. Martin and Sarah Goodman (Lincoln and London, 1983; reprinted, Nebraska, 1993) [hereafter *De Arte Cabalistica*]. Here at p. 7.
2. Spitz, 'Humanism in Germany', p. 204; S.E. Ozment, *Mysticism and Dissent: Religious Ideology and Social Protest in the Sixteenth Century* (New Haven and London, 1973), *passim*.
3. Spitz, 'Humanism in Germany', p. 205.
4. *Ibid.*, pp. 206–7.
5. *Ibid.*, pp. 209–210; N.L. Braun, 'Humanism in Germany' in Rabil, *Renaissance Humanism*, II, pp. 123–154.
6. Spitz, 'Humanism in Germany', p. 208.
7. *Ibid.*, p. 212.
8. J.H. Overfield, *Humanism and Scholasticism in Late-Medieval Germany* (Princeton, 1984) [hereafter Overfield], p. 159.
9. D.B. Ruderman, 'The Italian Renaissance and Jewish Thought' in Rabil, *Renaissance Humanism*, I, pp. 382–433.
10. Overfield, p. 159.
11. J. Reuchlin, *De Verbo Mirifico* (Basel, 1494), 5b, (Facsimile reprint, 1964), quoted in Overfield, p. 160.
12. Overfield, p. 159.
13. Pico della Mirandola, *Oration on the Dignity of Man*, trans. A.R. Caponigri (Washington D.C., 1956, reprinted, 1999), p. 65, quoted in *Renaissance Philosophy*, p. 252 and Lloyd Jones, p. 16.
14. *De Arte Cabalistica*, p. 45; Lloyd Jones, p. 17.
15. Lloyd Jones, p. 8.
16. *Ibid.*; see R. Weiss, 'England and the Decree of the Council of Vienne on the teaching of Greek, Arabic, Hebrew and Syriac', *Bibliothèque d'Humanisme et Renaissance*, Tome, 14, (1952), pp. 1 ff.
17. Lloyd Jones, p. 8; E. Zimmer, 'Jewish and Christian Hebraist Collaboration in Sixteenth-Century Germany', *Jewish Quarterly Review*, 71 (1980), pp. 71 ff.
18. *De Arte Cabalistica*, p. 123; Lloyd Jones, p. 20.
19. Lloyd Jones, p. 9.
20. *Ibid.*; *Marsilio Ficino: Opera Omnia*, ed. P.O. Kristeller (Turin, 1962), I, pp. 31–105.

21. Lloyd Jones, p. 10; *Corpus Reformatorum*, XI (Halle, 1943), 'Oratio continens historiam Ioannis Capnionis', column 1002.
22. Lloyd Jones, p. 10.
23. *Ibid.*, p. 11.
24. J. Reuchlin, *De Rudimentis Hebraicis* (Pforzheim, 1506, reprinted 1974), p. 123, quoted in Lloyd Jones, p. 12.
25. Overfield, pp. 247–8.
26. *Ibid.*, p. 249.
27. *Ibid.*
28. Lloyd Jones, p. 14; G. Kisch, 'The Jews and Mediaeval Law', *Essays on Antisemitism*, ed., K.S. Pinson, (second edition revised, New York, 1946), pp. 103 ff.
29. Overfield, p. 249.
30. Lloyd Jones, p. 14.
31. J. Reuchlin, *Warhafftige Entschuldigung Gegen und Wider ains Getaufften Juden Genant Pfefferkorn Vormals Getruckt...* (Tübingen, 1511).
32. J. Reuchlin, *Recommendation Whether to Confiscate, Destroy and Burn all Jewish Books: A Classic Treatise Against Anti-Semitism*, trans and ed. P. Wortsman (New York, 2000), p. 62.
33. *Ibid.*, p. 70.
34. Lloyd Jones, p. 15; H. Graetz, *History of the Jews* (London, 1892), IV, pp. 451 ff.
35. J. Reuchlin, *Defensio Johannis Reuchlin contra Calumniatores suos Coloniensis* (Tübingen, 1513), quoted in Overfield, p. 267.
36. H. Holborn, *Ulrich von Hutten and the German Reformation* (New York, 1965), p. 56. See also U. Von Hutten, *On the Eve of the Reformation: 'Letters of Obscure Men'* [*Epistolae Obscurorum Virorum*], *Ulrich von Hutten et al.*, trans. F.G. Stokes with introduction by H. Holborn (New York, 1964).
37. U. von Hutten, *Opera Omnia*, ed. e. Böcking, 7 vols. (Leipzig, 1859–1870), III, pp. 428 and 443, quoted in Overfield, p. 292.
38. Lloyd Jones, p. 16; *De Arte Cabalistica*, p. 137; J.L. Blau, *The Christian Interpretation of the Cabala in the Renaissance* (New York, 1944) [hereafter Blau], p. 19.
39. *De Arte Cabalistica*, pp 39–41.
40. *Ibid.*, p. 63.
41. Lloyd Jones, p. 18; Blau, pp. 49 ff.
42. Lloyd Jones, p. 21.
43. Lloyd Jones, p. 23; *Ulrich Hutteni Opera*, I, Letter 14, p. 29.
44. P. Smith, *The Life and Letters of Martin Luther* (London, 1911), p. 29; Lloyd Jones, p. 23.
45. *Luther's Works*, American edition, XLV (Philadelphia, 1962), p. 200.
46. Lloyd Jones, p. 24; Luther's anti-Jewish treatises of the 1520s are: *On the Jews and Their Lies, of the Shem Hamphoras and the Race of Christ*, and *The Last Words of David* (published 1543).
47. Lloyd Jones, p. 25; Allen, III, Letter 798, p. 253.

48. Lloyd Jones, p. 26; C. Zika, 'Reuchlin and Erasmus: Humanism and Occult Philosophy', *Journal of Religious History*, vol. 9 (1977), pp. 230 ff.

49. Lloyd Jones p. 26; *CWE*, IV, Letter 471, p. 85.

50. Lloyd Jones, p. 27; Lupton, p. 225; *CWE*, IV, Letter 593, p. 398.

51. J. Reuchlin, *De Rudimentis Hebraicis* (Pforzheim, 1506, reprinted 1974), p. 621, quoted in S.A. Hirsch, *A Book of Essays* (London, 1905), p. 143 and in Lloyd Jones, p. 11.

52. Erasmus, *Colloquies*, p. 86; quoted by Lloyd Jones, p. 7.

53. *Johann Reuchlin Briefwechsel*, ed. L. Geiger (Stuttgart, 1875), Letter 215, p. 245, quoted in Lloyd Jones, p. 15.

54. *De Arte Cabalistia*, p. 39, quoted in Moshe Idel, 'Introduction to the Bison Book Edition' [hereafter Idel] in *idem*, p. xiii.

Chapter 8: Philip Melanchthon

1. D. Steinmetz, *Reformers in the Wings* (Philadelphia, 1971) [hereafter Steinmetz], p. 49 citing *D. Martin Luthers Werke: Tischreden* (Weimar, 1912–21) [hereafter *D. Martin Luthers Werke*], V, no. 5511 and *Luther's Works*, ed. J. Pelikan, 55 vols., (Philadelphia and St. Louis, 1955–1986), LIV, pp. 339–40.

2. Steinmetz, p. 49, quoting *D. Martin Luthers Werke*, III, no. 3619 (1 August 1537): "*Res et verba Melanchthon; verba sine re Erasmus; res sine verbis Lutherus; nec res nec verba Carlostadius*".

3. For this brief biography of Melanchthon I am indebted to R. Stupperich, *Melanchthon: The Enigma of the Reformation*, translated by W.L. Jenkins (Cambridge, 1965; reprinted, Cambridge, 2006) [hereafter Stupperich], *passim*.

4. P. Melanchthon, *Corpus Reformatorum: Philippi Melanchthonis Opera Quae Supersunt Omnia*, ed. Karl Bretschneider and Heinrich Bindseil, 28 vols. (Halle, 1834–60) [hereafter *CR*], I, column 26.

5. Translation by R.A. Keen, *A Checklist of Melanchthon Imprints Through 1560* (St. Louis, 1988), p. 56, quoted in S. Kusukawa, *The Transformation of Natural Philosophy: The Case of Philip Melanchthon* (Cambridge, 1995) [hereafter Kusukawa], p. 38.

6. Kusukawa, p. 19. See Steinmetz, pp. 51–55.

7. P. Melanchthon, *Melanchthons Briefwechsel: Kritische und Kommentierte Gesamtansgabe*, ed. Heinz Scheible, (Stuttgart-Bad Cannstatt, 1975–2010) [hereafter *MBW*], no. 46, T-I, p. 110, quoted in Kusukawa, p. 40.

8. Kusukawa, p. 41.

9. P. Melanchthon, *Didymi Faventini Versus Thomam Placentinum pro M. Luthero Oratio* (Wittenberg, 1521), quoted in Stupperich, p. 43.

10. Kusukawa, p. 49.

11. R. Pauls, 'The World as Sin and Grace. The Theology of Melanchthon's *Loci Communes* of 1521' in *Christian Humanism*, pp. 469–478 [hereafter Pauls]. Here at p. 469.

12. Pauls, p. 470.

13. P. Melanchthon, *The Loci Communes of Philip Melanchthon*, trans. L.J. Satre (London, 1969), pp. 68–9.
14. Pauls, p. 471.
15. *Ibid.*, p. 478.
16. *MBW*, no. 209, T-I, 444, quoted in Kusukawa, p. 52.
17. Letter to Spalatin, 1522, *MBW*, no. 237, T-I, 492, quoted in Kusukawa, p. 54.
18. Kusukawa, p. 57.
19. *Ibid.*, p. 62.
20. *Ibid.*, p. 67.
21. A short disputation of Colossians, 2:8, quoted in *Ibid.*, p. 66.
22. *Ibid.*, p. 63.
23. *Ibid.*, p. 76.
24. *Ibid.*, p. 80.
25. Stupperich, p. 119.
26. *Ibid.*, p. 148.
27. *Ibid.*, p. 149.
28. *Ibid.*, p. 69.
29. Hildebrandt, *Melanchthon*, quoted in Steinmetz, p. 71.
30. G.B. Graybill, 'The Evolution of Philip Melanchthon's Thought on Free Will' (Unpublished D. Phil Thesis, University of Oxford, 2002), p. 228.
31. *Ibid.*, p. 230.
32. Steinmetz, p. 78.
33. D. Busogany, D., 'Melanchthon as a Humanist and a Reformer' [hereafter Busogany], in K. Maag (ed.), *Melanchthon in Europe: His Work and Influence Beyond Wittenberg* (Michigan, Grand Rapids, 1999), pp. 87–107 [hereafter Maag]. Here at p. 87.
34. *CR* 10, 908–9, quoted in Busogany, p. 88.
35. Q. Breen, 'Melanchthon's reply to Giovanni Pico della Mirandola', *JHI*, 13 (1952), pp. 413–26. Here at p. 413.
36. *Ibid.*, pp. 415–7.
37. J.R. Schneider, *Melanchthon's Rhetoric as a Context for Understanding his Theology*, in Maag, pp. 141–159. Here at p. 142.
38. *Ibid.*, pp. 145–6.
39. Kusukawa, p. 201.
40. For a full list of Melanchthon's works see Stupperich, pp. 172–175.

Chapter 9: John Colet

1. S. Knight, *The Life of Dr. John Colet* (London, 1724) [hereafter Knight], p. 1.
2. From Homerton in Huntingdonshire according to J.B. Trapp, 'John Colet' in H.C.G. Matthew and B. Harrison (eds.), *The Oxford Dictionary of National Biography in Association with the British Academy: From the Earliest Times to the Year 2000* [hereafter *New DNB*], XII (Oxford, 2004), pp. 601–9 [hereafter Trapp, *New DNB*], p. 601.

3. One child, Thomas, was buried in New Buckingham Church: '*Hic iacet Thomas filius Henrici Collet, civis et aldermanni Civitatis London., qui obiit die Nativitatis Sce Maree [sic] 1479*': Lupton, p. 14.

4. 'A Questionist was the scholar who was engaging in those exercises that accompanied his admissionto the bachelors' degree': John M. Fletcher, 'The Teaching of Arts in Oxford, 1400–1520', *Paedagogica Historica*, 7, 1967, p. 440; Gleason, p. 39 and p. 350, n. 33; R. Rex, *The Theology of John Fisher* (Cambridge, 1991) [hereafter Rex, *Fisher*].

5. For a view on Cambridge University during this time, see Gleason, pp. 38–41.

6. J.H. Lupton, *A Life of John Colet, D.D.* (London, 1887) [hereafter Lupton], p. 43.

7. Allen, II, pp. 268–70.

8. '*in transmarinis Academemiis*': M. Parker, *De Antiquitate Britannicae Ecclesiae Cantuariensis, cum Archiepiscopis Euisdem* (London, 1572) [*STC* 19292], p. 306.

9. Letter from Francis Deloynes to Erasmus: Allen, II, pp. 268–70. Deloynes expresses his pleasure at Colet having recalled the time they spent together at Orléans.

10. Colet to Erasmus, dated Oxford 1497. 'From 1494 the city [Paris] had an active circle of devotees of Ficino': Gleason, p. 60.

11. W.F. Hook, *The Lives of the Archbishops of Canterbury*, VI (London, 1868) [hereafter Hook], p. 285.

12. Gleason mistakenly suggests that Linacre studied only in Padua from 1487–92: Gleason, p. 44.

13. Jayne, pp. 16–17; G.B. Parks, *The English Traveller to Italy* (Stanford, 1954), I, pp. 423–94 and Appendix, pp. 621–40.

14. Lupton, p. 46 citing Johnson's *Life of Linacre*, pp. 141–6 and 151.

15. See Gleason, pp. 58–9 on Colet's lack of Greek: 'Though he could give a hearing to reformist sentiment, Colet apparently saw no connection between it and the study of the Greek New Testament, for while he was in Italy he showed no interest at all in studying Greek'.

16. For evidence that Colet was in Rome by September 1492, see W.K. Ferguson, 'An Unpublished Letter of John Colet', *The American Historical Review*, 34 (1934), pp. 696–9 [hereafter Ferguson]. Here at p. 699.

17. Jayne, p. 17; Ferguson, pp. 696–9; J.B. Trapp, 'Christopher Urswick and his Books: the Reading of Henry VII's Almoner', *Renaissance Studies*, I, 1987, pp. 48–71. Here at p. 50.

18. Colet was not enrolled for the following year; there is only one entry for him: Gleason, p. 45.

19. In his lectures on Romans, Colet quotes a long passage from Ficino's *Theologia Platonica* and declaims that 'there can be nothing finer in philosophy' than Ficino's writing: Colet, *Romans*, p. 32.

20. Jayne, pp. 17 and 70–5.

21. Lupton, pp. 53–6; J.A.R. Marriott, *The Life of John Colet* (London, 1933) [hereafter Marriott], *passim*; Ferguson, pp. 696–9.

22. Trapp, *New DNB*, p. 602.

23. Jayne, *passim*; Gleason, pp. 47–52. Gleason believes Colet may have been in Florence but missed meeting Ficino, who was then in exile: 'by the time he was settled there [Florence], Ficino was off to a self-imposed exile of indeterminate duration...Thus , there is no need to doubt that Colet passed in Florence at least a good part of the two years or more after he is last heard of in Rome', Gleason, p. 52.

24. Lupton, pp. 55–6.

25. *Ibid*., p. 61.

26. Gleason, p. 64.

27. Lupton, p. 61.

28. Gleason, p.43.

29. When he was elected Dean of St. Paul's on 2 June 1505 he was referred to as 'Professor of Sacred Theology', which meant that he had a D.D. by this time: Gleason, p. 43.

30. And following the author of the letter to the Hebrews, 11:4.

31. On which, see chapter 6 on Erasmus above.

32. Trapp, *New DNB*, p. 602.

33. All Souls' College, Oxford, MS AS infra. l.5.

34. Trapp, *New DNB*, p. 606.

35. John Bale mentions many more Colet texts extant at the end of the sixteenth century: J. Bale, *Index Britannicae Scriptorum: John Bale's Index of British and Other Writers*, ed. R.L. Poole and M. Bateson (Oxford, 1902) [hereafter Bale, *Index*], p. 602.

36. J. Colet, *Joannis Coleti Opuscula Quaedam Theologica: Letters to Radulphus on the Mosaic Account of Creation; On Christ's Mystical Body the Church; Exposition of St. Paul's Epistle to the Romans (Chapters I-V) by John Colet, D.D.*, trans. J.H. Lupton (London, 1876) [hereafter *Opuscula*], p. 81.

37. Lupton, p. 68.

38. *Opuscula*, p. 162.

39. *Hierarchies*, p. 123.

40. Lupton, p. 76; J. Colet, *Joannis Coleti Enarratio In Primam Epistolam S. Pauli ad Corinthios: An Exposition of St. Paul's First Epistle to the Corinthians, by John Colet*, trans. by J.H. Lupton (London, 1876) [hereafter *Corinthians*], p. 110.

41. *Corinthians*, p. 110.

42. Gleason, pp. 226–7.

43. *Corinthians*, p. 90 and J. Colet, *Opus De Sacramentis Ecclesiae: A Treatise on the Sacraments by John Colet*, translated in Gleason, pp. 270–333 [hereafter *De Sacramentis*].

44. Lupton, p. 78.

45. *Ibid*., p. 80. See chapters three and four above on Ficino and Pico.

46. Three orders: Bishops, Priests and Deacons; three sacraments: baptism, Holy Communion and Chrism; three classes: baptized, communicants and monks.

47. *Opuscula*, p. 40.

48. *Corinthians*, p. 125.

49. Colet, *Romans*, p. 127.

50. *Ibid.*

51. *Ibid.*, p. 86.

52. Allen, IV, pp. 507–528; D. Erasmus, *Christian Humanism and the Reformation: Selected Writings of Erasmus with the Life of Erasmus by Beatus Rhenanus*, ed. J.C. Olin (New York, second edition, 1975) [henceforth cited as Olin, *Erasmus*], pp. 164–91.

53. A. Fox, 'Facts and Fallacies: Interpreting English Humanism', in A. Fox and J. Guy, *Reassessing the Henrician Age: Humanism, Politics and Reform, 1500–1550* (Oxford, 1986) [hereafter Fox, 'Facts and Fallacies'], p. 21.

54. CUL, MS Gg.IV.26: fol. 86v; J. Colet, *John Colet's Commentary on First Corinthians: A New Edition of the Latin Text, with Translation, Annotations, and Introduction*, Medieval and Renaissance Texts and Studies, 21, ed. B. O'Kelly and C.A.L. Jarrott (Binghamton, New York, 1985) [hereafter Corinthians], p. 99. Latin, p. 98.

55. CUL, MS Gg.IV.26: fol. 86v; Corinthians, p. 99. Latin, p. 98.

56. British Library, London, Add. MS 63853: commentaries on Dionysius' *Celestial* and *Ecclesiastical Hierarchies* and his treatise *De Sacramentis Ecclesiae*.

57. For example in his lectures on Romans: CUL MS Gg.IV.26, fols. 2v-61r; Colet, *Romans*, p. 5, quoting Pico, and p. 29, quoting Ficino.

58. *CWE*, II, p. 235.

59. Anon., *The Cloud of Unknowing*, ed. J. Walsh (New York, 1981).

60. W. Hilton, *The Ladder of Perfection*, trans. L. Shirley-Price (Harmondsworth, 1957).

61. CUL, MS Gg.IV.26, fol. 67v; *Opuscula*, p. 31. Latin text, p. 185; fols. 64v-66r are missing in the CUL MS Gg.IV.26.

62. CUL, MS Gg.IV.26, fol. 68v; *Opuscula*, p. 34. Latin text, pp. 186-7.

63. CUL, MS Gg.IV.26, fol. 70v; *Opuscula*, p. 38. Latin text, p. 189.

64. E.M.W. Tillyard, *The Elizabethan World Picture* [henceforth Tillyard] (Harmondsworth, 1943; third edition, 1973).

65. Tillyard, p. 3.

66. *Ibid.*, p. 11.

67. CUL, MS Gg.IV.26, fol. 73v; *Opuscula*, p. 45. Latin text, p. 194.

68. *The Ecclesiastical* and *Celestial Hierarchies* of Dionysius, commented on in *Joannes Coletus Super Opera Dionysii: Two Treatises on the Hierarchies of Dionysius, by John Colet, D. D.*, trans. J.H. Lupton [hereafter Hierarchies] (London, 1869).

69. Hierarchies, p. xlvii.

70. *Ibid.*

71. This assertion is substantiated in a chapter on the dating of Colet's written works: J. Arnold, 'In Search of Perfection: Ecclesiology in the Life and Works of John Colet as Dean of St. Paul's Cathedral, 1505–1519'(Unpublished Ph.D. Thesis, University of London, 2004) [hereafter Arnold, 'In search of Perfection'], Chapter 2.

72. Dowling, *Fisher*, pp. 49–89.

73. Rex, *Fisher*, pp. 23–6 on Melton and Collingwood.

74. *Opuscula*, pp. xviii-xix on Collingwood; Lupton, *Life,* p.114.

75. S. Lander, 'Church Courts and the Reformation in the Diocese of Chichester 1500–58' in R. O'Day and F. Heal (eds.), *Continuity and Change: Personnel and Administration of the Church in England 1500–1642* (Leicester, 1976), pp. 215–37, reprinted in C. Haigh (ed.), *The English Reformation Revised* (Cambridge, 1987), pp. 34–55.

76. Gleason, *Colet*, pp. 217–234.

77. D. Lepine, *A Brotherhood of Canons Serving God: English Secular Cathedrals in the Later Middle Ages* (Woodbridge, 1995), pp. 108–132.

78. The dating of these works is not straightforward, but I believe Colet to have written most of them during his time at Oxford: see Arnold, 'In Search of Perfection', chapter 1 on dating, pp. 39–80.

   John Bale mentions many more Colet texts extant at the end of the sixteenth century: Bale, *Index* , p. 602.

79. CUL, MS Gg.iv.26, fol. 77v; *Corinthians*, p. 75/Latin, p. 74.

80. BL, Add. MS 63853, fol. 32r; *Hierarchies*, p. 49/Latin, p. 198.

81. CUL, MS Gg.iv.26, fol. 77r; *Corinthians,* p. 73/Latin, p. 72.

82. CUL, MS Gg.iv.26, fol. 67r; *Opuscula*, pp. 31–2/Latin, p. 185.

83. Gleason, p. 273/Latin, p. 272: '...*opus iustissimum*'. Like Plato, Colet saw justice as central to any decent society or virtuous soul: D. Forrester, 'Justice' in A. Hastings, A. Mason and H. Pyper (eds.), *The Oxford Companion to Christian Thought: Intellectual, Spiritual, and Moral Horizons of Christianity* (Oxford, 2000), p. 360.

Chapter 10: Thomas More

1. J. Guy, *Thomas More* (London, 2000) [hereafter Guy, *More*], p. 24.

2. *Ibid.*, p. 25.

3. *Ibid.*, p. 27.

4. *Ibid.*, p. 28.

5. *Ibid.*, pp. 21–39; R. Marius, *Thomas More* (New York, 1984) [hereafter Marius, *More*], pp. 34–43.

6. Arnold, *Dean John Colet*, pp. 1–2; Guy, *More*, p. 27. The phrase is taken from Dickens and Jones, pp. 3, 114.

7. *The Correspondence of Sir Thomas More*, ed. E.F. Rogers (Princeton, 1947) [hereafter More *Correspondence*], pp. 5.

8. *Ibid.*, p. 2.

9. *Acts of Court of the Mercers' Company, 1453–1527,* ed. L. Lyell and F.D. Watney (Cambridge, 1936) [hereafter *Acts of Court*], p. 320; Guy, *More*, p. 44; A.F. Sutton, *The Mercery of London: Trade, Goods and People, 1130–1578* (Aldershot, 2005) [hereafter Sutton, *Mercery*], p. 383; G.D. Ramsay, 'A Saint in the City: Thomas More at Mercers' Hall, London', *The English Historical Review*, 97 (1982), pp. 269–288 [hereafter Ramsay, 'Mercers'], p. 270; N. Harpsfield, *The Life and Death of Sir Thomas More, knight*, ed. E.V. Hitchcock and R.W. Chambers,

EETS, original series, 186, London (Oxford, 1932) [hereafter Harpsfield, *More*], pp. 312–3.

10. Ramsay, 'Mercers', p. 270.
11. W. Nelson, 'Thomas More: Grammarian and Orator' in *Essential Articles for the study of Thomas More*, ed. R.S. Sylvester and G.P. Marc'hadour (Hamden, Connecticut, 1977), pp. 150–60 [hereafter, Nelson, 'More'], p. 157.
12. *Acts of Court*, pp. 329–35; Ramsay, 'Mercers', p. 271.
13. Nelson, 'More', p. 157.
14. *Ibid.*, p. 158; Harpsfield, *More*, p. 312; Ramsay, 'Mercers', p. 271.
15. *Liber Albus: The White Book of the City of London*, ed. H.T. Riley (London, 1861), pp. 274–5; J. Guy, *The Public Career of Sir Thomas More* (New Haven and London, 1980) [hereafter Guy, *Public Career*], pp. 5–6.
16. An undersheriff also had a deputy, 'a clerk of the papers and four or five under-clerks.': Guy, *A Daughter's Love*, p. 33–4. For the duties of a sheriff see also Barron, *London*, pp. 159–71.
17. Guy, *Public Career*, p. 6.
18. Allen, IV, p. 20; Guy, *Public Career*, p. 6.
19. Guy, *Public Career*, p. 6.
20. N. Harpsfield, *The Life and Death of Sir Thomas Moore, knight, sometymes Lord high Chancellor of England*, ed. E.V. Hitchcock with an introduction by R. W. Chambers, Early English Texts Society, 186 (London, 1932) [hereafter Harpsfield, *More*], p. 313; W. Roper, *The Life of Sir Thomas More*, ed. R.S. Sylvester and D.P. Harding (1962) [hereafter Roper], pp. 8–9.
21. Nelson, 'More', pp. 150–60.
22. *Ibid.*; Guy, *Public Career*, p. 5.
23. Roper, p. 9.
24. *Ibid.*; Harpsfield, *More*, pp. 312–3; E. Surtz, 'St. Thomas More and his Utopian Embassy of 1515', *The Catholic Historical Review*, 29 (1953–4), pp. 272–97.
25. Sutton, *Mercery*, pp. 334–5.
26. The name of the deputy undersheriff is unknown: Harpsfield, *More*, p. 313.
27. Marius, *More*, pp. 62–3.
28. Sutton, *Mercery*, p. 335.
29. T. More, *Selected Letters*, ed. E.F. Rogers (New Haven, Connecticut and London) [hereafter Rogers, *Selected Letters*], p. 72. Letter dated 17 February 1516.
30. T. More, *Utopia*, ed. P. Turner (Harmondsworth, 1965) [hereafter *Utopia*], pp. 65–6.
31. Sutton, *Mercery*, p. 352; *The Complete Works of Thomas More*, ed. T.M.C. Lawler, G. Marc'hadour and R. Marius, 21 vols. (New Haven, Connecticut and London, 1963–c. 1997), IV, pp. 144–51.
32. The idea that More's attitude to equal prosperity in *Utopia* is not to be taken seriously is persuasively countered by Turner: in *Utopia*, pp. 149–51.

33. *Acts of Court*, p. 446.
34. See Arnold, *Dean John Colet*, pp.166–70.
35. Roper, p. 9.
36. Guy, *More*, p. 47.
37. Roper, pp. 10–11.
38. G. R. Elton, 'Thomas More: Councillor' in *St. Thomas More: Action and Contemplation*, ed. R. S. Sylvester (New Haven, Connecticut and London, 1972), p. 129.
39. *Ibid.*, p.131; *Letters and Papers, Foreign and Domestic, of the Reign of Henry VIII, 1509–47, Preserved in the Public Record Office, The British Museum, and Elsewhere in England, Arranged and Catalogued by J.S. Brewer, M.A., Under the Direction of the Master of the Rolls, and with the sanction of Her Majesty's Secretaries of State*; Volume I, Parts i and ii; Volume II, Parts i and ii (first edition, London, 1864; second edition, London, 1920) [hereafter *LP*], II, ii, no. 4025; Guy, *More*, pp. 53–4. For his oath to King's Council see National Archives, Kew, Chancery, Miscellaneous Books, 193/1, fol. 87v.
40. Harpsfield, *More*, p. 313; E. Hall, *Chronicle*, ed. H. Ellis (London, 1809), p. 593.
41. D. Halpin, 'Utopianism and Education: The Legacy of Thomas More' in *The British Journal of Educational Studies*, 49 (September, 2001), pp. 299–315 [hereafter Halpin, 'Utopianism'], p. 303.
42. P. Turner, 'Introduction' to More's *Utopia*, p. 7.
43. *Ibid.*
44. Gilles's letter to Busleiden, 1 November 1516, in More, *Utopia*, p. 33.
45. Nelson, p. 329.
46. *Ibid.*, p. 330.
47. *Ibid.*
48. Q. Skinner, 'More's Utopia', *Past and Present*, 38 (1967), pp. 153–68 [hereafter Skinner, 'Utopia'], pp. 154–5; B. Bradshaw, 'More on Utopia', *The Historical Journal*, 24:1 (1981), pp. 1–27; Guy, *More*, pp. 99–101; Halpin, 'Utopianism', p. 308.
49. Sowards, p. 80, citing D. Erasmus, 'The Abbot and the Learned Lady' in *The Colloquies of Erasmus*, ed. and trans. C.R. Thompson (Chicago, 1965), p. 223.
50. Sowards, p. 81; Allen VIII, Ep. 2133, March 24, 1529.
51. Allen, IV, Ep. 1233, p. 578.
52. More, *Correspondence*, p.96.
53. Harpsfield, p. 19.
54. *Christian Humanism*, p. 108.
55. J. Guy, *A Daughter's Love: Thomas and Margaret More* (London, 2008) [hereafter Guy, *A Daughter's Love*], pp. 59–60.
56. *Ibid.*, p. 60.
57. *Ibid.*
58. *Ibid.*, pp. 61–2; *CWE* 25, pp. 20–1.
59. Guy, *A Daughter's Love*, p. 62.
60. *Ibid.*, p. 64.

61. *Ibid.*, p. 68.
62. *Ibid.*, quoting Erasmus, *CWE*, XXV, p. 260.
63. *Ibid.*, p. 140.
64. D. Erasmus, *Precatio Dominica* (Basel, 1523).
65. Guy, *A Daughter's Love*, p. 149.
66. See chapter 6 on Erasmus above.
67. M. Roper, *A Deuoute treatise vpon the Pater noster, made first in latyn by the moost famous doctour mayster Erasmus Roterodamus, and tourned in to englisshe by a yong virtuous and well lerned gentylwoman of. Xix. Yere of age* (Second edition, London, *c.* 1525) [*STC* 10477], p. 104.
68. Guy, *A Daughter's Love*, p. 151.
69. Harpsfield, p. 92.
70. See a letter from More to his 'his whole school', which catered for more than his own family, including Ann Cresacre, Alice Middleton, William Rastall, Frances Staverton and Thomas Colt. See Rogers, *Selected Letters*, pp. 145–7 and Guy, *A Daughter's Love*, pp. 66–7.
71. More, *Utopia*, pp. 99–100.
72. Halpin, 'Utopianism', p. 305.
73. *Ibid.*, p. 304.
74. Letter to Oxford University, 1518, in Rogers, *Selected Letters*, pp. 95–103.
75. Rogers, *Selected Letters*, pp. 91–2. Extract from a Letter to his Daughters and Margaret Gyge, 1517? (Elizabeth, b. 1506, Cecily, b. 1507, John, b. *c.* 1509 [referred to as 'the pupil']. Margaret Gyge was Margaret More's age and possible the daughter of her wet nurse.)
76. D. Halpin, *Thomas More on Utopianism and William Hazlett on Plain Speaking* (London, 2003), p. 13; *idem*, 'Utopianism', pp. 306–7.
77. Hankins argues that humanist ideals can never work without a radical social reformation: J. Hankins, 'Humanism and the Origins of Modern Political Thought' in *CCRH*, pp. 118–141, here at p. 139.
78. Letter from Thomas More to Margaret Roper, 6 July 1535, in Rogers, *Selected Letters*, no. 66, quoted in Guy, *A Daughter's Love*, pp. 263–4.

Chapter 11: The English Erasmians

1. R.S. Schoeck, 'Humanism in England' in Rabil, *Renaissance Humanism*, II, pp. 5–38.
2. V. Nutton, 'Thomas Linacre' in *New DNB*, XXXIII, pp. 803–6.
3. A.B. Emden, *A Biographical Register of the University of Oxford to A.D. 1500* (Oxford, 1957) [hereafter Emden], II, 1147.
4. J.W. Bennett, 'John Morer's Will: Thomas Linacre and Prior Sellyng's Greek Teaching', *Studies in the Renaissance*, 15 (1968), pp. 70–91 [hereafter Bennett]. Here at p. 73; See C.H. Clough, 'Thomas Linacre, Cornelio Vitelli and Humanistic Studies in Oxford', [hereafter Clough] in F. Maddison, C. Pelling and C. Webster (eds.), *Essays on the Life*

and Work of Thomas Linacre c. 1460–1524 (Oxford, 1977) [hereafter *Essays on Linacre*], pp. 1–23. Here at p. 8.

5. Clough, p. 1.
6. *Ibid.*, pp. 1–23.
7. *Ibid.*, p. 22.
8. According to John Leland (*c.* 1503–52): J. Leland, *Commentarii de Scriptoribus Brittanicis*, ed. A. Hall, 2 vols. (Oxford, 1709), II, p. 483. Leland uses '*adolescentulum*', although Linacre was 26 in 1487; Clough, p. 3.
9. C.B. Schmitt, 'Thomas Linacre and Italy', in *Essays on Linacre*, pp. 36–75 [hereafter Schmitt]. Here at p. 37; R. Weiss, *Humanism in England during the Fifteenth Century* (Oxford, 1967, third edition), pp. 153–9.
10. Allen, II, 441–2: letter of 30 January 1517 from Latimer to Erasmus.
11. Schmitt, p. 38.
12. The dedication letter, *De Temperamentis* (Cambridge, 1521), is reprinted in J.N. Johnson, *The Life of Thomas Linacre*, ed. R. Graves (London, 1835), pp. 324–5.
13. J. Woolfson, *Padua and the Tudors: English Students in Italy, 1485–1603* (Cambridge, 1998) [hereafter Woolfson, *Padua*], p. 77; D.J. Geanakoplos, *Interaction of the 'Sibling' Byzantine and Western Cultures* (New Haven, Connecticut, London, 1976), pp. 231–64.
14. '*Item lego domino Thome Lynaker studenti Fflorence*', quoted in Bennett, p. 90 and Schmitt, p. 38, n. 1.
15. For Linacre's Florentine studies, see Allen, II, 441–2, letter 520: Letter from William Latimer (Linacre's friend) to Erasmus, 30 January 1517; *Liber* 17, fol. 18v, in the archives of the English College in Rome, gives a date of 4 November 1490 for Linacre's and William Lily's admission. Linacre's elevation to Warden is given as 3 May 1491 (fol. 19r). He held the position until 3 May 1492 – one year exactly. See V. Flynn, 'Englishmen in Rome during the Renaissance', *Modern Philology*, 36 (1938), pp. 136–7 and Clough p. 6.
16. Schmitt, p. 40.
17. Woolfson, *Padua*, p. 77; Fletcher, 'Linacre's Land', in Madison *et al.*, p. 118.
18. R.J. Mitchell, 'Thomas Linacre in Italy, *The English Historical Review*, l (1935), pp. 696–8; Richard Pace (1483–1536) studied at Padua shortly after Linacre and attested to Linacre's presence there in his *De Fructu qui ex Doctrina Percipiatur* (first edition, Basel, 1517), ed. F. Manley and R.S. Silvester (New York, 1967), pp. 96–7; Schmitt, p. 42.
19. A. Fox, 'Facts and Fallacies', p. 11; G.R. Elton, 'Humanism in England' in A. Goodman and A. Mackay (eds.), *The Impact of Humanism* (London, 1990), p. 260; Woolfson, *Padua*, p. 39. See also J.B. Trapp, *Erasmus, Colet and More: The Early Tudor Humanists and their Books* (London, 1991), p. 4.
20. Woolfson, *Padua*, p. 40.
21. All Souls' College, Oxford, MS. B. 29 (Bursars' Books, 1450–1520). Schmitt, p. 45.

22. Schmitt, p. 46.

23. *Ibid.*, pp. 56–7 citing *Statuta Dominorum Artistarum Achedemiae Patavinae*, (Venice, *c.* 1496), fol. 24v.

24. *Ibid.*, p. 58.

25. *Ibid.*

26. P.S. Allen, 'Linacre and Latimer in Italy', *The English Historical Review*, 18 (1903), pp. 514–7, here at p. 515. Letter from Latimer to Aldus reprinted in P. de Nolhac, 'Les correspondants d'Alde Manuce. Matériaux nouveaux d'histoire littéraire (1483–1514)', *Studi e documenti di storia e diretto*, 8 (Bologna, 1887), pp. 247–99; 9 (Bologna, 1888), pp. 203–48.

27. *Albertu Pii Carporum Comitis illustrisimi ad Erasmi Roterodami expostulationem Responsio accurate et paraenica Martini Lutheri et asseclarum eius haeresim vesanam magnis argumentis, et iustus rationibus confutans* (Paris, 1528?), fol. 3v; M.P. Gilmore, `Erasmus and Alberto Pio, Prince of Carpi' in T.K. Rabb and J.E. Siegel (eds.), *Action and Conviction in Early Modern Europe. Essays in Memory of E.H. Harbison* (Princeton, 1969), p. 306.

28. Published by the Aldine Press under the title *Astronomici Veteres*: Schmitt, p. 70.

29. Wolsey had suffered from the sweating sickness and was aware of the lack of medical regulation in the city. Moreover, Linacre was his personal physician: C. Webster, 'Thomas Linacre and the Foundation of the College of Physicians', in *Essays on Linacre*, pp. 198–222. [Hereafter Webster], p. 209.

30. J. Freind, *The History of Physick from the Time of Galen to the Beginning of the Sixteenth Century*, 2 vols., (London, 1725–6), II, 410–15 [hereafter Freind]. Here at 414.

31. Webster, p. 199. The Stone House passed to Merton College, Oxford in Linacre's Will, while the 'parlour adioyning to the sayd house and a chamber over the same adioyning to the street' were also given to the college: Merton College, Oxford, Roll no. 6697. Will of Thomas Linacre, 18 October 1524, reprinted in J.M. Fletcher, 'Linacre's Lands and Lectureships: Appendix B2', in *Essays on Linacre*, pp. 165–71.

32. Freind, p. 414, quoted in Webster, p. 199.

33. Webster, p. 200.

34. G. Clark and A.M. Cooke, *A History of the Royal College of Physicians of London*, 2 vols. (Oxford, 1964–6) [hereafter Clark], I, pp. 54–5; Webster, p. 208.

35. *Ibid.*, p. 209.

36. Clark, I, pp. 70–71.

37. *Ibid.*, p. 377; Webster, p. 216.

38. J.M. Fletcher, 'Linacre's Lands and Lectureships' in *Essays on Linacre*, pp. 107–147 [hereafter Fletcher]. Here at pp. 122–3. A. Wood, *Historia et Antiquitates Universitatis Oxoniensis*, 2 vols. (Oxford, 1674), II, pp. 34–6.

39. Merton College, Oxford, Roll. No. 6697. 18 October 1524.

40. Roll no. 6697, reprinted in Fletcher, appendix B, 'Will of Thomas Linacre', in *Essays on Linacre*, pp. 165–71 [hereafter Will]. Here at p. 169.

41. Fletcher, p. 130.

42. Merton Roll, Will, pp. 167–8.

43. *Ibid.*, p. 168.

44. *Ibid.*

45. Jackson was elected a fellow of St. John's College in April 1525 and died in 1528: T. Baker, *History of the College of St. John the Evangelist, Cambridge*, ed. J.E.B. Mayor, 2 vols. (Cambridge, 1869), I, p. 282; Fletcher, p. 136, no. 1.

46. Brass in St. John's College Chapel; Fletcher, p. 136.

47. *Acts of Court*, fol. 49.

48. Fletcher, p. 137.

49. For the full details see 'Appendix B9: Indenture between Cuthbert Tunstall and the Warden and Scholars of Merton College, Oxford, respecting the foundation of lectureships': Merton College, Oxford. Roll in envelope, E.2. 28s. (10 December 1549), reprinted in Fletcher, pp. 186–90. J.M. Fletcher, *Registrum Annalium Collegii Mertonensis* (Oxford, 1976), p. 192.

50. '*Admissus erat Georgius Iamis ad lectionem inferioris lectionis Linacri per litteras venerabilis viri domini Cuthberti Tonstawle, nuper Dunelmensis episcope, a domino custode presentibus omnibus sociis in domo custodies*', *Ibid.*, p. 192.

51. R.G. Lewis, 'The Linacre Lectureships Subsequent to their Foundation', in *Essays on Linacre*, pp. 223–64 [hereafter Lewis]. Here at p. 224.

52. W. Osler, *Thomas Linacre* (Cambridge, 1908), pp. 52, and 54–5, quoted in Lewis, p. 223.

53. H.D. Rolleston, *The Cambridge Medical School, a Biographical History* (Cambridge, 1932), p. 17; Lewis, p. 223.

54. For the life of Grocyn see article by J.B. Trapp, 'William Grocyn', in *New DNB*, XXIII, pp. 56–58.

55. Lupset defended Erasmus's *Novum Testamentum* along with Thomas More, in *Epistolae Aliquot Eruditorum, Nunquam Antheac Excuae* (Louvain 1519; republished, Froben, Basel, 1520).

56. Woolfson, *Padua*, p. 83.

57. B.L., Add. MS. 29549, fol. 7.; Woolfson, *Padua*, p. 189.

58. Woolfson, *Padua*, p. 108.

59. T.F. Mayer, 'Thomas Lupset', in the *New DNB*, XXXIV, p. 781.

60. J.A. Gee, *The Life and Works of Thomas Lupset: With a Critical Edition of the Original Treatises and the Letters* (New Haven and London, 1926) [hereafter Gee, *Lupset*], p. 228.

61. Mayer, in *New DNB*, XXXIV, p. 781.

62. Gee, *Lupset*, p. 139.

63. '*hic situs est Thomas Lupsetus vir Graece et Latine, atque in sacris literis eruditissimus*'.

64. For a full survey of Linacre's works, see G. Barber, 'Thomas Linacre: A bibliographical Survey of his Works', in *Essays on Linacre*, pp. 290–336.

65. Allen, I, p. 467: '*De Linacro cave ne cui temere credas; nam ego certis argumentis habeo compertum illum observantissimo in te esse animo, et de reiecta grammatical non magnopere laborare.*'

66. T.F. Mayer, 'Thomas Lupset', in *New DNB*, XXXIV, p. 781.

67. 'Both God is charity and charity is God', Gee, p. 231.

Chapter 12: Jacques Lefèvre D'Étaples

1. J. R. Veenstra, 'Jacques Lefèvre D'Étaples' in *Christian Humanism*, pp. 353–62 [hereafter Veenstra]. Here at p. 354.

2. Veenstra, pp. 356–7.

3. G. Bedouelle, 'Jacques Lefèvre d'Étaples (*c.* 1460–1536)' in Lindberg, pp. 19–33 [hereafter referred to as Bedouelle]. Here at p. 20.

4. M. Luther, *Annotationes Quincuplici Fabri Stapulensis Psalterio Manu ad Scriptae* (1513); J. Rilliet, *Zwingli: Third Man of the Reformation*, trans. H. Knight (Philadelphia, 1964), p. 99.

5. Bedouelle, p. 20.

6. Concerning this controversy, see A. Reeve (ed.), *Erasmus's Annotations on the New Testament: Galations to the Apocalypse* (Leiden, 1993), pp. 706–13.

7. Bedouelle, p. 21.

8. *Ibid.*

9. *Ibid.*, p. 23.

10. The proto-reformer theorists are: C.H. Graf (1842 and 1852); A.L. Herminjard (1868); E. Doumergue (1899); J. Bernaud (1900 and 1936); N. Weiss (1919); H. Doerries (1925); K. Spiess (1930); J. Panier (1935); F. Hahn (1938). The earliest claim made for Lefèvre as a proto-Protestant came from Bèze's 1580 *Icones*. As for the proponents of Lefèvre as a Catholic, conservative humanist leader, see E. Amann (1926); P. Imbert de la Tour (1944); and especially Richard Stauffer's 1967 article 'Lefèvre d'Étaples, artisan ou Spectateur de la Réforme?', in *Interprètes de la Bible* (Paris, 1980), p. 11–29.

11. J. Lefèvre d'Étaples, *The Prefatory Epistles of Jacques Lefèvre d'Étaples and Related Texts*, ed. E.F. Rice, Jr. (New York, 1972) [hereafter Lefèvre, *Prefatory Epistles*], p. 194.

12. *Ibid.*, p. 194.

13. *Ibid.*, p. 473.

14. F. Secret, *Les Cabalistes Chrétiens de la Renaissance* (Paris, 1964), pp. 150–64.

15. Lefèvre, *Prefatory Epistles*, p. 194.

16. D. Erasmus, *Apologia ad Fabrum Stapulensem* (Louvain, 1517), ed. A.W. Steenbeek (Amsterdam, 1994); Bedouelle, p. 25.

17. *LW*, 48: 26; *WA Br.* 1: 90.

18. Bedouelle, p. 26.

19. *Ibid.*, p. 27.
20. *Ibid.*, p. 28.
21. J. Lefèvre d'Étaples, '*Evangile de la Pentecote*' in G. Bedouelle and F. Giacore (eds.), *Epistres et Evangiles pour les cinquante-deux dimanches de l'an* (Leiden, 1976), p. 269, which is *Evangile du 8eme dimanche après la Pentecote, ajout de 1531/1532.*
22. *Ibid*, p. 251, which is *Evangile du 5eme dimanche après la Pentecot.*
23. Lefèvre, *Prefatory Epistles*, p. 461.
24. J. Lefèvre d'Étaples, *Jacques Lefévre d'Étaples and the Three Marys debates: On Mary Magdalen, on Christ's three days in the tomb, on the on Mary in place of the three: a discussion ; On the threefold and single Magdalen : a second discussion.* An edition of: *De Maria Magdalena, triduo Christi, et ex tribus una Maria disceptatio...Secunda emissio. Parisiis: Ex officina Henrici Stephani, 1518- De tribus et unica Magdalena disceptatio secunda...Parisiis: Ex officina Henrici Stephani, 1519,* introduction, Latin text, English translation and annotation by Sheila M. Porrer. (Genève, 2009) [hereafter Porrer]. Prior to 1969, scholarship on the subject was mainly confined to A. Clerval, *De J. Clichtovei Vita et Operibus* (Paris, 1894), pp. 27–30; M. Mann, *Erasme et les débuts de la Réforme Française (1517–1536)* (Paris, 1934), chapter 2; and E. Surtz, *The Works and Days of John Fisher* (Cambridge, Mass., 1967), pp. 5–7, 157–60, 274–89.
25. Porrer, pp. 1–3 and 20.
26. The idea of the three phases is Porrer's own: pp. 62–127.
27. R. Cameron, 'The Attack on the Biblical Work of Lefèvre D'Étaples, 1514–1521', *Church History*, 38 (1969) pp. 9–24 [hereafter Cameron], here at p. 10.
28. Cameron, pp. 9–10.
29. Faber Stapulensis, *De Maria Magdalena et Triduo Christi Disceptatio, ad Clarissimum virum D. Franciscum Molineum, Christianissimi Francorum Regis Francisci Primi Magistrum* (Paris, 1517); *idem, De Tribus et Unica Magdalena Disceptatio Secunda* (Paris, 1518).
30. A. Hufstader, 'Lefèvre d'Étaples and the Magdalen', *Studies in the Renaissance,* 16 (1969), pp. 31–60 [hereafter Hufstader], here at pp. 32–4.
31. Hufstader, pp. 35–6.
32. *Ibid.*, p. 34.
33. *Ibid.*, p. 33.
34. Porrer, p. 185; *De Maria Magdalena,* fol. 11r.
35. M. de Grandval, *Ecclesiae Catholicae non tres Magdalenas sed Unicum Colentis Apologia seu Defensorium* (Paris, 1518).
36. *Ibid.*, last folio (no folio numbers given).
37. J. Clichtove, Preface, *Disceptatio Prima, Secunda Emissio,* fol. 3v.
38. Porrer, p. 167.
39. M. de Grandval, *Apologiae seu Defensorii Ecclesiae Catholicae non Tres Sive Duas Magdalenas sed Uniam Celebrantis et Colentis Apologiae Marcum de Grandval* (Paris, 1519).

40. Lefèvre d'Étaples, *De Tribus et Unica Magdalena Disceptatio Secunda* (Paris, 1519); Hufstader, p. 37.

41. *Discpetatio Secunda*, fols. 3v-4r.

42. *Ibid.*, fol. 40r.

43. *Ibid.*

44. Hufstader, p. 37.

45. *Ibid.*, p. 38: *Evangelistarum Symphonia* (Venice, 23 November, 1519).

46. Cameron, p. 15.

47. J. Fisher, *Eversio Munitionis Quam Iodocus Clichtoveus erigere moliebatur adversus unicam Magdalenam per Ionnaem Roffensis Ecclesiae in Anglia Episcopum* (Louvain, 1519); J. Fisher, *Confutatio Secundae Disceptationis per Jacobum Fabrum Stapulensem habitae in qua tribus foeminis partiri molitur quae totius ecclesiae consuetude unicae tribuit Magdalenae* (Paris, September, 1519); J. Fisher, *De Unica Magdalena Libri Tres* (Paris, March, 1519) fol. 3r and *passim*.

48. Fisher, *De Unica Magdalena, Libri tres,* fol. A3v.

49. Allen, IV, p. 73 (Letter to Fisher, 4 October 1519).

50. Hufstader, p. 39.

51. *Ibid.*, p. 40.

52. Allen, IV, p. 323.

53. Bedouelle, p.31.

54. *Ibid.*, p. 20.

Chapter 13: Juan Luis Vives

1. Until recently biographical information on Vives was based upon the *Vita Vivis* of Gregorio Mayans, which prefaced the *Opera Omnia*, 8 vols. (Valencia, 1782–1790; reprinted London, 1964). This biography remained unchallenged by Adolfo Bonilla's *Luis Vives y la Filosofia del Renaciamiento* (Madrid, 1903) and a much later article by Emilie L. Bergmann, *Encyclopaedia of the Renaissance*, ed. Paul F. Grendler, 6 vols. (New York, 1999), IV, pp. 281–83. Revisionist scholarship has questioned the significance of Vives's conversion from scholasticism to humanism and emphasized his *Judeo-Converso* origin: E.J. Ashworth, *Language and Logic in the Post-Medieval Period* (Dordrecht and Boston, 1974) and Carlos G. Noreña, *Juan Luis Vives* (The Hague, 1970). Noreña's later work *Juan Luis Vives and the Emotions* (Carbondale and Edwardsville, 1989) gives an excellent biography of the humanist (pp. 3–68). The most recent and comprehensive guides to Vives are the series of articles contained in Charles Fantazzi (ed.), *A Companion to Juan Luis Vives* (Leiden, 2008) [hereafter Fantazzi, *Companion to Vives*].

2. E.G. González, 'Juan Luis Vives: Works and Days' in Fantazzi, *Companion to Vives*, pp. 15–64 [hereafter González]. Here at p. 25.

3. There were roughly three castes in Aragon: the working-class *moriscos*, the powerful 'old' Christians (*cristianos viejos*) and the *converses* (new Christians): González, p. 20.

4. C. Roth, *A History of the Marranos* (London and Philadelphia, 1932), p. 19, quoted in González, p. 22.

5. Benzion Netanyahu, *The Marranos of Spain. From the Late XIVth to the Early XVIth Century, According to Contemporary Hebrew Sources* (New York, 1966); González, p. 22.

6. González, pp. 19–20.

7. 2 November 1517, Allen, IV, Ep. 694.

8. González, p. 25.

9. *Ibid.*, p. 28.

10. *Ibid.*, p. 31.

11. Carlos G. Noreña, *Juan Luis Vives and the Emotions* (Carbondale and Edwardsville, 1989) [hereafter Noreña, *Vives*], p. 18.

12. González, p. 35.

13. *Ibid.*, p. 37.

14. *Ibid.*, p. 43.

15. E.G. González, 'The Encounter of Luis Vives (1492/3–1540) and Hadrianus Barlandus (1486–1538) in Louvain, 1514?-1515', *Lias* 30/2 (2003), pp. 177–212.

16. Noreña, *Vives*, pp. 23–5.

17. Del Nero, p. 182.

18. González, p. 42. Letter published by Bonilla in his *Luis Vives*, Appendix IX, pp. 733–34.

19. González, p. 43.

20. E. Grassi, *Rhetoric as Philosophy: The Humanist Tradition*, trans. J.M. Krois and A. Azodi (Southern Illinois, 1980; reprint, 2001), p. 11.

21. *Ibid.*, p. 12.

22. Vives succeeded Thomas Lupset in the post as lecturer, when Lupset set out on his Italian travels.

23. González, p. 56.

24. *Ibid.*, p. 46.

25. See M.L. Colish, 'The *De Veritate Fidei Christianae* of Juan Luis Vives' [hereafter Colish] in *Christian Humanism*, pp. 173–97: for Vives as a sceptic see J.A. Fernández Santamaría, *The Theater of Man: Juan Luis Vives on Society* (Philadelphia, 1998), pp. 11–37, 43–56, 119–124; Clements and Casini, however, disagree: R.D. Clements, 'A Sixteenth-Century Psychologist on the Immortality of the Soul: Juan Luis Vives', *Bibliothèque d'Humanisme et Renaissance*, 28 (1966), p. 82; L. Casini, 'Aristotelianism and Anti-Stoicism in Juan Luis Vives' in J. Kraye and R. Saarinen (eds.) in *Moral Philosophy and the Threshold of Modernity* (Dordrecht, 2005), pp. 283–305. For Vives on Judaism see H.A. Oberman, *The Role of Anti-Semitism in the Age of Renaissance and Reformation*, trans. J.I. Porter (Philadelphia, 1984), *passim*.

26. J.L. Vives, *De Veritate Fidei Christianae*, praef. 1.3 in *Opera Omnia*, ed. Mayans y Síscar, 8 vols. (Valencia, 1782–1790; reproduced, London, 1964), 5:9, VIII, p. 454, quoted in Colish, p. 196.

27. Colish, p. 196.

28. Allen, Ep. 2932, 10 May 1534: '*Tempora habemus difficilia, in quibus nec loqui nec tacere possumus absque periculo*'. González, p. 54.

29. Noreña, *Vives*, p. 33.

30. González, p. 64.

31. C. Fantazzi, 'Introduction' to *De Institutione*, p. 20 quoting. *Desiderii Erasmi Roteromdami Opera Omnia*, ed. J. Leclerc (Leiden, 1703–1706; reprint Hildesheim, 1961–2), V, 617D.

32. Fantazzi, 'Introudction' to *De Institutione*, p. 23.

33. Valerio Del Nero, 'The *De Disciplinis* as a model of a humanistic text', in Fantazzi, *Companion to Vives*, p. 177–226 [hereafter Del Nero]. Here at p. 177.

BIBLIOGRAPHY

INTRODUCTION

Manuscripts

All Souls' College, Oxford, Codrington Library, MS AS, h. infra 1.5: John
Colet's marginalia on a copy of Marsilio Ficino's *Epistolae*, Venice, 1495.
Cambridge University Library, MS Gg.iv.26: *Joannis Coleti Enarratio In
Epistolam S. Pauli ad Romanos* and other works by John Colet.

Printed Primary Sources

Breen, Q., 'Melanchthon's Reply to Giovanni Pico della Mirandola', *The
Journal of the History of Ideas*, 13 (1952), pp. 413–426.
——, 'Giovanni Pico della Mirandola on the Conflict of Philosophy and
Rhetoric', *The Journal of the History of Ideas*, 13 (1952), pp. 384–412
(correspondence between Pico della Mirandola and Ermolao Barbaro).
Foxe, J., *John Foxe's Book of Martyrs 1583: Acts and Monuments of Matters
Most Speciall and Memorable* [STC 11225]: Facsimile edition for C.D.
R.O.M., edited by D.G. Newcombe and M. Pidd (Oxford, 2001).
Nugent, E.M. (ed.), *The Thought and Culture of the English Renaissance: An
Anthology of Tudor Prose, 1481–1555* (Cambridge, 1956).
Pace, R., *De Fructu qui ex Doctrina Percipitur: The Benefit of a Liberal
Education*, translated and edited by F. Manley and R.S. Sylvester (New
York, 1967).
Plato, *The Republic*, trans. by H.D.P. Lee (Harmondsworth, 1955).
Plotinus, *The Enneads*, translated by S. Mackenna (Harmondsworth, 1991).
Pseudo-Dionysius: The Complete Works, trans. and ed. by C. Luibheid (New
York, 1987).
Tyndale, W., *An Answer to Sir Thomas More's Dialogue: The Supper of the
Lord after the True Meaning of John VI and 1 Corinthians XI; and W.
Tracy's Testament Expounded*, edited by H. Walter, Parker Society, 38
(Cambridge, 1850).

Secondary Sources

Amos, N. Scott, 'New Learning, Old Theology: Renaissance Biblical Humanism, Scripture, and the Question of Theological Method', *Renaissance Studies,* 17 (2003) pp. 47–54.

Baron, H., *The Crisis of the Early Italian Renaissance: Civic Humanism and Republican Liberty in an Age of Classicism and Tyranny,* 2 vols. (Princeton, 1966).

Black R., *Renaissance Thought: A Reader* (London and New York, 2001).

Borghesi, F., 'A Life in Works' in M.V. Dougherty (ed.), *Pico della Mirandola: New Essays* (Cambridge, 2008), pp. 202–219.

Bouwsma, W.J., 'The Two Faces of Humanism: Stoicism and Augustinianism in Renaissance Thought,' in H.A. Oberman with T.A. Brady, Jr (eds.), *Itinerarium Italicum: The Profile of the Italian Renaissance in the Mirror of Its European Transformations* (Leiden, 1975), pp. 3–60.

Brotton, J., *The Renaissance Bazaar: From the Silk Road to Michelangelo* (Oxford, 2002).

Cassirer, E., 'Giovanni Pico della Mirandola. A Study in the History of Renaissance Ideas', *The Journal of the History of Ideas,* 3 (1942), pp. 123–44 and 319–46.

——, *The Individual and the Cosmos in Renaissance Philosophy,* trans. M. Domandi (New York, 1963).

D'Amico, J., *Renaissance Humanism in Papal Rome – Humanists and Churchmen of the Eve of the Reformation* (Baltimore, 1983).

Dowling, M., *Fisher of Men: A Life of John Fisher, 1469–1535* (Basingstoke, 1999).

——, *Humanism in the Age of Henry VIII* (London, 1986).

Edelheit, A., 'Humanism and Theology in Renaissance Florence: Four Examples, Caroli, Savonarola, Ficino, and Pico', in *Verbum Analecta Neolatina,* 8 (2006), pp. 271–290.

——, *Ficino, Pico and Savonarola: The Evolution of Humanist Theology 1461/2–1498* (Leiden, 2008).

Ferguson, W.K., *The Renaissance in Historical Thought: Five Centuries of Interpretation* (Cambridge, Mass., 2006).

Flannery, K.L., SJ, 'Plato and Platonism' in A. Hastings, A. Mason and H. Pyper (eds.), *The Oxford Companion to Christian Thought* (Oxford, 2000), pp. 542–4.

Garin, E., *Italian Humanism: Philosophy and Civic Life in the Renaissance,* trans. P. Munz (Oxford, 1965).

Gleason, J.B., *John Colet* (Berkeley, 1989).

Goodman, A., and Mackay, A., *The Impact of Humanism on Western Europe* (London, 1990).

Grafton, A., 'Humanism and Political Theory', in J.H. Burns (ed.), *The Cambridge History of Political Thought, 1450–1700,* (Cambridge, 1991), pp. 20–29.

Hamilton, A., 'Humanists and the Bible' in J. Kraye (ed.), *The Cambridge Companion to Renaissance Humanism*, (Cambridge, 1996), pp. 100–117.

Hankins, J., 'Humanism, Scholasticism, and Renaissance Philosophy', in J. Hankins (ed.), *The Cambridge Companion to Renaissance Philosophy* (Cambridge, 2007), pp. 30–48.

——, 'The Significance of Renaissance Philosophy', *The Cambridge Companion to Renaissance Philosophy* (Cambridge, 2007), pp. 338–345.

Haskins, C.H., *The Renaissance of the Twelfth Century* (Cambridge, Mass., 1927).

Huizinga, J., *The Waning of the Middle Ages: A Study of the Forms of Life, Thought and Art in France and the Netherlands in the XIVth and XVth Centuries* (First Dutch edition, 1919; Second Dutch edition, 1921; English edition, London, 1924).

IJsseling, S., *Rhetoric and Philosophy in Conflict: A Historical Survey* (The Hague, 1976).

Jayne, S., *John Colet and Marsilio Ficino* (Oxford, 1963).

Jardine, L., 'Humanism and the Sixteenth Century Cambridge Arts Course', *The History of Education*, 4 (1975) pp. 16–31.

Kekewich, L., *The Renaissance in Europe: A Cultural Enquiry* (New Haven and London, 2000).

Kittelson, J.M., 'Humanism in the theological faculties of Lutheran Universities during the Late Reformation', in M.P. Fleischer (ed.), *The Harvest of Humanism in Central Europe. Essays in Honour of Lewis W. Spitz* (St. Louis, 1992), pp. 139–57.

Kraye, J. (ed.), *The Cambridge Companion to Renaissance Humanism* (Cambridge, 1996; Eighth edition, 2007).

Kristeller, P.O., 'Florentine Platonism and its Relations with Humanism and Scholasticism', *Church History*, 8 (1939) pp. 201–11.

——, *Renaissance Thought and its Sources*, ed. M. Mooney (Columbia, 1979).

——, 'The Scholar and his Public in the Late Middle-Ages' in E.P. Mahoney (ed.), *Medieval Aspects of Renaissance Learning: Three Essays by Paul Oskar Kristeller* (Durham, N. Carolina, 1974), pp. 3–28.

Levi, A., *Renaissance and Reformation: The Intellectual Genesis* (New Haven and London, 2002).

Livingstone, E.A., (ed.), *The Concise Dictionary of the Christian Church* (Oxford, 1977).

MacCulloch, D., *Reformation: Europe's House Divided (1490–1700)* (London, 2003).

MacDonald, A.A.M., Martels, Z.R.W.M von and Veenstra, J.R. (eds.), *Christian Humanism: Essays in Honour of Arjo Vanderjagt* (Leiden, 2009).

Mack, P., 'Montaigne and Christian Humanism' in A.A.M. MacDonald, Z.R.W.M. von Martels and J.R. Veestra (eds.), *Christian Humanism: Essays in Honour of Arjo Vanderjagt* (Leiden, 2009), pp. 199–209.

Mann, N., 'The Origins of Humanism' in J. Kraye (ed.), *The Cambridge Companion to Renaissance Humanism* (Cambridge, 1996).

McConica, J.K., *English Humanists and Reformation Politics Under Henry VIII and Edward VI* (first edition, Oxford, 1965; second edition, Oxford, 1967).

McGrath, A.E., *The Intellectual Origins of the European Reformation* (Oxford, 1987; second edition, Oxford, 2004).

Michelet, J., *Renaissance* (Paris, 1855).

Miles, L., 'Platonism and Christian Doctrine: The Revival of Interest in John Colet', *Philosophical Forum*, 21, 1964, pp. 87–103.

——, *John Colet and the Platonic Tradition*, (London, 1962).

Nauert, C.G., *Humanism and the Culture of the Renaissance* (Cambridge, 1995; second edition, Cambridge, 2006), pp. 151–167.

O' Malley, J., *Praise and Blame in Renaissance Rome –Rhetoric, Doctrine, and Reform in Sacred Orators of the Papal Court, 1450–1521* (Durham, North Carolina, 1979).

Panofsky, E., *Renaissance and Renascenes in Western Art* (London, 1969).

Pollard, A.W. and Redgrave, G.R., *A Short Title Catalogue of Books Printed in England, Scotland and Ireland and of English Books Printed Abroad, 1475–1640*, first compiled in 1926, second edition revised and enlarged by W.A. Jackson and F.S. Ferguson (1976–86), completed by K.F. Pantzer, The Bibliographical Society, I: A-H; II: I-Z; III: printers and publishers index, indices and appendices (London, 1976–91).

Rabil, A. (ed.), *Renaissance Humanism: Foundations, Forms and Legacy*, 3 vols. (Philadelphia, 1988).

Rex, R., 'Humanism' in A. Pettegree (ed.), *The Reformation World*, (London, 2000), pp. 51–70.

——, 'The New Learning', *The Journal of Ecclesiastical History*, 44 (1993), pp. 26–44.

——, 'The Role of English humanists in the Reformation up to 1559', in N. Scott Amos, A.D.M. Pettegree and H. Van Nierop (eds.)*The Education of a Christian Society: Humanism and the Reformation in Britain and the Netherlands* (Aldershot, 1999), pp. 19–40.

Schiffman, Z.S., *Humanism and the Renaissance* (Boston, 2002).

Scott Amos, N., Pettegree, A.D.M and Van Nierop, H. (eds.), *The Education of a Christian Society: Humanism and the Reformation in Britain and the Netherlands* (Aldershot, 1999).

Seigel, J., *Rhetoric and Philosophy in Renaissance Humanism* (Princeton, 1968).

Skinner, Q., *The Foundations of Modern Political Thought, I: The Renaissance* (Cambridge, 1978).

Spitz, L.W., 'The Renaissance: Humanism and Humanism Research', English version of 'Humanismus/Humanismusforschung' in *Theologische Realenzyklopädie*, 15, Berlin and New York, Walter der Gruyter, 1986, pp. 639–61; reprinted in L.W. Spitz, *Luther and German Humanism* (Hampshire, 1996), pp. 1–40.

Trinkaus, C., *In Our Image and Likeness: Humanity and Divinity in Italian Humanist Thought*, 2 vols. (Chicago, 1970).

——, *The Scope of Renaissance Humanism* (Ann Arbor, 1983).

Voigt, G., *Die Wiederbelebung des classischen Altertums oder das erste Jahrhundert des Humanismus* (1859) and V.R. Giustiani, 'Homo, Humanus, and the Meanings of "Humanism"', *The Journal of the History of Ideas*, 46 (1985), pp. 167–95.

Weiss, R., *The Dawn of Humanism in Italy* (London, 1947), revised and reprinted in *The Bulletin of the Institute of Historical Research*, 42 (1969), pp. 1–16.

Witt, R., 'Coluccio Salutati in the Footsteps of the Ancients' in A.A. MacDonald, Z.R.W.M. von Martels and J.R. Veenstra (eds.), *Christian Humanism: Essays in Honour of Arjo Vanderjagt* (Leiden, 2009), pp. 3–12.

——, 'The Humanism of Paul Oskar Kristeller' in J. Monfasani (ed.), *Kristeller Reconsidered. Essays on his Life and Scholarship* (New York, 2006), pp. 257–67.

PETRARCH

Printed Primary Sources

Bruni, L., *Laudatio Florentinae Urbis*, trans. R.G. Witt in B.G. Kohl and R.G. Witt, *The Earthly Republic: Italian Humanists on Gvernment and Society* (Philadelphia, PA, 1978).

Petrarch, F., *Epistolae Rerum Familiarium*, Book VI, no. 2 (*Le Familiari*, ed. V. Rossi and U. Bosco, Florence, 1933–42).

——, *Invectives*, ed. and trans. D. Marsh, The I Tatti Renaissance Library (Harvard, 2003).

——, *Le traité De sui ipsius et multorum ignorantia*, ed. L.M. Capelli (Paris, 1906).

——, *On His Own Ignorance and That of Many Others*, translated by H. Nachod, in *The Renaissance Philosophy of Man*, ed. E. Cassirer, P.O. Kristeller, and J.H. Randall, Jr. (Chicago, 1948), pp. 47–133.

——, *On Religious Leisure: De otio religioso*, ed. and trans. by S.S. Schearer, introduction by R.G. Witt (New York, 2002).

——, *Petrarch's Africa*, trans. T.G. Bergin and A.S. Wilson (New Haven, 1977).

——, *Canzoniere (Rerum vulgarium fragmenta): Petrarch's Lyric Poems: The 'Rime sparse' and Other Lyrics*, ed. and trans. R.M. Durling (Cambridge, Mass., 1976).

——, *Petrarch's Remedies for Fortune Fair and Foul*. A modern English translation of *De remediis utriusque fortune*, with commentary by C.H. Rawski, 5 vols. (Bloomington and Indianapolis, 1991).

——, *The Life of Solitude by Francis Petrarch*, ed. J. Zeitlin (Urbana, 1924).

——, *Invectives*, ed. and trans. D. Marsh (Cambridge, Mass., 2003).

——, *Rerum familiarum libri I-VIII.*, ed. A. Bernado (Albany, 1975–85).

——, *Letters on Familiar Matters: Books IX-XXIV*, 2 vols. (Baltimore, 1982).

Petrarch, F., *Petrarch's Secretum,* with Introduction, notes, and critical anthology by D.A. Carozza and H.J. Shey. Series 17: Classical Languages and Literature, VII (New York, 1989).

——, *I Tromphi,* ed. W.E.Hatch, *Triumphs* (Chicago, 1962).

Petrarch's *Epistle to Posterity,* printed in F. Petrarch, *Epistolae Seniles,* XIII, 3.

Petrarch's *Prose,* ed. Martellotti, *et al* (Milan and Naples, 1955).

Salutati, C., *Epistolario di Coluccio Salutati,* ed. F. Novati, 4 vols. (Rome, 1891–1911).

Secondary Sources

Bernardo, A.S., 'Petrarch, Dante, and the Medieval Tradition' in A. Rabil (ed.), *Renaissance Humanism: Foundations, Forms and Legacy,* 3 vols. (Philadelphia, 1988), I, pp. 115–140.

Bishop, M., *Petrarch and His World* (London, 1964).

Carducci, G. and Ferrari, S. (ed.), *Le Rime di Francesco Petrarca* (Florence, 1899).

Celenza, C.S., 'The Revival of Platonic Philosophy', in J. Hankins (ed.), *The Cambridge Companion to Renaissance Philosophy* (Cambridge, 2007), pp. 72–96.

Ferguson, W.K., *The Renaissance in Historical Thought: Five Centuries of Interpretation* (Cambridge, Mass., 1948; reprinted in Toronto, 2006).

Cassirer, E., Kristeller, P.O. and Randall, J.H., *The Renaissance Philosophy of Man* (Chicago, 1948).

Kallendorf, C. 'The Historical Petrarch', *The American Historical Review,* 101, (1996), pp. 130–141.

Kirkham, V. and Maggi, A., *Petrarch: A Critical Guide to the Complete Works* (Chicago, 2009).

Kohl, B.G., 'Francesco Petrarcha: Introduction: How a Ruler Ought to Govern His State,' in B.G. Kohl and R.G. Witt (eds.), *The Earthly Republic: Italian Humanists on Government and Society* (Philadelphia, 1978), pp. 25–78.

——, 'Petrarch's Prefaces to *De Viris Illustribus*', *History and Theory,* XIII (1974), pp. 132–44.

Kraye, J., 'The Revival of Hellenistic Philosophies' in J. Hankins (ed.), *The Cambridge Companion to Renaissance Philosophy* (Cambridge, 2007), pp. 97–111.

Kristeller, P.O., *Eight Philosophers of the Italian Renaissance* (Stanford, 1964).

Lorch, M., 'Petrarch, Cicero, and the Classical Pagan Tradition' in A. Rabil (ed.), *Renaissance Humanism: Foundations, Forms and Legacy,* 3 vols. (Philadelphia, 1988), I, pp. 71–94.

Mann, N., *Petrarch,* (Oxford, 1984).

Mortimer, A., (ed.), *Petrarch's Canzionere in the English Renaissance* (Revised and enlarged edition, Amsterdam and New York, 2005).

Nelson, E., 'The Problem of the Prince' in J. Hankins (ed.), *The Cambridge Companion to Renaissance Philosophy* (Cambridge, 2007), pp. 319–337.

Rabil, A., 'Petrarch, Augustine, and the Classical Christian Tradition' in A. Rabil (ed.), *Renaissance Humanism: Foundations, Forms and Legacy*, 3 vols. (Philadelphia, 1988), I, pp. 95–114.

——, 'The Significance of "Civic Humanism" in the Interpretation of the Italian Renaissance' in *Renaissance Humanism: Foundations, Forms and Legacy*, 3 vols. (Philadelphia, 1988), I, pp. 141–174.

Wilkins, E.H., *Life of Petrarch* (Chicago, 1961).

Witt, R., 'Coluccio Salutati in the Footsteps of the Ancients' in A.A.M MacDonald, ZR Martels, Z.R.W.M von and Veenstra, J.R. (eds.), *Christian Humanism: Essays in Honour of Arjo Vanderjagt* (Leiden, 2009), pp. 3–12.

VALLA

Printed Primary Sources

Calvin, J., *Institutes of the Christian Religion* (sixth edition, Philadelphia, 1932), Book III.

Erasmus, D., *De Libro Arbitrio Distriba Sive Collatio*, in *Opera Omnia* (Leyden, 1706), IX.

Valla, L., *De Falso Credita et Ementita Constantini Donatione Declamtio (1440)*, trans. C.B. Coleman (New Haven, 1922).

——, *De Professione Religiosorum*, ed. J. Vahlen (*Laurentii Vallae opuscula tria*, in 'Sitzungsberichte der Kaiserlichen Akademie der Wissenschaften, Philos. Und Hist. Kl.,' nos. 61 and 62 (Vienna, 1869).

——, *De Servo Arbitrio*, ed. A. Freitag (*Werke*, WA, Band XVIII 1908).

——, *De Voluptate ac Vero Bono Libri Tres* (Basel, 1519).

——, *Dialectice Laurentii Vallae Libri Tres seu Ejusdem Reconcinnatio Totius Dialectice et Fundamentorum Universalis Philosophiae; ubi Multa Adversus Aristotelem, Boetium, Porphyrium* etc. (Paris, 1509).

——, *Encomium sancti Thomae Aquinatis*, later published by Johannes Vahlen in *Vierteljahschrift für Kultur- und Litteraturgeschichte der Renaissance*, I (1886), pp. 387–96.

——, *Epistole*, ed. O. Besomi and M. Regoliosi (Padua, 1984).

——, *Laurentii Vallae De libero arbitrio edidit Maria Anfossi* 'Opusculi filosofici: testi e documenti inediti o rari pubblicati da Giovanni Gentile', VI (Florence, 1934).

——, *On Pleasure: De Voluptate (Of the True and the False Good)*, ed. M. Lorch, trans. A. Kent Hiett and M. Lorch, (New York, 1977).

——, *On the Donation of Constantine*, trans. G.W. Bowersock (The I Tatti Renaissance Library, Harvard, 2007).

——, *Repastinatio Dialectice et Philosophie*, ed. G. Zippel, 2 vols. (Padua, 1982).

Secondary Sources

Barozzi, L., *Lorenzo Valla*, printed with Remigio Sabbadini, in *Studi sul Panormita e sul Valla* ('R. Istituto di studi superiori ... in Firenze, Sezione di filosofia e filogia, Pubblicazioni', no. 25 (Florence, 1891).

Celenza, C.S., *The Lost Italian Renaissance: Humanists, Historians, and Latin's Legacy* (Baltimore and London, 2004).

Davies, J., *Florence and its University during the Early Renaissance*, Education and Society in the Middle Ages and Renaissance, 8 (Leiden, 1998).

Jardine, L., 'Lorenzo Valla and the Intellectual Origins of Humanist Dialectic', *Journal of the History of Philosophy*, 15 (1977), pp. 143–64.

Kraye, J., 'Lorenzo Valla and Changing Perceptions of Renaissance Humanism', *Comparative Criticism*, 23 (2001), pp. 37–55.

Langer, U., 'The Ring of Gyges in Plato, Cicero, and Lorenzo Valla: The Moral Force of Fictional Examples' in *Res et Verba in der Renaissance*, ed. E. Kessler and I. Maclean (Wiesbaden, 2002), pp. 131–45.

Lorch, M., 'Lorenzo Valla' in A. Rabil (ed.), *Renaissance Humanism: Foundations, Forms and Legacy*, 3 volumes (Philadelphia, 1988), I, pp. 332–349.

Nauta, L., *In Defence of Common Sense : Lorenzo Valla's Humanist Critique of Scholastic Philosophy* (Cambridge, Mass., 2009).

———, 'Lorenzo Valla and the Rise of Humanist Dialectic', in J. Hankins (ed.), *The Cambridge Companion to Renaissance Philosophy* (Cambridge, 2007), pp. 193–210.

Struever, N.S., *The Language of History in the Renaissance: Rhetoric and Historical Consciousness in Florentine Humanism* (Princeton, 1970).

Trinkhaus, C.E., 'Lorenzo Valla on Free Will to Garsia, Bishop of Lerida' in E. Cassirer, P.O. Kristeller and J.H. Randall (eds.), *The Philosophy of Renaissance Man* (Chicago, 1948), pp. 147–154.

Witt, R.G., *In the footsteps of the Ancients: The Origins of Humanism from Lovato to Bruni* (Leiden, 2000).

FICINO

Printed Primary Sources

Corpus Hermeticum, trans. C. Salaman, D. van Oyen and W. Wharton (eds.) in *The Way of Hermes* (London, 1999).

Ficino, M., *Marslii Ficini florentini disputatio contra iudicium astrologorum*, translated by members of the Language Department of the School of Economic Science, vol. III: *The Letters* (London, 1981).

———, *Platonic Theology*, trans. and ed. M.J.B. Allen and J. Warden, 6 vols.: Books I-IV, V-VIII, IX-XI, XII-XIV, XV-XVI, XVII-X-VIII (Cambridge, Mass., 2001–6), I.

———, *The Letters of Marsilio Ficino*, I, translated from the Latin by members of the Department of the School of Economic Science, London (London, 1975).

Ficino, M., *Theologia Platonica*, XIII.3, trans. C. Trinkhaus, 'Humanist Themes in Marsilio Ficino's Philosophy' in C. Trinkhaus, *In Our Image and Likeness* (London, 1970).

Ficinus, M., *Opera Omnia* (Basel, 1576, reprinted Turin, 1959).

Iamblichus, *On the Mysteries*, trans. E.C. Clarke, J.M. Dillon and J.P. Hershbell (Atlanta, 2003).

Secondary Sources

Allen, M.J.B., *Synoptic Art: Marsilio Ficino on the History of Platonic Interpretation* (Florence, 1998).

Allen, M.J.B. and Rees, V., *Marsilio Ficino: His Theology, his Philosophy, his Legacy* (Leiden, 2002).

Arnold, J., *Dean John Colet of St. Paul's: Humanism and Reform in Early Tudor England* (London, 2007).

Bedouelle, G., 'Jacques Lefèvre d'Étaples (c.1460–1536)' C. Lindberg (ed.), *The Reformation Theologians: An Introduction to Theology in the Early Modern Period* (Oxford, 2002), pp. 19–33.

Blum, P.R., 'The Immortality of the Soul' in *The Cambridge Companion to Renaissance Philosophy* (Cambridge, 2007), pp. 211–233.

Celenza, C., 'The Revival of Platonic Philosophy', in *The Cambridge Companion ot Renaissance Philosophy* (Cambridge, 2007), pp. 72–96.

Field, A., *The Origins of the Platonic Academy in Florence* (Princeton, 1988).

Gleason, J.B., *John Colet* (Berkeley, 1989).

Hankins, J., *Humanism and Platonism in the Italian Renaissance*, 2 vols. (Rome, 2003–4), II.

——, *Plato in the Italian Renaissance*, 2 vols. (Leiden, 1990).

Hough, S.J., 'An Early Record of Marsilio Ficino', *Renaissance Quarterly*, 30 (1977), pp. 301–4.

Jayne, S., *John Colet and Marsilio Ficino* (Oxford, 1963).

Kristeller, P.O., *Marsilio Ficino and his Work after Five Hundred Years* (Florence, 1987).

——, *Renaissance Thought and its Sources* (New York, 1979).

——, *The Classics and Renaissance Thought* (Cambridge, Mass., 1955).

Salaman, C., 'Introduction' in *Meditations of the Soul: Selected Letters of Marsilio Ficino*, translated from the Latin by Members of the Language Department of the School of Economic Science (London, 1975).

Stinger, C.L., 'Humanism in Florence' in A. Rabil (ed.), *Renaissance Humanism: Foundations, Forms and Legacy*, 3 vols (Philadelphia, 1988), I, pp. 175–208.

Trapp, J.B., 'An English Late Medieval Cleric and Italian Thought: The Case of John Colet, Dean of St. Paul's (1467–1519)' in G. Kratzmann and J. Simpson (eds.), *Medieval English Religious and Ethical Literature: Essays in Honour of G. H. Russell*, (Cambridge, 1986), pp. 233–50.

Trinkhaus, C., *In Our Image and Likeness* (London, 1970).

Voss, A., (ed.), *Marsilio Ficino* (Berkeley, 2006).

PICO

Printed Primary Sources

Pico della Mirandola, *900 Theses*, in *Syncretism in the West: Pico's 900 Theses (1486): The Evolution of Traditional Religious and Philosophical Systems,* ed. and trans. S.A. Farmer (Tempe, AZ, 1998), 183–553. Includes facing page Latin text.

——, *Commentary on Psalm 15*, translated by Clarence H. Miller, in 'Appendix A' of *The Complete Works of St. Thomas More*, vol. I, ed. Anthony S.G. Edwards, Katherine Gardiner Rodgers, and Clarence H. Miller (New Haven, 1997), 362–71. Includes facing page Latin text.

——, *Heptaplus or Discourse on the Seven Days of Creation*, trans. J.B. McGaw (New York, 1977).

——, *Of Being and Unity (De Ente et Uno)*, trans. Victor Michael Hamm (Milwaukee, 1943).

——, *Opera Omnia* (Turin, 1971).

——, *Oration on the Dignity of Man*, trans. A.R. Caponigri (Washington, 1956).

Secondary Sources

Blum, P.R., 'Pico, Theology, and the Church' in M.V. Dougherty (ed.), *Pico della Mirandola: New Essays* (Cambridge, 2008), pp. 37–60.

Borghesi, F., 'A Life in Works' in Dougherty, M.V. (ed.), *Pico della Mirandola: New Essays* (Cambridge, 2008), pp. 202–220.

Dougherty, M.V., 'Introduction' in Dougherty, M.V. (ed.), *Pico della Mirandola: New Essays* (Cambridge, 2008), pp. 1–12.

Edelheit, A., 'Humanism and Theology in Renaissance Florence: Four Examples (Caroli, Savonarola, Ficino, and Pico)', *Verbum Analecta Neolatina,* 8 (2006), pp. 271–290.

Farmer, S.A., *Syncretism in the West: Pico's 900 Theses (1486). The Evolution of Traditional Religious and Philosophical Systems, with text, translation and Commentary, by S.A. Farmer* (Tempe, Arizona, 1998).

Kirk, R., 'Introduction' to Pico's *Oration on the Dignity of Man* (Washington D.C., 1956), pp. 1–10.

Kraye, J., 'Pico on the Relationship of Rhetoric and Philosophy' in Dougherty, M.V. (ed.), *Pico della Mirandola: New Essays* (Cambridge, 2008), pp. 13–36.

Kristeller, P.O., 'Thomism and Italian Thought' in *idem, Medieveal Aspects of Renaissance Learning: Three Essays by Paul Oskar Kristeller,* ed. and trans. By E.P. Mahoney (Durham, N. Carolina, 1974), pp. 29–94.

Lehmberg, S.E., 'Sir Thomas More's Life of Pico della Mirandola', *Studies in the Renaissance*, 3 (1956), pp. 61–74.

Suddoth, M., 'Pico della Mirandola's Philosophy of Religion', in M.V. Dougherty (ed.), *Pico della Mirandola: New Essays* (Cambridge, 2008), pp. 61–80.

Thorndyke, L., *A History of Experimental Science*, IV: *Fourteenth and Fifteenth Centuries* (New York, 1934).

Yates, F.A., *Giodano Bruno and the Hermetic Tradition* (Chicago, 1964).

Zaccaria, R.M., 'Critiche e difesa dell' *Heptaplus*', in P. Viti, *Pico, Poliziano e L'Umanesimo di fine quattrocento* (Florence, 1994), pp. 76–7.

AGRICOLA

Printed Primary Sources

Agricola, R., *De Formando Studiis* (letter to Jacob Barbireau of 7 June 1484) in *Lucubrationes aliquot lectu dignissime* (Cologne, 1539), facsimile reprint *Opuscula Orationes Epistolae* (Frankfurt am Main, 1975).

——, *Letters*, ed. and trans. with notes, by Adrie Van Der Laan and Fokke Akkerman (Tempe, Arizona, 2002).

——, *Rudolphi Agricolae Phrisii De inventione dialectica libri omnes et integri et recogniti, etc. per Alardum Aemstelradamum*, II (Cologne, 1539).

Elyot, T., *The Boke named the Gouernour*, ed. H.H.S. Croft, 2 vols. (London, 1883; reprinted New York, 1967).

Valla, L., *Repastinatio dialecticae et philosophie*, ed. G. Zippel (Padua, 1982).

Secondary Sources

Brann, N.L., 'Humanism in Germany' in *Renaissance Humanism: Foundations, Forms and Legacy*, 3 vols. (Philadelphia, 1988), II, pp. 123–155.

Carroll, C., 'Humanism and English Literature in the Fifteenth and Sixteenth Centuries', in J. Kraye (ed.), *The Cambridge Companion to Renaissance Humanism* (Cambridge, 1996), pp. 246–268.

Leijenhorst, C.G., '*Rodolphus Agricola*, 17 February 1444- 27 October 1485' in A.E. Peter, G. Bietenholz and Thomas B. Deutsche (eds.), *Contemporaries of Erasmus: A Biographical Register of the Renaissance and Reformation*, I (Toronto, 1985), pp. 15–17.

Mack, P., 'Humanist Rhetoric and Dialectic' in J. Kraye (ed.), *The Cambridge Companion to Renaissance Humanism* (Cambridge, 1996), pp. 82–99.

Meerhoff, K., 'The Significance of Philip Melanchthon's Rhetoric in the Renaissance' in P. Mack (ed.), *Renaissance Rhetoric* (London, 1994), pp. 46–62.

Moss, A., *Renaissance Truth and the Latin Language* (Oxford, 2003).

Nauert, C.G., *Humanism and the Culture of Renaissance Europe* (Cambridge, 1995, second edition, Cambridge, 2006).

Nauta, L., 'Lorenzo Valla and the Rise of Humanist Dialectic', in J. Hankins (ed.), *The Cambridge Companion to Renaissance Philosophy* (Cambridge, 2007), pp. 193–210.

Spitz, L.W., 'Humanism in Germany', in A. Goodman and A. Mackay (eds.), *The Impact of Humanism on Western Europe* (London, 1990), pp. 202–219.

H. Van Ruler, 'The *Philosphia Christi*' in A.A.M. MacDonald, Z.R.W.M. von Martels and J.R. Veestra (eds.), *Christian Humanism: Essays in Honour of Arjo Vanderjagt* (Leiden, 2009), p. 236–54.

ERASMUS

Printed Primary Sources

Erasmus, D., *Christian Humanism and the Reformation: Selected Writings of Erasmus with The Life of Erasmus by Beatus Rhenanus,* ed. and trans. J.C. Olin (first edition, New York, 1965; second edition, New York, 1975).

——, *Opus Epistolarum Desiderii Erasmi Roterdami,* I-IV, ed. P.S. Allen and H.M. Allen (Oxford, 1906–22).

——, *The Collected Works of Erasmus,* trans. and ed. R.A.B. Mynors and D.F.S. Thomson; annotated by P.G. Bietnholz, W.K. Ferguson and J.K. McConica (Toronto, 1974–1988).

——, *The Colloquies of Erasmus,* trans. C.R. Thompson (Chicago, 1965).

——, *The Praise of Folly,* trans. B. Radice (Harmondswoth, 1971).

Luther, M., *De Servo Arbitrio,* translated as *The Bondage of the Will,* by P. Watson and B. Drewery in *Luther's Works,* XXXIII.

——, *Hyperaspistes: Diatribe Adversus Servum Abirtrium Martini Lutheri,* LB, X, 1423 B–C.

——, *Luther Works* 55 vols. (Philadelphia, 1955).

Secondary Sources

Allen, P.S., *The Age of Erasmus* (Oxford, 1914).

Augustijn, C., *Erasmus: His Life, Works and Influence* (Toronto, 1991).

Bietenholz, P. and Deutscher, T.B. (eds.), *Contemporaries of Erasmus: A Biographical Register of the Renaissance and Reformation,* I (Toronto, 1985) pp. 324–8.

Boyle, M. 'Rourke, *Erasmus on Language and Method in Theology* (Toronto, 1994).

——. O'Rourke, *Rhetoric and Reform: Erasmus' Civil Dispute with Luther* (Cambridge, 1983).

Carrington, J.L., 'Desiderius Erasmus (1460–1536)' in C. Lindberg (ed.), *The Reformation Theologians: An Introduction to Theology in the Early Modern Period* (Oxford, 2002), pp.34–48.

Dickens, A.G., *Martin Luther and the Reformation* (London, 1967).

Dickens, A.G. and Jones, W.R.D., *Erasmus the Reformer* (London, 1994).

Garrod, H.W., 'Erasmus and His English Patrons', *The Library,* 5th series, IV (1949) pp.1–13.

Gleason, J.B., 'The Birth Dates of John Colet and Erasmus of Rotterdam: Fresh Documentary Evidence', *Renaissance Quarterly*, 32 (1979) pp. 73–6.

Hoffmann, M., *Rhetoric and Theology: The Hermeneutic of Erasmus* (Toronto, 1994).

Huizinga, J., *Erasmus and the Age of Reformation* (London, 1957).

Hyma, A., 'Erasmus and the Oxford Reformers (1503–1519)', *Nederlands Archief voor Kerkgeschiedenis*, 38 (1951) pp. 65–85.

Jardine, L., *Erasmus, Man of Letters: The Construction of Charisma in Print* (Princeton, New Jersey, 1993).

Jarrott, C.A.L., 'Erasmus's Annotations and Colet's Commentaries on Paul: A Comparison of Some Theological Themes' in R.L. De Molen (ed.), *Essays on the Works of Erasmus* (New Haven, Connecticut, and London, 1978) pp. 125–44.

Loewenich, W. von., *Martin Luther: The Man and his Work*, trans. L.W. Denef (Minneapolis, 1986).

Mansfield, B., *Phoenix of His Age: Interpretations of Erasmus, c. 1550–1750* (Toronto, 1979).

McConica, J.K., *Erasmus* (Oxford, 1991).

O' Boyle, M., 'Erasmus and the "Modern" question: Was he Semi-Pelagian?', *Archiv für Reformationsgeschichte*, 75 (1984), pp. 59–77.

Olin, J.C., *Six Essays on Erasmus and a Translation of Erasmus' Letter to Corondelet, 1523* (New York, 1979).

Pabel, H.M. (ed.), *Erasmus' Vision of the Church* (Kirksville, 1995).

Payne, J.B., *Erasmus: His Theology of the Sacraments* (Richmond, Virginia, 1970).

Rabil, A., 'Desiderius Erasmus', in A. Rabil (ed.), *Renaissance Humanism: Foundations, Forms and Legacy*, 3 volumes (Philadelphia, 1988), II, pp. 216–264.

Reynolds, E.E., *Thomas More and Erasmus* (New York, 1965).

Rieger, J.H., 'Erasmus, Colet and the Schoolboy Jesus', *Studies in the Renaissance*, 9 (1962) pp. 187–94.

Rummel, E., 'Voices of Reform from Hus to Erasmus' in T.A. Brady Jr., H.A. Oberman and J.D. Tracy (eds.), *Handbook of European History, 1400–1600: Late Middle Ages, Renaissance and Reformation. Volume II: Visions, Programs and Outcomes* (Leiden, 1995) pp. 61–92.

——, *Erasmus and his Catholic Critics*, 2 vols. (Nieuwkoop, 1989).

——, *Erasmus' Annotations on the New Testament: From Philologist to Theologian* (Toronto, 1986).

Sauer, Joseph. 'Desiderius Erasmus' in *The Catholic Encyclopedia*, V (New York, 1909).

Stewart, A., 'The Trouble with English Humanism: Tyndale, More and Darling Erasmus' in J. Woolfson (ed.), *Reassessing Tudor Humanism* (Basingstoke, 2002) pp. 78–98.

Tracy, J.D., *Erasmus of the Low Countries* (Berkeley, 1996).

——, *Erasmus: The Growth of a Mind* (Geneva, 1972).

Trapp, J.B., 'Erasmus on William Grocyn and Ps-Dionysius: A Re-examination', *The Journal of the Warburg and Courtauld Institutes*, 59 (1996) pp. 294–303.

——, *Erasmus, Colet and More: The Early Tudor Humanists and Their Books* (London, 1991).

Watson, P.S., *Luther and Erasmus: Free Will and Salvation* (London, 1969).

Wengert, T.J., *Human Freedom, Christian Righteousness: Philip Melanchthon's Exegetical Dispute with Erasmus of Rotterdam* (New York, 1998).

REUCHLIN

Printed Primary Sources

Reuchlin, J., *Warhafftige Entschuldigung Gegen und Wider ains Getaufften Juden Genant Pfefferkorn Vormals Getruckt...* (Tübingen, 1514).

Erasmus, D., *The Colloquies of Erasmus*, English translation by C.R. Thompson (Chicago, 1965).

Hutten, U. von, Busche, H. von dem, Rubianus, C., Reuchlin, J., *Epistolae Obscurorum Vivorum* (Frankfurt-am-Main, 1570 edition).

Hutten, U. Von., *On the Eve of the Reformation: 'Letters of Obscure Men' [Epistolae Obscurorum Virorum]*, Ulrich von Hutten et al., trans. F.G. Stokes with intro. by H. Holborn (New York, 1964).

——, *Opera Omnia*, ed. E. Böcking, 7 vols. (Leipzig, 1859–1870), III.

Luther, M., *Luther's Works*, American ed., XLV (Philadelphia, 1962).

Reuchlin, J., *De Arte Cabalistica: On the Art of the Kabbalah*, trans. Martin and Sarah Goodman (Lincoln and London, 1983; reprinted Nebraska, 1993).

——, *Defensio Johannis Reuchlin contra Culumniatores suos Coloniensis* (Tübingen, 1513).

——, *De Verbo Mirifico* (Basel, 1494; facsimile reprint, Stuttgart, 1964).

——, *Johann Reuchlin Briefwechsel*, ed., L. Geiger (Stuttgart, 1875).

Secondary Sources

Blau, J.L., *The Christian Interpretation of the Cabala in the Renaissance* (New York, 1944).

Brann, N.L., 'Humanism in Germany' in *Renaissance Humanism: Foundations, Forms and Legacy*, 3 vols. (Philadelphia, 1988), II, pp. 123–155.

Graetz, H., *History of the Jews* (London, 1892), IV.

Hirsch, S.A., *A Book of Essays* (London, 1905).

Holborn, H., *Ulrich von Hutten and the German Reformation* (New York, 1965).

Idel, M., 'Introduction to the Bison Book Edition' in J. Reuchlin, *De Arte Cabalistica: On the Art of the Kabbalah*, trans. Martin and Sarah Goodman (Lincoln and London, 1983; reprinted Nebraska, 1993), pp. 1–6.

Kisch, G., 'The Jews and Mediaeval Law' in *Essays on Antisemitism*, ed., K.S. Pinson, (Second edition revised, New York, 1946), pp. 103 ff.

Lloyd Jones, G., 'Introduction', in J. Reuchlin, *De Arte Cabalistica: On the Art of the Kabbalah*, trans. Martin and Sarah Goodman (Lincoln and London, 1983; reprinted Nebraska, 1993), pp. 7–32.

Overfield, J.H., *Humanism and Scholasticism in Late-Medieval Germany* (Princeton, 1984).

Ozment, S.E., *Mysticism and Dissent: Relgious Ideology and Social Protest in the Sixteenth Century* (Yale, 1973).

Ruderman, D.B., 'The Italian Renaissance and Jewish Thought' in *Renaissance Humanism: Foundations, Forms and Legacy*, 3 vols. (Philadelphia, 1988), I, pp. 382–433.

Smith, P., *The Life and Letters of Martin Luther* (London, 1911).

Spitz, L.W., 'Humanism in Germany', in Goodman and Mackay (eds.), *The Impact of Humanism*, pp. 202–219.

Weiss, R., 'England and the Decree of the Council of Vienne on the teaching of Greek, Arabic, Hebrew and Syriac', *Bibliothèque d'Humanisme et Renaissance*, Tome 14, (1952), pp. 1 ff.

Zika, C., 'Reuchlin and Erasmus: Humanism and Occult Philosophy', *Journal of Religious History*, IX (1977), pp. 230 ff.

Zimmer, E., 'Jewish and Christian Hebraist collaboration in sixteenth-century Germany', *Jewish Quarterly Review*, 71 (1980), pp. 71 ff.

MELANCHTHON

Printed Primary Sources

Luther, M., *D. Martin Luthers Werke: Tischreden* (Weimar, 1912–21).

——, *Luther's Works*. 55 vols., (Philadelphia, 1955–1986), LIV.

Melanchthon, P., *Corpus Reformatorum: Philippi Melanchthonis Opera Quae Supersunt Omnia*, edited by Karl Bretschneider and Heinrich Bindseil, 28 vols. (Halle, 1834–60).

——, *Didymi Faventini Versus Thomam Placentinum pro M. Luthero Oratio* (Basel, 1521).

——, *Melanchthons Briefwechsel: Kritische und Kommentierte Gesamtansgabe*, edited by Heinz Scheible, 10 vols. to date (Stuttgart-Bad Cannstatt, 1977).

——, *The Loci Communes of Philip Melanchthon* trans. L.J. Satre (London, 1969).

Secondary Sources

Busogany, D., 'Melanchthon as a Humanist and a Reformer', in K. Maag (ed.), *Melanchthon in Europe: His Work and Influence Beyond Wittenberg* (Michigan, Grand Rapids, 1999), pp. 87–107.

Graybill, G.B., 'The Evolution of Philip Melanchthon's Thought on Free Will' (Unpublished D. Phil Thesis, University of Oxford, 2002).

Hildebrandt, F., *Melanchthon: Alien or Ally?* (Cambridge, 1946).

Keen, R.A., *Melanchthon* (St. Louis, 1988).

——, *A Checklist of Melanchthon Imprints Through 1560* (St. Louis, 1988).

Kusukawa, S., *The Transformation of Natural Philosophy: The Case of Philip Melanchthon* (Cambridge, 1995).

Pauls, R., 'The World as Sin and Grace: The Theology of Melanchthon's *Loci Commeunes* of 1521' in A.A.M. MacDonald, Z.R.W.M. von Martels and J.R. Veestra (eds.), *Christian Humanism: Essays in Honour of Arjo Vanderjagt* (Leiden, 2009), pp. 469–78.

Schneider, J.R., *Melanchthon's Rhetoric as a Context for Understanding his Theology*, in K. Maag (ed.), *Melanchthon in Europe: His Work and Influence Beyond Wittenberg* (Michigan, Grand Rapids, 1999), pp. 141–159.

Stupperich, R., *Melanchthon: The Enigma of the Reformation*, trans. W.L. Jenkins (Cambridge, 1965, reprinted 2006).

COLET

Manuscripts

British Library, Lansdowne Manuscript, 1030: White Kennett's notes on John Colet and others.

British Library, London, Additional MS 63853: Colet's Commentaries on Dionysius' *Celestial* and *Ecclesiastical Hierarchies* and his treatise *De Sacramentis Ecclesaie*.

Cambridge University Library, MS Gg.IV.26: Colet's Lectures on Romans; letter to the Abbot of Wynchcombe; treatise on the Mystical Body of Christ; commentary on 1 Corinthians; and commentary on the *Celestial Hierarchy* of Dionysius.

Printed Primary Sources

Anon., *The Cloud of Unknowing*, ed. J. Walsh (New York, 1981).

Bale, J., *Index Britannicae Scriptorum: John Bale's Index of British and Other Writers*, edited by R.L. Poole and M. Bateson, (Oxford, 1902).

Colet, J., *John Colet's Commentary on First Corinthians: A New Edition of the Latin Text, with Translation, Annotations, and Introduction*, ed. by B. O'Kelly and C.A.L. Jarrott (Medieval and Renaissance Texts and Studies 21, Binghamton, New York, 1985).

——, *Johannis Coleti Enarratio In Epistolam S. Pauli ad Romanos: An Exposition of St. Paul's Epistle to the Romans, delivered as Lectures in the University of Oxford about the year 1497, by John Colet, D. D.*, trans. by J.H. Lupton (London, 1873).

——, *Joannis Coleti Opuscula Theologica: Letters to Radulphus on the Mosiac Account of Creation; On Christ's Mystical Body the Church;*

Exposition of St. Paul's Epistle to the Romans (Chapters I-V) by John Colet D. D., trans. J.H. Lupton (London, 1876).

——, *Joannes Coletus Super Opera Dionysii: Two Treatises on the Hierarchies of Dionysius, by John Colet, D. D.*, trans. by J.H. Lupton (London, 1869).

——, *Oratio Habita a D. Joanne Colet ad Clerum in Convocatione. Anno. M.D.xj* (London, [1511–12] STC 5545).

——, (translated by [T. Lupset]) *The Sermon of Doctor Colete, made to the Conuocacion at Paulis* (London, [1530] STC 5550).

Hilton, W., *The Ladder of Perfection*, trans. L. Shirley-Price (Harmondsworth, 1957).

Parker, M., *De Antiquitate Britannicae Ecclesiae Cantuariensis, cum Archiepiscopis Euisdem* (John Daye, London, 1572) [STC 19292].

Registrum Statutorum et Consuetudinum Ecclesiae Cathedralis Sancti Pauli Londinensis, edited by W. Sparrow Simpson (London, 1873).

Secondary Sources

Arnold, J., 'Colet, Wolsey and the Poltics of Reform: St. Paul's Cathedral in 1518', *The English Historical Review*, 121, September, 2006.

——, *Dean John Colet of St. Paul's: Humanism and Reform in Early Modern England* (London, 2007).

——, 'In Search of Perfection: Ecclesiology in the Life and Works of John Colet, Dean of St. Paul's Cathedral, 1505–19' (Unpublished Ph.D. Thesis, King's College, London University, 2004).

——, 'John Colet and a Lost Manuscript of 1506', *History*, 89, (2004), pp. 174–92.

——, 'John Colet, Preaching and Reform at St. Paul's Cathedral, 1505–19', *Historical Research*, 76 (2003), pp. 450–68.

Chatterjee, K.K., *In Praise of Learning: John Colet and Literary Humanism in Education* (New Delhi, 1974).

Dowling, M., *Fisher of Men: A Life of John Fisher, 1469–1535* (Basingstoke, 1999).

Dugdale, W., *A History of St Paul's Cathedral in London, from its Foundation Until These Times* (London, 1658).

Ferguson, W.K., 'An Unpublished Letter of John Colet', *The American Historical Review*, 34, (1934), pp. 696–9.

Fletcher, J.M., 'The Teaching of Arts in Oxford, 1400–1520', *Paedagogica Historica*, 7 (1967), p. 440.

Fox, A., 'Facts and Fallacies: Interpreting English Humanism', in A. Fox and J. Guy, *Reassessing the Henrician Age: Humanism, Politics and Reform, 1500–1550* (Oxford, 1986).

Gleason, J.B., *John Colet* (Berkeley, 1989).

Godfrey, W.R., 'John Colet of Cambridge', *Archiv für Reformationsgeschichte*, 65 (1975), pp. 6–17.

Harper-Bill, C., 'Dean Colet's Convocation Sermon and the Pre-Reformation Church in England', *History*, 73 (1988), pp. 191–210.

Hook, W.F., *The Lives of the Archbishops of Canterbury*, VI, Richard Bentley, (London, 1868).

Hunt, E.W., *Dean Colet and His Theology* (London, 1956).

Jayne, S., *John Colet and Marsilio Ficino* (Oxford, 1963).

Kaufman, P.I., 'John Colet and Erasmus' *Enchiridion*', *Church History*, 46 (1977), pp. 296–312.

——, 'John Colet's *Opus de Sacramentis* and Clerical Anticlericalism: The Limitations of "Ordinary Wayes"', *Journal of British Studies*, 22 (1982), pp. 1–22.

——, *Augustinian Piety and Catholic Reform: Augustine, Colet, and Erasmus* (Macon, Georgia, 1982).

Knight, S., *The Life of Dr. John Colet* (London, 1724).

Lander, S., 'Church Courts and the Reformation in the Diocese of Chichester 1500–58' in R. O' Day and F. Heal (eds.), *Continuity and Change: Personnel and Administration of the Church in England 1500–1642* (Leicester, 1976), pp. 215–37, reprinted in C. Haigh (ed.), *The English Reformation Revised* (Cambridge, 1987), pp. 34–55.

Lepine, D., *A Brotherhood of Canons Serving God: English Secular Cathedrals in the Later Middle Ages* (Woodbridge, 1995).

Lupton, J., *A Life of John Colet, D.D.* (London, 1887).

Miles, L., *John Colet and the Platonic Tradition* (London, 1961).

Milman, H.H., *The Annals of St Paul's Cathedral* (London, 1868).

Nauert, C.G., 'Humanism as Method: Roots of Conflict with the Scholastics', *The Sixteenth Century Journal*, 29 (1998), pp. 426–38.

Parks, G.B., *The English Traveller to Italy* (Stanford, 1954), I.

Rex, R., *The Theology of John Fisher* (Cambridge, 1991).

Rice, E.F., 'John Colet and the Annihilation of the Natural', *Harvard Theological Review*, 45 (1952), pp. 141–63.

Seebohm, F., *The Oxford Reformers of 1498: Being a History of the Fellow- Work of John Colet, Erasmus, and Thomas More* (London, 1867).

Simpson, W. Sparrow, 'A Newly-Discovered Manuscript Containing Statutes Compiled by Dean Colet for the Government of the Chantry Priests and Other Clergy of St Paul's', *Archaeologia*, 52 (1890), pp. 144–74.

Tillyard, E.M.W., *The Elizabethan World Picture* (Harmondsworth, first edition, 1943; third edition, 1973).

Trapp, J.B., 'An English Late Medieval Cleric and Italian Thought: The Case of John Colet, Dean of St. Paul's (1467–1519)', in G. Kratzmann and J. Simpson (eds.), *Medieval English Religious and Ethical Literature: Essays in Honour of G. H. Russell* (Cambridge, 1986), pp. 233–50.

——, 'Christopher Urswick and his Books: the Reading of Henry VII's Almoner', *Renaissance Studies*, I, 1987, pp. 48–71.

——, 'John Colet and the *Hierarchies* of the Ps-Dionysius', in K. Robbins (ed.), *Religion and Humanism* Studies in Church History, 17 (Oxford, 1981), pp. 127–48.

——, 'John Colet, His Manuscripts and the Pseudo Dionysius', in R.R. Bolgar (ed.), *Classical Influences on European Culture 1500–1700: Proceedings* of an International Conference held at King's College Cambridge, April 1974 (Cambridge, 1976), pp. 205–215.

Trapp, J.B., 'John Colet' in H.C.G. Matthew and B. Harrison (eds.), *The Oxford Dictionary of National Biography in Association with the British Academy: From the Earliest Times to the Year 2000*, XII, (Oxford, 2004), pp. 601–9.

——, 'John Colet', in P. Bietenholz and T.B. Deutscher (eds.), *Contemporaries of Erasmus: A Biographical Register of the Renaissance and Reformation*, (3 vols.; Toronto, 1985–7), I, pp. 324–8.

——, *Erasmus, Colet and More: The Early Tudor Humanists and Their Books* (London, 1991).

Walker, G., 'The Renaissance in Britain', in P. Collinson (ed.), *The Short Oxford History of the British Isles: The Sixteenth Century, 1485–1603* (Oxford, 2002), pp. 145–188.

MORE

Printed Primary Sources

Acts of Court of the Mercers' Company, 1453–1527, ed. by L. Lyell and F.D. Watney, (Cambridge, 1936).

Hallett, P.E., trans. *The Life and Illustrious Martyrdom of Sir Thomas More.* By Thomas Stapleton. (London, 1928).

Hitchcock, E.V. (ed.), *The Life and Death of Sr Thomas Moore, knight, some-tymes Lord high Chancellor of England.* By Nicholas Harpsfield. With an introduction by R.W. Chambers. Early English Texts Society, 186 (London, 1932).

Letters and Papers, Foreign and Domestic, of the Reign of Henry VIII, 1509–47, Preserved in the Public Record Office, The British Museum, and Elsewhere in England, Arranged and Catalogued by J.S. Brewer, M.A., Under the Direction of the Master of the Rolls, and with the sanction of Her Majesty's Secretaries of State; Volume I, Parts i and ii; Volume II, Parts i and ii (first edition, London, 1864; second edition, London, 1920).

Liber Albus: The White Book of the City of London, ed. H.T. Riley (London, 1861.

More, T., *The Correspondence of Sir Thomas More*, ed. E.F. Rogers (Princeton, 1947).

——, *The Workes of Sir Thomas More Knyght, sometyme Lord Chancellour of England, wrytten by him in the Englysh tonge* (London, 1557).

——, *The Yale Edition of the Complete Works of St. Thomas More* (New Haven and London, 1963).

——, *Utopia*, ed. P. Turner (Harmondsworth, 1965).

——, *Opera omnia latina* (Frankfurt and Leipzig, 1689).

——, *Selected Letters*, edited by E.F. Rogers (New Haven and London, 1961).

——, *The English Works of Sir Thomas More.* Ed. W. E. Campbell and A. W. Reed, 2 vols. (London and New York, 1931). I: *Early Poems, Pico*

Della Mirandola, Richard III, The Four Last Things. II: *The Dialogue Concerning Tyndale.*

Secondary Sources

Barron, C.M., *London in the Later Middle Ages: Government and People, 1200–1500*, (Oxford, 2004).

Bradshaw, B., 'More on Utopia', *The Historical Journal*, 24, pp. 1–27.

Elton, G.R., 'Thomas More: Councillor' in *St. Thomas More: Action and Contemplation*, ed. R. S. Sylvester (Cambridge, Mass., 1972).

Gilmore, P., 'The Program of Christian Humanism: Sir Thomas More and his Friends, in *The World of Humanism, 1453–1517* (New York, 1952), pp. 211–15.

Guy, J., *Thomas More* (London, 2000).

——, *A Daughter's Love: Thomas and Margaret More* (London, 2008).

——, *Public Career of Sir Thomas More* (Cambridge, Mass., 1980).

Halpin, D., 'Utopianism and Education: The Legacy of Thomas More' in *The British Journal of Educational Studies*, 49 (September, 2001), pp. 299–315.

——, *Thomas More on Utopianism and William Hazlett on Plain Speaking* (London, 2003).

Hankins, J., 'Humanism and the Origins of Modern Political Thought' in J. Kraye (ed.), *The Cambridge Companion to Renaissance Humanism* (Cambridge, 1996, eighth printing, 2007), pp. 118–141.

Kristeller, P.O., 'Thomas More as a Renaissance Humanist', *Moreana*, 65 (1980), pp. 5–22.

Kristeller, P.O., and H. Maier. *Thomas Morus als Humanist. Zwei Essays.* Gratia, Bamberger Schriften zur Renaissanceforshung, 11 (Bamberg, 1982).

Marc'hadour, G., 'Thomas More and His Foursome of "Blessed Holy Women."' *Thomas–Morus–Gesellschaft Jahrbuch 1983/84.* Ed. H. Boventer (Düsseldorf, 1984), pp. 113–30.

Marius, R., *Thomas More* (New York, 1984).

McCutcheon, E., 'The Education of Thomas More's Daughters: Concepts and Praxis' in R.L. Hadlich and J.D. Ellsworth (eds.), *East Meets West: Homage to Edgar C. Knowlton, Jr.* (Honolulu, HI, 1988), pp. 193–207.

Nelson, W., 'Thomas More: Grammarian and Orator' in R.S. Sylvester and G.P. Marc'hardour (eds.), *Essential Articles for the study of Thomas More* (Hamden, Connecticut, 1977), pp. 150–60.

Ramsay, G.D., 'A Saint in the City: Thomas More at Mercers' Hall, London', *The English Historical Review*, 97 (1982), pp. 269–288.

Schoeck, R.J., 'Humanism in England' in A. Rabil (ed.), *Renaissance Humanism: Foundations, Forms, and Legacy* (Philadelphia, 1988), II, pp. 5–38.

Skinner, Q., 'More's Utopia', *Past and Present*, 38, pp. 153–68.

Sowards, J.K., 'Erasmus and the Education of Women', *The Sixteenth Century Journal,* 13 (1982), pp. 77–89.

Sowards, J.K., 'On Education: More's Debt to Erasmus', *Miscellanea Moreana*, pp. 103–23.

Surtz, E., 'St. Thomas More and his Utopian Embassy of 1515', *The Catholic Historical Review*, 29 (1953–4), pp. 272–97.

Sutton, A.F., *The Mercery of London: Trade, Goods and People, 1130–1578*, (Aldershot, 2005).

Thompson, C.R., 'The Humanism of More Reappraised', *Thought*, 52 (1977), pp. 231–48.

Trinkaus, C., 'Thomas More and Humanist Tradition: Martyrdom and Ambiguity', *The Scope of Renaissance Humanism* (Ann Arbor, 1983), pp. 422–36.

Warnicke, R., 'Women and Humanism in England', A. Rabil (ed.), *Renaissance Humanism: Foundations, Forms, and Legacy*, 3 vols. (Philadelphia, PA, 1988), II, pp. 39–54.

Weinberg, C., 'Thomas More and the Use of English in Early Tudor Education', *Moreana*, 59/60 (1978), pp. 21–30.

THE ENGLISH ERASMIANS

Manuscripts

All Souls' College, Oxford, Codrington Library, MS. B. 29 (Bursars' Books, 1450–1520).

Merton College, Oxford, Roll no. 6697. Will of Thomas Linacre (18 October 1524).

Printed Primary Sources

Freind, J., *The History of Physick from the Time of Galen to the Beginning of the Sixteenth Century*, 2 vols. (London, 1725–6), II.

Leland, J., *Commentarii de Scriptoribus Brittanicis*, ed. A. Hall, 2 vols. (Oxford, 1709), II.

Lupset, T., *Epistolae aliquot eruditorum, nunquam antheac excuae* (Thierry Martens, 1519; republished, Froben, 1520).

Pace, R., *De Fructu qui ex Doctrina Percipiatur* ed. F. Manley and R.S. Silvester (first edition, London, 1517), (New York, 1967).

Secondary Sources

Allen, P.S., 'Linacre and Latimer in Italy', *The English Historical Review*, 18 (1903), pp. 514–7.

Baker, T., *History of the College of St. John the Evangelist, Cambridge*, ed. J.E.B. Mayor, 2 vols. (Cambridge, 1869).

Barber, G., 'Thomas Linacre: A bibliographical Survey of his Works', in *Essays*, pp. 290–336.

Bennett, J.W., 'John Morer's Will: Thomas Linacre and Prior Sellyng's Greek Teaching', *Studies in the Renaissance*, XV, (1968), pp. 70–91.

Clark, G. and Cooke, A.M., *A History of the royal College of Physicians of London*, 2 vols. (Oxford, 1964–6).

Clough, C.H., 'Thomas Linacre, Cornelio Vitelli and Humanistic Studies in Oxford', in F. Maddison, C. Pelling and C. Webster (eds.) *Essays as the Life and Work of Thomas Linacre c. 1460–1524* (Oxford, 1977), pp. 1–23.

Elton, G.R., 'Humanism in England', in A. Goodman and A. Mackay (eds.), *The Impact of Humanism in Western Europe* (London, 1990), pp. 260–70.

Emden, A.B., *A Biographical Register of the University of Oxford to A.D. 1500*, I and II (Oxford, 1957).

Fletcher, J.M., 'Linacre's Lands and Lectureships: Appendix B2', in F. Maddison, C. Pelling and C. Webster (eds.) *Essays as the Life and Work of Thomas Linacre c. 1460–1524* (Oxford, 1977), pp. 165–71.

——, 'Linacre's Lands and Lectureships' in F. Maddison, C. Pelling and C. Webster (eds.) *Essays as the Life and Work of Thomas Linacre c. 1460–1524* (Oxford, 1977), pp. 107–147.

Flynn, V., 'Englishmen in Rome during the Renaissance', *Modern Philology*, 36 (1938), pp. 136–7.

Fox, A., 'Facts and Fallacies: Interpreting English Humanism' in A. Fox and J. Guy, *Reassessing the Henrician Age: Humanism, Politics and Reform, 1500–1550* (Oxford, 1986), pp. 9–25.

Geanakoplos, D.J., *Interaction of the 'Sibling' Byzantine and Western Cultures* (New Haven, Connecticut and London, 1976).

Gee, J.A., *The Life and Works of Thomas Lupset: With a Critical Edition of the Original Treatises and the Letters* (Cambridge, Mass., 1926).

Gilmore, M.P., 'Erasmus and Alberto Pio, Prince of Carpi', T.K. Rabb and J.E. Seigel (eds.), *Action and Conviction in Early Modern Europe. Essays in Memory of E.H. Harbison* (Princeton, 1969), pp. 306ff.

Johnson, J.N., *The Life of Thomas Linacre*, ed. R. Graves (London, 1835).

Lewis, R.G., 'The Linacre Lectureships Subsequent to their Foundation', in F. Maddison, C. Pelling and C. Webster (eds.) *Essays as the Life and Work of Thomas Linacre c. 1460–1524* (Oxford, 1977), pp. 223–64.

Mayer, T.F., 'Thomas Lupset', in H.C.G. Matthew and B. Harrison (eds.), *The Oxford Dictionary of National Biography in Association with the British Academy: From the Earliest Times to the Year 2000*, XXIV (Oxford, 2004), pp. 780–81.

Mitchell, R.J., 'Thomas Linacre in Italy', *The English Historical Review*, l (1935), pp. 696–8.

Nolhac, P. de., 'Les correspondants d'Alde Manuce. Matériaux nouveaux d'histoire littéraire (1483–1514)', *Studi e documenti di storia e diretto*, 8 (1887), pp. 247–99.

Nutton, V., 'Thomas Linacre' in H.C.G. Matthew and B. Harrison (eds.), *The Oxford Dictionary of National Biography in Association with the British Academy*, XXXIII (Oxford, 2004), pp. 803–6.

Osler, W., *Thomas Linacre* (Cambridge, 1908).

Rolleston, H.D., *The Cambridge Medical School, a Biographical History* (Cambridge, 1932).

Schoeck, R.J., 'Humanism in England' in A. Rabil (ed.), *Renaissance Humanism: Foundations, Forms and Legacy*, 3 vols. (Philadelphia, 1988), II, pp. 5–38.

Schmitt, C.B., 'Thomas Linacre and Italy', in F. Maddison, C. Pelling and C. Webster (eds.) *Essays as the Life and Work of Thomas Linacre c. 1460–1524* (Oxford, 1977), pp. 36–75.

Trapp, J.B., *Erasmus, Colet and More: The Early Tudor Humanists and their Books* (London, 1991).

——, 'William Grocyn' in H.C.G. Matthew and B. Harrison (eds.), *The Oxford Dictionary of National Biography in Association with the British Academy: From the Earliest Times to the Year 2000*, XXIII (Oxford, 2004), pp. 56–58.

Webster, C., 'Thomas Linacre and the Foundation of the College of Physicians', in F. Maddison, C. Pelling and C. Webster (eds.) *Essays as the Life and Work of Thomas Linacre c. 1460–1524* (Oxford, 1977), pp. 198–222.

Weiss, R., *Humanism in England during the Fifteenth Century* (third edition, Oxford, 1967).

Wood, A., *Historia et Antiquitates Universitatis Oxoniensis*, 2 vols. (Oxford, 1674).

Woolfson, J., *Padua and the Tudors: English Students in Italy, 1485–1603* (Cambridge, 1998).

LEFÈVRE D'ÉTAPLES

Printed Primary Sources

Erasmus, D., *Apologia ad Fabrum Stapulensem* (1517), ed. Andrea. W. Steenbeek (Amsterdam, 1994).

Faber Stapulensis, *De Maria Magdalena et Triduo Christi Disceptatio, ad Clarissimum virum D. Franciscum Molineum, Christianissimi Francorum Regis Francisci Primi Magistrum* (Paris, 1517).

Faber Stapulensis, *De tribus et unica Magdalena disceptatio secunda* (Paris, 1519).

Fisher, J., *Confutatio Secundae Disceptationis per Jacobum Fabrum Stapulensem habitae in qua tribus foeminis partiri molitur quae totius ecclesiae consuetude unicae tribuit Magdalenae* (Paris, 1519).

——, *De Unica Magdalena Libri Tres* (Paris, 1519).

——, *Eversio Munitionis Quam Iodocus Clichtoveus erigere moliebatur adversus unicam Magdalenam per Ionnaem Roffensis Ecclesiae in Anglia Episcopum* (Louvain, 1519).

Grandval, M. de., *Apologiae seu defensorii Ecclesiae Catholicae non tres sive duas Magdalenas sed uniam celebrantis et colentis apologiae Marcum de Grandval* (Paris, 1519).

——, *Ecclesiae Catholicae non tres Magdalenas sed unicum colentis apologia seu defensorium* (Paris, 1518).

Lefèvre d'Étaples, J., '*Evangile de la Pentecote*' in G. Bedouelle and F. Giacore (eds.), *Epistres et Evangiles pour les cinquante-deux dimanches de l'an* (Leiden, 1976), p.269, which is *Evangile du 8eme dimanche après la Pentecote, ajout de 1531/1532*.

——, *Jacques Lefévre d'Etaples and the three Maries debates: On Mary Magdalen, on Christ's three days in the tomb, on the on Mary in place of the three : a discussion ; On the threefold and single Magdalen : a second discussion*. An edition of: *De Maria Magdalena, triduo Christi, et ex tribus una Maria disceptatio ... Secunda emissio. Parisiis: Ex officina Henrici Stephani, 1518 – De tribus et unica Magdalena disceptatio secunda ... Parisiis: Ex officina Henrici Stephani, 1519*, introduction, Latin text, English translation and annotation by Sheila M. Porrer (Geneva, 2009).

——, *The Prefatory Epistles of Jacques Lefèvre d'Étaples and Related Texts*, ed. E.F. Rice, Jr. (New York, 1972).

Luther, M., *Annotationes Quincuplici Fabri Stapulensis Psalterio Manu ad Scriptae* (1513).

Secondary Sources

Bedouelle, G., *Jacques Lefèvre d'Étaples (c. 1460–1536)* in C. Lindberg (ed.), *The Reformation Theologians: An Introduction to Theology in the Early Modern Period* (Oxford, 2002), pp. 19–33.

Cameron, R., 'The Attack on the Biblical Work of Lefèvre D'Étaples, 1514–1521', *Church History*, 38 (March, 1969) pp. 9–24.

Clerval, A., *De J. Clichtovei Vita et Operibus* (Paris, 1894).

Hufstader, A. 'Lefèvre d'Étaples and the Magdalen', *Studies in the Renaissance*, 16 (1969), pp. 31–60.

Mann, M., *Erasme et les débuts de la Réforme Française (1517–1536)* (Paris, 1934).

Reeve, A. (ed.), *Erasmus's Annotations on the New Testament: Galations to the Apocalypse* (Leiden, 1993).

Rice, E.F., 'Humanism in France' in A. Rabil (ed.), *Renaissance Humanism: Foundations, Forms and Legacy*, 3 vols. (Philadelphia, 1988). II, pp. 109–122.

Rice, E.F. Jr., 'Humanist Aristotelianism in France: Jacques Lefèvre d'Étaples and his Circle' in A.H.T. Levi (ed.), *Humanism in France at the End of the Middle Ages and in the Early Renaissance* (Manchester, 1970), pp. 132–49.

——, 'The Humanist Idea of Christian Antiquity: Lefèvre d'Étaples and his Circle' in *Studies in the Renaissance*, 9 (1962) pp. 126–60, reprinted in W.L. Gundersheimer (ed.), *French Humanism, 1470–1600* (London, 1969), pp. 163–80.

Rilliet, J., *Zwingli: Third Man of the Reformation*, trans. H. Knight (Philadelphia, 1964).

Secret, F., *Les Kabbalistes Chrétiens de la Renaissance* (Paris, 1964).

Stauffer, R., 'Lefèvre d'Étaples, artisan ou Spectateur de la Réforme?' in *Interprètes de la Bible* (Paris, 1980), p. 11–29.

Surtz, E., *The Works and Days of John Fisher* (Harvard, 1967).

VIVES

Printed Primary Sources

Desiderii Erasmi Roteromdami Opera Omnia, ed. J. Leclerc (Leiden, 1703–1706; reprint Hildesheim, 1961–2).

Vives, J.L., *Adversus Pseudodialecticos. Ejusdem Pomepeius Fugiens* (Selestadii, 1520).

——, *De Veritate Fidei Christianae*, praef. 1.3 in *Opera Omnia*, ed. Mayans y Síscar, 8 vols. (Valencia, 1782–1790; reproduced, London, 1964).

——, *Early Writings: De Initiis Sectis et Laudibus Philosophiae, Veritas Fucata, Anima Senis*, ed. C. Mattheeussen, C. Fantazzi and E. George (Leiden, 1987).

——, *Opera Omnia*, 8 vols. (Valencia, 1782–1790).

——, *The Education of a Christian Woman: A Sixteenth-Century Manual*, edited and translated by C. Fantazzi (Chicago, 2000).

Secondary Sources

Anon. 'Juan Luis Vives', in P.F. Grendler (ed.), *Encyclopaedia of the Renaissance* (New York 1999), VI, pp. 281–83.

Ashworth, E.J., *Language and Logic in the Post-Medieval Period* (Dordrecht and Boston, 1974).

Bonilla, A., *Luis Vives y la filosofia del Renaciamiento* (Madrid, 1903).

M.L. Colish, 'The *De Veritate Fidei Christianae* of Juan Luis Vives' in *Christian Humanism*, pp. 173–97.

Camillo, O. Di., 'Humanism in Spain' in A. Rabil (ed.), *Renaissance Humanism: Foundations, Forms and Legacy*, 3 vols. (Philadelphia, 1988). II, pp. 55–108.

Casini, L., 'Aristotelianism and Anti-Stoicism in Juan Luis Vives' in J. Kraye and R. Saarinen (eds.), *Moral Philosophy and the Threshold of Modernity* (Dordrecht, 2005), pp. 283–305.

Clements, R.D., 'A Sixteenth-Century Psychologist on the Immortality of the Soul: Juan Luis Vives', *Bibliothèque d'Humanisme et Renaissance*, 28 (1966), p. 82.

Fantazzi, C. (ed.), *A Companion to Juan Luis Vives* (Leiden, 2008).

——, 'Introduction' to *The Education of a Christian Woman: A Sixteenth-Century Manual*, ed. and trans. C. Fantazzi (Chicago, 2000).

González, E.G., 'Juan Luis Vives Works and Days', translated into English by Alexandre Coroleu and Charles Fantazzi in Charles Fantazzi (ed.), *A Companion to Juan Luis Vives* (Leiden, 2008), pp. 15–64.

——, 'Juan Luis Vives: Works and Days' in C. Fantazzi, *A Companion to Juan Luis Vives* (Leiden, 2008), pp. 15–64.

González, E.G., 'The Encounter of Luis Vives (1492/3–1540) and Hadrianus Barlandus (1486–1538) in Louvain, 1514?-1515', *Lias* 30/2 (2003), pp. 177–212.

Mayans, G., 'Life of Vives', preface to J.L. Vives, *Opera Omnia*, 8 vols. (Valencia, 1782–1790).

Nero, V. Del., 'The *De Disciplinis* as a model of a humanistic text', in *A Companion to Juan Luis Vives*, ed. Charles Fantazzi (Leiden, 2008), pp. 177–226.

Netanyahu, B., *The Marranos of Spain. From the Late XIVth to the Early XVIth Century, according to Contemporary Hebrew Sources* (New York, 1966).

Noreña, C.G., *Juan Luis Vives* (The Hague, 1970).

——, *Juan Luis Vives and the Emotions* (Carbondale and Edwardsville, 1989).

Oberman, H.A., *The Role of Anti-Semitism in the Age of Renaissance and Reformation*, trans. J.I. Porter (Philadelphia, 1984).

Roth, C., *A History of the Marranos* (London, Philadelphia, 1932).

INDEX